Mobile 3D Graphics: Learning 3D Graphics with the Java™ Micro Edition

Claus Höfele

THOMSON

COURSE TECHNOLOGY

Professional ■ Technical ■ Reference

© 2007 Thomson Course Technology, a division of Thomson Learning Inc. All rights reserved. No part of this book may be reproduced or transmitted in any form or by any means, electronic or mechanical, including photocopying, recording, or by any information storage or retrieval system without written permission from Thomson Course Technology PTR, except for the inclusion of brief quotations in a review.

The Thomson Course Technology PTR logo and related trade dress are trademarks of Thomson Course Technology, a division of Thomson Learning Inc., and may not be used without written permission.

Java™ is a trademark of Sun Microsystems. MascotCapsule® is a registered trademark of HI Corporation. OpenGL® is a registered trademark of Silicon Graphics, Inc. Python® is a registered trademark of the Python Software Foundation (PSF). All other trademarks are the property of their respective owners.

Important: Thomson Course Technology PTR cannot provide software support. Please contact the appropriate software manufacturer's technical support line or Web site for assistance.

Thomson Course Technology PTR and the authors have attempted throughout this book to distinguish proprietary trademarks from descriptive terms by following the capitalization style used by the manufacturer.

Information contained in this book has been obtained by Thomson Course Technology PTR from sources believed to be reliable. However, because of the possibility of human or mechanical error by our sources, Thomson Course Technology PTR, or others, the Publisher does not guarantee the accuracy, adequacy, or completeness of any information and is not responsible for any errors or omissions or the results obtained from use of such information. Readers should be particularly aware of the fact that the Internet is an ever-changing entity. Some facts may have changed since this book went to press.

Educational facilities, companies, and organizations interested in multiple copies or licensing of this book should contact the Publisher for quantity discount information. Training manuals, CD-ROMs, and portions of this book are also available individually or can be tailored for specific needs.

ISBN-10: 1-59863-292-2
ISBN-13: 978-1-59863-292-7
Library of Congress Catalog Card Number: 2006904575
Printed in the United States of America
07 08 09 10 11 TW 10 9 8 7 6 5 4 3 2 1

Publisher and General Manager, Thomson Course Technology PTR:
Stacy L. Hiquet

Associate Director of Marketing:
Sarah O'Donnell

Manager of Editorial Services:
Heather Talbot

Marketing Manager:
Heather Hurley

Senior Acquisitions Editor:
Emi Smith

Marketing Assistant:
Adena Flitt

Project Editor:
Kezia Endsley

Technical Reviewer:
Henrik Enqvist

PTR Editorial Services Coordinator:
Erin Johnson

Copy Editor:
Kezia Endsley

Interior Layout Tech:
ICC Macmillan Inc.

Cover Designer:
Mike Tanamachi

CD-ROM Producer:
Brandon Penticuff

Indexer:
Sharon Shock

Proofreader:
Dan J. Foster

THOMSON
COURSE TECHNOLOGY
Professional ■ Technical ■ Reference

Thomson Course Technology PTR,
a division of Thomson Learning Inc.
25 Thomson Place
Boston, MA 02210
http://www.courseptr.com

To Ben

Acknowledgments

Writing a book can be a challenging experience. I survived it thanks to Rachel, the better writer of the two of us, who provided encouragement and valuable comments; and Ben, the better track builder of the two of us, who provided welcome distractions from software development. I couldn't do what I do without them.

This book wouldn't exist if it weren't for the fine staff at Thomson Course Technology PTR. I thank Emi Smith for selecting my book proposal, making it happen, and for providing excellent guidance through the publishing process. Thanks to Kezia Endsley for helping me refine the words that are so hard to come by and managing all the little details that make a good book. Thanks also to Brandon Penticuff who created the CD-ROM that ships with the book.

In Henrik Enqvist, I found a superb technical reviewer. His experience gained at Digital Chocolate in wrangling with the myriad of mobile devices hardened this book's technical foundation.

I was also fortunate to receive help from the following people:

Gerhard Völkl, who is the author of the M3G Exporter Script that I use in Part III of this book. He was also kind enough to review Chapter 10 despite a challenging schedule of his own.

Rob Teixeira from HI Corporation reviewed and provided valuable input to Appendix B about the MascotCapsule V3 API.

Roger Riggs arranged access for me to an engineering copy of Sun's Java Wireless Toolkit with JSR 239 support. This enabled me to write about the Java Binding for OpenGL in Appendix C. Thanks also to the Wireless Toolkit Team, particularly E-ming Saung, Ariel Levin, Amihai Cohen, Dov Zandman, and Benny Fridschtein.

The wireframe example in Chapter 5 is based on an idea posted by Mik Bry on the Sony Ericsson developer forum.

Tomi Aarnio from Nokia helped me get the permission to reprint the reference geometry and fragment pipelines illustrations in Appendix A.

I'd also like to give credit to Mayang's Free Textures library and Hemera, The Big Box of Art, where I found images for illustrations and the example applications; Martin Newell, who created the Utah Teapot model, which I use throughout the book; NaN, the original creator of Blender and the monkey model Suzanne used in Chapter 10; and the companies that allowed me to ship versions of their software on the CD-ROM.

My sincere thanks to all who provided input to this book.

About the Author

Claus Höfele is a software engineer and writer. Throughout his career, he has specialized in software for devices with constrained memory and processing power, but plenty of challenges and opportunities. Over the years, Claus has developed for Web browsers, PDAs, smart cards, mobile phones, and game consoles.

Claus has worked in various roles for Sony Ericsson in Japan and Europe. This experience gives him unique insights and understanding of the Java platform on mobile phones. His involvement with Java began more than 10 years ago and Java continues to be one of his favorite tools. Claus now lives and works in Australia. You can contact him at claus@claushoefele.com.

Contents

	Introduction xiv
PART I	OVERVIEW 1
Chapter 1	The Mobile 3D Graphics API 3
	Java on Mobile Devices............................ 3
	Tailoring the Java Platform...................... 4
	The Java Micro Edition........................ 4
	Collection Standards.......................... 6
	M3G's Architecture........................... 7
	M3G Feature Overview 8
	M3G's Pedigree 8
	Features in M3G 1.0.......................... 9
	What's New in M3G 1.1 10
	Additional Clarifications from the MSA.............. 11
	The Future of M3G........................... 11
	Alternatives to M3G 12
	Summary 12
Chapter 2	Hello, World! 13
	Developing a MIDlet.............................. 13
	MIDlet States 14
	Displaying Screens 15
	Drawing Graphics........................... 17

vii

viii   Contents

     Receiving User Input 19
     Animating Your World. 22
   Running Your Application on the Emulator 24
     The Build Process. 24
     The Java Wireless Toolkit and the KToolbar 26
     Integrated Development Environments 32
   Downloading Your Application to the Phone. 32
     Installing Over the Air 32
     Alternative Methods of Installation. 33
   Summary 33

Chapter 3 **Before You Start** 35
   Getting to Know Your Device 35
     Does Your Phone Support M3G?. 35
     Implementation-Specific M3G Properties. 36
     Important MIDP Properties. 39
     Key Layouts 39
   Programming for Different Devices 41
     Hardware Considerations 41
     Device Fragmentation 43
   Summary 43

PART II **3D FUNDAMENTALS** 45

Chapter 4 **Rendering Geometric Objects** 47
   Coordinate Systems. 47
     3D 48
     2D 48
   Creating Meshes 49
     Mesh Overview 50
     Vertex Buffers and Arrays. 51
     Building Geometry. 53
     Polygon-Level Attributes. 58
     Colors 61
   Immediate Mode Rendering 63
     Graphics3D 63
     Defining a Background 68
     Render Targets. 71

	A Shapes Library	77
	Using Fractional Positions	78
	Cylinder and Sphere	80
	Bézier Surfaces	81
	Summary	93
Chapter 5	**Transformations**	**95**
	Transforming Vectors	95
	Transformation Matrices	96
	Homogeneous Coordinates	97
	Matrix Operations Using Transform	98
	Orientation Representations	102
	Stages of Vertex Transformation	107
	Modeling Transformations	109
	A Transformation Framework	109
	Translation	114
	Scaling	116
	Rotation	117
	Combining Transformations	119
	Generic Transformations	120
	Viewing Transformations	122
	Describing a Camera	122
	Switching Between Portrait and Landscape Mode	123
	Projection Transformations	129
	Setting the Viewing Volume	129
	Using Parallel and Perspective Projection	131
	The Viewport Transformation	134
	The Depth Buffer	136
	Using the Depth Buffer	137
	Depth Buffer Resolution	139
	Handling Transparent Objects	140
	Manually Transforming 3D Coordinates	141
	A Wireframe Engine	142
	Transforming 3D Coordinates	143
	Drawing Triangles	145
	Summary	149
Chapter 6	**Textures**	**151**
	Image2D	151
	Pixel Formats	151

Contents

Creating Images	153
Reading PNG Images	155
Reading JPEG Images	158
Using Textures	158
Texture Mapping	158
Creating Textures	161
Working with Texture Coordinates	167
Texture Quality	171
Sprite3D	174
Cheap Environment Mapping	176
The Real Thing	176
A Fast Alternative	177
Applying Environment Mapping to Meshes	182
Summary	186

Chapter 7 Blending and Transparency 187

Compositing	187
Fragment Tests	188
Blending Modes	190
Multi-Texturing	195
Texture Blending	196
Blending Modes	197
Adding Fog for Realism	198
Creating Fog	198
Fog Modes	202
Creating an Emboss Effect	206
Creating the Emboss Image	206
Embossing a Texture	207
Using the Emboss Effect	211
Summary	214

Chapter 8 Lighting 215

Lighting in M3G	215
M3G's Lighting Model	216
Finding Normals	216
Computing Normals	219
Lighting Quality	220
Light Sources	221
Creating Lights	221

		Ambient Light.................................	227
		Directional Light..............................	227
		Omnidirectional Light.........................	228
		Spot Light....................................	230
	Materials...		231
		Creating Materials............................	231
		Defining Material Properties..................	237
	Emulating Light.....................................		239
		Texture Baking...............................	239
		Vertex Colors................................	241
		Light Maps...................................	243
	Summary..		245
PART III	ADVANCED TOPICS................................		247
Chapter 9	Scene Graphs..		249
	Retained Mode......................................		249
		Creating a Scene Graph.......................	250
		Node Transformations.........................	254
		Rendering a World............................	255
	Retained versus Immediate Mode......................		258
	Node Properties.....................................		260
	Selecting Nodes.....................................		261
		Traversing a Scene Graph......................	261
		User IDs.....................................	262
		Picking......................................	263
		Scoping......................................	269
	Aligning Nodes......................................		270
	Billboards...		271
		Screen-Aligned Billboards......................	271
		Axis-Aligned Billboards........................	273
	Summary..		279
Chapter 10	M3G's File Format..................................		281
	Creating M3G Files with Blender......................		281
		Setting Up the Environment....................	282
		Getting to Know Blender......................	282
		Monkey Business.............................	286
		Exporting the Scene...........................	289

xii Contents

Using M3G Files in Your Application	290
Loading and Displaying the Contents	290
Finding Nodes	294
Coordinate Axes	295
Improving the Result	297
Export Options	297
Adjusting the Render Preview	299
Producing the Minimum Number of Vertices	300
Reducing the Poly Count	303
Analyzing M3G Files	305
File Structure	305
Contents of the Blender Generated File	308
Extending the M3G Exporter Script	311
Writing Blender Scripts	311
Data-Driven Applications	314
Playing Memory	322
Summary	324

Chapter 11   Keyframe Animations   325

Keyframes	325
Creating Keyframe Sequences	326
Interpolation Modes	328
Animation Targets	329
Controlling Animations	334
The Animation Loop	335
World versus Sequence Time	339
Moving Images	342
Drawing into Textures	342
UV Animations	344
UV Animations in Action	350
Alternatives	355
Summary	355

Chapter 12   Dynamic Meshes   357

Morphing	357
Basic Morphing	358
Creating a MorphingMesh	359
Animating Morph Targets	362

	Skinned Meshes	366
	Creating Skin and Skeleton	366
	Attaching the Skin to the Skeleton	368
	Rotating Bones with Quaternions	373
	Animating the Skeleton	376
	An Articulated Robot	382
	Rigging the Robot Model	382
	Skinning the Mesh	385
	Posing the Walk Animation	387
	Importing the Robot Model	389
	Switching Between Animation Sequences	393
	Summary	399
Appendix A	Reference Geometry and Fragment Pipelines	401
Appendix B	MascotCapsule V3 API	405
Appendix C	Java Binding for the OpenGL ES API	415
Appendix D	What's on the CD-ROM	429
	Index	433

Introduction

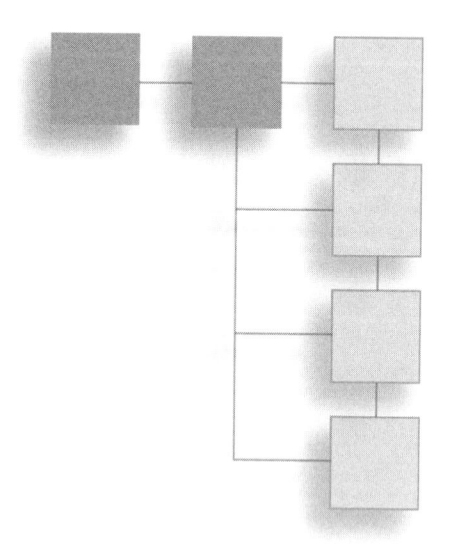

Mobile 3D Graphics: Learning 3D Graphics with the Java Micro Edition introduces you to the world of 3D graphics programming. What was formerly the domain of high-end computers is now readily available in mobile devices.

In this book, you'll learn about 3D graphics by using the Mobile 3D Graphics API, standardized as part of the Java Community Process in Java Specification Request 184. This API addresses the needs of developers who want to use Java for 3D graphics programming on devices with little memory and processing power.

These devices are the domain of the Java Platform, Micro Edition (previously known as the Java 2 Platform, Micro Edition, or J2ME). More specifically, this book focuses on the Connected, Limited Device Configuration (CLDC) and the Mobile Information Device Profile (MIDP). Both are part of the Java Micro Edition and together provide the application environment that's used in this book. If you buy a mobile phone today, chances are high that it includes such a Java environment and you can use it for 3D graphics programming. (See Chapter 3 to find out more about your device.)

Who Are You?

I assume you are eager to apply your programming skills to 3D graphics. You might be a student who needs an inexpensive programming environment to learn 3D graphics, a software developer who wants to work for the game industry, or an enthusiast who wants to create his or her own killer game. This book contains the basics you'll need to understand the complex topic of 3D graphics; many of the concepts in this book also apply to other 3D platforms.

But this book isn't for beginners alone. You might have already developed a game or have previous experience with 3D graphics in another environment. If you have already mastered the basics, you'll find plenty of examples in the book that will guide you to more advanced topics.

If you are new to the Java Micro Edition, you'll find an overview of this environment and an introduction to MIDP development in the first part of this book. You might want to complement this information with an introductory text in Java if you haven't used it before. Fortunately, Java has plenty of documentation freely available.

Tip

For a start, have a look at the trail Learning the Java Language in The Java Tutorials at http://java.sun.com/docs/books/tutorial/java/index.html. Note that this tutorial covers the Java Standard Edition. The Java Micro Edition used in this book allows most, but not all, programming concepts of its bigger cousin.

This book is not specifically about game programming, although it contains many examples that will help you in this context. For an introduction to this topic, I recommend *J2ME Game Programming* by Martin J. Wells, from the same publisher as this book.

What's in the Book?

Part I introduces you to the environment this book uses to create mobile 3D graphics applications:

Chapter 1, **The Mobile 3D Graphics API**, contains an overview of the Java Micro Edition and the Mobile 3D Graphics API.

Chapter 2, **Hello, World!**, explains more about CLDC and MIDP. In this chapter you'll develop your first 3D application and get a review of the CLDC/MIDP tool chain.

Chapter 3, **Before You Start**, will tell you how to find out more about a device and the challenges you will face when programming for the many devices that exist in the mobile space.

Part II covers the fundamentals of 3D graphics: creating geometry, transforming meshes, texturing models, blending operations, and lighting your scene:

Chapter 4, **Rendering Geometric Objects**, explains how you construct meshes and render them in immediate mode. You'll create a library of 3D shapes that will come in handy throughout the book.

Chapter 5, **Transformations**, shows you how to position a mesh in a scene. It also covers all other transformations in the geometry pipeline that your mesh will go through until it ends up on the screen, including viewing, projection, and viewport transformations.

Chapter 6, **Textures**, describes how you can wrap an image around a mesh to create realistic-looking models.

Chapter 7, **Blending and Transparency**, gives you the tools to create composites of different rendering sources. It also includes descriptions on how you can layer several textures on top of each other and create fog.

Chapter 8, **Lighting**, shows you how to shade your scene. Lighting adds depth and realism.

After covering the basics, you are ready to jump into the advanced topics in **Part III**:

Chapter 9, **Scene Graphs**, introduces a data structure that you can use to organize your scene. It will also introduce an alternate rendering mode that's closely related to scene graphs: retained mode.

Chapter 10, **M3G's File Format**, talks about creating and using files with serialized scene data. You'll see how you can export such files from Blender, an open-source 3D content-creation tool, and import the data into your own applications.

Chapter 11, **Keyframe Animations**, discusses how the Mobile 3D Graphics API helps you create animations and control the playback.

Chapter 12, **Dynamic Meshes**, describes two advanced features relating to meshes: morphing, which blends one mesh into another, and skinning, which is a technique to animate vertebrates such as humans and animals. Both features help you create articulated characters.

In the **appendixes**, you'll find the following complementary information:

Appendix A, **Reference Geometry and Fragment Pipelines**, shows M3G's official order of operation. You can use this as a handy index to the classes used in this book.

Appendix B, **MascotCapsule V3 API**, compares M3G with an alternate Java API by Japan-based HI Corporation. This API is successful for low-end devices.

Appendix C, **Java Binding for the OpenGL ES API**, provides an example using JSR 239. This API defines a Java mapping that resembles OpenGL ES's C interface, making it easy to port existing OpenGL content.

Appendix D, **What's on the CD-ROM**, outlines in detail what you'll find on the book's CD and describes how the CD is laid out.

What's on the CD-ROM?

The CD-ROM contains the book's source code, along with any graphics resources and data files you'll need to build and run the examples in this book. You'll also find software and links to Web sites that I find useful when developing my own 3D graphics applications.

I recommend that you play along with the examples while reading the chapters. Many are interactive and you can adjust different parameters to get a better understanding of the theory behind the examples. For updates, please visit the publisher's Web site (http://www.courseptr.com) and the author's home page (http://www.claushoefele.com). See Appendix D for a detailed list of what you'll find on the CD-ROM.

Part I

Overview

CHAPTER 1

The Mobile 3D Graphics API

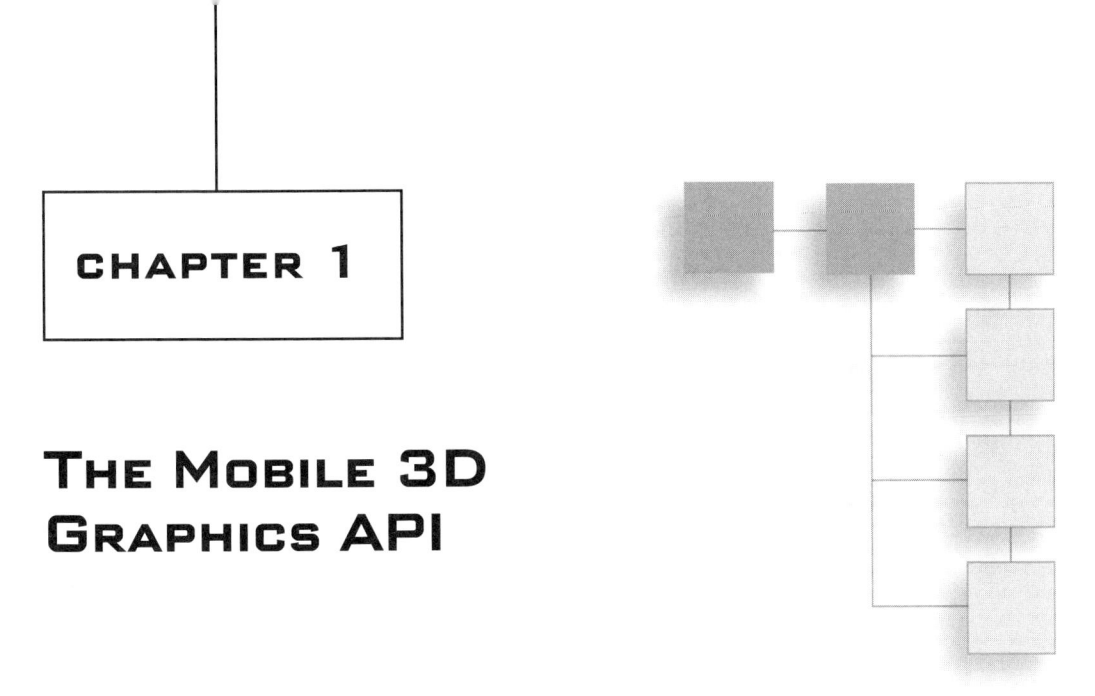

The Mobile 3D Graphics API, or M3G for short, provides a 3D graphics library for devices with little memory and processing power. Such devices pose unique challenges to application developers, but reward you with a huge potential market for your applications.

In this chapter, you will learn how Java and M3G help you create 3D content for constrained devices. I introduce you to:

- The Java Micro Edition.
- The different standards that surround Java and M3G.
- M3G's pedigree and features.
- Alternatives and how they compare to M3G.

Java on Mobile Devices

Java's device independence makes it particularly suitable to run on heterogeneous consumer devices. However, the same Java platform that works great on desktop systems is too large to fit the memory constraints of a mobile phone. On the other hand, important interfaces that only make sense on a mobile device are not included. To accommodate the different systems that run Java, Sun Microsystems,

Inc. created three editions that bundle the right set of Java language support, virtual machine, and class libraries to fit the needs of a particular environment.

Tailoring the Java Platform

The Java editions are the Java Platform, Standard Edition for desktop computers, the Java Platform, Enterprise Edition for server-side applications, and the Java Platform, Micro Edition for constrained devices.

Note

Beginning with Java 1.2, Sun included the number 2 in the names of the editions, such as Java 2 Micro Edition. With the advent of Java 5 (actually Java 1.5), Sun dropped the number again. Although the official name changed, you will still find lots of references on the Web to the old name and its abbreviation J2ME.

On the Java Standard Edition, you'll find 3D APIs that offer access to the power of desktop computers and the advanced features of 3D accelerated graphics cards. M3G, on the other hand, was specifically designed for devices with limited resources that might not have hardware support for 3D graphics or even floating-point math. On such devices, the dominate Java platform is the Java Micro Edition.

The Java Micro Edition

Even with the Java Micro Edition targeted toward constrained devices, the overwhelming number of appliances that fit this criterion requires more refined sub-categories. That's why the Java Micro Edition is further divided into configurations, profiles, and optional packages. The Java Community Process creates the specifications for these components.

In the Java Community Process, Sun works together with members of the industry to agree on new Java APIs. If there's a missing feature, a process member can suggest a new Java Specification Request (JSR) and establish an expert group that works together to produce a new standard. At the end, the JSR results in a specification, a reference implementation, and a technology compatibility kit. The reference implementation and the compatibility kit help companies verify their implementation's compliance to the specification.

Tip

Each JSR has a number assigned. You can use this number to find documentation and further information for it on the Java Community Process Web site at http://jcp.org.

Configurations

A configuration details the Java virtual machine and a base set of Java classes for devices that share similar hardware characteristics. The Java Micro Edition knows two configurations—the Connected Device Configuration (CDC) and the Connected, Limited Device Configuration (CLDC).

CDC targets devices with several megabytes of memory such as set-top boxes and PDAs. On CDC, you more or less have a standard Java environment, albeit with a subset of Java's class libraries. As mobile phones become more and more powerful, CDC will be increasingly viable for these devices. So far, however, the majority of mobile phones support CLDC.

CLDC defines a subset of the Java language and the Java Virtual Machine Specification; for example, there is no finalization support for classes or user-defined class loaders. These omissions together with a restricted standard library make it possible to implement Java on devices with as little as several hundred kilobytes of memory.

With CLDC, everything is optimized for constrained devices. To save the time and memory it takes to process an application at runtime, Java classes must be specially formatted. For this reason, you have to perform an additional step at development time, called *preverification*. You will learn more about the CLDC tool chain and preverification in Chapter 2.

CLDC 1.0 (JSR 30) was the first CLDC standard and was superseded by CLDC 1.1 (JSR 139). The major addition of the latter version was floating point support. In other words, you can use `float` and `double` variables in your application. For a device that supports M3G, CLDC 1.1 is a requirement because M3G's interface uses `float` types.

Profiles

On top of a configuration, you need a profile that provides a complete runtime environment for applications. Among other APIs, a profile defines classes for the user interface and access to persistent storage. The profile used in this book is the Mobile Information Device Profile (MIDP), which targets mobile phones and similar devices. Applications written for this profile are also called *MIDlets* because the specification requires you to follow a specific application model, which is introduced in Chapter 2.

MIDP 1.0 (JSR 37) brought its own user interface API called LCDUI, which was streamlined to work well on mobile devices. For example, most phones have a number pad and a navigation key as their input devices instead of a full keyboard and mouse. MIDP 1.0 also features the Record Management System to persist data and support for HTTP and other network protocols.

Most notably for game developers, MIDP 2.0 (JSR 118) introduced an enhanced audio API and classes that simplify the development of 2D games. MIDP 2.1 was a maintenance release of the same JSR that provided clarifications for the specification.

Optional Packages

Although a configuration and a profile define all that's necessary to create applications, optional packages extend a platform with APIs for a very specific purpose. As their name indicates, it's up to the manufacturer which packages you will find on the device. M3G is such an optional package defined in JSR 184. M3G's initial version is 1.0, which was later extended in a maintenance release to create version 1.1.

If you are developing a game, you might also be interested in the Mobile Media API (JSR 135), which defines a superset of MIDP 2.0's audio API, or the Java APIs for Bluetooth (JSR 82), for multiplayer games.

Collection Standards

As you have seen, there are a lot of possible ways to configure the Java platform for a particular device. Because of the overwhelming number of JSRs targeting the Java Micro Edition, the industry saw the need to create bundles of configurations, profiles, and optional packages. These collections provide a common set of APIs that reduce the variety of Java implementations. In addition, they come with an additional set of clarifications and requirements to improve interoperability between devices.

The first such initiative was the Java Technology for the Wireless Industry (JTWI; JSR 185). It includes CLDC 1.0, MIDP 2.0, and the Wireless Messaging API 1.1 (JSR 120). Optionally, a JTWI compliant device includes CLDC 1.1 and the Mobile Media API 1.1 (JSR 135).

The Mobile Service Architecture (JSR 248) is the successor to JTWI and raised the bar in terms of supported APIs. A compliant device can either implement the MSA Subset that includes eight component JSRs or the full MSA specification with 16 JSRs. Some of these APIs are conditionally mandatory, which means that a device must support them only if the underlying system provides the feature. For example, Bluetooth support (JSR 82) is mandatory only if the necessary hardware is present.

Whether JTWI devices include M3G is up to the device manufacturer. Conversely, all MSA compliant devices must support M3G 1.1. This makes the latter viable targets for your 3D applications, but you will also have to cope with older devices. Chapter 3 explains how you can find out which APIs a mobile phone supports.

M3G's Architecture

M3G is compatible with several editions and configurations. This book, however, focuses on the CLDC/MIDP class of devices. It is these appliances that represent the majority of mobile phones. Figure 1.1 provides an overview of the Java architecture on such a device.

MIDP subsumes the functionality of installing, selecting, and running an application under the term *application management software*. When the user asks the application manager to start a Java application, it begins executing inside the virtual machine where your application can access all APIs installed on the system. If your application wants to use M3G, this must consist of at least CLDC 1.1 and a version of MIDP, typically MIDP 2.0. These APIs are implemented with the help of the phone's system software that provides access to resources such as the display or 3D hardware acceleration if it exists.

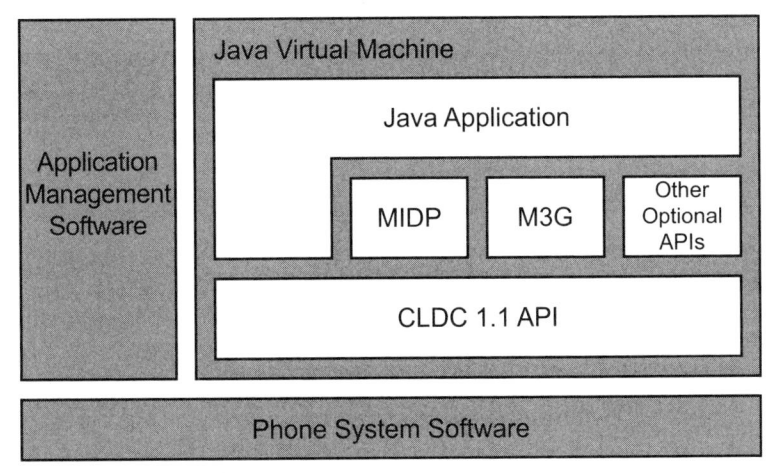

Figure 1.1
The architecture of a typical M3G device.

M3G Feature Overview

Java doesn't exist in isolation. For non-Java applications, the *de facto* standard for 3D graphics on constrained devices is OpenGL ES. OpenGL ES is a streamlined version of the widely known OpenGL 3D library. When creating M3G, the expert group set the goal to define M3G so that it can be implemented on top of OpenGL ES.

M3G's Pedigree

Although it's up to the M3G implementer whether to actually use OpenGL ES underneath, defining M3G based on OpenGL ES features ensures that many devices are able to support it. OpenGL ES is also a natural path toward hardware acceleration because many graphics processing units (GPUs) come with a driver for this API. Figure 1.2 shows how OpenGL relates to M3G and other influences that went into the definition of M3G.

As I have already mentioned, M3G requires CLDC 1.1 because it uses float types in its interface. Floating point numbers are a lot more convenient to work with than fixed point numbers. The drawback is that most CPUs used on mobile phones don't have a floating point unit to execute such calculations in hardware. If floating point calculations are executed in software, they are painfully slow.

However, the use of float in Java doesn't necessarily require the M3G implementation to use floating point numbers internally. Implementations are allowed to represent floats with fixed point numbers instead. This isn't completely transparent to the application developer because fixed and floating point numbers differ in range and accuracy.

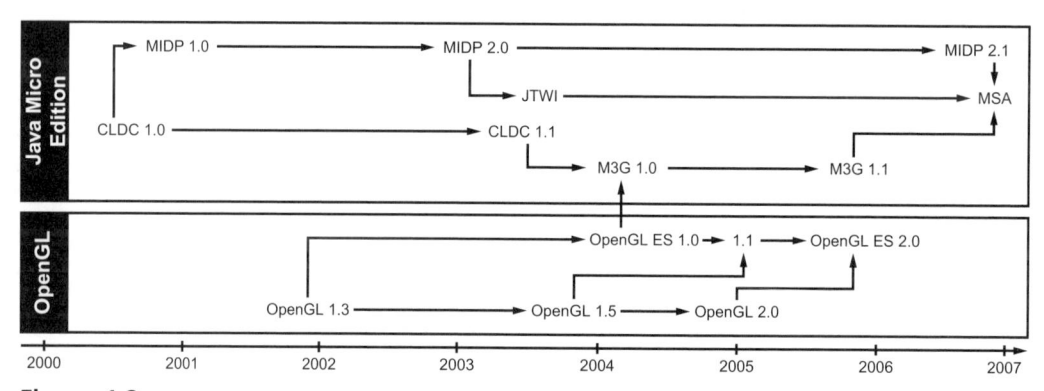

Figure 1.2
M3G requires CLDC 1.1 and has influences from OpenGL ES 1.0 and OpenGL 1.3.

> **Note**
>
> The package description in M3G's javadoc contains a section called "Numeric Range and Accuracy" that details the requirements for fixed and floating point support.

For application developers it's also important that M3G integrates well with MIDP as it provides the application shell around M3G code that you can execute. As an example of the integration, M3G makes it possible to mix 2D and 3D graphics on the same drawing context if certain preconditions are fulfilled. Although M3G works with both MIDP 1.0 and 2.0, most devices with M3G support the newer MIDP version. Chapter 3 explains how you can determine which MIDP version is installed on your device.

Features in M3G 1.0

The heritage to OpenGL and OpenGL ES means that if you know these libraries, you will recognize many of M3G's features, albeit in an object-oriented disguise. As an overview, here's a quick run-down of the OpenGL subset that M3G supports:

- Rendering of indexed triangle lists.
- Parallel, projective, or generic camera transformations.
- Lighting model with ambient, diffuse, emissive, and specular components.
- Minimum of eight light sources.
- Fog.
- Frame buffer compositing with alpha blending.
- Multi-texturing (optional).

But M3G's expert group didn't rest on the merits of OpenGL alone. M3G contains additional features that make an application developer's life easier. Most notably, this includes a scene graph API to structure your 3D objects and a file format to read in 3D models created in digital content creation tools. Chapter 9 tells you more about scene graphs and Chapter 10 more about M3G's binary format.

Other high-level features include:

- Keyframe animations.
- Skinned and morphing meshes to facilitate character animation.

- Intersection testing and alignment of meshes.
- Background and screen aligned images.

M3G is a general purpose 3D API. Although games are the main attraction, you might also want to use M3G for applications such as map visualization software or screen savers.

What's New in M3G 1.1

M3G 1.1 was a maintenance release that introduced few new features, but instead concentrated on tightening the specification and improving the existing API.

If you scan the documentation for added methods, you will find many new getter methods to query existing object properties. As each M3G class is introduced in this book, a class table shows you its interface. In this table, you'll find an indication as to whether a method is new for version 1.1. That way, you can either take advantage of the new methods or write applications that use M3G 1.0 exclusively. The examples in this book work on either version.

Other changes include:

- In M3G 1.1, Sprite3Ds now also inherit an ancestor's alpha factor in the same way as other meshes do. With the alpha factor, you can blend groups of meshes in and out. You will read more about Sprite3Ds in Chapter 6. Chapter 9 introduces scene graphs and discusses how to group objects.

- M3G defines runtime exceptions to signal error states. In many places, the API now throws fewer exceptions than before.

- The API clarified how Loader converts PNG images to M3G's image format and that it must treat file names as case sensitive. Also, M3G 1.1 now specifies how mutable and immutable MIDP images convert to M3G images. Chapter 6 contains more information about M3G's image format and how to read PNG files.

- There's a new OVERWRITE hint flag for Graphics3D.bindTarget(). When specified, the contents of the render target when binding are undefined, which can improve performance. Otherwise, existing contents in the target before binding are preserved. Target surfaces used in bindTarget()

are now restricted to the maximum viewport size. You learn how to use `bindTarget()` in Chapter 4.

- Several smaller resolved interoperability issues.

Using new features obviously causes a problem on older devices, but you have to be careful the other way around as well. If you rely on M3G 1.0's definition of features that changed in version 1.1, your code might not run as expected on newer devices. Either avoid these features or switch your code based on the M3G version. Chapter 3 explains how to determine which M3G version a device supports.

Additional Clarifications from the MSA

Devices that are compatible with the Mobile Service Architecture (JSR 248) support the following additional requirements:

- In addition to PNG, JPEG is a mandatory image format for M3G. Chapter 6 contains more information about image formats and how you can put them to use.

- When loading a file in M3G's binary format from the network, the device must comply with the security checks mandated by MIDP. That means that the user must confirm access to the network before you can use it. Also, an `IOException` is thrown if M3G encounters a file format that is not supported by the implementation. Reading resources with M3G is covered in Chapters 6 and 9.

- If a Java application goes to paused state, M3G must not automatically release any resources. You will see the different application states in Chapter 2.

The Future of M3G

Version 2.0 of M3G is underway in the form of JSR 297. As the capabilities of mobile devices improve, you can expect to see more features from the latest versions of OpenGL ES come to M3G. Goals defined for the new standard include the improvement of 3D art asset compression and the addition of features from OpenGL ES 1.1 and 2.0.

Tip

Check back at JSR 297's Web site at http://jcp.org/en/jsr/detail?id=297 to find the latest developments. Before new specifications become final, there's also a review phase where you can give feedback.

Alternatives to M3G

M3G is not the only Java 3D library for mobile phones. Two alternative contenders are HI Corporation's MascotCapsule V3 API and the Java Bindings for OpenGL ES (JSR 239).

MascotCapsule is a 3D rendering engine developed by Japan based HI Corporation, which offers its own Java interface from version V3 of the engine. The API has a simplified set of features that result in increased performance on low-end devices. You can see an example of how to use MascotCapsule V3 API in Appendix B.

JSR 239 defines a Java API that resembles OpenGL ES's interface as much as possible, making it easy to port existing OpenGL content. It offers direct access to OpenGL ES operations. However, it doesn't offer anything comparable to M3G's high-level features such as scene graph support. Appendix C contains an example that uses JSR 239.

Although the supported features differ between APIs, the underlying principles of 3D graphics stay the same. Appendixes B and C serve as references on how you can translate your know-how from M3G to these alternatives.

Summary

In this chapter, you have seen where M3G comes from and what it includes.

M3G was designed to run on devices with little memory and processing power. Such devices usually have the Java Micro Edition installed, which is further divided into configurations, profiles, and optional packages.

The configuration and profile provide the application environment. All applications in this book are written for CLDC/MIDP devices, which represent the majority of mobile phones. A device is complemented by optional packages such as M3G. M3G is based on OpenGL for standard 3D graphics features but also adds its own high-level APIs that make an application developer's life easier.

To help you get used to CLDC/MIDP, the next chapter illustrates how you can write an application in this environment.

CHAPTER 2

Hello, World!

M3G provides a 3D graphics library, but not an application model. That's where CLDC and MIDP come in, which define a host environment to create applications for mobile phones. Whereas CLDC takes care of class compilation and execution, MIDP provides the user interface and the deployment model. In this chapter, you develop a MIDlet that you can use as a framework for your own 3D applications.

This chapter shows you how to:

- Use the MIDP application framework.
- Display graphics and receive user input.
- Create a render loop for animated applications.
- Build and test a MIDlet with the Java Wireless Toolkit.
- Download a MIDlet to a phone.

Developing a MIDlet

The application management software controls the lifecycle of your application. To make this possible, you have to derive a class from `javax.microedition.midlet.MIDlet` and implement methods that allow the Java platform to interact with your program.

MIDlet States

Figure 2.1 shows the possible lifecycle states of a MIDlet. Right at the start, your application transfers to the paused state. When paused, a MIDlet should minimize its use of system resources. Instead, allocating resources should be done in the active state, which indicates that your application is ready for execution. Your application enters the destroyed state when it's terminating, which typically happens when the user ends your application.

By overriding the following MIDlet interfaces, you can add custom behavior to the state transitions:

- new: When creating a new instance of your MIDlet derived class, the application management software calls the no-argument constructor. However, the MIDlet is in a paused state, which means it shouldn't hold any expensive resources. You should postpone these initializations until startApp() is called.

- startApp(): The application management software calls this method to signal that the MIDlet has entered the active state. In contrast to new, this can happen more than once during the lifetime of an application because a MIDlet can transition between the paused and active states any time.

- pauseApp(): When entering the paused state, the application management software wants your application to free resources. A paused state might indicate that another application now has the focus.

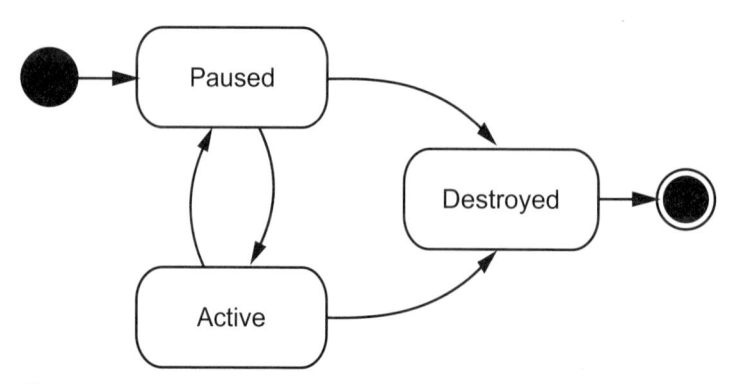

Figure 2.1
A MIDlet can be in one of three states.

Releasing resources allows this application to use them again. If you do this, make sure to reallocate the resources in `startApp()`.

- `destroyApp()`: When the MIDlet has entered the destroyed state, this is your last chance to clean up and save application data for the next start.

State transitions don't complete until the respective method has returned. To avoid blocking the user interface, any lengthy task should be offloaded to a thread. You will see an example of using a thread later in this chapter.

The previously mentioned state transitions are initiated by the application management software. Conversely, your application can also notify the application manager to trigger state changes. `notifyPaused()` and `notifyDestroyed()` signal that your application wants to enter paused and destroyed states. Neither of these methods calls `pauseApp()` and `destroyApp()`; you must make sure to call any methods that release resources. `resumeRequest()` indicates that your application wants to change from paused to active state. If this request is successful, the application management software will call `startApp()`.

Displaying Screens

To display something on the screen, you can use your MIDlet's `startApp()` method as a starting point. The following code illustrates this:

```
/*
 * Mobile 3D Graphics
 * Learning 3D Graphics with the Java Micro Edition
 */

package m3g02;

import javax.microedition.midlet.*;
import javax.microedition.lcdui.*;

/**
 * MIDlet for <code>HelloWorldSample</code>.
 *
 * @author Claus Hoefele
 */
public class Main extends MIDlet {
  /** The sample. */
  private HelloWorldSample sample;
```

```java
/**
 * Constructor.
 */
public Main() {}

/**
 * Enters the active state. Displays the sample.
 */
public void startApp() {
  if (sample == null) {
    sample = new HelloWorldSample();
    sample.init();
    Display.getDisplay(this).setCurrent(sample);
  }
}

/**
 * Enters the paused state.
 */
public void pauseApp() {}

/**
 * Enters the destroyed state.
 *
 * @param unconditional if true, MIDlet is required to exit
 *                      unconditionally.
 */
public void destroyApp(boolean unconditional) {
  if (sample != null) {
    sample.destroy();
  }
 }
}
```

`Main` derives from `MIDlet`, so it has to implement the abstract methods that signal a state change: `startApp()`, `pauseApp()`, and `destroyApp()`. In `startApp()`, the MIDlet creates a new `HelloWorldSample` instance that represents the screen used to show your application's user interface. `startApp()` then brings `HelloWorldSample` to the foreground by calling `Display.getDisplay(this).setCurrent()`.

`HelloWorldSample` and any class used for display must inherit from one of `Displayable`'s subclasses. These come in two flavors: those you can use for high-level user interfaces and those you can use for low-level graphics access to the screen.

`Screen` is the common superclass of high-level screens, which you can use to create user interfaces out of pre-configured building blocks. For example, MIDP offers lists, dialogs, and forms. With forms, you can configure a custom screen out of items such as text fields and choice groups.

High-level user interfaces are convenient for the programmer because you don't have to worry about how to draw the individual components. If, however, you want more direct access to the screen, you have to use `Canvas` or its subclass `GameCanvas`. They put every pixel on the screen under your control.

Drawing Graphics

MIDP 2.0 introduced `GameCanvas`. It inherits all features of `Canvas` but is also always double-buffered—you first draw in an off-screen buffer and once you are finished, you copy the complete contents to the screen. This avoids the flickering that occurs when the system updates the screen in between drawing calls. Conversely, `Canvas` supports double-buffering only if the device implemented this feature. In this case, `Canvas.isDoubleBuffered()` returns `true`.

The implementation of `HelloWorldSample` demonstrates how to use `GameCanvas`. `HelloWorldSample` gives you a jumpstart on the usage of M3G, which will be complemented by more detailed explanations later in this book.

```java
package m3g02;

import javax.microedition.lcdui.*;
import javax.microedition.lcdui.game.*;
import javax.microedition.m3g.*;

/**
 * Animates a three-dimensional Hello, World! text that's stored in a
 * binary file.
 *
 * @author Claus Hoefele
 */
public class HelloWorldSample extends GameCanvas {
  /** File that stores the 3D scene. */
  private static final String M3G_FILE = "/m3g02/helloworld.m3g";
  /** User ID to find the mesh inside the scene graph. */
  private static final int USER_ID_MESH = 1;

  /** Object that represents the 3D world. */
  private World world;
```

```java
/** Text mesh. */
private Mesh mesh;

/** 3D graphics singleton used for rendering. */
private Graphics3D graphics3d;
/** 2D graphics singleton used for rendering. */
private Graphics graphics;

/**
 * Constructor.
 */
public HelloWorldSample() {
  super(true);  // suppress game key events received in key handlers
}

/**
 * Initializes the sample.
 */
public void init() {
   // Get the singletons for rendering.
   graphics3d = Graphics3D.getInstance();
   graphics = getGraphics();

  try {
   // Load World from M3G binary file.
   Object3D[] objects = Loader.load(M3G_FILE);
   world = (World) objects[0];

   // Change the camera's properties to match the current device.
   Camera camera = world.getActiveCamera();
   float aspect = (float) getWidth() / (float) getHeight();
   camera.setPerspective(60, aspect, 1, 1000);

   // Find mesh in scene graph.
   mesh = (Mesh) world.find(USER_ID_MESH);
  } catch (Exception e) {
   System.out.println("Error loading" + M3G_FILE + ".");
   e.printStackTrace();
  }

   // Display scene.
   render(graphics);
   flushGraphics();
 }
```

```
/**
 * Destroys the sample.
 */
public void destroy() {
}

/**
 * Renders the sample.
 *
 * @param graphics graphics context for rendering.
 */
protected void render(Graphics graphics) {
  graphics3d.bindTarget(graphics);
  graphics3d.setViewport(0, 0, getWidth(), getHeight());
  graphics3d.render(world);
  graphics3d.releaseTarget();
}
}
```

You have already seen the different states of a MIDlet that you can use to react on external events. In `HelloWorldSample`, `init()` and `destroy()` serve to relay this information from the MIDlet to the display class. Whereas `init()` is called by `Main.startApp()` to create all M3G resources, `destroy()` is called by `destroyApp()` when the application exits.

Part of the resource allocation in `init()` is to get access to a graphics context by calling `getGraphics()`. The returned `Graphics` object provides 2D drawing methods such as `drawLine()` that write in the off-screen buffer. `HelloWorldSample` also creates a `Graphics3D` object that provides 3D drawing methods. Both objects are stored in the class for later use.

Most other M3G parameters are hidden in helloworld.m3g, which is a binary file that contains a 3D scene. (The mechanism for creating such files is fully explained in Chapter 10.) `init()` reads the file's contents into a `World` object and draws it on the screen by calling `render()`. This method binds the `Graphics3D` object to the `Graphics` context to tell M3G where to write the output. When `render()` returns, the off-screen buffer contains the graphics output, which is then copied to the screen by calling `GameCanvas.flushGraphics()`. You can see the result in Figure 2.2.

Receiving User Input

For classes derived from `Canvas`, MIDP offers two mechanisms to receive user input: commands that tie soft keys to actions and key handlers.

Figure 2.2
The rendered Hello, World! example.

Commands

A `Command` object describes the functionality of a soft key and can be added to any `Displayable`. To receive an event, you write a class that implements `CommandListener` and register it with `Displayable.setCommandListener()`:

```
public class Main extends MIDlet implements CommandListener {
  /** Exit command. */
  private Command exitCommand = new Command("Exit", Command.EXIT, 1);

  ...

  /**
   * Enters the active state. Displays the sample.
   */
  public void startApp() {
    if (sample == null) {
      sample = new HelloWorldSample();
      sample.init();
      sample.addCommand(exitCommand);
```

```
    sample.setCommandListener(this);
    Display.getDisplay(this).setCurrent(sample);
  }
}

...
/**
 * Receives command actions.
 *
 * @param command command.
 * @param displayable source of the command.
 */
public void commandAction(Command command, Displayable displayable) {
  if (command == exitCommand) {
    destroyApp(true);
    notifyDestroyed();
  }
 }
}
```

A `Command` contains a soft key's label, type, and priority. Many devices have a standard way of displaying typical operations such as exit and back. If you indicate the correct type, the MIDP implementation can place your command in accordance with the user interface guidelines of your device. The priority describes the importance of the command. A MIDP implementation might make a high-priority command accessible with one button click, whereas a low-priority command might be hidden in a submenu.

A command is added to a `Displayable` with `addCommand()`. After registering a class that implements the `CommandListener` interface, pressing a soft key will result in a call to `commandAction()` in the observing class. `Main` uses this mechanism to exit the application.

Key Events and Game Actions

Unlike commands, you will receive key events without registering a listener. However, key events are unique to subclasses of `Canvas`, which can override `keyPressed()` and `keyReleased()` to implement a key handler.

When choosing which key to use for your application, you will run into the problem whereby different devices have different key layouts. A key to fire a bullet might be conveniently located on one device, but not on another. To this end, MIDP introduced game actions that abstract common operations. Instead of listening to the number eight key for example, you can listen to `Canvas.DOWN`. The device manufacturer ensures that the action is mapped to a convenient location such as the navigation key most devices have.

One key event maps to one game action, but not necessarily the other way around. For example, a device might map the same game action to two locations so that the user has a choice. To convert from a key code to a game action, call `Canvas.getGameAction()` in your key handler. Another convenient method is `getKeyName()`, which returns a textual representation of a key code.

When using `GameCanvas` instead of `Canvas`, you can suppress receiving game key events in `keyPressed()` and `keyReleased()`. The device then stops delivering such events, which might speed up your application. Because `HelloWorldSample` doesn't need these events, it calls `super(true)` in its constructor. If you want to receive them, call the superclass's constructor with `false` instead.

Animating Your World

In a game, you usually have constant animations going on to make some interesting effects. This requires an independently running task that updates the animation in regular intervals. In Java, such an independent task is a subclass of `Thread`. However, because `HelloWorldSample` already derives from `GameCanvas`, it implements the interface `Runnable` instead.

```
public class HelloWorldSample extends GameCanvas implements Runnable {
  /** Flag for stopping the animation thread.*/
  private boolean isRunning;
  ...

  /**
   * Initializes the sample.
   */
  public void init() {
    ...

    // Start animation.
    Thread thread = new Thread(this);
    isRunning = true;
    thread.start();
  }
```

```
/**
 * Destroys the sample.
 */
public void destroy() {
  isRunning = false;
}

/**
 * Drives the animation.
 */
public void run() {
   while(isRunning) {
      // Advance the animation by rotating the mesh.
      if (mesh != null) {
         mesh.postRotate(-1, 0, 0, 1);
      }

      // Display scene.
      render(graphics);
      flushGraphics();

    try {
       Thread.sleep(20);                    // max 50 fps
    } catch (Exception e){}
   }
  }
  ...
}
```

In `init()`, the `Runnable` is turned into a `Thread` and started. This causes the call of the `run()` method where you implement your animation. In `HelloWorldSample`, this method consists of rotating the 3D text, rendering the result to the screen, and waiting for 20 milliseconds. The latter limits your frame rate to a maximum of 50 frames per second. Depending on the time it takes to render the world and the accuracy of `sleep()`, the actual frame rate is slower than that.

When implementing an animation loop, it's inconvenient to receive key events asynchronously via `keyPressed()`. You'll have to think about synchronization because one thread animates the game, and the system delivers key events on another. To make game, development easier, `GameCanvas` provides `getKeyStates()` that synchronously retrieves the currently pressed keys. You can test the resulting int value against bit patterns stored in GameCanvas such as FIRE_PRESSED. With this method, you avoid synchronization issues by calling getKeyStates() as part of your animation loop inside run().

Running Your Application on the Emulator

Before you can run your application, you have to build it. Sun provides you with the Java Wireless Toolkit, which contains the tools necessary to build your application and execute the result in an emulator.

The Build Process

CLDC and MIDP govern different parts of the tool chain to build an application: whereas CLDC specifies how to prepare the class files, MIDP defines how to package your application and deliver it to a device.

The CLDC Tool Chain

The build process of CLDC-based applications differs from the Java Standard Edition in order to accommodate the memory and speed constraints of embedded devices. To decrease the resources necessary to process an application when it's executed, the class file verification is split into an offline part that's done at development time and an online part done at runtime. Class file verification ensures that only valid Java classes are executed.

Figure 2.3 shows the CLDC tool chain. After compilation, all classes must go through the preverifier. This tool prepares the classes by replacing some bytecodes with easier to verify, equivalent substitutions and adding information that speeds up the online verification process. The tradeoff is that this process results in an increased file size. Non-CLDC class file verifiers simply ignore the additional information, so the classes are still valid input to conventional VMs.

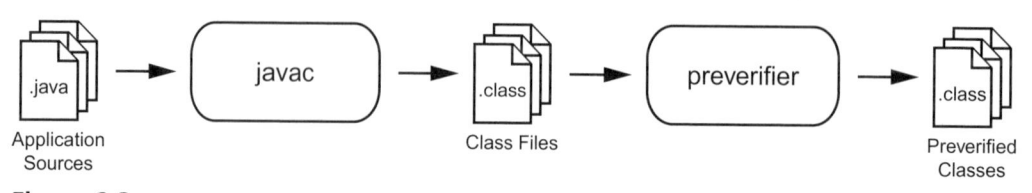

Figure 2.3
Java classes have to be compiled and preverified before using them on a CLDC device.

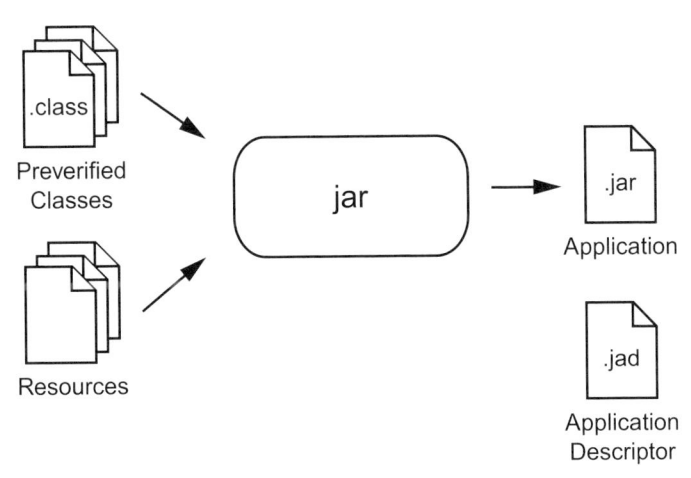

Figure 2.4
The application's classes and resources are packed into a JAR file.

Creating a MIDlet Suite

The application management software deals with *MIDlet suites*, which consist of one or more MIDlets. A MIDlet suite comprises all preverified classes, resources, and other data that is necessary to run your applications in a Java archive file (JAR). MIDlets in the same suite can share this data. Figure 2.4 depicts the process of creating a JAR file from your files.

Tip
> You can use a standard zip utility to look into your JAR file to check that all the files are included.

You can accompany the JAR file with an optional Java application descriptor with the file ending .jad. With this file, a device checks whether it can execute your application successfully before starting the possibly lengthy process of downloading the application itself.

The following is the contents of the JAD file for the example in this chapter:

```
MIDlet-1: HelloWorld, HelloWorld.png, m3g02.Main
MIDlet-Jar-Size: 7048
MIDlet-Jar-URL: HelloWorld.jar
MIDlet-Name: HelloWorld
MIDlet-Vendor: Unknown
MIDlet-Version: 1.0
MicroEdition-Configuration: CLDC-1.1
MicroEdition-Profile: MIDP-2.0
```

The JAD file consists of name value pairs separated by a colon. `MIDlet-1` identifies the MIDlet's name, icon, and `MIDlet` derived class. Because you can have several MIDlets in one suite, you can add additional entries with increasing values for the `MIDlet-<n>` parameter. The suite itself has a name specified in the `MIDlet-Name` attribute.

`MIDlet-Jar-URL` and `MIDlet-Jar-Size` indicate where to download your application's JAR file and how big it is. Based on the size, the device can reject applications that won't fit on the device. In a similar way, a device will download your application only if the minimum versions specified in `MicroEdition-Configuration` and `MicroEdition-Profile` are met. Also when downloading, the `MIDlet-Version` can be used to check whether the same version is already installed. Finally, you can add some information about yourself in the `MIDlet-Vendor` attribute.

> **Tip**
>
> You can add your own named properties to the JAD file and read the values with `MIDlet.getAppProperty()`.

The JAD file is optional because the same information can also be added to the MANIFEST.MF file stored inside the JAR file. This is Java's standard way of providing meta information about applications. However, this prevents the device from checking your application before downloading it.

> **Tip**
>
> Avoid conflicts between attributes in the JAD and the MANIFEST.MF file by always providing the same values.

The Java Wireless Toolkit and the KToolbar

Fortunately, you don't have to execute the steps to create your application deliverables manually. Sun offers the Java Wireless Toolkit that comes with a MIDlet emulator as well as tools to make a developer's life easier. Among them is the KToolbar, which serves as a dashboard to build and run MIDlet applications.

Installing the Software

Before you install the Wireless Toolkit, you need a Java Standard Edition Development Kit. Make sure to download the Development Kit rather than the Runtime Environment because you need the Java compiler to build your MIDlets.

The Wireless Toolkit supports the M3G 1.0 API since version 2.2 and supports M3G 1.1 since 2.5. The examples in this book are compatible with either M3G version.

Note

You can find the Java SDK at http://java.sun.com/javase/ and the Wireless Toolkit at http://java.sun.com/products/sjwtoolkit/.

Tip

The Java Wireless Toolkit only supports Windows XP. If you are a Mac OS X or Linux user, try the mpowerplayer (http://www.mpowerplayer.com/).

After installation, you will have a new entry for the Wireless Toolkit in the Windows Start menu. Among the new applications, you will also find the KToolbar.

Creating a New Project

Figure 2.5 shows the dialog box that opens after you start the KToolbar and click the New Project button. Enter the project name and the MIDlet's class name in the upcoming dialog box.

The project name decides the name of the folder where your application resides, the name of the JAR and JAD files, and the MIDlet's name as it will show up in the phone's menu. Except for the application folder, you can give each setting individual values after you have finished creating the project.

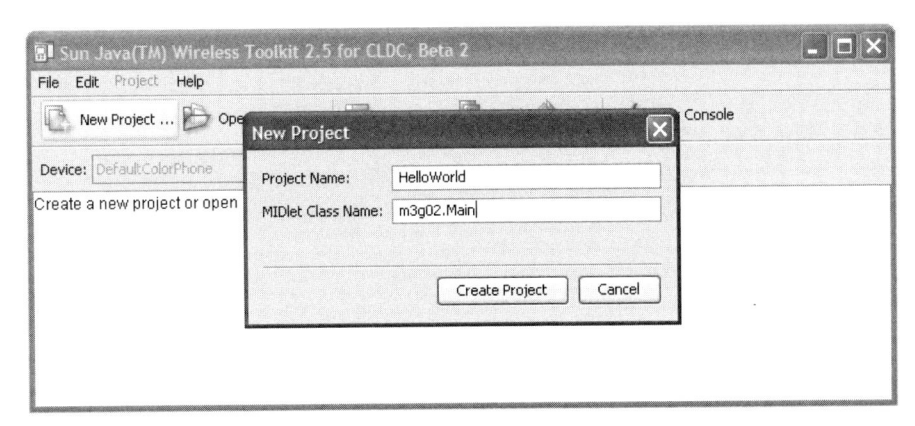

Figure 2.5
Creating a new project.

In the second text box, you have to enter the fully qualified name of a class derived from `MIDlet`. Because the samples in this book each live in a chapter specific package, the correct setting in this case is "m3g02.Main." In the previous section, you find this value in the package definition in the source code. Initially, you'll have one MIDlet in the suite, but you can add more later on.

After entering the project and MIDlet name, the KToolbar will automatically open the settings dialog box. The API Selection page, shown in Figure 2.6, allows you to select which APIs your application can use. Make sure that Mobile 3D Graphics for J2ME (JSR 184) is included in the list of APIs. If it's missing, you will

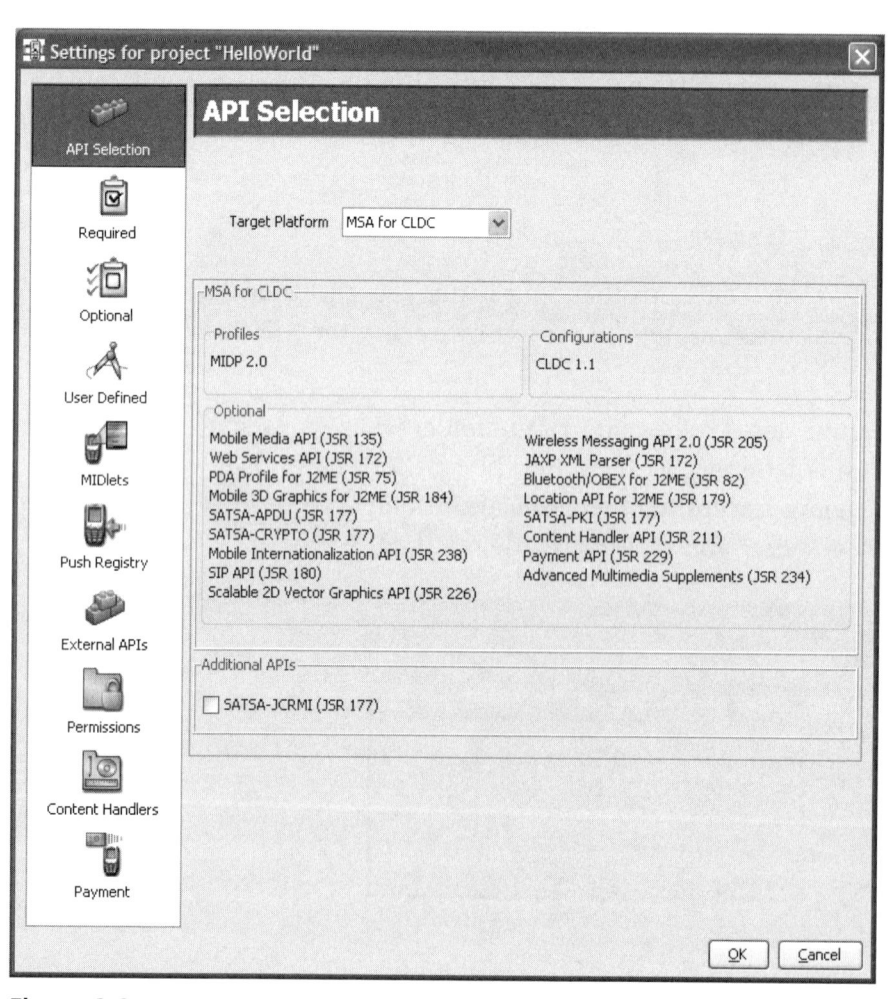

Figure 2.6
The API Selection dialog box.

get compilation errors. The default selection for target platform, the Mobile Service Architecture for CLDC, is fine.

Note

The Java Wireless Toolkit 2.5 doesn't allow you to choose between M3G 1.0 and 1.1. Be careful which methods you call in your application when targeting older devices that only support version 1.0. Alternatively, you can install the toolkit in version 2.3 in parallel to the newer version. This software supports M3G 1.0 exclusively.

Should you need to go back to this dialog box, you can open it by clicking the Settings button in the KToolbar's main screen. The MIDlet has sensible default values, but you might want to have a look at the different pages in the settings dialog box if you want to add another MIDlet to your suite, for example. These settings are written to the JAD file and determine the properties of your application.

Adding Source Code and Resources

After you closed the settings dialog box with the OK button, the KToolbar will create a new directory for your project. This directory is located below the installation directory where you installed the Wireless Toolkit. In there, you will find a directory called apps that contains all the applications. Your application lives in its own folder that has the same name as the project.

Note

The KToolbar doesn't allow you to change where the applications reside; it's always below the apps folder. Neither can you import an existing project from another directory or change the project's directory structure.

Copy the source code of your Java application to the src folder and the resources to res. The sample in this chapter uses two Java classes (Main.java and HelloWorldSample.java) and one resource file (helloworld.m3g). You should end up with a directory structure like this:

```
<Wireless Toolkit Installation Directory>\
  - apps\
    - HelloWorld\
      - bin\
        - HelloWorld.jad
        - MANIFEST.MF
```

```
- lib\
- res\
  - m3g02\
    - helloworld.m3g
- src\
  - m3g02\
    - HelloWorldSample.java
    - Main.java
- project.properties
```

Note

You can find all the files of the sample application on the CD-ROM. The files are already sorted in the proper directory structure so you can simply copy the complete folder. Don't forget to copy helloworld.m3g or the application will stop with a `java.io.IOException`.

Building and Running

You are now ready to execute the application. Simply click the Build button and then choose Run. Figure 2.7 shows the emulator's startup screen. You start the MIDlet by using the Select button.

Figure 2.7
You can select a MIDlet of your suite for execution when starting the emulator.

In Figure 2.7, you can see the DefaultColorPhone device. The Wireless Toolkit allows you to customize the skin of the emulator to adapt to different looks, screen sizes, and key layouts. You usually get a skin adapted to a specific device from the device manufacturer.

You can select skins in the KToolbar with the drop-down list labeled Device. I like the DefaultColorPhone device because it has a large screen, which makes it ideal for the screenshots in this book.

Tip

If you want to do your own customizations, have a look at the Basic Customization Guide that comes with the Wireless Toolkit's documentation.

The build step reports any errors in the KToolbar's console window. The same window also displays all system output of your application. However, the toolkit doesn't come with a code editor. For this, you have to install a separate application.

Packaging Your Application

When the KToolbar builds your application, it will automatically compile and preverify all classes so the emulator can execute the application. To create a binary delivery of your application, you have to do one additional step. Figure 2.8 shows the Create Package menu item that triggers this process.

The Create Package command creates a JAR file with all preverified classes and the resources in it and puts it in the bin directory. Together with the JAD file in the same directory, these two files are the binaries for deployment on your device.

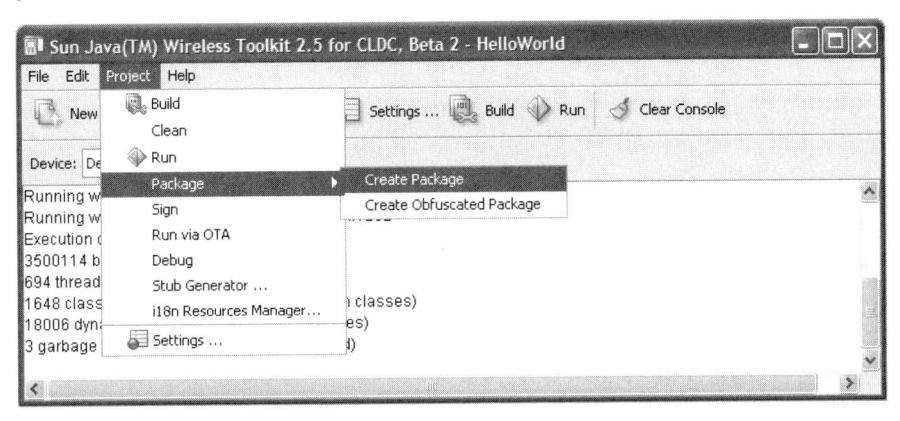

Figure 2.8
Packaging an application for distribution.

Integrated Development Environments

The KToolbar is an effective development environment, but if you prefer to edit, build, debug, and execute MIDlet applications in one comfortable user interface, you might want to look into a full-featured IDE. Two great IDEs are the open source packages NetBeans and Eclipse.

The NetBeans Mobility Pack extends NetBeans with support for MIDP applications. The Mobility Pack includes a version of the Wireless Toolkit, so it's very easy to set up. NetBeans also supports advanced features such as conditional compilation of code and a GUI editor. Eclipse is an alternative to NetBeans, and the free plug-in EclipseME adds MIDP development capabilities.

Note

To get the latest versions of the IDEs, have a look at http://www.netbeans.org/ and http://www.eclipse.org/. You can find EclipseME at http://eclipseme.org/.

The plug-ins for NetBeans and Eclipse internally use the tools that come with the Wireless Toolkit. If there is a new version, you can install the latest version in parallel to older versions and select which one to use to test your applications. Best of all, both IDEs support source code debugging—an invaluable tool to verify your MIDlets.

Downloading Your Application to the Phone

Now that you have the JAR file with your application and the JAD file with the application's properties, you can install your software on a device.

Installing Over the Air

An extra section in the MIDP standard, the Over the Air User Initiated Provisioning Specification, describes how MIDlet suites can be deployed wirelessly over a mobile phone network. Installing over the air requires you to have a properly set up network connection for your mobile phone's browser.

The application's JAR and JAD files must reside on a Web server that the device's mobile browser can access. You have to configure the Web server to map JAD files to the MIME type `text/vnd.sun.j2me.app-descriptor` and JAR files to `application/javaarchive`. These settings tell the receiving device what kind of files it downloads, so it can initiate the installation of Java applications. How to configure MIME types depends on your Web server. If you use a hosted Web server, make sure you talk to your service provider to determine whether these settings are already done.

Next, type the URL of your JAD file into the mobile phone's browser. Your phone will download and inspect the properties of your application and check whether the application is acceptable for download. For example, it will check whether it can provide the MIDP version that your application requires and that is specified in the JAD's `MicroEdition-Profile` attribute. You are also usually given the option to display the application's properties such as size and vendor name.

If you accept the application, the phone will download the JAR file from the URL specified in the JAD's `MIDlet-Jar-URL` attribute. If everything went fine, the application is installed and ready to execute.

Alternative Methods of Installation

To test applications on real devices at development time, it's better to install applications offline because it's fast and cheap. What tools exist and how they work is highly specific to a particular phone and its manufacturer.

Many phones now come with a software suite and a data cable that allows you to back up the phone's memory. In the same way, Java applications can find their way to the phone, although some manufacturers require you to install separate software to do this.

If your phone doesn't come pre-packaged with a data cable, you might be able to buy it as an accessory. Another possibility is to send an application via infrared connection or Bluetooth. You might also want to check whether you can copy an application to a removable memory card and use this medium to install software.

Tool support varies widely; check your manufacturer's developer Web site to determine what's available for your specific phone.

Summary

Well done. You have successfully created and executed your first M3G application.

This chapter introduced developing M3G applications with the MIDP framework. To create a new application, you have to write a class that derives from `MIDlet`. This is the entry point that allows the application management software to control the lifecycle of your application. To display something on the screen, you have to create another class that derives from `Displayable`. The example in this chapter used `GameCanvas`, which provides double-buffered access to the screen.

If you need user input, you can use `Commands` that define soft key actions and receive key events. Key events are delivered asynchronously via `keyPressed()` or synchronously via `getKeyStates()`.

When you have finished coding your application, you can build and test it on the emulator. The Java Wireless Toolkit provides all necessary tools. To install the application on real devices, you can either download it or use device specific tools for offline installation. Testing your application on a device is important to avoid any incompatibilities that the emulator didn't catch.

This chapter provided you with an application that you can use as a framework for your own experiments. In the remainder of this book, you learn how to add more M3G functionality to it.

CHAPTER 3

BEFORE YOU START

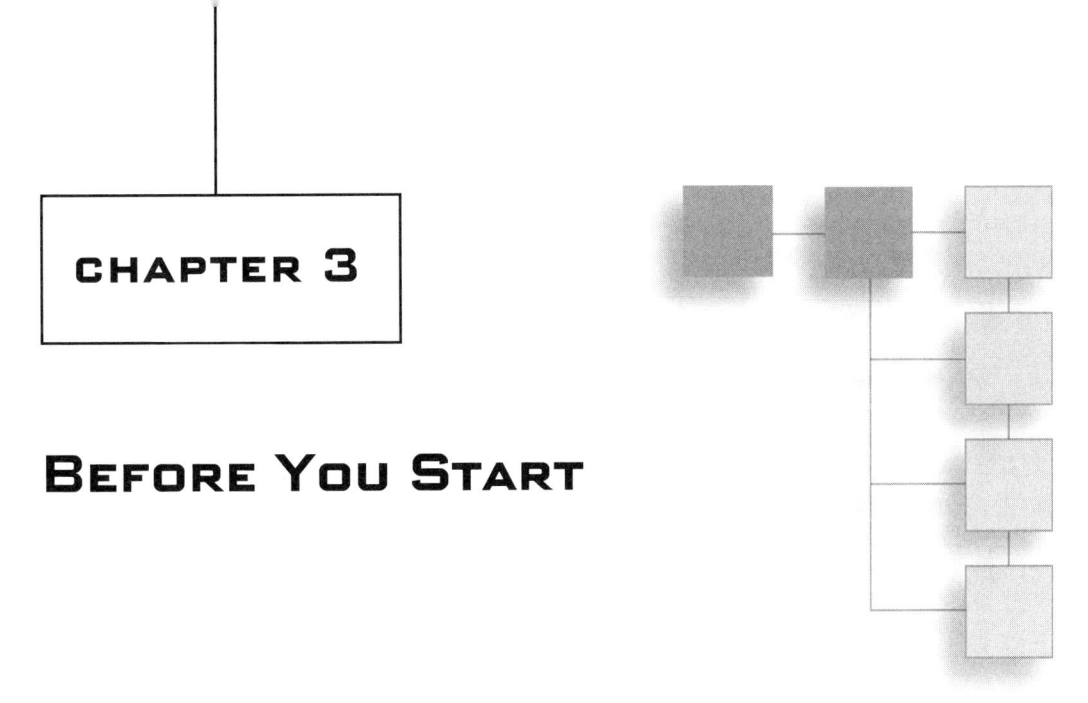

Over the course of the next nine chapters, you will learn the ins and outs of the M3G library. But before you start, this chapter covers a handful of tips that will make your journey smoother:

- How to find out whether your device supports M3G.
- Implementation-specific M3G properties.
- MIDP properties that tell you about important device characteristics.
- How to cope with device differences.

Getting to Know Your Device

Differing hardware support, device capabilities, and optional features inevitably lead to variations in devices. This section gives you some handy tools to find out about these differences.

Does Your Phone Support M3G?

If you want to find out about a phone's M3G support, the best starting point is the manufacturer's or operator's developer Web site. It's in general a good idea to check out these places, because they often host detailed information and tips about how to use a specific mobile phone at its best.

> **Tip**
> Also check out Web sites that list common properties of Java devices such as http://developers.sun.com/techtopics/mobility/device/ and http://www.j2mepolish.org/devices-overview.html.

If you already own a device or have access to it, you can query the system properties to check for M3G support:

```
String m3gVersion = System.getProperty("microedition.m3g.version");

// Does this phone support M3G?
if (m3gVersion != null) {
  // Hooray, it does!
  // m3gVersion contains the version number.
} else {
  // Unfortunately not.
}
```

The property `microedition.m3g.version` will contain the version number if M3G is installed. Otherwise, the property will be undefined and `System.getProperty()` returns `null`.

If you pack this code into a MIDlet, you can quickly find out whether a device supports M3G. Figure 3.1 shows the result when running such an application on the Wireless Toolkit 2.5, which includes the M3G library, and on an older version of the software, which doesn't.

> **Note**
> You will find this MIDlet on the CD-ROM. It's implemented in Main.java in the `m3g03.midp1` package and written so you can also execute it on MIDP 1.0 devices.

Implementation-Specific M3G Properties

Once you know that your device supports M3G, you can start querying for implementation-specific properties. Variations among M3G devices concern maximum values or optional features.

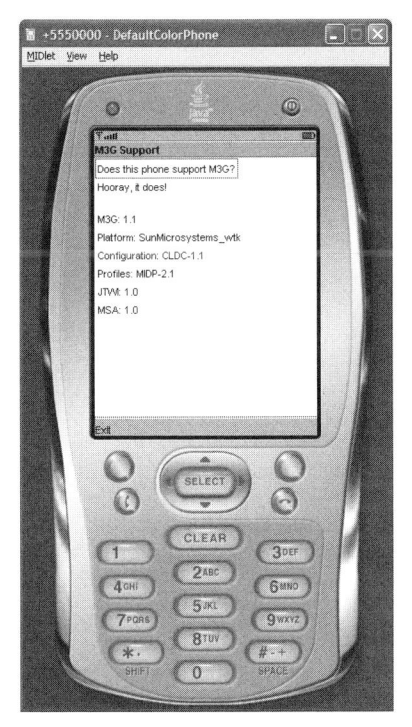

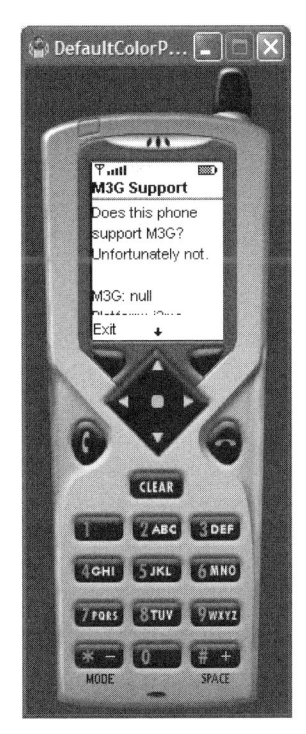

Figure 3.1
By querying the system properties, you can find out whether your device supports M3G.

You can retrieve M3G's properties with the following code:

```
import java.util.Hashtable;
import javax.microedition.m3g.Graphics3D;

Hashtable properties = Graphics3D.getProperties();
for (Enumeration elements = properties.keys();
    elements.hasMoreElements();) {
  String property = (String) elements.nextElement();
  System.out.println(property + ": " + properties.get(property));
}
```

Table 3.1 lists the different properties that exist and for each property, its value type, and the minimum requirement. Individual chapters in this book discuss these properties in more detail.

Note

By sticking to the minimum requirements, you ensure that your application works on any device. Sometimes, however, you want to exceed these values to achieve a particular effect. If so, make sure your device supports the feature you need. You will find a MIDlet that displays the M3G properties on the CD-ROM. It's implemented in M3gPropertiesSample.java in the `m3g03.midp2` package.

Table 3.1 Implementation-Specific Properties

Key	Value Type	Minimum Requirement	Description
supportAntialiasing	Boolean	false	If true, implementation supports antialiasing when calling Graphics3D.bindTarget() with hint ANTIALIAS.
supportTrueColor	Boolean	false	If true, implementation calculates with true color internally even if the display color resolution is lower. To enable this feature, you have to call Graphics3D.bindTarget() with the hint TRUE_COLOR.
supportDithering	Boolean	false	If true, dithering is used to increase the perceived color resolution when calling Graphics3D.bindTarget() with hint DITHER.
supportMipmapping	Boolean	false	If true, implementation supports mipmap images to improve the quality of texturing.
supportPerspectiveCorrection	Boolean	false	If true and enabled with PolygonMode.setPerspectiveCorrectionEnable(), implementation uses a perspective correction technique to reduce artifacts caused by interpolation.
supportLocalCameraLighting	Boolean	false	If true and enabled with PolygonMode.setLocalCameraLightingEnable(), implementation calculates lighting based on true camera position instead of an approximation.
maxLights	Integer	8	Maximum number of lights that are used for the lighting calculation.
maxViewportWidth	Integer	256	Maximum viewport width that can be used in Graphics3D.setViewport(). (Since M3G 1.1.)
maxViewportHeight	Integer	256	Maximum viewport height that can be used in Graphics3D.setViewport(). (Since M3G 1.1.)
maxViewportDimension	Integer	256	The minimum of maxViewportWidth and maxViewportHeight.

Table 3.1 (Continued)

Key	Value Type	Minimum Requirement	Description
maxSpriteCropDimension	Integer	256	Maximum width and height for the visible area of a `Sprite3D`.
maxTextureDimension	Integer	256	Maximum width and height for textures.
numTextureUnits	Integer	1	Maximum number of textures that can be assigned to `Appearance`.
maxTransformsPerVertex	Integer	2	Maximum number of bones that can have an effect on a single vertex of a `SkinnedMesh`.

Important MIDP Properties

M3G requires CLDC 1.1 because it requires floating-point number support. Although it's possible to support M3G on a MIDP 1.0 device, you will be hard pressed to find one.

You can read this and other information about your device from the system properties and through MIDP specific methods. Table 3.2 lists important properties and how you can get them. The values of MIDP properties—same as the M3G properties—depend on the specific device you are using. Many device manufacturers provide customizations to the Wireless Toolkit that more closely reflect the real values of their devices.

Note

The CD-ROM contains a MIDlet that displays these values. The test is implemented in MidpProperties.java in the `m3g03.midp2` package.

Key Layouts

Although phones traditionally come with number keypads, specialized devices might sport full keyboards or other input devices. To cope with the diversity, MIDP introduced game actions. The device manufacturer ensures that actions map to keys that are convenient for a game player. All examples in this book use game actions instead of physical keys for user input.

Figure 3.2 shows the game action mappings of Sun's Java Wireless Toolkit. To learn where your phone places the game actions, you can find two test applications on the CD-ROM.

Table 3.2 MIDP Properties

Property	Description
System	
`System.getProperty("microedition.platform")`	Device-specific name.
`System.getProperty("microedition.configuration")`	Supported configuration.
`System.getProperty("microedition.profiles")`	Supported profiles.
`System.getProperty("microedition.jtwi.version")`	JTWI support
`System.getProperty("microedition.msa.version")`	MSA support.
`System.getProperty("microedition.locale")`	The device's locale.
`System.getProperty("microedition.encoding")`	Default character encoding.
Display	
`Display.isColor()`	If `true`, device supports colors.
`Display.numColors()`	Number of colors supported if device has color support. Otherwise, number of grayscales supported.
`Display.numAlphaLevels()`	Number of alpha levels for transparency. (Since MIDP 2.0.)
Canvas	
`Canvas.getWidth()`	Canvas width for drawing.
`Canvas.getHeight()`	Canvas height for drawing.
`Canvas.getWidth()`(full screen)	Canvas width when in full screen mode (`Canvas.setFullScreenMode(true)`). (Since MIDP 2.0.)
`Canvas.getHeight()`(full screen)	Canvas height when in full screen mode. (Since MIDP 2.0.)
`Canvas.isDoubleBuffered()`	If `true`, `Canvas` is double buffered to avoid flickering.
`Canvas.hasRepeatEvents()`	If `true`, device generates key events repeatedly when a key is held down.
`Canvas.hasPointerEvents()`	Returns `true` if the device supports a pointing device and you can receive press and release events.
`Canvas.hasPointerMotionEvents()`	Returns `true` if the device supports a pointing device and you can receive motion events.

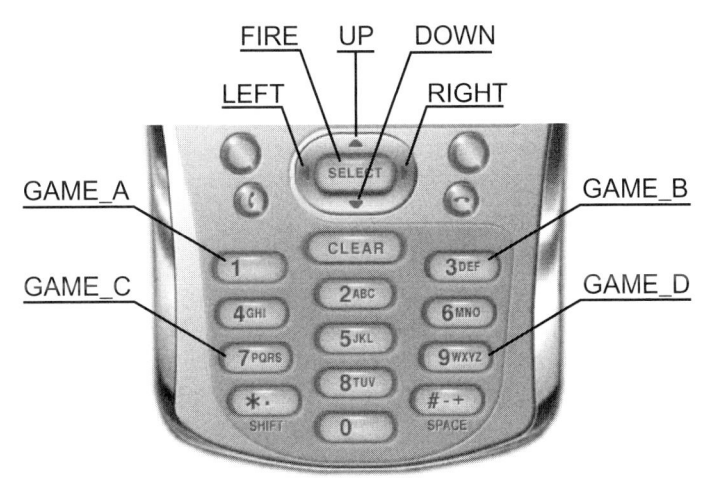

Figure 3.2
The game action mappings of the Java Wireless Toolkit.

`CanvasKeyEvents` displays the code, the name, and the action mapping of a key received in `keyPressed()`. `GameCanvasKeyStates` on the other hand, reads key states from `GameCanvas.getKeyStates()`.

Note

The tests are implemented in CanvasKeyEvents.java and GameCanvasKeyStates.java in the `m3g03.midp2` package.

With these tools, you can also find out whether your device allows you to press several keys at the same time. This is handy when you want to maneuver your spaceship and shoot simultaneously.

Programming for Different Devices

Each manufacturer has its own idea about what comprises a great phone. Network operator requirements, user wishes, and new ideas produce a wealth of variations. Inevitably, you have to plan how you will cope with the differences among devices.

Hardware Considerations

3D applications have one huge advantage: you can adapt the output of the rendering to any screen size. This is similar to vector graphics that scale to any size.

Of course, the more pixels on the screen, the harder the device has to work to reach the same frame rate. In Chapter 5, you will learn more about transformations, how you can adapt the render output to the screen size, and how to switch between landscape and portrait display.

Another hardware consideration is application performance that will vary according to CPU speed, VM performance, and 3D hardware support. Most mobile phones aren't purpose-built for 3D graphics; you have to live with the fact that M3G applications compete with other applications for hardware attention.

Because modern phones second as multimedia computers, CPU performance is on the rise, although most still lack hardware floating-point support because of the additional cost and energy consumption. For Java execution, it's also crucial whether your code is interpreted, compiled to native code, or a mixture of both.

Tip

JBenchmark provides several benchmarking software programs that measure MIDP and M3G performance. You can find the result database at http://www.jbenchmark.com/.

If the device supports 3D hardware acceleration, you can expect a performance boost. However, mobile GPUs are optimized for small size, low cost, and high-energy efficiency. For this reason, they will always lag behind their more advanced desktop counterparts. Nevertheless, 3D hardware support provides two main advantages: speed and visual quality.

With increased performance, you can pack more features in your application, achieve a higher frame rate for the same features, or save battery use if you execute the same operations in less time. Energy efficiency is important because most of the time the 3D application isn't the main purpose of the device.

Apart from the performance, a mobile GPU also leads to higher visual fidelity. A GPU can compute high-quality algorithms in hardware that might otherwise be too slow in software. An improvement you often notice first is better looking texture images. Chapter 6 provides more information about texture quality such as perspective correction and texture filters.

Ideally, you write your application so it will benefit from enhanced hardware but also adapt to low-end devices. Chapter 4 contains ideas how you can adapt the level of detail of a 3D model to device capabilities by generating it parametrically.

Device Fragmentation

The difficult part starts when you enter the domain of device variations because of an ambiguous specification or bugs. Every standard of the Java Community Process comes with a reference implementation and a test suite called the *Technology Compatibility Kit*. Together, they provide implementers the means to check that their implementation is compliant to the specification. M3G 1.1 introduced updates to version 1.0 that tightened the specification further.

From the beginning, you should plan enough time to test your application on real devices. The earlier you find a problem, the easier it is to solve it. If you find that a device has a bug, you should contact the respective manufacturer. There might already be a firmware update or a workaround available. Many manufacturers' Web sites also host forums where you can discuss your issues with fellow developers.

Tip

> Many CLDC/MIDP developers discuss phone-related issues on the KVM-Interest mailing list hosted by Sun. You can look at the archives and subscribe at http://archives.java.sun.com/archives/kvm-interest.html. It's quite possible that someone has already had the same problem as you.

Summary

Programming for the many existing devices in the mobile space can be fun and challenging at the same time. M3G applications have the advantage that you can easily adapt the rendering output to the screen size. Nevertheless, your application has to take care of performance differences and optional M3G features.

In general, you should strive to create applications that run on any device. Flexible algorithms that adapt to a device can help you. If you need to distinguish between devices, you can query MIDP's or M3G's properties for supported features.

Part II

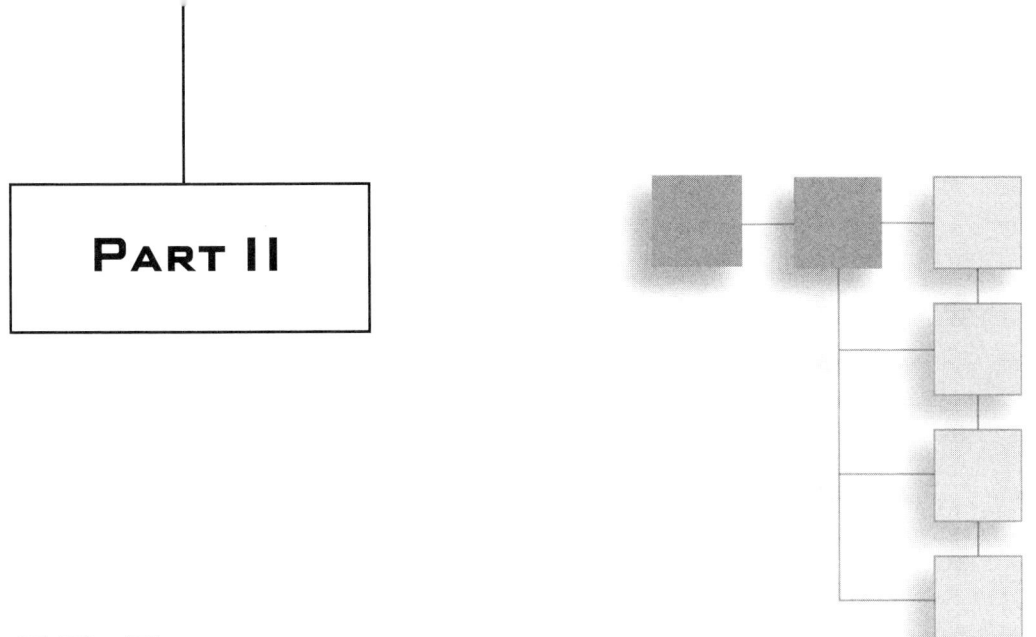

3D Fundamentals

Chapter 4

Rendering Geometric Objects

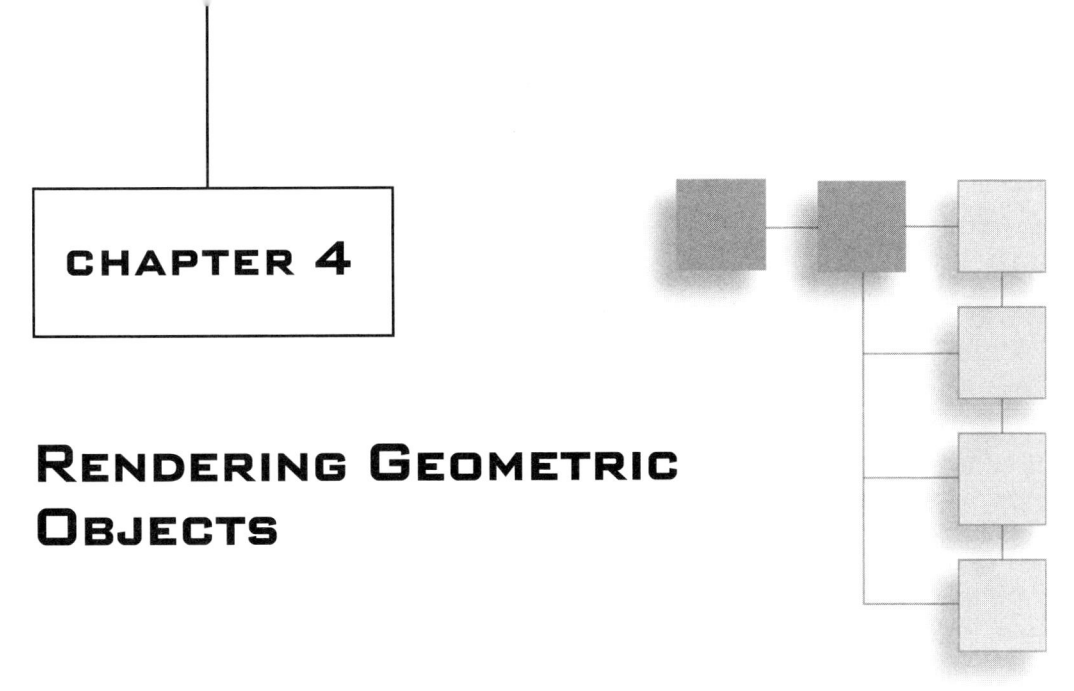

Much as you can draw an image from points and lines, a complex 3D object consists of simple graphics primitives at its lowest level. In this chapter, you learn how to create geometry and render the result to the screen.

You learn how to:

- Store vertex data.
- Build a mesh's geometry.
- Apply colors.
- Use a background image.
- Render your meshes onto the screen.
- Create shapes from parametric equations.

Coordinate Systems

When using M3G, you'll work with two coordinate systems: 3D for placing objects in your scene and 2D for rendering the result to the screen. Coordinates in two and three dimensions use Cartesian coordinates where each axis is orthogonal to each other axis. From this basic setup, different graphics systems have found several ways of aligning the axes.

3D

M3G's coordinate system is right-handed. If you take your right hand and stretch out your thumb, index finger, and middle finger so that each finger is in a right angle to the two others, then the thumb is your x axis, the index finger the y axis, and the middle finger the z axis. This is called the right-hand rule and there are analogous definitions for left-handed coordinate systems. Figure 4.1 shows how M3G orients the axes: the x axis is to the right, the y axis up, and the z axis points toward you.

M3G inherited its conventions from OpenGL. In comparison, DirectX uses a left-handed coordinate system, and 3D modeling tools often use a right-handed coordinate system where the y axis (the index finger) points away from you and the z axis (the middle finger) is up. You'll have to transform your coordinates when exchanging data with these systems.

2D

Although 3D objects live in M3G's coordinate system, the final product of the rendering will end up on a two-dimensional canvas. In most cases, you'll draw on a MIDP graphics context `Graphics` obtained from `javax.microedition.lcdui.Canvas` or its subclass `GameCanvas`, but M3G is flexible on the target of its output. The important part for now is that Java uses a coordinate system where the positive x axis extends to the right and the positive y axis extends down. Coordinates refer to a pixel's upper-left edge.

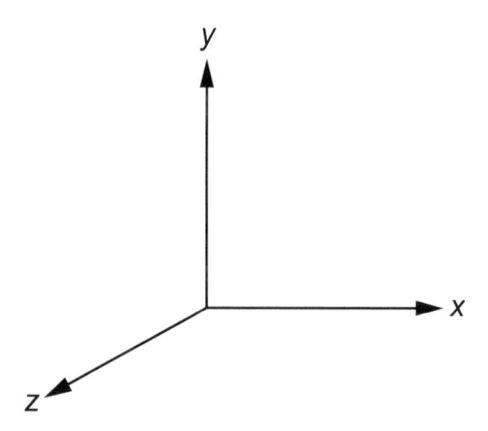

Figure 4.1
M3G's coordinate system.

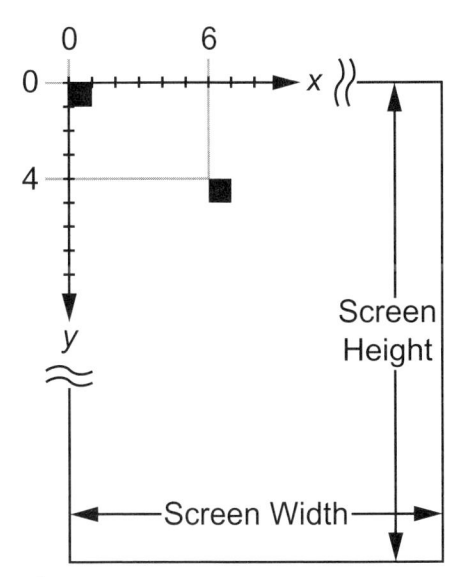

Figure 4.2
Java's 2D coordinate system.

The default origin is located in the upper-left corner, but you can move it anywhere you like by using Graphics.translate(). Figure 4.2 shows the case when you use a graphics context with the default settings to draw on the screen.

M3G uses Java's 2D coordinate system for example when rendering to the screen or when using images. How the 3D coordinate system maps to 2D for rendering will become clear in Chapter 5, which includes a description of the camera projection.

When porting from platforms other than Java, you have to check whether the coordinate systems match. For example GLUT, the OpenGL Utility Toolkit library that's often used in connection with OpenGL, defines the origin in the lower-left corner of the screen instead.

Creating Meshes

Meshes represent visible objects in a 3D scene. It's somewhat arbitrary how you map your objects to meshes, but usually you'd create a separate mesh for each object that needs to be transformed independently. As an example, you could model a complete car as one mesh, but if you wanted to move the tires independently, you'd probably create separate meshes for them.

Mesh Overview

Mesh is the class that represents a visible 3D object in M3G. It's a convenient container for a VertexBuffer that stores the vertex data, one or several IndexBuffers that define the geometry, and one or several Appearance objects that encapsulate the appearance of a mesh. Figure 4.3 shows how the objects are associated with each other, and Table 4.1 defines the interface for Mesh.

A *vertex* is a corner point of a mesh that can have several attributes associated with it. Apart from a position, a vertex can have a color, a normal, and texture coordinates. Vertex positions and colors will follow in this chapter. Texture coordinates will play a role in Chapter 6 for texture mapping, and normals appear in Chapter 8 about lighting. The idea is to put each kind of vertex data in its own VertexArray and then assign the arrays to a VertexBuffer.

A VertexBuffer with the positions is the main ingredient for the geometry of the mesh, but to build a shape, you have to tell M3G how to connect the vertices. M3G's only drawing primitive is a triangle; several of them can be concatenated into strips.

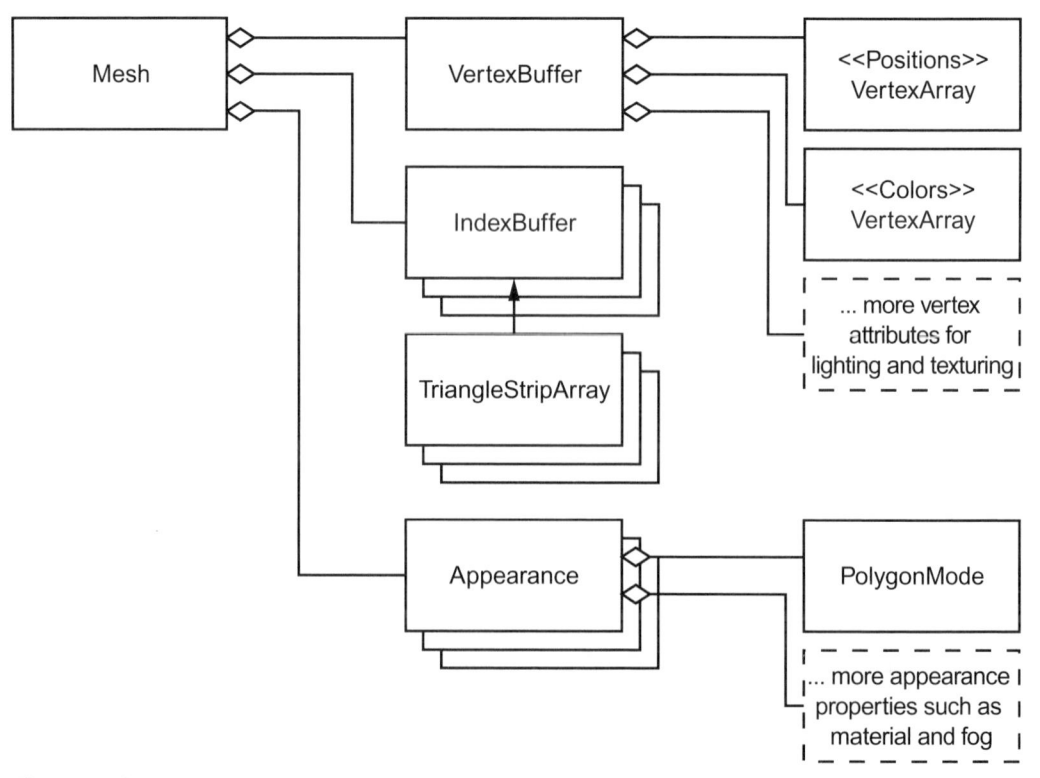

Figure 4.3
Mesh associations.

Table 4.1 Mesh Class Description

Method	Description
`Mesh(VertexBuffer vertices, IndexBuffer[] submeshes, Appearance[] appearances)`	Initializes the class with vertex data and submeshes.
`Mesh(VertexBuffer vertices, IndexBuffer submesh, Appearance appearance)`	Initializes the class with vertex data and one submesh.
`int getSubmeshCount()`	Returns the number of submeshes.
`IndexBuffer getIndexBuffer(int index)`	Returns the triangle strip definitions for a submesh.
`VertexBuffer getVertexBuffer()`	Getter for vertex data.
`void setAppearance(int index, Appearance appearance)`	Setter for appearance.
`Appearance getAppearance(int index)`	Getter for the appearance of a submesh.

Like in a dot-to-dot drawing, you have to connect vertices with triangles until you see the shape. The resulting triangle definitions are stored in a `Triangle StripArray`, which is a subclass of the abstract `IndexBuffer`.

`Appearance` comes in when you want to change the look of a mesh. Color itself is a vertex-specific attribute, but the appearance decides how to apply a texture (see Chapter 6), how a mesh is blended into the scene and affected by fog (see Chapter 7), and how the colors are modified by lights (see Chapter 8). In this chapter, you find explanations of triangle-specific attributes stored in `PolygonMode`. They allow you to distinguish between front and back face as well as determine the shading of colors inside a triangle.

As indicated in Figure 4.3 with stacked boxes, the combination of `IndexBuffer` and `Appearance` can exist several times, where each pair defines a submesh that shares the vertices in `VertexBuffer`. For example, you could create the model of a car with two sets of triangle strips: one that uses many vertices and one that uses few. When your game shows the car very closely, you can use the highly detailed model. Otherwise, you can save rendering time by using the low detailed one. By default, M3G renders all submeshes, but you can disable a submesh by setting its `Appearance` component to `null`.

Vertex Buffers and Arrays

Because of the differing data structures for each kind of vertex data, `VertexArray` was designed to be flexible. When creating a `VertexArray`, you specify the number of vertices, the number of components, and the component size. A component is one element of a vertex data. For example the number of components for a position would be three—one for each of the coordinate axes. A color can have either three or four components depending on the use of transparency. Texture coordinates are either two- or three-dimensional.

The component size specifies the range of numbers a component can use as well as how much memory it occupies. Colors have a fixed component size of one byte, but all other vertex data can choose between one and two bytes. The following is a summary of the types of vertex data with the possible number of components and component sizes:

Vertex Data	Components	Component Size
Position	3 (x, y, z)	1 or 2 bytes
Color	3 (R, G, B) or 4 (R, G, B, A)	1 byte
Normal	3 (x, y, z)	1 or 2 bytes
Texture coordinate	2 (s, t) or 3 (s, t, r)	1 or 2 bytes

The different vertex data types explain `VertexArray`'s interface, listed in Table 4.2. It consists of getters and setters for the vertex data, component numbers, and component sizes.

Once you have created your `VertexArrays`, you can put them into a `VertexBuffer`. Each kind of vertex data has its own setter and getter method as Table 4.3 shows. All `VertexArrays` in the same `VertexBuffer` must have the same number of vertices. When setting the data of a `VertexArray`, the values are copied in, which can waste quite a lot of memory if you need the same definitions several times. An easy way to circumvent this problem is to share `VertexArray` instances between buffers.

The method signatures for setting positions and texture coordinates differ slightly from the others because they take a *scale* and a *bias* argument. You might have noticed that a `VertexArray` allows integer elements only. Instead of `float` elements that use four bytes each, the array is made of `bytes` (one byte) or `shorts` (two bytes). Each element is then divided by the scaling factor so you can still have fractional numbers. The other parameter, the bias, is simply an offset that's added to the element. `setTexCoords()` has an index parameter because you can have several textures. Chapter 6 explains more about textures.

Table 4.2 VertexArray Class Description

Method	Since	Description
Data Type		
VertexArray(int numVertices, int numComponents, int componentSize)		Initializes the VertexArray with the number of vertices, number of components per vertex, and the component size.
int getVertexCount()	1.1	Returns the number of vertices.
int getComponentCount()	1.1	Returns the number of components (2, 3, or 4).
int getComponentType()	1.1	Returns the number of bytes per component (1 or 2).
Vertex Data		
void set(int firstVertex, int numVertices, byte[] values)		Setter for vertex data with component size of one byte. Copies input data.
void get(int firstVertex, int numVertices, byte[] values)	1.1	Getter for vertex data with component size of one byte.
void set(int firstVertex, int numVertices, short[] values)		Setter for vertex data with component size of two bytes. Copies input data.
void get(int firstVertex, int numVertices, short[] values)	1.1	Getter for vertex data with component size of two bytes.

Building Geometry

To put `VertexArray` and `VertexBuffer` into action, the following sample shows you how to create a cube. Figure 4.4 displays this cube, which has its center at the origin and an edge length of two units.

The cube has eight vertices, which you store in a `VertexArray`. Because the geometry is so simple, `bytes` suffice to store the vertex positions.

Note

Over the course of the next two sections, I show you how to create the cube, add colors, and render the result onto the screen. The sample is implemented in ColoredGeometrySample.java and you can find it together with a working MIDlet on the accompanying CD-ROM.

In this section, I implement `createCube()`, which creates a `Mesh` object for rendering. In the next major section, "Immediate Mode Rendering," I show you how to display the cube on the screen.

Table 4.3 VertexBuffer Class Description

Method	Description
Construction	
VertexBuffer()	Initializes class. All VertexArray members are null by default; the default color is opaque white (0xFFFFFFFF).
Default Color	
void setDefaultColor(int ARGB)	Sets the mesh's default color.
int getDefaultColor()	Returns the mesh's default color.
Vertex Data	
int getVertexCount()	Number of vertices. All VertexArrays in the VertexBuffer must have the same length.
void setColors(VertexArray colors)	Sets the vertex colors.
VertexArray getColors()	Returns the vertex colors.
void setNormals(VertexArray normals)	Sets the vertex normals.
VertexArray getNormals()	Returns the vertex normals.
void setPositions(VertexArray positions, float scale, float[] bias)	Sets the vertex positions.
VertexArray getPositions(float[] scaleBias)	Returns the vertex positions.
void setTexCoords(int index, VertexArray texCoords, float scale, float[] bias)	Sets the vertex texture coordinates.
VertexArray getTexCoords(int index, float[] scaleBias)	Returns the vertex texture coordinates.

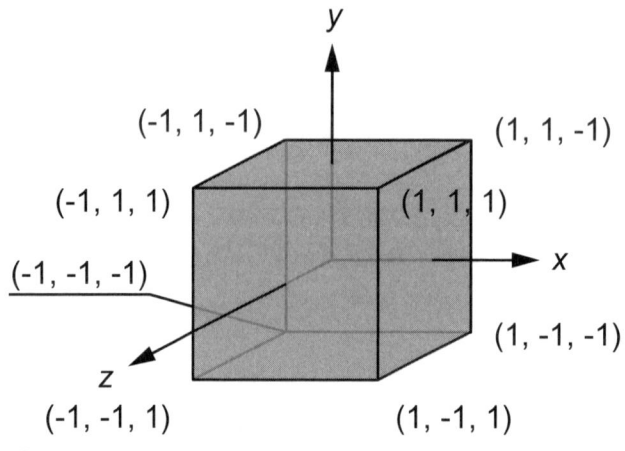

Figure 4.4
Cube vertex positions.

Creating Meshes

```java
/**
 * Creates a cube with eight vertices, one triangle strip, and
 * per-vertex colors.
 *
 * @return cube wrapped in a Mesh object.
 */
private Mesh createCube() {
  // Create vertex data.
  VertexBuffer cubeVertexData = new VertexBuffer();

  // The cube's vertex positions (x, y, z).
  byte[] positions = {
    -1, -1,  1,   1, -1,  1,   -1, 1,  1,   1, 1,  1,
    -1, -1, -1,   1, -1, -1,   -1, 1, -1,   1, 1, -1
  };

  VertexArray vertexPositions =
      new VertexArray(positions.length/3, 3, 1);
  vertexPositions.set(0, positions.length/3, positions);
  cubeVertexData.setPositions(vertexPositions, 1, null);

  // The triangles that define the cube's geometry; the indices
  // point to array elements in positions.
  int[] indices = { 0, 1, 2, 3, 7, 1, 5, 4, 7, 6, 2, 4, 0, 1 };

  TriangleStripArray cubeTriangles
      = new TriangleStripArray(indices, new int[] {indices.length});
  ...
}
```

For the geometry of the cube, you'll need 12 triangles to describe the six sides. Many triangles have common vertices, so it's natural to reuse them. That's why the triangle definitions are stored separately from vertices in a `TriangleStripArray`. Its content references indices of the `VertexArray` with the vertex positions. Tables 4.4 and 4.5 summarize `TriangleStripArray`'s interface as well as its superclass `IndexBuffer`.

Table 4.4 IndexBuffer Class Description

Method	Since	Description
int getIndexCount()	1.1	Returns the number of indices.
void getIndices(int[] indices)	1.1	Returns the indices.

Table 4.5 TriangleStripArray Class Description

Method	Description
TriangleStripArray(int[] indices, int[] stripLengths)	Initializes the class with explicit indices.
TriangleStripArray(int firstIndex, int[] stripLengths)	Initializes the class with implicit indices.

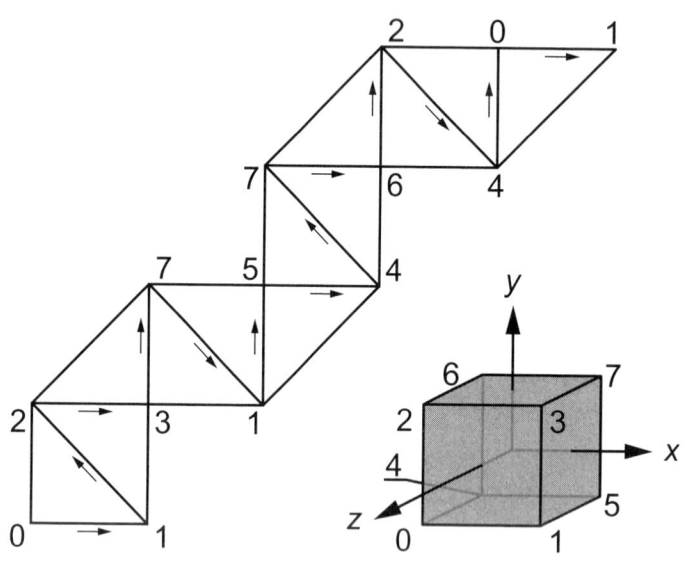

Figure 4.5
The cube's triangle strip.

3D libraries like triangles because they are always planar and you can define any polygon as a set of triangles. Most render algorithms work with triangles as the basic drawing operation and using the same set of data speeds up processing. That said, for defining geometry, triangles are sometimes cumbersome to use. IndexBuffer exists to allow future revisions of M3G to add more types of geometry definitions.

To further improve memory consumption, TriangleStripArray lets you reduce the number of indices by using strips. With a triangle strip, new triangles reuse the preceding triangle's last two indices. For example, the triangle strip (0, 1, 2, 3) will translate to two triangles: (0, 1, 2) and (1, 2, 3). Figure 4.5 shows how the triangle definitions in indices wrap a single triangle strip around the cube.

The strip meanders around the cube to avoid the definition of several triangle strips. In the end, the cube has eight vertex positions (three bytes each) and 14 indices (four bytes each). Because the positions use `bytes`, an index takes more memory than a vertex position, which defeats the purpose of reusing vertices to save memory in this simple case. However, once you assign more data to the vertex such as colors, the ratio will turn around. In addition, M3G has to calculate transformations for each vertex, which means that decreasing the vertex count will make this process faster.

Tip
To improve performance, try to put your into as few strips as possible. If the geometry of your mesh doesn't allow you to have one single strip, you can concatenate strips with *degenerate triangles*. These are triangles that have two or more vertices at the same position. Because the vertices of a degenerate triangle lie on a line, it has no volume and won't be displayed. M3G explicitly allows this behavior.

The previous code example uses a `TriangleStripArray` with *explicit* indices. With *implicit* indices, on the other hand, you define a starting index and M3G builds triangles by adding one to every succeeding index. The following code defines a `TriangleStripArray` with implicit indices that has one strip with the length of four indices and starts at index 0:

```
TriangleStripArray cubeTriangles
   = new TriangleStripArray(0, new int[] {4});
```

In this case, M3G creates a triangle strip with the indices (0, 1, 2, 3). The strip itself would be interpreted as in the explicit case. Implicit indices hence use fewer indices. However, if you want to use the same index more than once in the strip definition, as is the case for the cube, you have to use explicit indices. However, you can split the strip into several parts and reorder the vertices in the `VertexArray` to use implicit indices. Independent of the way you define the indices, the order they are stored in `TriangleStripArray` isn't arbitrary.

Unless you own the electronic version, the book you are reading has a front and a back—3D graphics makes the same distinction. By default, vertices defined in a counterclockwise order indicate the front side of a triangle; that's why the strip for the cube starts with the indices (0, 1, 2). If you look at the arrows in Figure 4.5, you can see this order. You can also see that the way a strip is structured, every odd triangle automatically changes the orientation. For a triangle strip, the first triangle always defines the orientation of the whole strip. By starting the strip with a front-sided triangle, the outside of the cube serves as the front and the inside as the back.

The purpose of this definition is to save rendering time by drawing only the faces you can see. For this reason, M3G doesn't display the back side of a triangle by default, although you can change this behavior with the methods in `PolygonMode`.

Polygon-Level Attributes

The only polygon you'll work with in M3G is a triangle. When used in defining the geometry of a mesh, its two sides are called *front face* and *back face*. Polygon-specific attributes are defined in `PolygonMode` whose interface Table 4.6 shows.

The order of the vertices in the triangle defines its *winding*. As you've seen, counterclockwise wound triangles are front-facing by default. The side of a

Table 4.6 PolygonMode Class Description

Method	Description
Culling	
static int CULL_BACK	Back faces are culled.
static int CULL_FRONT	Front faces are culled.
static int CULL_NONE	All faces are rendered.
Winding	
static int WINDING_CCW	Counterclockwise wound triangles are considered front-facing.
static int WINDING_CW	Clockwise wound triangles are considered front-facing.
Shading	
static int SHADE_FLAT	Flat shading.
static int SHADE_SMOOTH	Smooth shading.
Construction	
PolygonMode()	Initializes class. Default values are CULL_BACK, WINDING_CCW, and SHADE_SMOOTH. All other properties (two-sided lighting, local camera lighting, and perspective correction) are disabled.
Face-Specific Attributes	
void setWinding(int mode)	Setter for winding (WINDING_CCW, WINDING_CW)

Table 4.6 (Continued)

Method	Description
int getWinding()	Getter for winding.
void setCulling(int mode)	Setter for culling mode (CULL_BACK, CULL_FRONT, CULL_NONE).
int getCulling()	Getter for culling mode.
void setTwoSidedLightingEnable(boolean enable)	Enables separate lighting for back and front face.
boolean isTwoSidedLightingEnabled()	Getter for two-sided lighting.

Attributes That Influence Both Faces

Method	Description
void setShading(int mode)	Setter for shading mode (SHADE_FLAT, SHADE_SMOOTH).
int getShading()	Getter for shading mode.
void setLocalCameraLightingEnable(boolean enable)	Hint for implementation to enable lighting based on true camera position instead of approximation.
boolean isLocalCameraLightingEnabled()	Getter for local camera lighting. (Since M3G 1.1.)
void setPerspectiveCorrectionEnable(boolean enable)	Hint for implementation to enable techniques to reduce artifacts caused by interpolation.
boolean isPerspectiveCorrectionEnabled()	Getter for perspective correction. (Since M3G 1.1.)

polygon plays a role because you can instruct M3G to cull front or back faces. In other words, if you cull the back face of the cube, you'll see the outside; if you cull the front face, the inside. You should disable faces that you can't see because it speeds up rendering, but you might want to display both sides if you can open the lid of the cube and see both inside and outside at the same time.

You'll have the least effort with `PolygonMode`, if you accept that front faces are wound counterclockwise and stick to the intuitive approach to define the outside of your meshes as the front. Here's a code snippet showing how to create a `PolygonMode` instance:

```
private Mesh createCube() {
  ...
  // Set the polygon mode, which is part of the appearance. The
  // default values are: SHADE_SMOOTH, CULL_BACK, and WINDING_CCW.
  polygonMode = new PolygonMode();
  Appearance appearance = new Appearance();
```

```
    appearance.setPolygonMode(polygonMode);

    // Put vertex data and triangle definitions in a Mesh object. The
    // Appearance attribute must not be null, or the mesh won't
    // display.
    return new Mesh(cubeVertexData, cubeTriangles, appearance);
}
```

Similar to `VertexBuffer` being the container for `VertexArrays`, `Appearance` stores references to objects that change a mesh's look, including `PolygonMode`. Don't worry about `Appearance`'s many attributes in Table 4.7 for now; they'll become clear in the following chapters. For the moment, only `setLayer()` and `setPolygonMode()` are of interest.

By using `Appearance.setLayer()` with a layer ID between −63 and 63, M3G supports rendering of submeshes in a specific order.

Table 4.7 Appearance Class Description

Method	Description
Construction	
Appearance()	Initializes class. All object members are set to null; the layer is set to 0 by default.
Layer	
void setLayer(int layer)	Sets the layer (−63 to 63)
int getLayer()	Gets the layer information.
Appearance Attributes	
void setPolygonMode(PolygonMode polygonMode)	Setter for polygon-level attributes.
PolygonMode getPolygonMode()	Getter for polygon-level attributes.
void setCompositingMode (CompositingMode compositingMode)	Setter for per-pixel compositing attributes.
CompositingMode getCompositingMode()	Getter for per-pixel compositing attributes.
void setFog(Fog fog)	Setter for fog attributes.
Fog getFog()	Getter for fog attributes.
void setMaterial(Material material)	Setter for material.
Material getMaterial()	Getter for material.
void setTexture(int index, Texture2D texture)	Setter for texture information.
Texture2D getTexture(int index)	Getter for texture information.

As mentioned in the `Mesh` overview, one `IndexBuffer/Appearance` pair builds a submesh. When you group several meshes together, the layer also affects all meshes in a group.

`setPolygonMode()` assigns the polygon-level attributes to `Appearance`. Once a `PolygonMode` object is instantiated, you can change settings such as the culling with `setCulling()` and the winding rule with `setWinding()`. If you are happy with `PolygonMode`'s default values, you can also skip the creation of the instance. `Appearance` then behaves as if a `PolygonMode` instance created by the class' no-argument constructor had been registered. The previous code example sets the `PolygonMode` property in order to change polygon-specific attributes later.

> **Tip**
> If your mesh is invisible with `CULL_BACK`, but displays with `setCulling(PolygonMode.CULL_NONE)`, check whether the winding of your triangles is correct. Use `CULL_NONE` only if you have to because it decreases performance.

Another face-specific property in `PolygonMode` is two-sided lighting, which you can enable or disable with a call to `setTwoSidedLightingEnable()`. Depending on the current state, M3G computes the lighting color separately for the front and back faces.

Attributes that are polygon-specific but not dependent on the side are local camera lighting, perspective correction, and the polygon shading mode. Perspective correction plays a role for texturing in Chapter 6, and lighting follows in Chapter 8. The shading parameter determines the colors inside triangles. You learn this in the following section about colors.

The definition of `Appearance` completes the geometry of the cube, and you can construct a new `Mesh` instance out of the `VertexBuffer`, the `TriangleStripArray`, and the `Appearance`. You do need an instance of `Appearance`, even if you accept its default settings, because a `null` property in the `Mesh` disables rendering. Although you could render the cube in the current state to the screen, you would just see a white blob—white being the default color. That will change in the next section.

Colors

You can assign several kinds of information to a vertex—colors for example. Vertex colors replace the default color set with `VertexBuffer.setDefaultColor()`

with per-vertex specific values. Here is an example:

```
private Mesh createCube() {
  // Create vertex data.
  VertexBuffer cubeVertexData = new VertexBuffer();
  ...

  // The cube's vertex colors (R, G, B).
  byte c1 = (byte) 255;
  byte c2 = (byte) 128;
  byte[] colors = {
     0, c1, 0,    0, c1, c1,   c1, 0, 0,    c1, 0, c1,
     c1, c1, 0,   c1, c1, c1,  0, 0, c2,    0, 0, c1
  };

  VertexArray vertexColors =
      new VertexArray(colors.length/3, 3, 1);
  vertexColors.set(0, colors.length/3, colors);
  cubeVertexData.setColors(vertexColors);

  ...
}
```

The previous code adds another VertexArray to the cube's VertexBuffer. Note that a color value goes from 0 (minimum brightness) to 255 (maximum brightness), but byte has a range from –128 to 127. The previous code handles this by casting values greater than 127; M3G will automatically interpret the values correctly.

The component number of the VertexArray is three because transparency is omitted—M3G then implicitly sets the alpha value to opaque (255). If you want to define the transparency separately, don't forget to update the number of components to four. The order for color components in a VertexArray is R, G, B, A.

Note

You can find more information about transparency and blending in Chapter 7.

If you assign colors to vertices, what happens to the pixels inside the triangles? One possibility is to use one vertex color for the whole triangle; another is to interpolate the colors between two vertices and create a color ramp. M3G lets you choose between both options. In flat-shading mode (`PolygonMode.SHADE_FLAT`), M3G draws the entire triangle in the color of its third vertex. In the cube's triangle strip, the first triangle starts with the indices (0, 1, 2). If you look up the vertex two's color in `colors`, you'll find that it's red (255, 0, 0). In smooth-shading mode on the other hand (`PolygonMode.SHADE_SMOOTH`), each pixel inside the triangle gets its own color by interpolation. The pixels between vertex 0 and 2 would start with green (0, 255, 0) and slowly change to red. The default value in `PolygonMode` is smooth shading; you can change it to flat shading by calling:

```
polygonMode.setShading(PolygonMode.SHADE_FLAT);
```

The drawback of a triangle strip that reuses vertices is that triangles with common vertices will also share the color. This leads to the conclusion that, although the geometry doesn't need it, sometimes you have to duplicate vertices for the sake of flexibility.

With the definition of colors, the cube's now ready for rendering. The next section shows you how to actually display the mesh.

Immediate Mode Rendering

M3G divides rendering in *immediate* and *retained mode*. The difference lies in the way you organize your data. Immediate mode lets you render 3D objects immediately to the screen, hence the name. In retained mode on the other hand, you first define a scene graph of your 3D world, including cameras and lights, and then render the complete data structure to the screen. In this part of the book, the samples use immediate mode. Retained mode and scene graphs come in Part III.

Graphics3D

Analogous to `Graphics` for 2D drawing, M3G's graphics context `Graphics3D` provides methods to render your meshes in 3D. You can see its interface in Table 4.8.

`Graphics3D` is a singleton instance, which you retrieve by calling `Graphics3D.getInstance()`.

Table 4.8 Graphics3D Class Description

Method	Since	Description
General Functionality		
`static Graphics3D getInstance()`		Returns the singleton instance for 3D rendering.
`static java.util.Hashtable getProperties()`		Returns implementation-specific properties.
Render Target		
`void bindTarget(java.lang.Object target)`		Binds the render target.
`void bindTarget(java.lang.Object target, boolean depthBuffer, int hints)`		Binds the render target with the option to switch off the depth buffer and to pass additional rendering hints.
`void releaseTarget()`		Flushes the 3D render result to the render target and releases the target.
`int getHints()`	1.1	Getter for rendering hints.
`boolean isDepthBufferEnabled()`	1.1	Returns `true` if depth buffer is enabled.
`java.lang.Object getTarget()`	1.1	Getter for render target.
`void clear(Background background)`		Clears the background in immediate mode. Use `null` to clear to black.
Rendering		
`void render(Node node, Transform transform)`		Immediate mode rendering of `Node` objects.
`void render(VertexBuffer vertices, IndexBuffer triangles, Appearance appearance, Transform transform)`		Immediate mode rendering of a submesh.
`void render(VertexBuffer vertices, IndexBuffer triangles, Appearance appearance, Transform transform, int scope)`		Immediate mode rendering of a submesh in the defined scope.
`void render(World world)`		Retained mode rendering.
Camera (Immediate Mode)		
`void setCamera(Camera camera, Transform transform)`		Sets the current camera.
`Camera getCamera(Transform transform)`	1.1	Getter for camera.
Light (Immediate Mode)		
`int addLight(Light light, Transform transform)`		Adds a light.
`void setLight(int index, Light light, Transform transform)`		Sets a light at index `index`.

Table 4.8 (Continued)

Method	Since	Description
`Light getLight(int index, Transform transform)`	1.1	Getter for light at index `index`.
`int getLightCount()`	1.1	Getter for number of lights.
`void resetLights()`		Deletes all lights.
Depth Range		
`void setDepthRange(float near, float far)`		Allows setting the depth buffer resolution to a specific area.
`float getDepthRangeFar()`	1.1	Getter for depth range far value.
`float getDepthRangeNear()`	1.1	Getter for depth range near value.
Viewport		
`void setViewport(int x, int y, int width, int height)`		Setter for viewport position and size.
`int getViewportHeight()`	1.1	Getter for viewport height.
`int getViewportWidth()`	1.1	Getter for viewport width.
`int getViewportX()`	1.1	Getter for viewport *x* position.
`int getViewportY()`	1.1	Getter for viewport *y* position.

To use it in immediate mode, you have to execute the following steps:

1. Construct a `Camera` object, which defines the view point of your scene, and assign it to `Graphics3D` by calling `setCamera()`.

2. Tell `Graphics3D` what graphics context to use as the render target with `bindTarget()`. This could be the screen, a double buffer, or an image.

3. Set the viewport rectangle, which defines the size of the render output with `setViewPort()`.

4. Clear the background with `clear()`.

5. Draw your 3D objects with `render()`.

6. Flush the result to the render target and release the target with `releaseTarget()`.

In the following sample code, `ColoredGeometrySample` derives from `GameCanvas` and defines instance members for the mesh, the mesh's `PolygonMode`, and a `Background` object. It also stores the graphics contexts for 3D and 2D rendering.

Graphics3D is for rendering the 3D scene; Graphics is the render target where the result ends up.

> **Note**
>
> In the previous section, you saw how createCube() was used to construct a mesh. In this section, you learn how to render the cube to the screen.

```
/**
 * Sample displaying a cube with per-vertex colors.
 *
 * @author Claus Hoefele
 */
public class ColoredGeometrySample extends GameCanvas
    implements Sample {
  /** The cube's mesh object. */
  private Mesh mesh;

  /** The cube's polygon-level attributes such as winding and
   *  culling. */
  private PolygonMode polygonMode;

  /** The sample's background. */
  private Background background;

  /** 3D graphics singleton used for rendering. */
  private Graphics3D graphics3d;
  /** 2D graphics singleton used for rendering. */
  private Graphics graphics;

  /**
   * Constructor.
   */
  public ColoredGeometrySample() {
    super(false);
  }
  ...
}
```

The Sample interface that ColoredGeometrySample implements defines the methods init() and destroy(). The MIDlet that executes the sample calls the former method when the class is initialized and the latter when it's destroyed.

Tip

Have a look at Main.java in the m3g04 package to learn how this chapter's MIDlet is implemented and look at Sample.java to see the interface. All examples in this book use a similar structure.

In `ColoredGeometrySample`, `init()` creates the member variables just before the `GameCanvas` is displayed:

```
/**
 * Initializes the sample.
 */
public void init() {
  // Get the singletons for rendering.
  graphics3d = Graphics3D.getInstance();
  graphics = getGraphics();

  // Create mesh.
  mesh = createCube();

  // Create a camera with perspective projection.
  Camera camera = new Camera();
  float aspect = (float) getWidth() / (float) getHeight();
  camera.setPerspective(60, aspect, 1, 1000);
  Transform cameraTransform = new Transform();

  // Transform camera so it's looking at one of the cube's corners.
  cameraTransform.postTranslate(4, 2, 4);
  cameraTransform.postRotate(45, 0, 1, 0);
  cameraTransform.postRotate(-20, 1, 0, 0);

  // Activate camera.
  graphics3d.setCamera(camera, cameraTransform);

  // Create background.
  background = createBackground();

  // Render mesh.
  render(graphics);
  flushGraphics();
}
```

`init()` obtains references to the graphics contexts and creates a cube mesh. `createCube()` is the method from the last section and the resulting `Mesh` contains the cube's `VertexBuffer`, `TriangleStripArray`, and `Appearance` objects.

Next, there's a bit of magic for setting up and positioning the camera. When calling `setPerspective()`, you ask M3G to render your scene with perspective projection. This will draw objects smaller the farther their distance from the camera. The `Transform` object in the variable called `cameraTransform` is used to place the camera so it looks at one of the corners of the cube. Chapter 5 contains the full explanation how to set up a camera.

The last lines of `init()` create a new `Background` object for the background settings and trigger the drawing of the mesh. The next two sections explain `createBackground()` and `render()` in more detail.

Defining a Background

You can fill a background either with a color or an image. The former you can set by calling `Background.setColor()`, the latter by calling `setImage()`. `setImage()` also switches the background mode. If you pass `null`, the color will be used, if you pass an image, the image will be used instead. Table 4.9 shows `Background`'s methods.

`Graphics3D.clear()` with a `Background` object as a parameter draws the background according to your settings. You typically do this at the beginning of each frame, before drawing any other objects. Setting a background image is a convenient way to simulate a landscape without defining any geometry.

Tip

> The only image format supported by every M3G implementation is PNG. Although devices that comply with the Mobile Service Architecture (JSR 248) support JPEG and some devices also support additional image formats, you'll run into problems if you execute your application on a device that doesn't.

The image is stored in an `Image2D` object, which, unlike `javax.microedition.lcdui.Image`, holds a format identifier. Chapter 6 explores the different image formats such as luminance and how you can use them with textures. A background image, however, can only be RGB or RGBA and must also match the format of the rendering target. This rule restricts background images for MIDP graphics contexts to RGB because MIDP restricts mutable images to RGB format.

You can convert a MIDP `Image` to `Image2D` with one of its constructors:

```
Image image = Image.createImage("/background.png");
Image2D image2d = new Image2D(Image2D.RGB, image);
```

Table 4.9 Background Class Description

Method	Description
Image Mode	
static int BORDER	Uses background color when the background image is too small to cover the whole screen.
static int REPEAT	Tiles background image when the image is too small to cover the whole screen.
Construction	
Background()	Initializes class. By default, the background color is transparent black (0x00000000), color clear and depth clear enabled, background image null, image mode in *x* and *y* direction BORDER, and the crop rectangle undefined.
Background Color	
void setColor(int ARGB)	Setter for background color.
int getColor()	Getter for background color.
Image	
void setImage(Image2D image)	Setter for background image. Setting null disables image mode and the background color is used instead.
Image2D getImage()	Getter for background image.
void setImageMode(int modeX, int modeY)	Sets image mode for *x* and *y* direction (BORDER, REPEAT).
int getImageModeX()	Getter for image mode in *x* direction.
int getImageModeY()	Getter for image mode in *y* direction.
Cropping	
void setCrop(int cropX, int cropY, int width, int height)	Sets the cropping rectangle. The cropping rectangle is initialized to the background image size when calling setImage().
int getCropX()	Getter for the cropping rectangle's *x* position.
int getCropY()	Getter for the cropping rectangle's *y* position.
int getCropWidth()	Getter for the cropping rectangle's width.
int getCropHeight()	Getter for the cropping rectangle's height.
Framebuffer Tests	
void setColorClearEnable (boolean enable)	Enables/disables color clearing.
boolean isColorClearEnabled()	Returns true if color clearing is enabled.
void setDepthClearEnable (boolean enable)	Enables/disables depth buffer clearing.
boolean isDepthClearEnabled()	Returns true if depth buffer clearing is enabled.

However, this would create the image data twice; first for the Image object, and a second time when copied into Image2D. The fastest and most memory efficient way to create an Image2D is to use Loader, as in the following example:

```
/**
 * Creates a new background with an image.
 *
 * @return background object.
 */
private Background createBackground() {
  Background background = new Background();

  try {
    // Load image from file directly into Image2D object.
    Image2D image=(Image2D) Loader.load("/m3g04/background.png")[0];
    background.setImage(image);
  } catch (Exception e) {
    System.out.println("Error loading image.");
    e.printStackTrace();
  }

  return background;
}
```

Loader is mostly used to read scene graphs stored in a binary file (see Chapter 10), but it can load images as well, thus avoiding the copy operation. Unfortunately, Loader doesn't let you specify the image format. Hence you have to rely on M3G to interpret the image as Image2D.RGB data.

Tip

> Make sure that your image doesn't contain transparency when using Loader to read a background image. Otherwise, some devices will interpret the image as Image2D.RGBA and throw an IllegalArgumentException when calling clear().

The background image is static and not affected by any camera movements. You can however crop and pan the image by calling setCrop(). Be aware of the memory necessary to decode large images though. If you can compromise on quality, a way to reduce memory is to decrease the image resolution. When passing an image to setImage(), M3G sets the crop rectangle to the image size and stretches the contents to cover the visible area of your 3D scene.

If the cropping rectangle is larger than the image, a call to `setImageMode()` determines what to do with the pixels not covered by the image: BORDER fills the space with the background color; REPEAT tiles the image. You can set the mode for *x* and *y* direction separately.

The two last properties in `Background` concern the *frame buffer*. This term relates to memory areas allocated to hold pixel-specific data. The color buffer holds the color information of the rendered scene. If you pass `true` to `setColorClearEnable()`, M3G clears the color buffer with the background color or image. Another part of the frame buffer is the depth buffer, which is cleared with `setDepthClearEnable()`. The depth buffer contains information, so meshes that are closer to the camera obscure objects farther away. Chapter 5 contains more about this; for the moment, the default setting is fine.

> **Note**
>
> M3G only knows color and depth buffers, but OpenGL has additional ones: the stencil buffer (restricts drawing to certain areas of the screen), the accumulation buffer (collects several rendering results), and the auxiliary color buffers.

This completes the initialization of `ColoredGeometrySample`, the definition of the camera view point, and the background creation. You only have to do this once before `ColoredGeometrySample` is displayed. By calling `init()` again, you can reset your scene. Conversely, the remaining steps to draw the cube must be executed each time you render your scene. The `Background` object constructed in `createBackground()` is then applied with `Graphics.clear()` before the cube is rendered. This follows in the next section.

Render Targets

The following code shows how to render your 3D objects:

```
/**
 * Renders the sample.
 *
 * @param graphics graphics context for rendering.
 */
private void render(Graphics graphics) {
    // Bind the render target.
    graphics3d.bindTarget(graphics);
```

```
    // Set the visible area to cover the entire screen.
    graphics3d.setViewport(0, 0, getWidth(), getHeight());

    // Clear the background with the settings in a Background
    // object. If you specify null, the background will be cleared to
    // black.
    graphics3d.clear(background);

    // Render mesh. null as the second parameter means the cube will
    // be rendered at the origin, without transformation.
    graphics3d.render(mesh, null);

    // Release render target.
    graphics3d.releaseTarget();

    // After the rendering target is released, the 2D graphics
    // context can be used again. This method displays the current
    // key assignment.
    drawMenu(graphics);
}
```

First, `render()` selects the render target with `bindTarget()`. You can use any graphics context for this purpose, for example the one you get in `Canvas`'s `paint()` method or one you obtained from a mutable image with `Image.getGraphics()`. `bindTarget()` takes a parameter of type `Object` because M3G is compatible with other Micro Edition profiles and Java editions. In case you are using the Abstract Windowing Toolkit, you can pass a `java.awt.Graphics` object instead of `javax.microedition.lcdui.Graphics`. M3G also lets you pass `Image2D`, M3G's own image class, directly to `bindTarget()`.

An overloaded version of `bindTarget()` takes two more parameters: a `boolean` value that enables or disables the depth buffer and rendering hints for the M3G implementation.

Table 4.10 lists the rendering hints. With `ANTIALIAS`, `TRUE_COLOR`, and `DITHER`, you can trade rendering performance for quality. Passing one or several of them combined with bitwise OR (|) enables smoothing jagged edges, calculating with true color resolution internally, and increasing the perceived color resolution with dithering. A hint in this case means that it's optional whether an implementation supports it. If it does, the properties returned by `Graphics3D.getProperties()` return `true` for `supportAntialiasing`, `supportTrueColor`, and `supportDithering`, respectively.

Table 4.10 Rendering Hints in `Graphics3D`

Hint	Since	Description
`static int ANTIALIAS`		Instructs implementation to use techniques that avoid jagged edges.
`static int TRUE_COLOR`		Implementation should internally calculate colors with a higher color resolution than supported by the display. The implementation should only reduce the number of colors to the display resolution when rendering to the screen.
`static int DITHER`		Implementation should increase the perceived number of colors by juxtaposing pixels. This can be used in combination with `TRUE_COLOR` hint to reduce the number of colors by dithering.
`static int OVERWRITE`	1.1	Implementation doesn't need to preserve the original contents of the rendering target.

`OVERWRITE` was introduced in M3G 1.1. When specified, the contents of the render target when binding are undefined, which can improve performance. Otherwise, existing contents in the target before binding are preserved.

After the render target is bound, rendering can commence by setting the viewport by calling `setViewport()`. This is the rectangular area that M3G uses for the render output, which the previous code sets to cover the entire screen. This area is then initialized with a call to `clear()`, which draws the background.

`Graphics3D` knows four `render()` methods. Which one you call decides whether you are using immediate mode or retained mode. When you call `render()` with a `World` object, you are in retained mode, otherwise you are in immediate mode. `World` is the mentioned scene graph representation, which plays a role in Chapter 9.

The immediate mode `render()` methods either take a submesh consisting of a `VertexBuffer`, an `IndexBuffer`, and an `Appearance`, or a `Node`. For convenience, the cube constructed with `createMesh()` is stored in a `Mesh` object, which is the only class derived from `Node` that you know at the moment. Later chapters introduce `Sprite3D` and `Group`, which are the other two classes that you can use here. All immediate mode `render()` calls have a `Transform` object in the parameter list. It defines whether the mesh changes its shape or position. Passing `null` means you aren't changing the mesh in any way.

The scoping parameter only exists for one of the `render()` calls. A mesh is visible only if its scope matches the scope of the `Camera` object. The scope of a mesh is usually stored by calling `setScope()` in classes derived from `Node`, such as `Mesh` or `Camera`. M3G builds the bitwise AND (&) of the camera's and the mesh's scope and renders the mesh only if the result doesn't equal 0. Scoping helps grouping objects without defining a direct object association. Because a `VertexBuffer` doesn't inherit the scope property from `Node`, M3G allows you to set it for a submesh when calling `render()`.

Finally, `releaseTarget()` signals the end of rendering. This transfers the rendering result to the render target. However, because `ColoredGeometrySample` is a `GameCanvas`, you have to call `Graphics.flushGraphics()` to flush the contents of its double buffer to the screen. If you go back to the previous section, you'll find a call to this method at the end of the `init()` method, right after calling `render()`.

Releasing the target is important because it allows you to bind the target again the next time. In a scenario where you set a wrong parameter in `Graphics3D` or in your mesh, `bindTarget()` or `render()` will throw a runtime exception and `releaseTarget()` might be skipped. If you are scared of this, you can wrap your calls with `throw/catch`. In M3G 1.0, `releaseTarget()` itself could again throw an exception, but this has been removed in revision 1.1.

Tip

I usually don't bother catching these exceptions, because most of the time it means that I have an intrinsic problem with my code and need to fix the actual problem. Catching exceptions makes sense only if you have a way to recover from the problem.

Unfortunately, the exceptions thrown by `render()` don't contain much detail about the cause. As soon as something's wrong with your mesh, `render()` will answer with an `IllegalStateException`. This includes problems that were caused when creating the mesh but checked only at render time, such as triangle strips that refer to non-existing indices.

Releasing the render target means that you can use the `Graphics` object for 2D rendering. The following code displays an on-screen menu of the key assignments:

```
private void render(Graphics graphics) {
  // Bind the render target.
  graphics3d.bindTarget(graphics);
  ...
```

```
    // Release render target.
    graphics3d.releaseTarget();

    // After the rendering target is released, the 2D graphics
    // context can be used again. This method displays the current
    // key assignment.
    drawMenu(graphics);
}

/**
 * Draws a menu for the current key assignments.
 *
 * @param graphics graphics context for drawing.
 */
private void drawMenu(Graphics graphics) {
    graphics.setColor(0xFFFFFFFF);
    graphics.setFont(Font.getFont(Font.FACE_SYSTEM,
        Font.STYLE_PLAIN, Font.SIZE_SMALL));
    int fontHeight = graphics.getFont().getHeight();

    // Upper half menu.
    int height = 0;
    graphics.drawString(getKeyName(getKeyCode(FIRE)) +
        ": Reset", 0, height, 0);
    ...
}
```

This is only part of `drawMenu()`, but it gives you an idea of how you can draw on top of the 3D render output. In a similar fashion, you could draw a heads-up display for your in-game statistics.

Tip

Each bind/release cycle has an associated performance overhead, which, depending on the device, can be more or less significant. To maximize performance, bind and release only once per frame and draw all 2D operations in one go. For screen-aligned images inside your 3D scene, consider textured quads or `Sprite3D`s (see Chapter 6).

To make the key assignments functional, `keyPressed()` handles user input. `ColoredGeometrySample` allows you to change the shading, culling, and winding parameters in `PolygonMode`:

```
/**
 * Handles key presses.
 *
 * @param keyCode key code.
 */
protected void keyPressed(int keyCode) {
  switch (getGameAction(keyCode)) {
    case FIRE:
      init();
      break;

    case GAME_A:
      if (polygonMode.getShading() == PolygonMode.SHADE_FLAT) {
        polygonMode.setShading(PolygonMode.SHADE_SMOOTH);
      } else {
        polygonMode.setShading(PolygonMode.SHADE_FLAT);
      }
      break;

    case GAME_B:
      if (polygonMode.getCulling() == PolygonMode.CULL_BACK) {
        polygonMode.setCulling(PolygonMode.CULL_FRONT);
      } else {
        polygonMode.setCulling(PolygonMode.CULL_BACK);
      }
      break;

    case GAME_C:
      if (polygonMode.getWinding() == PolygonMode.WINDING_CCW) {
        polygonMode.setWinding(PolygonMode.WINDING_CW);
      } else {
        polygonMode.setWinding(PolygonMode.WINDING_CCW);
      }
      break;

    // no default
  }

  render(graphics);
  flushGraphics();
}
```

Figure 4.6
Rendered cube with background.

This completes `ColoredGeometrySample`. If you build and run the sample, you can see the cube as in Figure 4.6.

A Shapes Library

Now that you know how to display a mesh, you'll learn different ways of generating them. The goal is to create a library of sample objects to demonstrate M3G's features. Until Chapter 10, where you see how to import data from 3D modeling software, this is the only viable approach.

But even if you had the information already, there is a good reason to avoid importing model data: application size. By generating shapes procedurally, you trade time (the time needed to generate the shapes) against size (the size needed to otherwise store the data for the model). Even better, you can adjust how many vertices you generate. For mobile devices with a 3D hardware accelerator, you might want to have many vertices to make the 3D models look smooth. For low-end devices, on the other hand, you might prefer the improved rendering speed of low-polygon models.

Most of the time, you'll either use static data for simple shapes or generate the geometry based on parametric equations. The first is easy to specify and the latter uses little memory. As you'll see, there's also a middle way of using static data as the basis for procedurally created geometry, which then allows you to combine the best of both worlds.

Using Fractional Positions

A disc is a simple example of a shape. A circle's parametric equation is given as

$$x = r \cos(t)$$

$$y = r \sin(t)$$

t is the angle that runs from 0 to 2π and r is the radius. To create a disc, you calculate two points on the circumference of the circle and connect them with the circle's center to create a triangle. The smaller the distance between the points on the circumference and the more triangles, the closer it will resemble a disc. Figure 4.7 shows the disc in the x-y plane.

Because the values for the circle are real numbers, but VertexArray can only store integers, you have to use the scale parameter. When generating the positions, you multiply them with the scale and then use the inverse of the scale value when calling VertexBuffer.setPositions(). To find the scale, you divide the maximum value range by the maximum possible value. If you choose a radius of 1 for the disc and shorts for the positions, the scale for the circle is Short.MAX_VALUE. The following code snippet details this method. The number of slices determines the subdivisions of the circle.

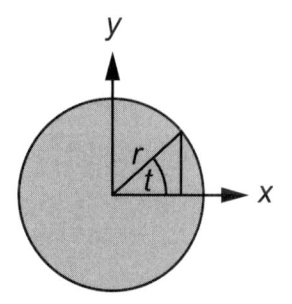

Figure 4.7
The parametric equation of a circle can be used to create a disc shape.

> **Note**
>
> The disc is implemented as the static method createDisc() in m3g04\mesh\MeshFactory2D.java. This class also contains methods to create a triangle (createTriangle()) and a quad (createQuad()). Each of these functions creates a shape with the origin at its center and extending in *x* and *y* directions with one unit.

```
/**
 * Creates a disc with radius one on the x-y plane. The disc's
 * center is at the origin (0, 0, 0).
 *
 * @param slices number of slices
 * @return mesh.
 */
public static Mesh createDisc(int slices) {
  final double angle = 2*Math.PI/slices;
  final float scale = Short.MAX_VALUE;         // because radius = 1

  short[] positions = new short[(slices+1)*3];
  int[] triangleIndices = new int[slices*3];
  int[] triangleLengths = new int[slices];

  // Center vertex is (0, 0, 0) by default and located at index
  // slices.

  for (int i=0; i<slices; i++) {
    // Calculate circle positions and convert to short using the
    // scale value.
    positions[i*3 + 0] = (short) (scale*Math.cos(angle*i));   // x
    positions[i*3 + 1] = (short) (scale*Math.sin(angle*i));   // y
    positions[i*3 + 2] = 0;                                   // z

    // Triangles.
    triangleIndices[i*3 + 0] = slices;
    triangleIndices[i*3 + 1] = i;
    triangleIndices[i*3 + 2] = (i + 1) % slices;
    triangleLengths[i] = 3;
  }

  VertexBuffer vertexBuffer = new VertexBuffer();

  VertexArray vertexPositions
      = new VertexArray(positions.length/3, 3, 2);
  vertexPositions.set(0, positions.length/3, positions);
```

```
vertexBuffer.setPositions(vertexPositions, 1/scale, null);

TriangleStripArray triangles
    = new TriangleStripArray(triangleIndices, triangleLengths);

return new Mesh(vertexBuffer, triangles, new Appearance());
}
```

Cylinder and Sphere

In a similar way to the disc, you can generate a cylinder and a sphere. Figure 4.8 shows the two shapes.

A cylinder is a straightforward extension of the disc: with the same equation for the circle you create two discs with different z coordinates for the top and bottom lids. Triangles connect the lids to form the body.

For maximum flexibility, the hard edge of the cylinder where the lids meet the body has double vertices. This allows you to assign different colors to the lid and the body. In addition, extra vertices at the seam where the longitudinal lines start and end become handy for texturing where each end of an image will be attached to the same location.

Note

Cylinder (`createCylinder()`) and sphere (`createSphere()`) are implemented as static methods in m3g04\mesh\MeshFactory3D.java. I also included a cube (`createCube()`) defined from static data.

The implementations are already prepared for the next chapters and include normals and texture coordinates. These parts are explained in the following chapters. You can use GeometricShapes Sample.java on the accompanying CD-ROM to display the shapes.

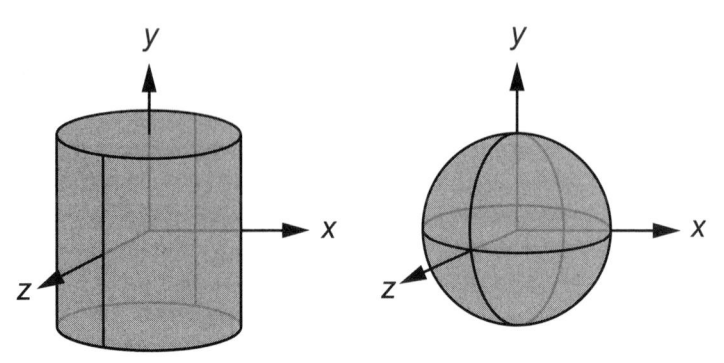

Figure 4.8
Cylinder and sphere.

A sphere can be created with the following parametric equation:

$$x = r \cos(s) \sin(t)$$
$$y = r \cos(t)$$
$$z = -r \sin(s) \sin(t)$$

s is the longitude running from 0 to 2π, t is the colatitude from 0 to π, and r is the radius. As with the cylinder, the seam has duplicate vertices for texturing. Then, for each longitude section, one triangle strip connects the vertices.

Bézier Surfaces

Parametric equations are easy to use, but restricted in the shapes that you can create. While designing cars, Pierre Bézier came up with a way to describe a curve based on control points and a formula to interpolate between them. With this tool, you can combine the advantages of static data with the flexibility of procedurally generated models. Bézier surfaces extend the same idea to 3D. Instead of one curve, four different curves restrict the sides of a surface.

Bézier Curves

Bézier curves are intuitive to use because the definition of the control points makes it easy to predict the curve's shape. Figure 4.9 shows a cubic Bézier curve, which uses four control points: P_0 and P_3 determine start and end of the curve; P_1 and P_2 bend the curve in its shape.

In the cubic example, the line segment $\overline{P_0 P_1}$ is tangent to P_0 and $\overline{P_2 P_3}$ is tangent to P_3. Thus, the four control points define the *convex hull* of the curve.

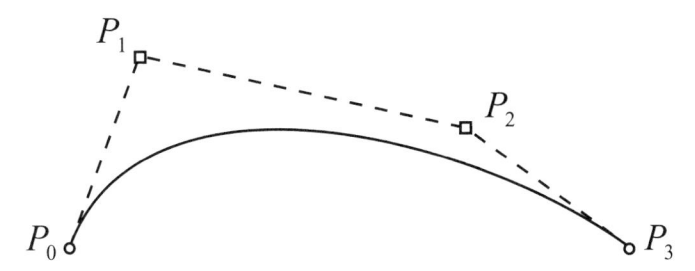

Figure 4.9
A Bézier curve with four control points.

Although you can use more or less than four control points, cubic Bézier curves build a good compromise between the amount of data required and flexibility of shape.

Given the four control points, you compute the points on the curve with the following formula:

$$Q(s) = (1-s)^3 P_0 + 3s(1-s)^2 P_1 + 3s^2(1-s)P_2 + s^3 P_3$$

The parameter s determines the point on the curve. For $s = 0$, you get P_0; for $s = 1$, P_3. The number of steps between zero and one decides the number of points on the curve that you receive.

Forward Differencing

Plugging the control points into the formula for Bézier curves isn't the fastest way to compute points. Because you are dealing with slow devices, it's important that you speed up the process. The algorithm described here is called *forward differencing*.

The formula given for Bézier curves can be rewritten as

$$Q(s) = As^3 + Bs^2 + Cs + D$$

Where

$$A = 3(P_1 - P_2) - P_0 + P_3$$
$$B = 3(P_0 + P_2) - 6P_1$$
$$C = 3(P_1 - P_0)$$
$$D = P_0$$

Instead of computing the expensive cubic equation for each point, forward differencing works by taking a point on the curve and adding a pre-calculated difference to get the next point. The following are the forward differences for a cubic curve:

$$P = P_0$$
$$\Delta P = As^3 + Bs^2 + Cs$$
$$\Delta\Delta P = 6As^3 + 2Bs^2$$
$$\Delta\Delta\Delta P = 6As^3$$

After the initial effort to get the delta values, each next value is computed by simple additions. In pseudo code, you'd use:

```
compute three forward differences
current point on curve is P0
for number of required steps
  use current point
  add first forward difference to current point
  add second forward difference to first
  add third forward difference to second
```

Because this algorithm uses the same forward differences in each step, the increments will all be equal. For example, if you evaluate four steps, *s* would be 0.25 and you'll receive five points at 0, 0.25, 0.5, 0.75, and 1.0.

Note

The algorithms for calculating Bézier curves are implemented in m3g04\mesh\Bezier.java.

```java
/**
 * Evaluates a cubic Bezier curve (four control points).
 *
 * Minimum of subdivisions is one, which will return the start and
 * end points of the Bezier curve. Each additional step will
 * increase the number of vertices by one.
 *
 * @param cpoints array with control points.
 * @param p0 index to first control point.
 * @param p1 index to second control point.
 * @param p2 index to third control point.
 * @param p3 index to fourth control point.
 * @param result evaluated points.
 * @param offset offset into the result array.
 * @param steps number of interpolation steps.
 * @param step1 pre-computed step value (1.0f/steps).
 * @param step2 pre-computed step value (1.0f/steps*steps).
 * @param step3 pre-computed step value (1.0f/steps*steps*steps).
 */
public static void evaluateCubicCurve(
    short[] cpoints, int p0, int p1, int p2, int p3, short[] result,
    int offset, int steps, float step1, float step2, float step3) {
  // Copy first and last control point unchanged because they lie
```

```java
      // on the surface.
      System.arraycopy(cpoints, p0, result, offset, 3);
      System.arraycopy(cpoints, p3, result, offset + steps*3, 3);

      // Interpolate remaining points using forward differencing.
      if (steps > 1) {
        long axs3 = (long) (((3*(cpoints[p1+0] - cpoints[p2+0]) -
            cpoints[p0+0] + cpoints[p3+0]) * step3));
        long ays3 = (long) (((3*(cpoints[p1+1] - cpoints[p2+1]) -
            cpoints[p0+1] + cpoints[p3+1]) * step3));
        long azs3 = (long) (((3*(cpoints[p1+2] - cpoints[p2+2]) -
            cpoints[p0+2] + cpoints[p3+2]) * step3));

        long bxs2 = (long) (((3*(cpoints[p0+0] + cpoints[p2+0]) -
            6*cpoints[p1+0]) * step2));
        long bys2 = (long) (((3*(cpoints[p0+1] + cpoints[p2+1]) -
            6*cpoints[p1+1]) * step2));
        long bzs2 = (long) (((3*(cpoints[p0+2] + cpoints[p2+2]) -
            6*cpoints[p1+2]) * step2));

        long cxs1 = (long) ((3*(cpoints[p1+0] - cpoints[p0+0]) *step1));
        long cys1 = (long) ((3*(cpoints[p1+1] - cpoints[p0+1]) *step1));
        long czs1 = (long) ((3*(cpoints[p1+2] - cpoints[p0+2]) *step1));

        long x = cpoints[p0+0];
        long y = cpoints[p0+1];
        long z = cpoints[p0+2];

        long xdelta1 = axs3 + bxs2 + cxs1;
        long ydelta1 = ays3 + bys2 + cys1;
        long zdelta1 = azs3 + bzs2 + czs1;

        long xdelta2 = 6*axs3 + 2*bxs2;
        long ydelta2 = 6*ays3 + 2*bys2;
        long zdelta2 = 6*azs3 + 2*bzs2;

        long xdelta3 = 6*axs3;
        long ydelta3 = 6*ays3;
        long zdelta3 = 6*azs3;

        int index = offset;
        for (int i=1; i<steps; i++) {
          index += 3;
```

```
        x += xdelta1;
        xdelta1 += xdelta2;
        xdelta2 += xdelta3;
        result[index + 0] = (short) x;

        y += ydelta1;
        ydelta1 += ydelta2;
        ydelta2 += ydelta3;
        result[index + 1] = (short) y;

        z += zdelta1;
        zdelta1 += zdelta2;
        zdelta2 += zdelta3;
        result[index + 2] = (short) z;
      }
    }
  }
```

After the initial setup, each point requires only additions, which makes this algorithm very fast. One problem with forward differencing is that rounding errors in the calculation of the delta values add up. This isn't helped by the fact that `evaluateCubicCurve()` calculates everything as `long` values. However, with a small number of steps this doesn't create visible artifacts and the increased performance is preferable. If you wanted higher precision, you could compute the values as `float` instead.

Rendering Bézier Surfaces

To create a surface from cubic curves, you use a grid of 16 control points. These points are interpolated with the algorithm depicted in Figure 4.10.

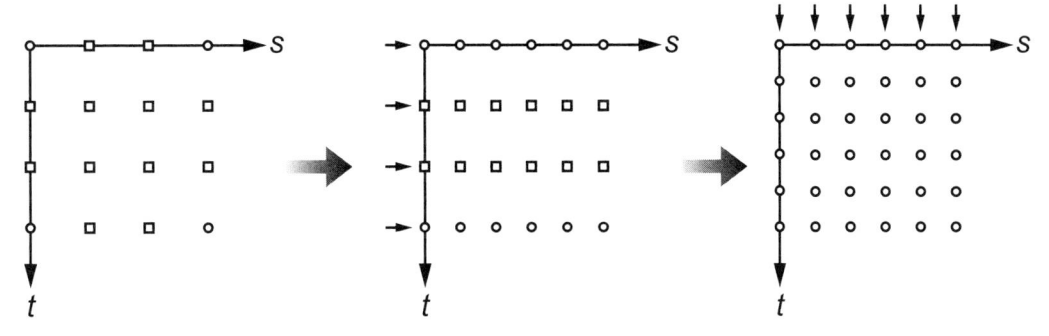

Figure 4.10
Rendering Bézier surfaces.

Initially, only the four corner points lie on the surface. Figure 4.10 indicates surface points with circles and all other points with squares. As a first step, you evaluate four Bézier curves in *s* direction. In the example, the step size is five, which results in six points for each curve. All points on the two outer curves lie on the surface, whereas all points on the two middle curves don't. The remaining step is to evaluate these intermediate points in *t* direction. Because *s* and *t* directions have the same step size, you'll receive a square grid of 36 surface points.

```
/**
 * Calculations for Bezier surfaces.
 *
 * @author Claus Hoefele
 */
public class Bezier {
  /** Number of interpolation steps. */
  private int steps;
  /** Number of vertices per curve. */
  private int numVertices;

  /** Pre-computed values for curve evaluation. */
  private float step1, step2, step3;

  /** Buffers for storing intermediate data. */
  private short[] intermediatePointsS;

  /**
   * Initializes class. If normals are created, extra memory buffers
   * are allocated to hold intermediate values.
   *
   * @param steps number of interpolation steps.
   * @param createNormals true to create normals, false otherwise.
   */
  public Bezier(int steps, boolean createNormals) {
    // Store often used values.
    this.steps = steps;
    numVertices = verticesPerCurve(steps);
    step1 = 1.0f/steps;
    step2 = step1*step1;
    step3 = step2*step1;

    // Allocate buffers.
    intermediatePointsS = new short[4*numVertices*3];
```

```
      ...
  }

  /**
   * Calculates the vertex positions of a cubic Bezier surface
   * (16 control points).
   *
   * @param controlPoints array of control points.
   * @param controlIndices array of indices to the control points.
   * @param positions resulting vertex positions.
   * @param offset offset into the positions array.
   */
  public void createPositions(short[] controlPoints,
      short[] controlIndices, short[] positions, int offset) {
    // Evaluate in s direction.
    for (int j=0; j<4 ; j++) {
      evaluateCubicCurve(controlPoints,
          controlIndices[j + 0]*3, controlIndices[j + 4]*3,
          controlIndices[j + 8]*3, controlIndices[j + 12]*3,
          intermediatePointsS, j*numVertices*3,
          steps, step1, step2, step3);
    }

    // Evaluate in t direction.
    for (int j=0; j<numVertices; j++) {
      evaluateCubicCurve(intermediatePointsS, j*3,
          (j+numVertices)*3, (j+2*numVertices)*3,
          (j+3*numVertices)*3, positions,
          offset + j*numVertices*3,
          steps, step1, step2, step3);
    }
  }
  ...
}
```

All you have to do to render the points is connect them with triangle strips.

```
  /**
   * Calculates triangle strips for the evaluated Bezier surface.
   *
   * @param offset offset to the array with vertex positions.
   * @param triStrips resulting triangle strips.
   * @param triLengths resulting triangle lengths.
```

```
 * @param triOffset offset to the triangle arrays.
 * @param windingCcw true to connect triangles counter-clockwise,
 *                   false otherwise.
 */
public void createTriStrips(int offset, int[] triStrips,
    int[] triLengths, int triOffset, boolean windingCcw) {
  final int stripLength = numVertices*2;

  for (int i=0; i<steps; i++) {
    int index = i*numVertices;

    for (int j=0; j<=steps; j++) {
      int triIndex = (triOffset + i)*stripLength + j*2;
      int index1 = offset/3 + index + j;
      int index2 = index1 + numVertices;

      // Swivel the indices depending on the winding.
      if (windingCcw) {
        triStrips[triIndex + 0] = index2;
        triStrips[triIndex + 1] = index1;
      } else {
        triStrips[triIndex + 0] = index1;
        triStrips[triIndex + 1] = index2;
      }
    }

    triLengths[triOffset + i] = stripLength;
  }
}
```

The Utah Teapot

No 3D graphics system is complete without the Utah Teapot (Figure 4.11). In the early days of 3D graphics, Martin Newell at the University of Utah created the model of a real teapot to have a familiar yet moderately complex object to work with. He published the data set and, when colleagues started to use the teapot, it eventually became an icon for 3D graphics. The original teapot now lives in the Computer History Museum in Mountain View, California. The Utah Teapot uses Bézier surfaces to describe the shape and is an excellent test object to try with the previously introduced algorithms.

Figure 4.11
The Utah Teapot uses Bézier surfaces to describe its shape.

Note

There are slightly different versions of the data set around. I downloaded the teapot definitions from http://www.sjbaker.org/teapot/, which is the same data that the OpenGL GLUT implementation uses. Including the bottom, this set consists of 10 unique patches. Because the teapot is symmetric, some patches are reflected to create the complete model. The handle and spout are reflected once on the y axis; the rim, body, lid, and bottom three times on the y, the x, and both the x and y axis. This results in 32 surfaces in the end.

Note

The teapot is implemented in m3g04\mesh\Teapot.java and uses the previously introduced Bezier.java. You can find all classes on the CD-ROM, together with GeometricShapesSample.java, which displays the teapot.

```
/**
 * Creates a new mesh based on the Bezier patches for the Utah Teapot.
 * The teapot data is taken from http://www.sjbaker.org/teapot/ and
 * includes the patches for the teapot's bottom.
 *
 * @see Bezier
 * @author Claus Hoefele
 */
public class Teapot {
```

Chapter 4 ■ Rendering Geometric Objects

```java
/** Number of patches, including reflected ones. */
private final static int NUMBER_OF_PATCHES = 32;
...

/**
 * Constructor has private access because class contains static
 * methods exclusively.
 */
private Teapot() {}

/**
 * Creates a new teapot with the given subdivisions in s and t
 * direction. Minimum values are one for each direction.
 *
 * The teapot is oriented so the lid's knob points in the positive z
 * direction, the spout in the positive x direction, and the center
 * of the teapot's bottom sits at (0, 0, 0).
 *
 *
 * @param steps number of subdivisions.
 * @param addNormals true to generate normals, false otherwise.
 * @param addTexCoords true to generate texture coordinates, false
 *                     otherwise.
 * @return teapot mesh.
 */
public static Mesh create(int steps, boolean addNormals,
    boolean addTexCoords) {
  if (steps < 1) {
    throw new IllegalArgumentException(";Step size must be >1.)");
  }

  // Allocate memory based on the number of subdivisions.
  final int verticesPerCurve = Bezier.verticesPerCurve(steps);
  final int verticesPerPatch = verticesPerCurve*verticesPerCurve;
  short[] positions
      = new short[verticesPerPatch*NUMBER_OF_PATCHES*3];
  int[] triangleIndices
      = new int[steps*verticesPerCurve*NUMBER_OF_PATCHES*2];
  int[] triangleLengths = new int[steps*NUMBER_OF_PATCHES];

  Bezier bezier = new Bezier(steps, addNormals);
```

```
// The offsets indicate the current position in the arrays.
final int deltaOffset = verticesPerPatch*3;
final int deltaTriOffset = steps;
int offset = 0;
int triOffset = 0;
int newOffset = 0;

// Loop through the patch data.
for (int i=0; i<PATCH_DATA.length; i++) {
   // Create a new patch from the control points.
   bezier.createPositions(CONTROL_POINTS, PATCH_DATA[i],
      positions, offset);

  bezier.createTriStrips(offset, triangleIndices, triangleLengths,
      triOffset, true);

  newOffset = offset + deltaOffset;
  triOffset += deltaTriOffset;

  // Reflect the previously created patch as necessary.
  for (int j=0; j<REFLECT_DATA[i].length; j++) {
    bezier.reflect(positions, offset, newOffset, deltaOffset,
        REFLECT_DATA[i][j]);

    bezier.createTriStrips(newOffset,
        triangleIndices, triangleLengths, triOffset,
        REFLECT_DATA[i][j] ==
        (Bezier.REFLECT_Y | Bezier.REFLECT_X) ? true : false);

    newOffset += deltaOffset;
    triOffset += deltaTriOffset;
  }

  offset = newOffset;
}

// Create a Mesh out of the generated data.
VertexBuffer vertexBuffer = new VertexBuffer();

VertexArray vertexPositions
    = new VertexArray(positions.length/3, 3, 2);
```

```
        vertexPositions.set(0, positions.length/3, positions);
        vertexBuffer.setPositions(vertexPositions, 1.0f/SCALE, null);

        TriangleStripArray triangles
            = new TriangleStripArray(triangleIndices, triangleLengths);

        return new Mesh(vertexBuffer, triangles, new Appearance());
    }
    ...
}
```

`create()` uses `Bezier` to calculate the surfaces. Each unique patch is created with a call to `Bezier.createPositions()` and `createTriStrips()`. To save time, the mirrored surfaces are reflected rather than recalculated. `createTriStrips()` is used in both cases with a `boolean` parameter to change the winding order.

The teapot data itself consist of three arrays: one that specifies which axes are used to reflect the surface, one that defines the 16 control points of each surface as indices, and one that contains the actual control points. The control points are pre-scaled to fit into `short` values.

Here are the array definitions:

```
/** The scale of the vertices in CONTROL_POINTS. */
public final static float SCALE = Short.MAX_VALUE/4;

/** Specifies on what axis a patch needs to be reflected. Handle
 * and spout are reflected on the x axis only, all other patches
 * on x, y, and x/y axis. The data must be in the same order as
 * PATCH_DATA. */
private final static int[][] REFLECT_DATA = {
    // rim
    {Bezier.REFLECT_Y, Bezier.REFLECT_X, Bezier.REFLECT_Y | Bezier
            .REFLECT_X},
    ...
};

/** Defines the Bezier patches for the teapot. Indices point to
 * vertices in CONTROL_POINTS. */
private final static short[][] PATCH_DATA = {
    // rim
    {102, 103, 104, 105, 4, 5, 6, 7, 8, 9, 10, 11, 12, 13, 14, 15},
    ...
```

```
};

/** The actual control points of the teapot. The original data was
 * scaled with the value defined in SCALE. */
private final static short CONTROL_POINTS[] = {
    1638, 0, 22115,
    1638, -917, 22115,
    917, -1638, 22115,
    0, -1638, 22115,
    ...
}
```

Using Bézier surfaces, you adjust the smoothness of your shapes to the device capabilities; just increase the number of steps to add more vertices. The control points use little storage memory and Bézier surfaces are easy to use for artists.

The disadvantage is that it takes some time to generate the surfaces. You also have to think about how to connect two or more patches to each other. To create a smooth transition, you have to choose the same tangents for two adjacent surfaces. A more general problem is that even though you can improve the smoothness of your shape by adding more vertices, this will never add more detail. That's why edgy objects need many surfaces to look good.

Summary

You've seen a lot of new classes in this chapter. VertexArray and VertexBuffer store vertex-specific data such as positions and colors. To build a mesh's geometry, you have to connect the vertex positions with triangle strips and put them into a TriangleStripArray. PolygonMode, a member of Appearance, defines which side of a triangle is back or front and other polygon-specific attributes. If you need to draw an image behind your 3D scene, you can use Background. Finally, you bind Graphics3D to a render target such as the screen's canvas to display your meshes.

This chapter explained how to render meshes in immediate mode and also showed you how to create common geometric objects. These shapes will help to demonstrate M3G's APIs throughout the book. You'll also see Graphics3D, Mesh, and Appearance again because these classes build the foundation of more features. In the next chapter, you see how to place and orient meshes and cameras with transformations.

Chapter 5

Transformations

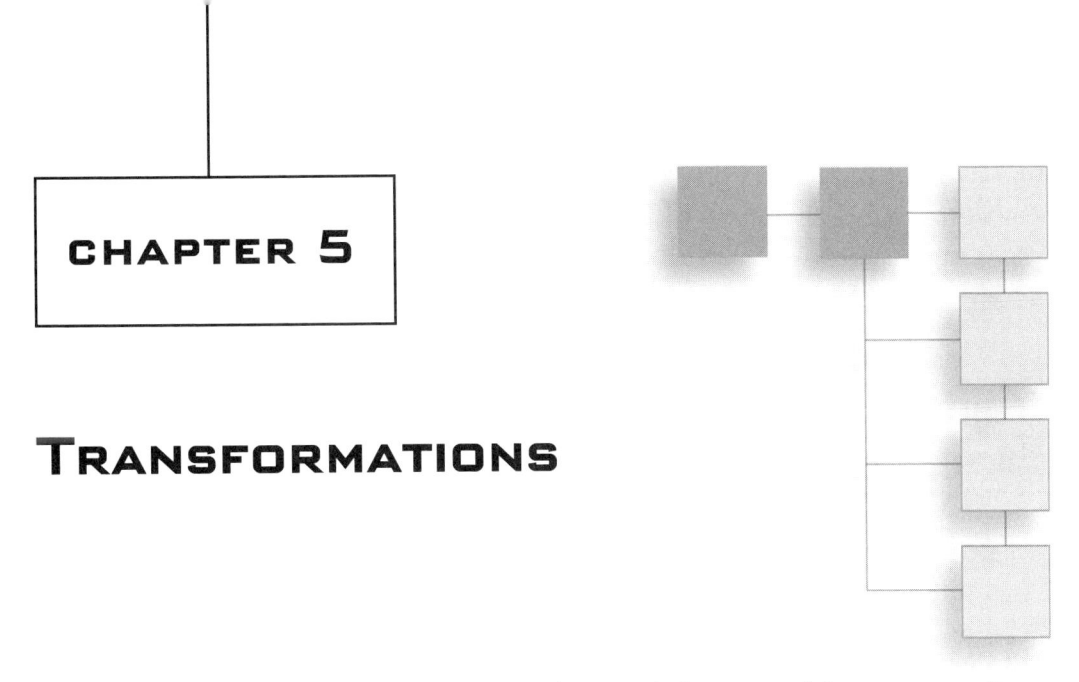

Chapter 4 showed you how vertex coordinates define a mesh's geometry. Once you put your mesh into a scene together with other 3D objects, you'll need a way to place them relative to each other and find a viewpoint from which you'd like to watch the scene. It's also clear that a three-dimensional scene doesn't map to a two-dimensional screen without conversion. Placing 3D objects, finding a viewpoint, and converting from 3D to 2D are examples of transformations that exist in 3D graphics, and linear algebra gives you the tools to compute them.

This chapter shows you:

- How M3G calculates transformations.
- What types of transformations M3G applies to a mesh.
- How you can use transformations to modify your scene.
- What the depth buffer is good for.
- How to draw wireframe meshes.

Transforming Vectors

Because the vertices of every mesh object that you draw on the screen go through a transformation process, it's important to compute it efficiently. Matrix multiplications do the majority of work here because they have unique properties that make them ideal for this purpose. If you already know about transformation matrices, homogeneous coordinates, and quaternions, you can skip this section. Otherwise, please stay with me for an introduction to the mathematical background of transformations.

Transformation Matrices

Matrices have two important properties: a matrix multiplication transforms a vector, and several matrices multiplied together represent a series of transformations.

According to the rules of linear algebra, a matrix multiplication is defined only if the number of columns of the first matrix is the same as the number of rows of the second. Thus, in order to multiply a matrix with a 3D vector that results in a vector with the same size, you need a 3-by-3 matrix.

You multiply matrices by multiplying each row of the first matrix with each column of the second. More formally, each element c of the resulting matrix at row i and column j is given by

$$c_{i,j} = \sum_{k=0}^{n-1} a_{i,k} b_{k,j} = a_{i0}b_{0j} + a_{i1}b_{1j} + \ldots + a_{i(n-1)}b_{(n-1)j}$$

Consider this example:

$$\mathbf{NMv} = \mathbf{N}\,(\mathbf{Mv}) = \begin{bmatrix} 0 & -1 & 0 \\ 1 & 0 & 0 \\ 0 & 0 & 1 \end{bmatrix} \begin{bmatrix} 2 & 0 & 0 \\ 0 & 3 & 0 \\ 0 & 0 & 4 \end{bmatrix} \begin{bmatrix} 1 \\ 0 \\ 0 \end{bmatrix} = \begin{bmatrix} 0 & -1 & 0 \\ 1 & 0 & 0 \\ 0 & 0 & 1 \end{bmatrix} \begin{bmatrix} 2 \\ 0 \\ 0 \end{bmatrix} = \begin{bmatrix} 0 \\ 2 \\ 0 \end{bmatrix}$$

First, the matrix **M** is multiplied from the right by the vector **v**, transforming (1, 0, 0) into (2, 0, 0). In other words, the operation scales **v** by the factor 2. Then, the matrix **N** is multiplied from the right by the result. This transforms the vector (2, 0, 0) into (0, 2, 0), which is a rotation by 90 degrees around the z axis. The result is a vector that is first scaled by **M**, and then rotated by **N**. Because you can equally well multiply the matrices first and the vector afterward by calculating (**NM**)**v**, you can combine transformation matrices from several steps and apply all transformations to a vector in one go. In a mesh that consists of many vertices, this saves a lot of time.

The order of multiplication is important. If you swapped **N** with **M** and calculated **MNv**, you would first rotate the vector and then scale it. The resulting vector (0, 3, 0) is clearly not the same. I'll give you some more practical examples of combining transformations later in this chapter, but it's important to remember that matrix multiplications aren't commutative (**NM** ≠ **MN**) and the matrix that's next to the vector transforms it first.

By convention, I always use column vectors and put them at the right end of the equation. This maps naturally to M3G's interface, which collects all transformations, multiplies them together, and then transforms the vertices. So, when I write a vector in the text, I really mean a column vector, but write it in a row for convenience.

The problem with the current 3-by-3 matrix is that it's restricted to a set of mathematical operations called *linear transformations*. Linear transformations include operations such as scaling and rotations, but not translations and projection. You could just add something to the vector to translate it, but ideally, a single matrix could express all of the transformations. Enter homogenous coordinates.

Homogeneous Coordinates

The coordinates of a vector in three dimensions (*x*, *y*, *z*) map to the homogenous coordinates (*x*, *y*, *z*, *w*) by picking a scalar *w*, scaling *x*, *y*, and *z* with it, and using *w* as the fourth coordinate. To convert from homogenous coordinates back to 3D, you divide the first three coordinates by *w*. Consider the following example, where *w* is set to 1 initially:

$$\mathbf{Mv} = \begin{bmatrix} 1 & 0 & 0 & 2 \\ 0 & 1 & 0 & 0 \\ 0 & 0 & 1 & 0 \\ 0 & 0 & 0 & 1 \end{bmatrix} \begin{bmatrix} 1 \\ 0 \\ 0 \\ 1 \end{bmatrix} = \begin{bmatrix} 3 \\ 0 \\ 0 \\ 1 \end{bmatrix}$$

The upper-left 3×3 block is labeled "Linear transformation such as rotation and scaling" and the right column (above the bottom row) is labeled "Translation".

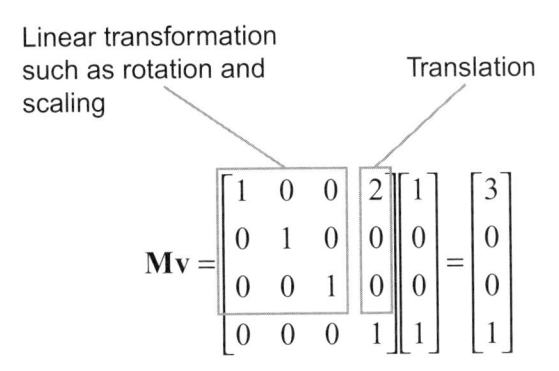

Here, the vector (1, 0, 0) is converted to homogeneous coordinates by setting the fourth coordinate to 1, which results in (1, 0, 0, 1). After multiplication with the 4-by-4 matrix, you have (3, 0, 0, 1). The first three coordinates divided by w yields (3, 0, 0): the original vector was moved by two units on the x axis.

I indicated in the equation which sub-matrices are used for which kind of transformation. The 3-by-3 matrix in the upper-left corner is the linear transformation matrix that you saw in the previous section. In addition, the upper-right 3-by-1 matrix is for a translation. The combination of a linear transformation with a translation is called an *affine transformation*. By adding a fourth coordinate, homogenous coordinates extend matrix multiplications to operations that weren't possible before.

In the previous example, the division by w wasn't really necessary. However, there are cases when this isn't the case, for example when computing a perspective projection. The perspective projection matrix is more complex than affine transformations and also uses the lower row of the 4-by-4 matrix.

The division by w is defined only if $w \neq 0$. Thus, for transforming vertices, the transformation multiplication must be defined so this can never happen. That's why I initially set the w coordinate to 1 when converting the vector from 3D to homogeneous coordinates. However, there are cases when setting w to 0 is useful as well.

In addition to a point, a vector can also be interpreted as a direction. For a direction, the length of a vector isn't important, thus scaling and dividing by w isn't necessary. Setting w to 0 indicates that you want M3G to interpret the vector as a direction instead of a point. This will be useful when you come to lighting, which needs an indication of the direction of a surface to work. When using `VertexArray`, you don't need to set the w coordinate explicitly because M3G automatically interprets its elements correctly, depending on the context in which they are used.

An infinite number of transformations are possible, but most of the time you'll only work with a few for which M3G defined easy-to-use interfaces. `Transform` has methods for translation, rotation, and scaling; `Camera` encapsulates the projection matrix. But in both classes, you can also specify a generic matrix for unusual transformations.

Matrix Operations Using Transform

`Transform` is M3G's class for matrix calculations. It can store arbitrary 4-by-4 matrices; Table 5.1 lists its interface.

Table 5.1 Transform Class Description

Method	Description
Setting/Getting Matrix Elements	
Transform()	Initializes the object to the identity matrix.
Transform(Transform transform)	Constructs a new Transform object by copying the values from another matrix.
void set(float[] matrix)	Copies the matrix values from a float array in row major order.
void get(float[] matrix)	Copies the matrix values to a float array in row major order.
void set(Transform transform)	Copies the matrix values from another matrix.
Transforming Vectors	
void transform(float[] vectors)	Multiplies an array of homogeneous vectors by this matrix.
void transform(VertexArray in, float[] out, boolean w)	Multiplies the elements of the VertexArray by this matrix and copies the result to a float array.
General Matrix Operations	
void setIdentity()	Sets the identity matrix.
void invert()	Inverts the matrix, if possible.
void transpose()	Transposes the matrix.
Matrix Multiplications	
void postMultiply(Transform transform)	Multiplies this matrix from the right by another matrix.
void postRotate(float angle, float ax, float ay, float az)	Multiplies this matrix from the right by a rotation matrix.
void postRotateQuat(float qx, float qy, float qz, float qw)	Multiplies this matrix from the right by a rotation matrix. The parameters are given in quaternion format.
void postScale(float sx, float sy, float sz)	Multiplies this matrix from the right by a scale matrix.
void postTranslate(float tx, float ty, float tz)	Multiplies this matrix from the right by a translation matrix.

The identity matrix is similar to the number 1: multiplying a matrix by the identity matrix results in the same matrix. Consider this 4-by-4 identity matrix **I**, which consists of a diagonal line of 1s and all other elements set to 0:

$$\mathbf{I} = \begin{bmatrix} 1 & 0 & 0 & 0 \\ 0 & 1 & 0 & 0 \\ 0 & 0 & 1 & 0 \\ 0 & 0 & 0 & 1 \end{bmatrix}$$

With the default constructor, a `Transform` object contains the identity matrix as the starting point. If you modified a `Transform` object, you can reset the matrix to the identity with `setIdentity()`.

To set the contents of a `Transform` object, you can either copy another `Transform` or use an array of `float`s. In the latter case, the contents of the array are assigned in row major form: starting from the upper-left corner, elements of the array are copied to the matrix left to right, top to bottom. In other words, if you declare a `float` array and initialize your `Transform` object like this:

```
float[] matrixElements = new float[] {
    0,  1,  2,  3,
    4,  5,  6,  7,
    8,  9, 10, 11,
   12, 13, 14, 15
};
Transform transform = new Transform();
transform.set(matrixElements);
```

You'll end up with this matrix:

$$\begin{bmatrix} 0 & 1 & 2 & 3 \\ 4 & 5 & 6 & 7 \\ 8 & 9 & 10 & 11 \\ 12 & 13 & 14 & 15 \end{bmatrix}$$

Tip
Be careful when working with matrices stored in arrays from OpenGL, because it requires the elements of the matrix column by column instead.

With the two `transform()` methods, you can multiply a number of vectors by a matrix. The first form takes an array of `float`s; each vector has to hold four elements (x, y, z, w). As explained in the previous section, if you are working with vectors that represent positions, you'll want to set w to 1; for directions, set w to 0.

The second form multiplies all vertices stored in a `VertexArray` by a matrix; the result is stored in a `float` array. This method is also a convenient way to copy out values from a `VertexArray` in M3G 1.0 because `VertexArray.get()` exists only in M3G 1.1. You can influence whether the w element of the input vertices is set to 1 or 0 with a `boolean` parameter.

Apart from the already mentioned setIdentity(), two general matrix operations need further explanation: invert() and transpose().

There's no division operation defined for a matrix; however, you can multiply a matrix with the inverse of another matrix. The inverse of a matrix is defined so that multiplying a matrix by its inverse results in the identity matrix ($MM^{-1}=I$). For example, the inverse M^{-1} of the Matrix M that I used previously for translating a vector in homogenous coordinates is:

$$M = \begin{bmatrix} 1 & 0 & 0 & 2 \\ 0 & 1 & 0 & 0 \\ 0 & 0 & 1 & 0 \\ 0 & 0 & 0 & 1 \end{bmatrix} \quad M^{-1} = \begin{bmatrix} 1 & 0 & 0 & -2 \\ 0 & 1 & 0 & 0 \\ 0 & 0 & 1 & 0 \\ 0 & 0 & 0 & 1 \end{bmatrix}$$

Intuitively, if you translate something in one direction, the inverse will have to move it in the other. Not all matrices have an inverse though; invert() will throw a java.lang.ArithmeticException if this is the case. The simplest example of a non-invertible matrix is one with all elements set to 0. No matter what you multiply, you'll never be able to come to the identity matrix. Rotation and translation pose no problem, but multiplying a matrix by a scale matrix or by a generic matrix might. Of course, you have to consider inversion only if such a matrix is needed, but this is more often the case than you'd think. Even if you don't work with the inverse of a matrix yourself, M3G might need it for internal calculations. The API reference guides you with its declarations for ArithmeticExceptions.

Tip
Your matrix will always be invertible if you use postTranslate(), postRotate(), and postRotateQuat(). postScale() is fine if you avoid 0 values in the parameters.

The transpose is a very simple operation that swaps the rows of a matrix with its columns. In some circumstances, a matrix's transpose is the same as its inverse, thus saving a more complicated calculation.

$$M = \begin{bmatrix} 0 & 1 & 2 & 3 \\ 4 & 5 & 6 & 7 \\ 8 & 9 & 10 & 11 \\ 12 & 13 & 14 & 15 \end{bmatrix} \quad M^T = \begin{bmatrix} 0 & 4 & 8 & 12 \\ 1 & 5 & 9 & 13 \\ 2 & 6 & 10 & 14 \\ 3 & 7 & 11 & 15 \end{bmatrix}$$

Finally, you can multiply a matrix with another one by using the methods starting with `post`, such as `postMultiply()`, which multiplies arbitrary matrices. All these methods multiply the parameter of the method from the right, hence the name. If **A** and **B** are matrices, you would code **AB** as `A.postMultiply(B)`.

For the most often used transformations, M3G defined convenience methods that construct the respective transformation matrix and multiplies it with a matrix. I'll give you code examples of how to use `postTranslate()` and `postScale()` later in the chapter. Rotation needs more explanation. For a start, there are two methods: `postRotate()` and `postRotateQuat()`. In the next chapter, I show you the difference between these methods.

Orientation Representations

When you take aim on your enemy, you have to change the orientation of your gun with a rotation. Animations often use a series of rotations to store the movements of arms and legs. In this case, the space needed to store them is an issue as is performance of the calculations. Ideally, a rotation uses little memory, is efficient to compute with, and results in a smooth rotation.

A rotation must in one way or another end up as a matrix in a `Transform` object, because that's the only way M3G allows clients to modify 3D objects. This makes sense because it's efficient to concatenate different transformation matrices into one and apply the result to a vector in one go. With the goal set, let's look at different possibilities to come to such a rotation matrix.

Axis-Angle Format

The axis-angle format consists of a vector that specifies a rotation axis and an angle that describes the amount of rotation. `Transform` has a method `postRotate()` that takes exactly these four values. The rotation is clockwise if you look along the positive rotation axis. The easiest way to remember this is to use the right hand and point your thumb in the direction of the positive axis. As Figure 5.1 shows, your object will rotate in the same direction as you can roll in the fingers of your right hand.

Check out this pseudo code as an example how to use the axis-angle format:

```
private float angle, axisX, axisY, axisZ;
private Transform transform = new Transform();
```

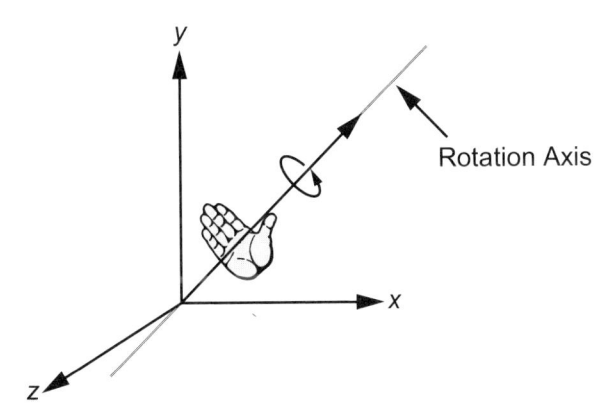

Figure 5.1
Rotation in axis-angle format.

```
// Receive key press, add delta value to angle, and call repaint()

public void paint(Graphics g) {
    // ... initialize and bind Graphics3D

    transform.setIdentity();
    transform.postRotate(angle, axisX, axisY, axisZ);
    graphics3D.render(mesh, transform);

    // ... release Graphics3D
}
```

In the example, you initialize the transformation to the identity matrix each time and build a new matrix from the rotation angles. This avoids problems that would occur if you multiplied the last rotation with a matrix that represents the delta rotation. Because of the finite numerical resolution of the matrix, rounding errors introduced with each multiplication would add up, causing the matrix to *drift*.

Drifting is actually a twofold problem. First of all, your object shouldn't deviate from the arc of rotation. If your object rotates off by an error, it's still undergone a rotation, although not the one you intended. Second, a matrix can represent many kinds of transformations that are not rotations at all. For example, a scale factor can creep in, causing the shape of your object to change. There are ways to force a matrix to obey constraints, but they are computationally expensive—basically, you want to avoid drifting.

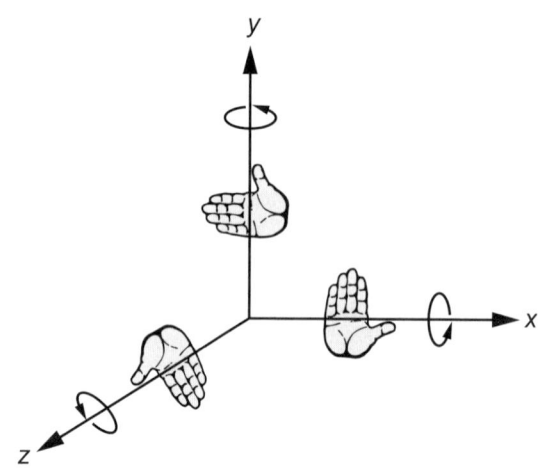

Figure 5.2
Rotation with Euler angles.

The general advice for any transformation is to store the original transformation values and initialize the matrix to new values every time.

Coming back to the discussion of the axis-angle format, you can see that it's quite memory efficient: it takes four `floats` to represent a rotation. Concatenating several axis-angle values to one rotation is difficult though. One method is to convert both rotations in a matrix and multiply them. Another problem is that the axis-angle format requires a single rotation axis. When you fly an airplane simulator, for example, you want to be able to control three axes separately.

Euler Angles

The alternative to a single rotation axis is to rotate your object three times in succession around a set of orthogonal axes, as Figure 5.2 depicts. The rotation angles are called *Euler angles*.

The following example rotates first around the *z*, then the *y*, and finally the *x* axis, although other sequences are possible.

```
private float rotX, rotY, rotZ;
Transform transform = new Transform();

// Receive key press, add delta value to rotX, rotY, or rotZ,
// and call repaint()
```

```
public void paint(Graphics g) {
   // ... initialize and bind Graphics3D

   transform.setIdentity();
   transform.postRotate(rotX, 1, 0, 0);
   transform.postRotate(rotY, 0, 1, 0);
   transform.postRotate(rotZ, 0, 0, 1);
   graphics3D.render(mesh, transform);

   // ... release Graphics3D
}
```

In the example, `postRotate()` builds a rotation matrix out of each Euler angle and multiplies the matrices in the order $\mathbf{R}_x\mathbf{R}_y\mathbf{R}_z$. You can't express an arbitrary rotation with fewer than three values, which makes Euler angles very memory efficient. However, Euler angles share the problem of concatenation with the axis-angle format. They also suffer from another major problem: *gimbal lock*.

The gimbal lock problem occurs when two axes of rotation align. Suddenly, only two degrees of freedom are left. Imagine rotating an airplane in the sequence *x-y-z* and the nose points initially toward the positive *z* axis. Dip the nose down (*x* axis rotation), rotate it 90 degrees to the right around the horizontal axis (*y* axis rotation), and now do the *z* axis rotation. The last rotation will be around the same rotation axis as the first one.

Because Euler angles are intuitive to use, they are often used for rotation despite their shortcomings. Most of the examples in this book use Euler angles.

Quaternions

Quaternions, on the other hand, use little memory and are efficient to compute with. To explain what quaternions are, consider a comparison. If you regard homogenous coordinates as a mathematical tool that helps with transformations, you can regard quaternions as a tool that helps with rotations.

Quaternions comprise the four values *x*, *y*, *z*, and *w*. (Don't mix up these four values with homogeneous coordinates; they are not related.) If you consider (*x*, *y*, *z*) a vector and *w* a scalar, you can also write quaternions in the following notation:

$$\mathbf{q}_N = [\mathbf{v}, w]$$

Only unit quaternions represent rotations. You come to a unit quaternion q_N by dividing it by its length.

$$\|q\| = \sqrt{x^2 + y^2 + z^2 + w^2}$$

$$q_N = \frac{q}{\|q\|}$$

You can divide a quaternion by a scalar by simply dividing each element with the scalar.

The following equation converts a rotation in axis-angle format to a quaternion, where θ is the angle of rotation and **v** a unit vector that specifies the rotation axis:

$$q = [v\sin(\frac{\theta}{2}), \cos(\frac{\theta}{2})]$$

The good news about unit quaternions is that they have similar properties as matrices—you can concatenate rotations by multiplying them. A multiplication is given by

$$pq = [w_p v_q + w_q v_p + v_p \times v_q, w_p w_q - v_p \cdot v_q]$$

The result **pq** would represent the rotation **q** followed by **p**. Similar to matrices, there's also an identity quaternion, which is (0, 0, 0, 1). And again, multiplication is not commutative because of the vector cross product involved.

So far, quaternions are just a complicated way of encoding rotations. What's the point then? If you study books about computer graphics, they'll tell you that, whereas matrices are computationally more efficient in transforming several vertices than quaternions, multiplying quaternions is more efficient than multiplying matrices. Hence, by first calculating rotations with quaternions and then converting them into a matrix, you get the best out of both worlds. The advantage of quaternions is that they use up only four `floats` and, because unit quaternions always represent a rotation, quaternions avoid drift. On top of that, quaternions also avoid gimbal lock.

Quaternions really start to shine when used in animations because they can be efficiently interpolated. In a third-person game, for example, you want the camera to always show the main character. However, if the camera follows the character immediately, the camera makes very sudden movements. Instead, you define the initial and the final camera orientation with quaternions. By interpolating the orientations with quaternion calculations, you can create an animation that slowly pans the camera to the final destination.

I've presented the whole slew of equations because M3G doesn't offer you any help for quaternion calculations. Later, I'll implement a quaternion class myself and need these definitions.

Note

In Chapter 12, you learn how to use quaternions for animating rotations.

What M3G does provide is a way to convert a quaternion to a matrix and multiply it with another matrix: `Transform.postRotateQuat()`. This method also normalizes the quaternion before the conversion. As I mentioned previously, only unit quaternions represent rotations. When a quaternion undergoes many multiplications, it might lose this property and will have to be readjusted.

Stages of Vertex Transformation

Now that you know how to compute transformations, I'll explain what kind of transformations a mesh goes through until it's displayed. In each step, the mesh is transformed so that in the end, a rendered image appears on the screen. Figure 5.3 shows the different steps and calls them according to the OpenGL naming conventions. You'll find many references to this naming in M3G's documentation.

The process starts with a mesh whose vertices are defined in object coordinates. Chapter 4 explained how to construct a mesh and put the vertex positions in a `VertexBuffer`. As a first step, the mesh undergoes the model/view transformation

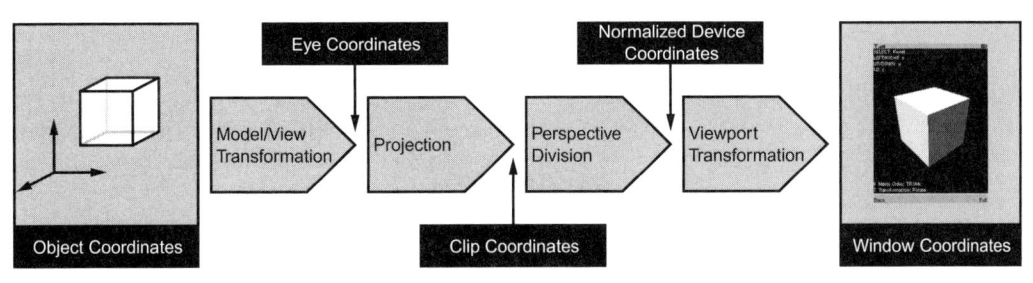

Figure 5.3
Stages of vertex transformation.

which yields eye coordinates. Modeling refers to operations you apply to the mesh itself, whereas viewing shows the model from the perspective of the camera's position. Sometimes, object coordinates are also referred to as local coordinates, which are then transformed to world coordinates by the modeling transformation.

Modeling and viewing is what you would do when taking a snapshot of your friend in front of Buckingham Palace. Either you, holding the camera, or your friend has to move until the scene contains everything you want to depict. In reality, it's a big difference whether you walk around your friend or your friend moves around you. But for a 3D scene without the earth as a fixed reference point, it doesn't matter. Hence, moving the camera 10 units backward or moving the model 10 units forward results in the same outcome.

For convenience, M3G lets you specify both transformations separately. It's sometimes easier to think of moving an object from the point of view of a camera, for example in a first-person shooter. Usually, you transform the meshes in your scene with model transformations until they are correctly placed relative to each other. Then, transforming the camera will change all the meshes to the view of the observer. The model transformation is part of the `Graphics3D.render()` call and the viewing transformation part of `Graphics3D.setCamera()`.

Next, the scene is projected onto the screen. The projection has two influences on the rendered scene: it defines the field of view and how the scene is mapped onto a 2D screen. Changing the field of view is similar to using different lenses with your camera. With a wide-angle lens, you can fit more of Buckingham Palace on your photo. With a telephoto lens, you can zoom in to a detail of the palace's decoration.

The second part of the projection transformation is the actual projection itself. M3G provides two in-built types of projection for you: perspective and parallel. Perspective projection works like the real world: when you look along a wall of Buckingham Palace, it seems that the wall's boundaries meet at a point on the horizon. Objects alongside the wall become smaller the farther their distance from the camera. When using parallel projection on the other hand, you ignore perspective and draw all objects the same size, no matter how far away they are. This can make sense for applications such as CAD programs, where it is easier to work on drawings without perspective. You can set the perspective and parallel projection parameters as part of M3G's `Camera` interface. After the projection transformation, the mesh is in clip coordinates because this is where M3G removes objects that aren't visible.

The next step, perspective division, converts the vertices back from homogeneous coordinates. Before M3G can draw the vertices, it must divide x, y, and z by the additional fourth coordinate w that homogeneous coordinates introduced. M3G does the perspective division automatically for you; there's no API for it. The perspective division results in normalized device coordinates which is only one step away from the final window coordinates used for drawing the scene onto the screen.

The viewport transformation does the same operation that you ask for when developing holiday snapshots in different sizes. You might want to have large prints to hang on the wall, whereas other prints need to be small so you can send them by mail. The viewport transformation scales and positions the rendered scene to the parameters you specify in `Graphics3D.setViewport()`. Usually, this would be the upper-left corner and the screen size of your mobile phone.

With the viewport transformation, the process of transforming geometry ends and M3G can use the resulting coordinates to render the scene. Now that you have an overview, I'll show you in detail how to influence the different stages.

Modeling Transformations

Changing the models in your 3D scene is probably the most common type of transformation you'll work with directly. Games allow you to control spaceships, ruthless pirates, or your favorite soccer star. `ModelTransformationsSample` starts modestly with a cube. I'll show you the skeleton of the application and then introduce various kinds of model transformations step by step.

A Transformation Framework

`ModelTransformationsSample` can switch between different kinds of transformations and transform the cube about any axis. Figure 5.4 shows three example screenshots.

Note

You can find ModelTransformationsSample.java together with a working MIDlet on the accompanying CD-ROM.

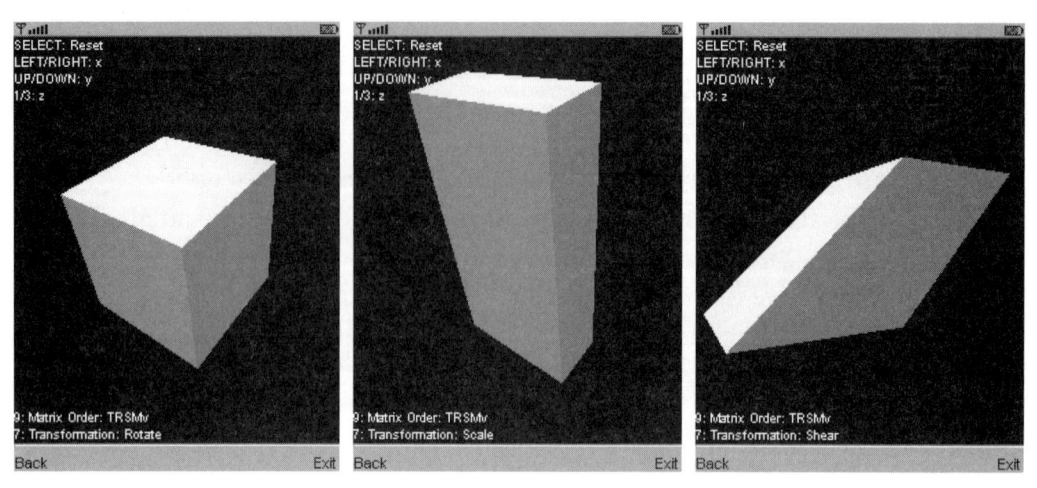

Figure 5.4
Screenshots of model transformations from left to right: Rotate, Scale, and Shear.

ModelTransformationsSample declares the mesh for drawing in mesh and its transformation in meshTransform. The sample uses the various constant values defined in the class to distinguish between the current transformation type stored in currentTransformation.

```
/**
 * Sample displaying a cube that can be transformed interactively.
 *
 * @author Claus Hoefele
 */
public class ModelTransformationsSample extends GameCanvas
    implements Sample{
  ...

  /** Mesh for display. */
  private Mesh mesh;
  /** The mesh's transformation. */
  private Transform meshTransform = new Transform();

  /** Indicates transformation along x axis. */
  private static final int TRANSFORMATION_X_AXIS = 0;
  /** Indicates transformation along y axis. */
  private static final int TRANSFORMATION_Y_AXIS = 1;
  /** Indicates transformation along z axis. */
  private static final int TRANSFORMATION_Z_AXIS = 2;
```

```
/** Indicates translation. */
private static final int TRANSFORMATION_TRANSLATE = 0;
/** Indicates rotation. */
private static final int TRANSFORMATION_ROTATE =   1;
/** Indicates scaling. */
private static final int TRANSFORMATION_SCALE  =   2;
/** Indicates shearing. */
private static final int TRANSFORMATION_SHEAR  =   3;
/** Current transformation. */
private int currentTransformation;

/** 3D graphics singleton used for rendering. */
private Graphics3D graphics3d;
/** 2D graphics singleton used for rendering. */
private Graphics graphics;

/**
 * Constructor.
 */
public ModelTransformationsSample() {
  super(false);
}
...
}
```

init() creates the cube and initialize the camera. The explanation of the camera parameters will follow in a later section. The focus here is on the modelling transformation, which is set by default to TRANSFORMATION_TRANSLATE.

```
/**
 * Initializes the sample.
 */
public void init() {
  // Get the singletons for rendering.
  graphics3d = Graphics3D.getInstance();
  graphics = getGraphics();

  // Create mesh and reset transformation parameters.
  mesh = MeshFactory3D.createCube(true, false, false);
  currentTransformation = TRANSFORMATION_TRANSLATE;
  ...

  // Create a camera with perspective projection.
  Camera camera = new Camera();
```

```
    float aspect = (float) getWidth() / (float) getHeight();
    camera.setPerspective(60, aspect, 1, 1000);
    Transform cameraTransform = new Transform();
    cameraTransform.postTranslate(0, 0, 5);
    graphics3d.setCamera(camera, cameraTransform);

    render(graphics);
    flushGraphics();
  }
```

`render()` calls `transform()` to apply the current transformation to the mesh's Transform object and draws the cube on the screen.

```
  /**
   * Renders the sample.
   *
   * @param graphics graphics context for rendering.
   */
  private void render(Graphics graphics) {
    graphics3d.bindTarget(graphics);
    graphics3d.setViewport(0, 0, getWidth(), getHeight());
    graphics3d.clear(null);
    transform(meshTransform);
    graphics3d.render(mesh, meshTransform);
    graphics3d.releaseTarget();

    drawMenu(graphics); // displays the current key assignment
  }
```

In its current state, `transform()` sets the transformation to the identity matrix. In the following sections I'll add something more useful here.

```
  /**
   * Applies the current transformation values to the given Transform
   * object.
   *
   * @param transform Transform object
   */
  private void transform(Transform transform) {
    transform.setIdentity();
    ...
  }
```

Modeling Transformations

`ModelTransformationsSample` implements `keyPressed()` to change the transformation values. For each transformation, LEFT/RIGHT changes the *x* axis, UP/RIGHT the *y* axis, and GAME_A/GAME_B the *z* axis. You can change the type of transformation with GAME_C and change the order of transformation with GAME_D. Figure 5.5 shows the application flow when a key press happens.

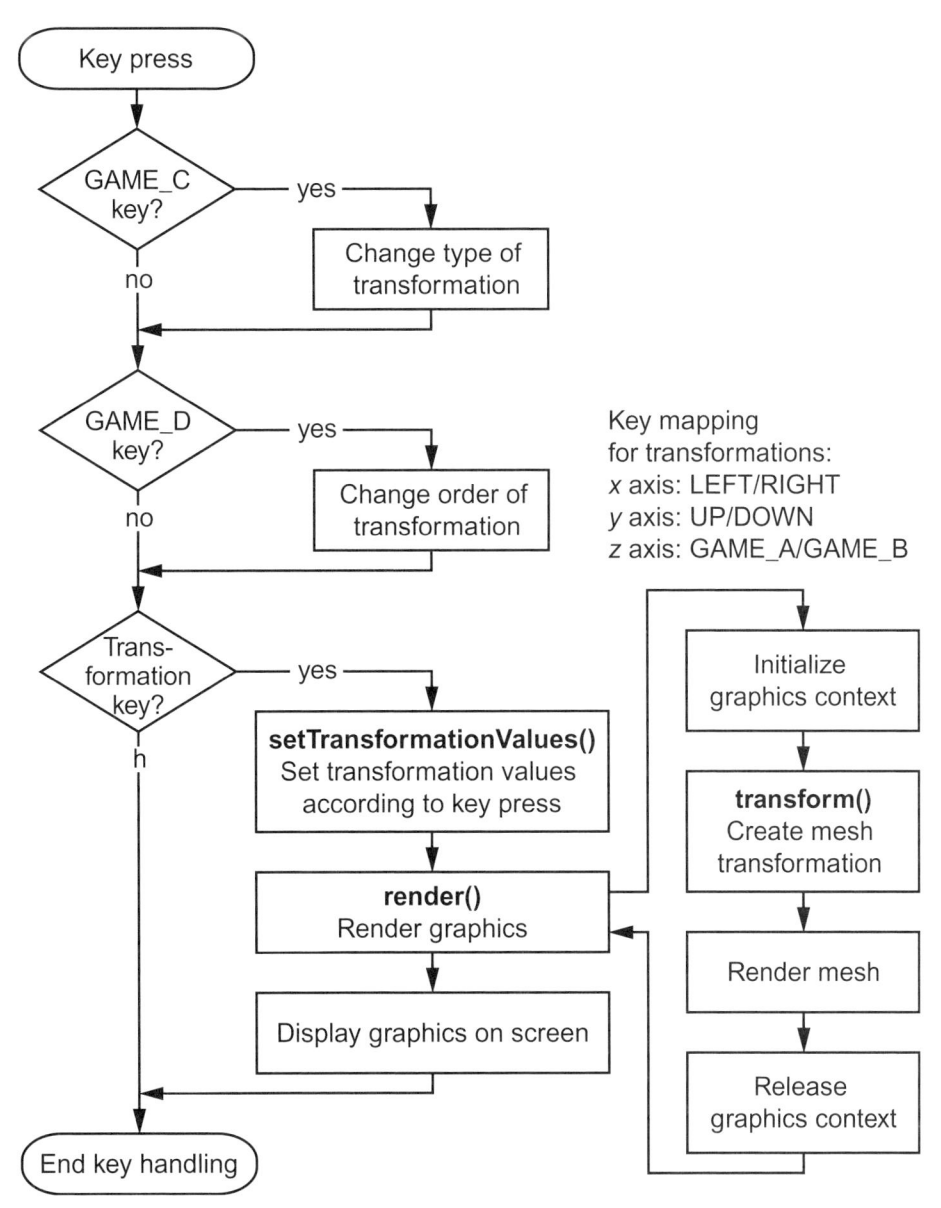

Figure 5.5
Application flow in `ModelTransformationsSample`.

When you press a key, `keyPressed()` will either switch to another type of transformation or call `setTransformationValues()` with the axis information to change the values of the current transformation. Afterward, a call to `render()` draws the mesh on the screen. This method initializes the graphics context, calls `transform()` to create the current mesh transformation, renders the mesh on the screen, and finally releases the graphics context. The image is then flushed to the screen.

That's the complete framework for the following transformations. For each type of transformation, I expand `init()` to initialize the transformation's values, add a key handler to `setTransformationValues()`, and apply the transformation in `transform()`. I show how to do translations next.

Translation

Translation is the simplest of all transformations: it moves the mesh by a value in the *x*, *y*, or *z* direction. Positive values move the mesh in the direction of the positive axis, negative values do the opposite. Figure 5.6 shows a cube translated along the *x* axis.

To move the cube, I added three translation values to `ModelTransformationsSample`, one for each axis. The values are set to 0 in `init()`.

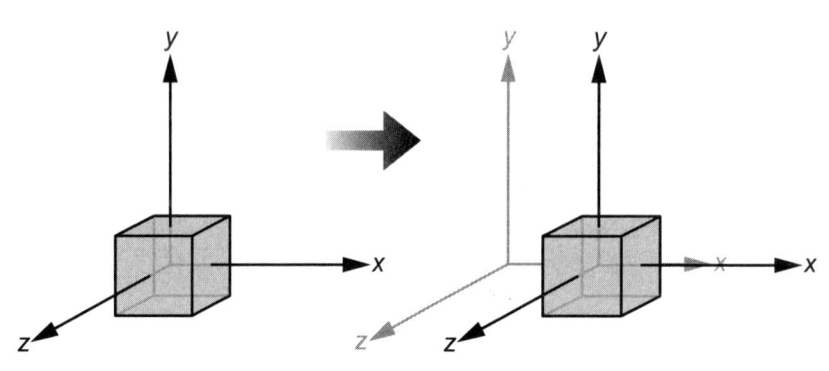

Figure 5.6
Translation in the *x* direction.

```java
/** Current translation value. */
private float transX, transY, transZ;
public void init() {
   ...
   transX = transY = transZ = 0;
   ...
}
```

If the example is in translation mode, depending on the axis, a key press will either add or subtract a small value to transX, transY, or transZ.

```java
private void setTransformationValues(int transformation, int axis,
    boolean positiveDirection) {
  ...
  if (transformation == TRANSFORMATION_TRANSLATE) {
    float amount = 0.2f * (positiveDirection ? 1 : -1);

    switch (axis) {
      case TRANSFORMATION_X_AXIS:
        transX += amount;
        break;

      case TRANSFORMATION_Y_AXIS:
        transY += amount;
        break;

      case TRANSFORMATION_Z_AXIS:
        transZ += amount;
        break;

      // no default
    }
  }
  ...
}
```

Once it's time to transform the mesh, postTranslate() takes the translation values and applies the transformation.

```java
private void transform(Transform transform) {
  ...
  transform.postTranslate(transX, transY, transZ);
  ...
}
```

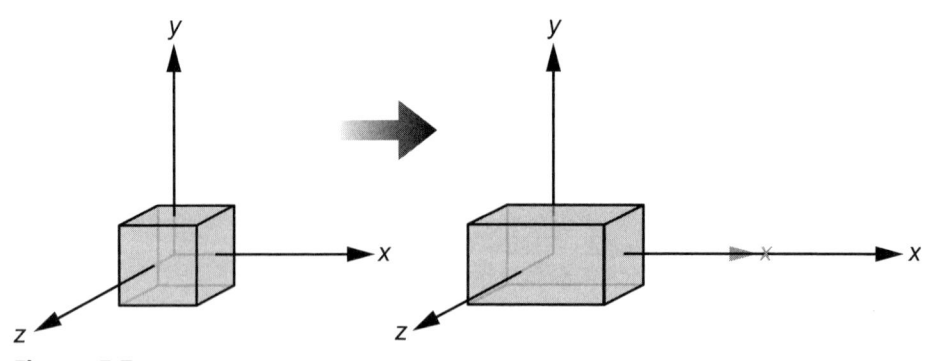

Figure 5.7
Scaling along the x axis.

Scaling

With scaling, you'll change the size of a mesh. Values greater than 1 will enlarge it, whereas values between 0 and 1 will shrink it. Negative values scale and reflect your mesh at the same time. You should avoid scaling by 0 because your mesh will vanish. Figure 5.7 shows a cube scaled along the *x* axis.

For each of the axes, `ModelTransformationsSample` owns a value that stores the current scaling value. `init()` sets these values to 1.

```
/** Current scale value. */
private float scaleX, scaleY, scaleZ;

private void init() {
  ...
  scaleX = scaleY = scaleZ = 1;
  ...
}
```

`setTransformationValues()` changes the current scaling value. For each key press, the scaling will change the mesh by the same percentage.

```
private void setTransformationValues(int transformation, int axis,
    boolean positiveDirection) {
  ...
  if (transformation == TRANSFORMATION_SCALE) {
    float amount = positiveDirection ? 1.2f : 0.8f;
```

```
    switch (axis) {
      case TRANSFORMATION_X_AXIS:
        scaleX *= amount;
        break;

      case TRANSFORMATION_Y_AXIS:
        scaleY *= amount;
        break;

      case TRANSFORMATION_Z_AXIS:
        scaleZ *= amount;
        break;

      // no default
    }
  }
  ...
}
```

In `transform()`, the scaling values are applied to the mesh's transformation.

```
private void transform(Transform transform) {
  ...
  transform.postScale(scaleX, scaleY, scaleZ);
  ...
}
```

Rotation

Rotation with Euler angles needs three angles, one for each axis of rotation. Remember the right hand rule to work out which direction the rotation will take place. Figure 5.8 shows a negative rotation around the *z* axis.

Analogous to the other transformations, `ModelTransformationsSample` defines a `float` value for each of the rotation axes and initialize them to 0 in `init()`.

```
/** Current rotation value. */
private float rotX, rotY, rotZ;

public void init() {
  ...
  rotX = rotY = rotZ = 0;
  ...
}
```

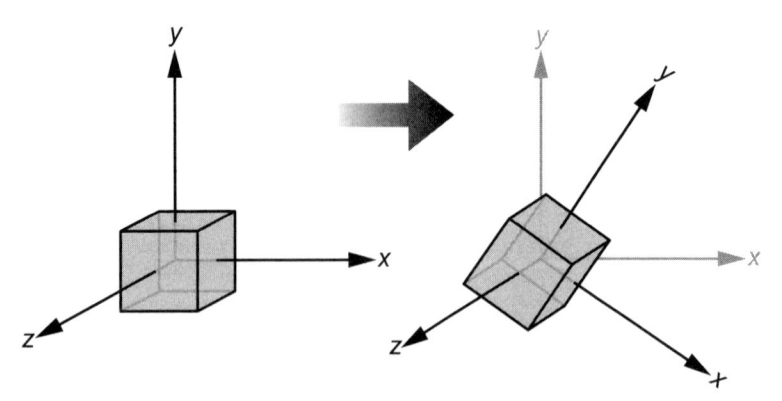

Figure 5.8
Rotation around the z axis.

The rotation values are then changed in setTransformationValues() and applied to the mesh with postRotate() in transform().

```
private void setTransformationValues(int transformation, int axis,
    boolean positiveDirection) {
  ...
  if (transformation == TRANSFORMATION_ROTATE) {
    float amount = 10 * (positiveDirection ? 1 : -1);

    switch (axis) {
      case TRANSFORMATION_X_AXIS:
        rotX += amount;
        break;

      case TRANSFORMATION_Y_AXIS:
        rotY += amount;
        break;

      case TRANSFORMATION_Z_AXIS:
        rotZ += amount;
        break;

      // no default
    }
  }
  ...
}

private void transform(Transform transform) {
  ...
```

```
    transform.postRotate(rotX, 1, 0, 0);
    transform.postRotate(rotY, 0, 1, 0);
    transform.postRotate(rotZ, 0, 0, 1);
    ...
}
```

Combining Transformations

When you apply different transformations to the same mesh, you have to consider the order. `ModelTransformationsSample` allows you rotate the cube either around its center or around the origin of the coordinate system by changing the order of the rotate and translate commands. Figure 5.9 shows what happens if you apply the rotation matrix **R** first and the translation matrix **T** afterward; the matrix multiplication is **TRv**. Figure 5.10 is the opposite case: **RTv**. Remember that the matrix next to the vector transforms it first.

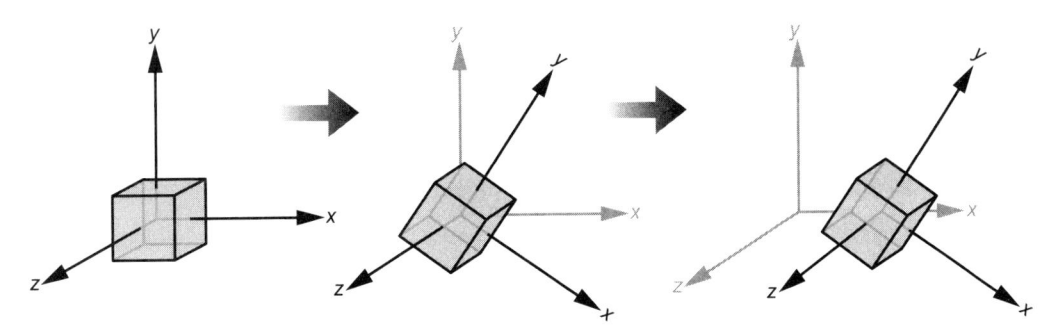

Figure 5.9
Combined transformations: first rotate and then translate.

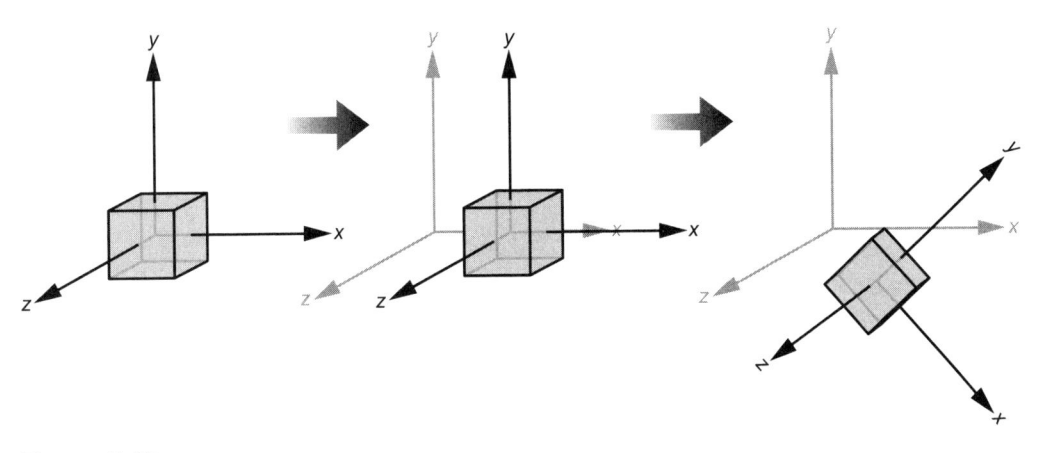

Figure 5.10
Combined transformations: first translate and then rotate.

To toggle between both cases, `ModelTransformationsSample` includes a `boolean` value `rotateBeforeTransform`, which `init()` sets to true.

```
/** Flag for swapping order of rotation and translation. */
private boolean rotateBeforeTransform;

public void init() {
  ...
  rotateBeforeTransform = true;
  ...
}
```

You can switch the order with the `GAME_D` key. `transform()` applies the transformations accordingly.

```
private void transform(Transform transform) {
  ...
  if (rotateBeforeTransform) {
    // Order of multiplication is TR.
    transform.postTranslate(transX, transY, transZ);
    transform.postRotate(rotX, 1, 0, 0);
    transform.postRotate(rotY, 0, 1, 0);
    transform.postRotate(rotZ, 0, 0, 1);
  } else {
    // Order of multiplication is RT.
    transform.postRotate(rotX, 1, 0, 0);
    transform.postRotate(rotY, 0, 1, 0);
    transform.postRotate(rotZ, 0, 0, 1);
    transform.postTranslate(transX, transY, transZ);
  }
  ...
}
```

Generic Transformations

In general, you should use the convenience methods `postTranslate()`, `postRotate()`, `postRotateQuat()`, and `postScale()` because an M3G implementation can optimize the calculations based on the reduced number of parameters needed for the operation. As an example of an operation that you can't perform with the standard methods, Figure 5.11 shows shear.

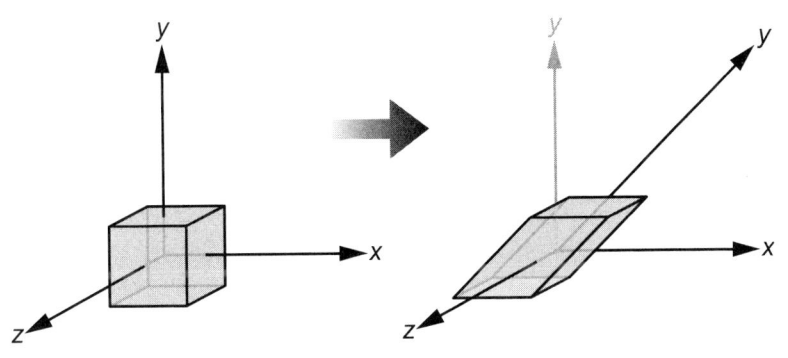

Figure 5.11
Shear along the x axis.

The matrix $\mathbf{M}_{shear}$ that shears the y coordinates of a mesh's vertices along the x axis by the value a is defined by

$$\mathbf{M}_{shear} = \begin{bmatrix} 1 & a & 0 & 0 \\ 0 & 1 & 0 & 0 \\ 0 & 0 & 1 & 0 \\ 0 & 0 & 0 & 1 \end{bmatrix}$$

`shearTransform` is a `float` array that stores the current shear matrix. `init()` copies the identity matrix into the array:

```
/** Current shear matrix. */
private float[] shearTransform = new float[16];

public void init() {
   ...
   new Transform().get(shearTransform); // stores identity matrix
   ...
}
```

When it's time to transform, `setTransformationValues()` updates the element that changes the amount of shearing. The sample only implements shearing along the x axis; the respective shearing value is located at index 1 in the `float` array.

```
private void setTransformationValues(int transformation, int axis,
     boolean positiveDirection) {
```

```
    ...
    if (transformation == TRANSFORMATION_SHEAR) {
      float amount = 0.5f * (positiveDirection ? 1 : -1);
      shearTransform[1] += amount;
    }
    ...
  }
```

`transform()` then creates a new `Transform` object out of the `float` array and multiplies it with the mesh's transformation.

```
  private void transform(Transform transform) {
    ...
    // Generic transformation by M (shear).
    Transform transform2 = new Transform();
    transform2.set(shearTransform);
    transform.postMultiply(transform2);
  }
```

Viewing Transformations

In the viewing transformation, you position the camera. If you recall, you can achieve the same outcome with either model or view transformations, but sometimes it's easier to transform your scene in relation to the camera. That's because the camera transformation applies to all meshes in a scene; the player movements in a first-person shooter are an intuitive example.

Describing a Camera

When translating a camera, you move your camera and look for a good viewpoint to take a picture. Similarly, rotation will turn the camera and change what you can see. By default, M3G positions the camera at the origin and the camera looks toward the negative z axis, as Figure 5.12 shows. This is what you'd get if you called `Graphics3D.setCamera(Camera, Transform)` with an identity matrix as the second parameter or `null`, which has the same meaning. I'll leave the first parameter, the camera, aside for a moment. I'll discuss this later when I come to projection transformations. The second parameter, however, concerns the viewing transformation, which I'll show you in detail.

The view transformations work the same as the model transformations: you create a new `Transform` object and build a transformation matrix with its methods.

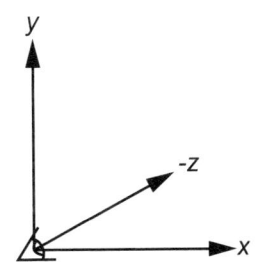

Figure 5.12
Camera in coordinate system.

There's one difference though: the camera's transformation is inverted before it's multiplied with the model transformations. The reason is that you position and rotate a camera as you would a model. You thus specify the transformation from the camera's local coordinates to world coordinates. What you want in the end, however, is exactly the opposite: a transformation that takes models from world coordinates to camera coordinates. This has the implication that the camera's transformation matrix must be invertible. This should be easy to achieve because postTranslate(), postRotate(), and postRotateQuat() can't cause your matrix to become non-invertible.

To demonstrate viewing transformations, the next section implements a common requirement in mobile games: switching between portrait and landscape mode. You get this feature nearly for free by simply rotating the camera.

Switching Between Portrait and Landscape Mode

If you turn your mobile phone so the width of the screen is greater than its height, you'll have the widescreen view that comes with modern TV sets. In landscape mode, more of your scene will fit on the screen horizontally, which looks great if you have scenery in the background such as in a golf game. Figure 5.13 shows a screenshot of three triangles in portrait mode and Figure 5.14 shows the same scene in landscape mode.

Note

You can find ViewTransformationsSample.java together with a working MIDlet on the accompanying CD-ROM.

ViewTransformationsSample starts with declaring the necessary member variables. Notable here is the boolean value orientationPortrait, which contains

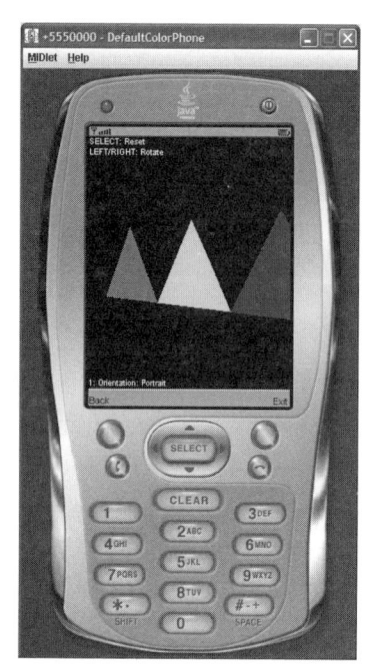

Figure 5.13
Display in portrait mode.

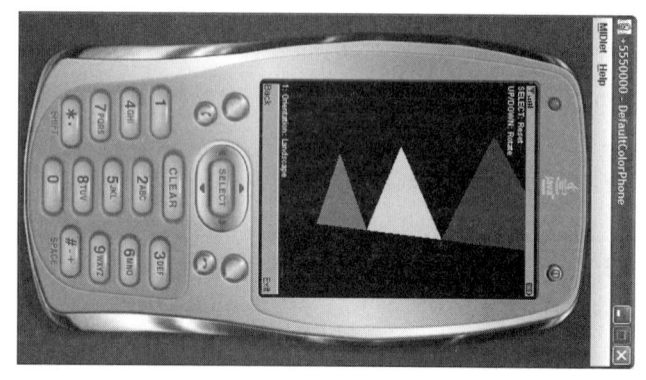

Figure 5.14
Display in landscape mode.

information as to whether portrait or landscape mode is active. The sample keeps the current rotation of the camera around the *y* axis in `rotY`.

```
/**
 * Demonstrates switching between portrait and landscape rendering
 * by changing the camera transformation.
```

```java
 *
 * @author Claus Hoefele
 */
public class ViewTransformationsSample extends GameCanvas
    implements Sample {
  /** True indicates portrait orientation, false landscape. */
  private boolean orientationPortrait;

  /** Mesh for display. */
  private Mesh mesh;
  /** The mesh's transformation. */
  private Transform meshTransform;

  /** Camera. */
  private Camera camera;
  /** The camera's transformation. */
  private Transform cameraTransform;
  /** Current rotation value. */
  private float rotY;

  /** 3D graphics singleton used for rendering. */
  private Graphics3D graphics3d;
  /** 2D graphics singleton used for rendering. */
  private Graphics graphics;

  /**
   * Constructor.
   */
  public ViewTransformationsSample() {
    super(false);
  }
  ...
}
```

`init()` sets the display mode to portrait. For rendering, this method also creates a triangle that points up with `MeshFactory.createTriangle()` and disables back face culling because it's a flat triangle and you want to see both sides when rotating the camera around it.

```java
  /**
   * Initializes the sample.
   */
```

```
public void init() {
  // Get the singletons for rendering.
  graphics3d = Graphics3D.getInstance();
  graphics = getGraphics();

  // Create camera.
  camera = new Camera();
  rotY = 0;
  cameraTransform = new Transform();
  orientationPortrait = true;
  setCamera();

  // Create mesh.
  mesh = MeshFactory2D.createTriangle();
  PolygonMode polygonMode = new PolygonMode();
  polygonMode.setCulling(PolygonMode.CULL_NONE);
  mesh.getAppearance(0).setPolygonMode(polygonMode);
  meshTransform = new Transform();

  render(graphics);
  flushGraphics();
}
```

The actual camera setup happens in setCamera(), which sets the camera rotation matrix to the current rotation value and also moves the camera backward so the triangles are visible. Afterward, this method rotates the camera around the z axis if the application is in landscape mode. The meshes will undergo the landscape rotation first, which means that you don't need to worry about orientation modes when positioning the camera or the meshes. The rotation is −90 degrees because game pads have the digipad controls on the left side. Hence, for mobile phones, you'll also want the keypad, and maybe a joystick-like device, on the left side. (This is in contrast to cameras, where the controls are on the right side.)

```
/**
 * Sets the camera in the <code>Graphics3D</code> context and
 * initializes it with the current orientation and transformation
 * parameters.
 */
private void setCamera() {
  cameraTransform.setIdentity();
  cameraTransform.postRotate(rotY, 0, 1, 0);
```

```
  cameraTransform.postTranslate(0, 0, 5);

  if (!orientationPortrait) {
    // Rotate camera in landscape mode.
    cameraTransform.postRotate(-90, 0, 0, 1);
  }

  float aspectRatio = (float) getWidth() / (float) getHeight();
  camera.setPerspective(60, aspectRatio, 1, 1000);
  graphics3d.setCamera(camera, cameraTransform);
}
```

render() then draws three triangles on the screen. Conveniently, the mesh transformations are independent of the current display mode because the camera rotation does all the work.

```
/**
 * Renders the sample.
 *
 * @param graphics graphics context for rendering.
 */
private void render(Graphics graphics) {
  graphics3d.bindTarget(graphics);
  graphics3d.setViewport(0, 0, getWidth(), getHeight());
  graphics3d.clear(null);

  meshTransform.setIdentity();
  meshTransform.postTranslate(-2, 0, 0);
  mesh.getVertexBuffer().setDefaultColor(0xFF0000); // red
  graphics3d.render(mesh, meshTransform);

  meshTransform.postTranslate(2, 0, 0);
  mesh.getVertexBuffer().setDefaultColor(0x00FF00); // green
  graphics3d.render(mesh, meshTransform);

  meshTransform.postTranslate(2, 0, 0);
  mesh.getVertexBuffer().setDefaultColor(0x0000FF); // blue
  graphics3d.render(mesh, meshTransform);

  graphics3d.releaseTarget();
  drawMenu(graphics); // displays the current key assignment
}
```

The interactive part happens in keyPressed(). First of all, you can rotate the camera around the *y* axis. Don't forget that in landscape mode, you have to swap the game controls from left/right to up/down, because you hold the mobile phone in a different position. Finally, the GAME_A key switches between portrait and landscape mode.

```
/**
 * Handles key presses.
 *
 * @param keyCode key code.
 */
protected void keyPressed(int keyCode) {
  switch (getGameAction(keyCode)) {
    case LEFT:
      if (orientationPortrait) {
        rotY -= 10;
      }
      break;

    case RIGHT:
      if (orientationPortrait) {
        rotY += 10;
      }
      break;

    case UP:
      if (!orientationPortrait) {
        rotY += 10;
      }
      break;

    case DOWN:
      if (!orientationPortrait) {
        rotY -= 10;
      }
      break;

    case GAME_A:
      orientationPortrait = !orientationPortrait;
      break;

    case FIRE:
      init();
      break;
```

```
    // no default
  }

  setCamera();
  render(graphics);
  flushGraphics();
}
```

Projection Transformations

Once you have finished positioning model and camera, you have to define a matrix that describes how the 3D model is projected onto a 2D screen and store this information in Camera. This is the first parameter of Graphics3D. setCamera(Camera, Transform).

Setting the Viewing Volume

Table 5.2 summarizes Camera's API. You can set the projection transformation in three ways: an arbitrary matrix with setGeneric(), a matrix with parallel projection with setParallel(), and a matrix with perspective projection with setPerspective().

Table 5.2 Camera Class Description

Method	Description
Fields	
static int GENERIC	Indicates a generic projection matrix.
static int PARALLEL	Indicates a parallel projection.
static int PERSPECTIVE	Indicates a perspective projection.
Setting/Getting the Projection Matrix	
Camera()	Constructs a camera and initializes the projection matrix to the identity.
void setPerspective(float fovy, float aspectRatio, float near, float far)	Sets a perspective projection matrix.
void setParallel(float fovy, float aspectRatio, float near, float far)	Sets a parallel projection matrix.
void setGeneric(Transform transform)	Sets a generic projection matrix.
int getProjection(float[] params)	Copies the current projection parameters to the float array and returns the type of projection.
int getProjection(Transform transform)	Copies the current projection matrix and returns the type of projection.

Once set, the projection transformation defines a viewing volume that describes how to project your scene onto the screen and defines a clipping area. Everything inside the viewing volume is visible, everything else is not. setGeneric() is reserved for unusual projections, for example looking at a scene from an oblique perspective. You'll mostly deal with setParallel() and setPerspective(); Figures 5.15 and 5.16 show the respective viewing volumes.

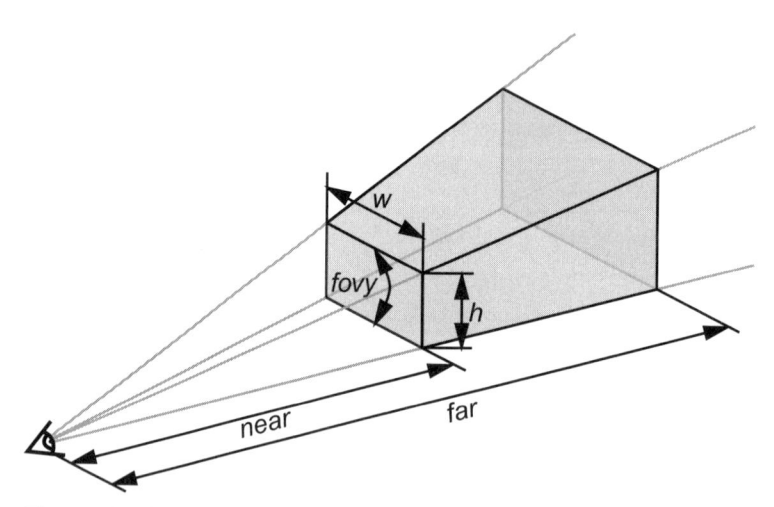

Figure 5.15
Viewing volume for perspective projection.

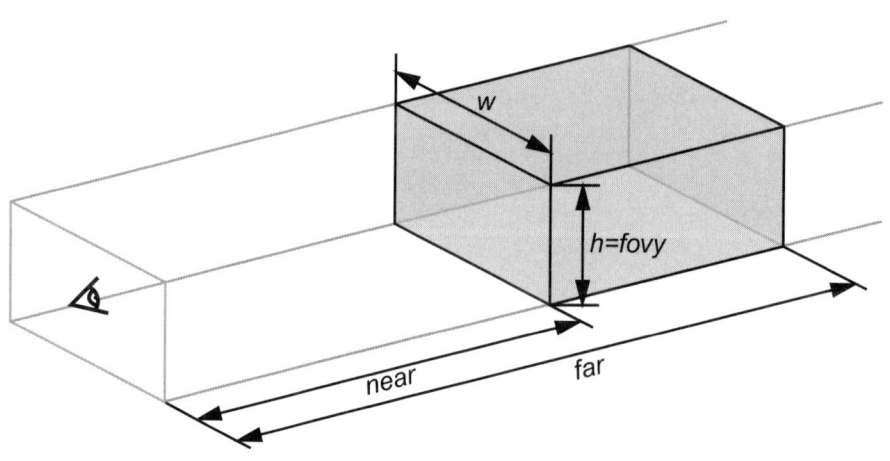

Figure 5.16
Viewing volume for parallel projection.

When using perspective projection, objects become smaller the farther away from the camera they are. `setPerspective()` takes the viewing angle in the *y* direction (`fovy`) and the aspect ratio of width and height. These two values form a pyramid that is truncated by the near and far clipping planes. You'd usually set the aspect ratio to the same value as the screen aspect ratio. Similar to the objective of a camera, the field of view determines how far you zoom into your 3D scene.

Parallel projection, on the other hand, ignores perspective and draws all objects the same size, no matter how far away they are. The viewing volume is a box with all opposing sides parallel. `setParallel()` takes the same parameters as `setPerspective()`, but instead of an angle, the `fovy` parameter specifies the height of the viewing volume in *y* direction.

Using Parallel and Perspective Projection

Figure 5.17 shows the difference between perspective and parallel projection. Both projections show the same three quads with varying *z* coordinates. In the left screenshot, you can see how the perspective projection foreshortens the left and middle quad because they are farther away from the camera than the right one. In the right screenshot, on the other hand, parallel projection draws all quads the same size no matter how far away.

Note

You can find ProjectionSample.java together with a working MIDlet on the accompanying CD-ROM.

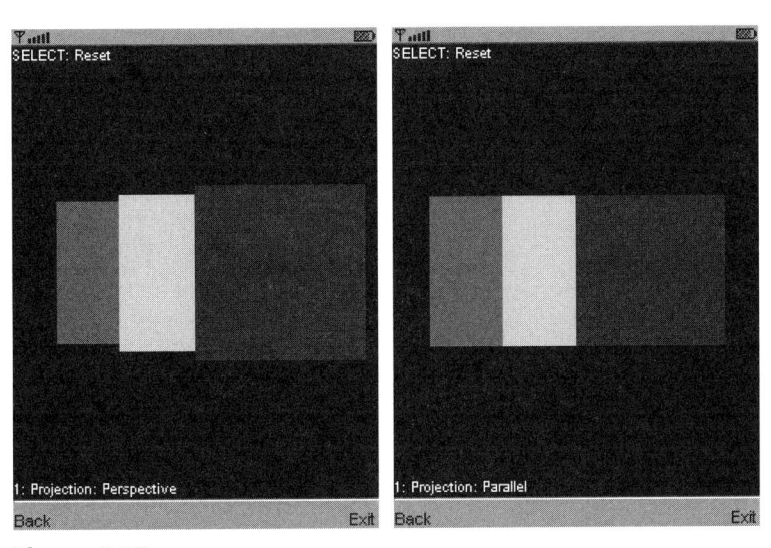

Figure 5.17
Quads with different distances to the camera in perspective (left) and parallel projection (right).

`ProjectionSample` stores two camera objects `cameraPerspective` and `cameraParallel` for both kinds of projection as well as the flag `isPerspective` to keep the information about which one is current.

```
/**
 * Sample demonstrating parallel and perspective projection.
 *
 * @author Claus Hoefele
 */
public class ProjectionSample extends GameCanvas implements Sample {
  /** Mesh to display. */
  private Mesh mesh;
  /** The mesh's transformation. */
  private Transform meshTransform;

  /** Camera with perspective projection. */
  private Camera cameraPerspective;
  /** Camera with parallel projection. */
  private Camera cameraParallel;
  /** The camera's transformation. */
  private Transform cameraTransform;

  /** Flag whether perspective or parallel projection is used. */
  private boolean isPerspective;

  /** 3D graphics singleton used for rendering. */
  private Graphics3D graphics3d;
  /** 2D graphics singleton used for rendering. */
  private Graphics graphics;

  /**
   * Constructor.
   */
  public ProjectionSample() {
    super(false);
  }
  ...
}
```

`init()` sets up the `Camera` objects for both projection modes. The perspective camera has a field of view of 60 degrees, which—based on experience—is a good starting point. The height parameter for parallel projection causes the quad in the middle to end up being about the same size in both projection modes.

The remaining camera parameters, such as the aspect ratio, which `init()` sets to the same ratio as the screen, are common to both modes. In order to see the quads, the value for the near clipping plane must be smaller than the distance between camera and the quads. Likewise, the distance to the far clipping plane must reach beyond the quads. You might want to adjust the far distance to clip away objects that are too tiny to see in the background.

```
/**
 * Initializes the sample.
 */
public void init() {
  // Get the singletons for rendering.
  graphics3d = Graphics3D.getInstance();
  graphics = getGraphics();

  // Create vertex data.
  mesh = MeshFactory2D.createQuad(false);
  meshTransform = new Transform();

  // Create parallel and perspective cameras.
  cameraPerspective = new Camera();
  float aspect = (float) getWidth() / (float) getHeight();
  cameraPerspective.setPerspective(60, aspect, 1, 1000);
  cameraTransform = new Transform();
  cameraTransform.postTranslate(0, 0, 5);

  cameraParallel = new Camera();
  cameraParallel.setParallel(6, aspect, 1, 1000);
  graphics3d.setCamera(cameraPerspective, cameraTransform);
  isPerspective = true;

  render(graphics);
  flushGraphics();
}
```

`render()` draws the three quads with varying z coordinates:

```
/**
 * Renders the sample.
 *
 * @param graphics graphics context for rendering.
 */
private void render(Graphics graphics) {
```

```
        graphics3d.bindTarget(graphics);
        graphics3d.setViewport(0, 0, getWidth(), getHeight());
        graphics3d.clear(null);

        // Draw meshes.
        meshTransform.setIdentity();
        meshTransform.postTranslate(-1, 0, -0.5f);
        mesh.getVertexBuffer().setDefaultColor(0xFF0000); // red
        graphics3d.render(mesh, meshTransform);

        meshTransform.setIdentity();
        mesh.getVertexBuffer().setDefaultColor(0x00FF00); // green
        graphics3d.render(mesh, meshTransform);

        meshTransform.setIdentity();
        meshTransform.postTranslate(1, 0, 0.5f);
        mesh.getVertexBuffer().setDefaultColor(0x0000FF); // blue
        graphics3d.render(mesh, meshTransform);

        graphics3d.releaseTarget();

        drawMenu(graphics); // displays the current key assignment
    }
```

You can switch the projection mode with the GAME_A button on your device. This will flip isPerspective and swap the current camera from perspective to parallel and vice versa.

The Viewport Transformation

Because you can't influence the perspective division, I come immediately to the final step of the geometry pipeline: the viewport transformation. You have already chosen which part of your scene to display. The viewport, however, defines the size of the rendered image. The benefit of separating between projection and viewport is that you can display your 3D scene on phones with screens of any size without changing the camera setup. You just stretch the rendered scene so it fits.

The viewport is automatically set to the clipping rectangle of the rendering target when you bind the graphics context, which means that you have to call setViewport() after bindTarget() to have any effect.

> **Tip**
>
> Don't assume that the clipping rectangle of your graphics context is always set to the complete drawing area of your screen. If you set the camera to the aspect ratio with getWidth()/getHeight(), you should also set the viewport with setViewport(0, 0, getWidth(), getHeight()). Otherwise, your rendered image might be distorted.

To experiment with the viewport, take ModelTransformationsSample from the beginning of this chapter and uncomment one of the calls to setViewport():

> **Note**
>
> To experiment with the viewport, you can edit ModelTransformationsSample.java on the accompanying CD-ROM. Have a look at the render() method.

```
// Aspect ratio of camera is set to
// (float) getWidth() / (float) getHeight().
private void render(Graphics graphics) {
  graphics3d.bindTarget(graphics);

  // Uncomment one of the calls to setViewport() below if you want
  // to experiment with other viewport settings.

  // Undistorted view.
  graphics3d.setViewport(0, 0, getWidth(), getHeight());

  // Reduces the rendered scene to a quarter of the screen size.
//    graphics3d.setViewport(0, 0, getWidth()/2, getHeight()/2);

  // Because the camera is using an aspect ratio of
  // getWidth()/getHeight(), this viewport setting will distort
  // the scene on the x axis.
//    graphics3d.setViewport(0, 0, getWidth(), getHeight()/2);

  graphics3d.clear(null);
  transform(meshTransform);
  graphics3d.render(mesh, meshTransform);
  graphics3d.releaseTarget();

  drawMenu(graphics); // displays the current key assignment
}
```

The viewport settings in combination with the camera's aspect ratio enable you to display your render output in arbitrary sizes.

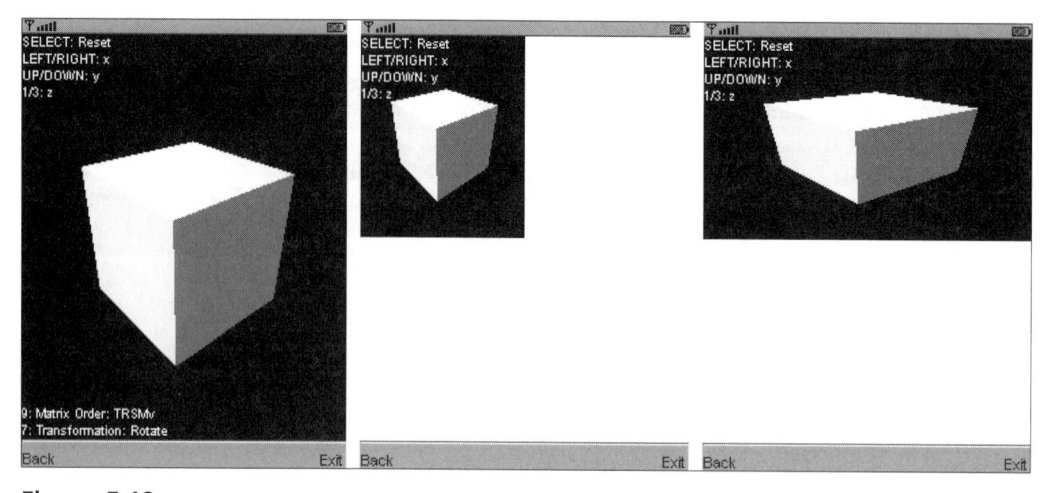

Figure 5.18
Cube with different viewport settings: Left image is same as screen size, middle image is quarter of screen size, and right image is distortion caused by different aspect ratio of camera and viewport.

An example of when this might be useful is a game that uses a split screen to display the views of several players at the same time.

Width and height of the viewport should have the same aspect ratio as the camera. Otherwise, the resulting image will be distorted. That's shown in Figure 5.18, which has screenshots of different viewport settings. In the left-most screenshot, the viewport is mapped to the full screen, the second screenshot uses `graphics3d.setViewport(0, 0, getWidth()/2, getHeight()/2)`, and the third `graphics3d.setViewport(0, 0, getWidth(), getHeight()/2)`.

The viewport respects the origin and the clipping region of the rendering target. In MIDP, `Graphics.translate()` sets the origin of the graphics context and `Graphics.clipRect()` the clipping rectangle. If set before calling `Graphics3D.bindTarget()`, M3G will render the viewport relative to the translated origin and clip the render result to the intersection of the viewport settings in `Graphics3D` and the clipping rectangle of `Graphics`.

The Depth Buffer

You might assume that M3G discards the z coordinate after the viewport transformation. After all, the whole purpose of the transformation process is to convert from 3D to 2D. However, the z coordinate still fulfills an important purpose because in window coordinates, an object's z coordinate specifies its distance from the camera. If you render several 3D objects, you would of course expect objects closer to the camera to obscure objects farther away. You can achieve this behavior by enabling the depth buffer.

Using the Depth Buffer

After M3G finished transforming the vertex data, the triangles that comprise your mesh are converted into pixel values. At this stage, these values are called fragments because they undergo further modification before they are displayed on the screen.

The depth buffer is a memory area that has the same width and height as the screen but holds depth values of the fragments instead of color values. For all the fragments drawn on the screen, it stores their distances to the near plane. Depending on where the near plane is located, this value is more or less different than the distance of the pixel to the camera. M3G draws a fragment only if it's closer to the camera than the existing one at the same position. You can test this by comparing the incoming fragment's depth with the value that's already in the depth buffer. Thus, enabling the depth buffer renders objects according to their 3D position, independent of the order of `Graphics3D.render()` commands. Conversely, if you disable the depth buffer, you have to pay attention to the order in which you draw your 3D objects.

You enable or disable the depth buffer test when you bind the target graphics to `Graphics3D`. When you use the overloaded version of `bindTarget()` that takes one parameter, you enable the depth buffer by default. When using `bindTarget()` with three parameters, you can explicitly switch the depth buffer on and off by using a `boolean` value as the second parameter. The following example demonstrates this.

Note

You can find DepthBufferSample.java together with a working MIDlet on the accompanying CD-ROM.

```
/**
 * Sample demonstrating the depth buffer.
 *
 * @author Claus Hoefele
 */
public class DepthBufferSample extends GameCanvas implements Sample {
    ...
```

```java
/**
 * Renders the sample.
 *
 * @param graphics graphics context for rendering.
 */
private void render(Graphics graphics) {
  // Create transformation objects for shapes.
  Transform origin = new Transform();
  Transform behindOrigin = new Transform(origin);
  behindOrigin.postTranslate(-1, 0, -0.5f);
  Transform inFrontOfOrigin = new Transform(origin);
  inFrontOfOrigin.postTranslate(1, 0, 0.5f);

  // Disable or enable depth buffering when target is bound.
  graphics3d.bindTarget(graphics, isDepthBufferEnabled, 0);
  graphics3d.setViewport(0, 0, getWidth(), getHeight());
  graphics3d.clear(null);

  // Draw shapes front to back. If the depth buffer is enabled,
  // they will be drawn according to their z coordinate. Otherwise,
  // according to the order of rendering.
  mesh.getVertexBuffer().setDefaultColor(0x0000FF); // blue
  graphics3d.render(mesh, inFrontOfOrigin);
  mesh.getVertexBuffer().setDefaultColor(0x00FF00); // green
  graphics3d.render(mesh, origin);
  mesh.getVertexBuffer().setDefaultColor(0xFF0000); // red
  graphics3d.render(mesh, behindOrigin);

  graphics3d.releaseTarget();

  drawMenu(graphics); // displays the current key assignment
}
  ...
}
```

render() draws three circles with varying z coordinates. The circle on the right is in front of the origin and rendered first. The circle in the middle is placed at the origin, and the left-most circle behind the origin. If everything works according to the z coordinates, the right-most circle should be in front even though the other circles are drawn later. The image on the left in Figure 5.19 shows this behavior if the depth buffer is enabled in the call to Graphics3D.bindTarget(). On the other hand, a disabled depth buffer results in the circles being drawn

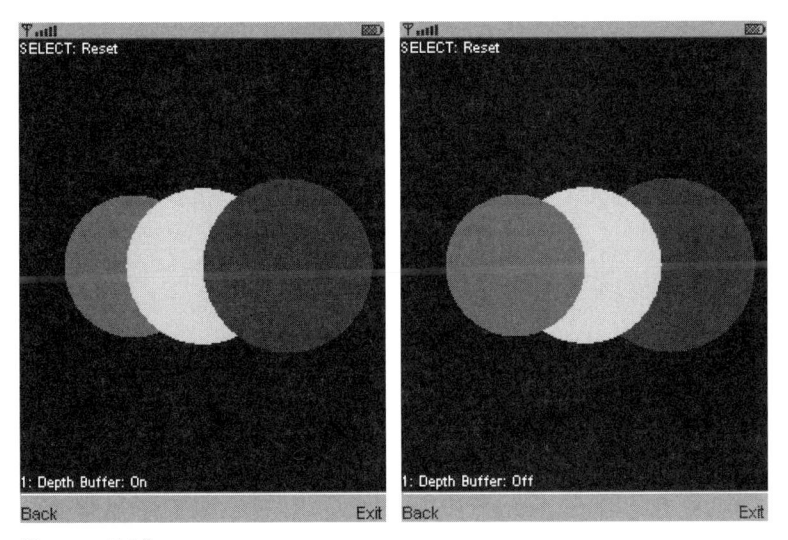

Figure 5.19
Left image shows discs drawn according to distance from the camera with enabled depth buffer; right image shows discs drawn in the order of render commands with disabled depth buffer.

according to the order of the render() calls, as depicted in the image in Figure 5.19 on the right.

In addition to bindTarget(), which enables or disables the depth buffer until you call releaseTarget(), you can also set a depth buffer flag per mesh by using CompositingMode, which is an attribute of the mesh's Appearance object. The depth buffer for a mesh is enabled if the depth buffer is enabled in bindTarget() and CompositingMode.isDepthTestEnabled() is set to true. Conversely, the depth buffer is disabled if it's disabled in bindTarget() or if CompositingMode.isDepth TestEnabled() is set to false. Also make sure that you enabled clearing the depth buffer in the current Background with setDepthClearEnable().

Depth Buffer Resolution

Because the depth buffer operates on a pixel level, it works nicely even if triangles intersect each other. However, the depth buffer also has its restrictions. For one, it has a finite resolution. In certain cases, rounding errors might result in incorrectly placed objects.

As a first step toward a better depth buffer resolution, you can try to decrease the distance between near and far plane. If that's not possible or still not enough, you can map a subset of the range of normalized device coordinates to the depth buffer with Graphics3D.setDepthRange().

Alternatively, instead of changing the depth buffer range, you can give an object an offset with `CompositingMode.setDepthOffset()`. With this method, two objects, despite having the same *z* coordinates, can have different depth values.

Handling Transparent Objects

There's another problem with the depth buffer: It doesn't work correctly with transparent objects. If you first rendered a half-transparent quad in front of an opaque quad, both objects should be visible and blended where they overlap. However, the depth buffer will store the *z* coordinates of the transparent quad and from there on ignore everything that's behind.

The solution is to first render opaque meshes. Then, you sort the transparent ones according to the depth and render them in a second batch. Because this is rather a lot of effort, `Appearance.setLayer()` guarantees that all opaque meshes in the same layer are rendered before any transparent ones. If you have several meshes, you have to group them, which I explain in Chapter 9. This at least partly helps the problem, but might lead to one transparent mesh hiding another because the depth buffer is enabled all the time.

Tip

You can also use `Appearance.setLayer()` to tell M3G in which order you want to draw your meshes.

Another method involves rendering opaque meshes first with enabled depth buffer. Then, you disable writing to the depth buffer, but not reading from it, and render the transparent objects. The *z* coordinates of the opaque meshes are taken into account, but the transparent meshes can't change them. Hence, opaque and transparent objects are blended together. You can disable writing to the depth buffer by setting `CompositingMode.isDepthWriteEnabled()` to `false` in your object. Chapter 7 introduces `CompositingMode` and discusses blending and transparency in more detail.

The one drawback to this method is that transparent meshes might be blended the wrong way around. If you had two transparent meshes behind each other and rendered the one closer to the camera first, the second mesh would be blended into the one before. What you really want is the mesh closer to the camera to be blended into the one behind, but most of the time this problem isn't noticeable.

Manually Transforming 3D Coordinates

You've seen how to influence M3G's transformation process. Conveniently, it works like a black box where you can influence parameters but don't need to care about the process itself. Once you have created all the necessary objects and parameters, you call `render()` and M3G takes over the hard work. However, this also means that you can't access the results of the transformation process.

Imagine a 3D billiard game where you want to give the player the opportunity to see where the ball will roll when it's hit by the cue. To assist the shot, you want to draw a line from the ball in the direction of the pocket. Unlike OpenGL, M3G doesn't allow you to render lines, only filled triangles. You could model the line with a thin quad strip, but with the knowledge of the transformation process, you can also compute the positions of the ball and the pocket on the screen yourself and draw lines between them by using MIDP's graphics interface.

Combining 2D with 3D graphics often needs the results from the transformation process. The following example shows you how to transform 3D coordinates to 2D manually and how to draw a wireframe representation of an arbitrary mesh. This is useful for checking that the triangles of your mesh are correctly built. Figure 5.20 shows screenshots from meshes rendered as wireframes.

Note
The sample is implemented in WireframeEngine.java and WireframeSample.java, which you can find together with a working MIDlet on the accompanying CD-ROM.

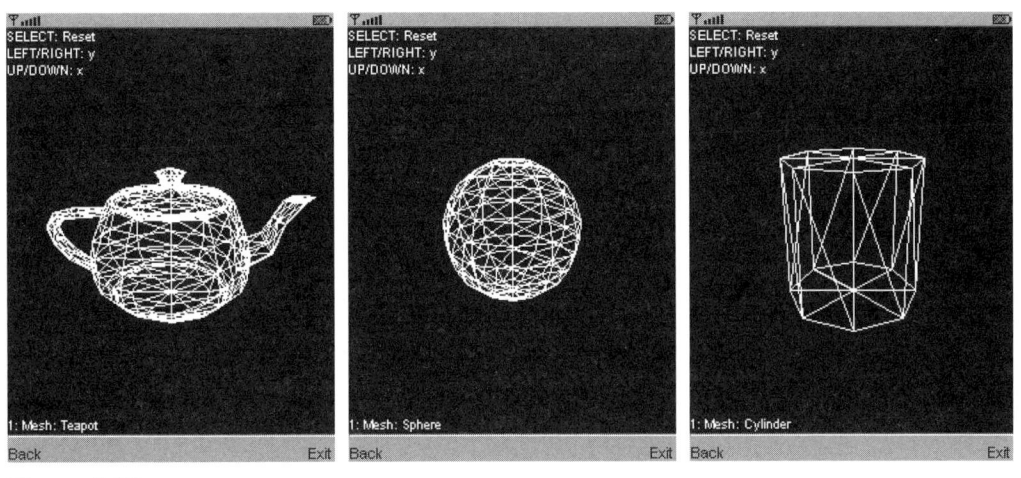

Figure 5.20
Wireframe meshes.

A Wireframe Engine

I'll start by defining a class `WireframeEngine` that computes the 2D coordinates and draws the lines. Its constructor takes the viewport position and size.

```
/**
 * Wireframe engine that displays 3D models as line drawings. It uses
 * M3G's matrix operations to transform 3D vertex coordinates to a 2D
 * screen representation and draws the model on a MIDP graphics
 * context.
 *
 * @author Claus Hoefele
 * @see WireframeSample
 */
public class WireframeEngine {
  /** Viewport x. */
  private int viewportX;
  /** Viewport y. */
  private int viewportY;
  /** Half the viewport width. */
  private int halfViewportWidth;
  /** Half the viewport height. */
  private int halfViewportHeight;

  /** Camera object that represents the viewer of the 3D scene. */
  private Camera camera;
  /** Transformation for camera. */
  private Transform invertedCameraTransform;

  /**
   * Creates a new WireframeEngine with the given viewport attributes.
   * The viewport defines the size and position of the rendered image.
   *
   * @param viewportX viewport x position.
   * @param viewportY viewport y position.
   * @param viewportWidth viewport width.
   * @param viewportHeight viewport height.
   */
  public WireframeEngine(int viewportX, int viewportY,
      int viewportWidth, int viewportHeight) {
    this.viewportX = viewportX;
    this.viewportY = viewportY;
    halfViewportWidth = viewportWidth / 2;
```

```
    halfViewportHeight = viewportHeight / 2;
  }
  ...
}
```

`WireframeEngine` needs only half the size of the viewport for the calculations, so that's what the constructor stores in the object. `WireframeEngine` also needs a camera that defines the view point of the spectator and the definition of the projection matrix:

```
/**
 * Sets the camera that's used to represent the viewer of the scene.
 *
 * @param camera camera.
 * @param cameraTransform camera transformation.
 */
public void setCamera(Camera camera, Transform cameraTransform) {
  this.camera = camera;

  // Copy transformation because we need to modify it.
  invertedCameraTransform = new Transform(cameraTransform);
  invertedCameraTransform.invert();
}
```

The camera matrix is copied in. It contains the transformation from the camera's local coordinates to the world. `WireframeEngine` has to transform meshes from world coordinates to camera coordinates and therefore stores the inverted matrix.

Transforming 3D Coordinates

Before a mesh can be displayed as wireframe model, `WireframeEngine` must transform its vertices from object coordinates to window coordinates. For this process, `transform()` computes the model/view transformation, projection, perspective division, and viewport transformation:

```
/**
 * Transforms vertices from 3D to 2D.
 *
 * @param mesh mesh to be transformed.
 * @param invertedCameraTransform inverted camera transformation.
```

```
 * @param meshTransform the mesh's transformation.
 * @param camera camera object that represents the viewer of the 3D
 *               scene.
 * @return transformed vertices.
 */
protected float[] transform(Mesh mesh, Transform meshTransform,
    Camera camera, Transform invertedCameraTransform) {
  int numVertices = mesh.getVertexBuffer().getVertexCount();
  float[] vertices = new float[numVertices * 4];
  Transform transform = new Transform();
  float[] scaleBias = new float[4];
  VertexArray vertexArray3d
      = mesh.getVertexBuffer().getPositions(scaleBias);

  // Projection transformation.
  camera.getProjection(transform);

  // Model/view transformation.
  transform.postMultiply(invertedCameraTransform);
  transform.postMultiply(meshTransform);

  // Scale vertices.
  transform.postTranslate(scaleBias[1], scaleBias[2], scaleBias[3]);
  transform.postScale(scaleBias[0], scaleBias[0], scaleBias[0]);

  // Apply concatenated transformation to vertices; transforms from
  // object coordinates to clip coordinates.
  transform.transform(vertexArray3d, vertices, true);

  // Clip coordinates to windows coordinates loop.
  for (int i = 0; i < numVertices; i++) {
    // Perspective division.
    float w = 1.0f / vertices[i * 4 + 3];
    vertices[i * 4 + 0] *= w; // x
    vertices[i * 4 + 1] *= w; // y
    // Also calculate the z coordinate if you need it for depth
    // calculations such as the depth buffer.
    //vertices[i * 4 + 2] *= w; // z

    // Viewport transformation.
    vertices[i * 4 + 0] = vertices[i * 4 + 0] * halfViewportWidth
        + halfViewportWidth; // x
    vertices[i * 4 + 1] = -vertices[i * 4 + 1]
```

```
                * halfViewportHeight + halfViewportHeight; // y
    }
    return vertices;
}
```

`transform()` collects all transformations from object coordinates to clip coordinates into one matrix. This includes projection, model/view transformation, and an operation that takes the scale and bias of the mesh into account. The scale and bias are what you can define when setting the positions in `VertexBuffer.setPositions()`. Note the order of the matrix multiplications. Because of the post-multiplication, the matrix that is used first ends up on the left side of the equation and is applied last to the vertices.

The last step of the clip coordinate transformation multiplies the `VertexArray` with the vertices and copies them out to an array of `float`s. M3G 1.0 doesn't yet have a method for actually getting vertices from a `VertexArray`. Copying vertices out by transforming them in the process is the only way. (In M3G 1.1, you can use `VertexArray.get()`.)

After the matrix multiplication comes the perspective division. You can't calculate the perspective division with matrices, which is why `transform()` loops through the vertices array and divides each of the elements by the *w* coordinate. At the same time, the loop stretches the result to fit the viewport size, which completes the conversion from clip coordinates to window coordinates.

Drawing Triangles

Once transformed, you can connect the vertices with lines to draw the triangles on the screen, which is done in `draw()`.

```
/**
 * Draws a wireframe model on the given graphics context.
 *
 * @param graphics graphics context for drawing.
 * @param vertices transformed vertices of the model.
 * @param triangleIndices triangle indices that define how to draw
 *        the model.
 * @param triangleLengths lengths of the triangle array.
 */
protected void draw(Graphics graphics, float[] vertices,
    int[] triangleIndices, int[] triangleLengths) {
  // Stores the current position in the vertex array.
  int position = 0;
```

```java
    // Set viewport position.
    graphics.translate(viewportX, viewportY);

    // Loop through triangle strips.
    for (int i = 0; i < triangleLengths.length; i++) {
      // Loop through triangles in strip.
      int numberOfTriangles = triangleLengths[i] - 2;
      for (int j = 0; j < numberOfTriangles; j++) {
        int vertex1 = triangleIndices[position] * 4;
        int vertex2 = triangleIndices[position + 1] * 4;
        int vertex3 = triangleIndices[position + 2] * 4;

        // Draw first line only if it's the first triangle in the
        // strip.
        if (j == 0) {
          graphics.drawLine((int) vertices[vertex1],
              (int) vertices[vertex1 + 1], (int) vertices[vertex2],
              (int) vertices[vertex2 + 1]);
        }

        graphics.drawLine((int) vertices[vertex2],
            (int) vertices[vertex2 + 1], (int) vertices[vertex3],
            (int) vertices[vertex3 + 1]);
        graphics.drawLine((int) vertices[vertex3],
            (int) vertices[vertex3 + 1], (int) vertices[vertex1],
            (int) vertices[vertex1 + 1]);

        position++;
      }

      // Triangle strip is finished, advance position to next strip.
      position += 2;
    }

    // Unset viewport position.
    graphics.translate(-viewportX, -viewportY);
  }
```

WireframeEngine contains a convenience method render() to do the transformation and drawing in one step. Clients that want to use the class call this method.

```java
  /**
   * Renders a 3D model as wireframe.
   *
```

```
 * @param graphics graphics context used for drawing.
 * @param mesh mesh to be drawn.
 * @param meshTransform the mesh's transformation.
 * @param triangleIndices triangle indices that define how to draw
 *                        the model.
 * @param triangleLengths lengths of the triangle array.
 */
public void render(Graphics graphics, Mesh mesh,
    Transform meshTransform, int[] triangleIndices,
    int[] triangleLengths) {
  // Transform vertices from 3D to 2D.
  float[] vertices = transform(mesh, meshTransform, this.camera,
      invertedCameraTransform);

  // Draw triangles.
  draw(graphics, vertices, triangleIndices, triangleLengths);
}
```

To demonstrate the engine, `WireframeSample` provides the rendering canvas and calls `WireframeEngine` with a mesh. This will then draw the mesh as wireframe object. Again, there's a restriction in M3G 1.0, which doesn't allow you to access the triangle strip definition in a `Mesh`, so you have to pass the information to `render()` directly. (In M3G 1.1, you can use `IndexBuffer.getIndices()`.) Because the sample uses the shape library from Chapter 4, the triangle strips are available and stored in a class called `MeshUtils`.

In the finished example, you can rotate the mesh around the *x* and *y* axes as well as switch between different kinds of meshes.

```
/**
 * Demonstrates manual transformation of vertices by displaying
 * wireframe objects.
 *
 * @author Claus Hoefele
 * @see WireframeEngine
 */
public class WireframeSample extends GameCanvas implements Sample {
  /** The mesh for display. */
  private Mesh mesh;
  ...
  /**
   * Initializes the sample.
   */
```

```
  public void init() {
    // Any mesh can be used, for example
    // mesh = Teapot.create(3, false, false);
    ...
  }

  /**
   * Renders the sample.
   *
   * @param graphics graphics context for rendering.
   */
  private void render(Graphics graphics) {
    graphics.setColor(0); // black
    graphics.fillRect(0, 0, getWidth(), getHeight());

    meshTransform.setIdentity();
    meshTransform.postRotate(rotX, 1, 0, 0);
    meshTransform.postRotate(rotY, 0, 1, 0);

    if (currentMesh == MESH_TEAPOT) {
      // Orient the teapot so its lid points up.
      meshTransform.postTranslate(0, -1, 0);
      meshTransform.postRotate(-90, 1, 0, 0);
      meshTransform.postScale(0.6f, 0.6f, 0.6f);
    }

    graphics.setColor(0xFFFFFF); // white
    graphics.setStrokeStyle(Graphics.SOLID);
    wireframeEngine.render(graphics, mesh, meshTransform,
        MeshUtils.getLastTriangleIndices(),
        MeshUtils.getLastTriangleLengths());

    drawMenu(graphics); // displays the current key assignment
  }
  ...
}
```

Instead of drawing triangle strips, you can also use quads, which avoids the diagonal lines of the wireframe. This looks better, but also means that you have to create a separate data structure when drawing in 3D and in wireframe mode. If you want to stick to the triangle strip format but avoid the diagonal lines, you could do something similar to OpenGL and pass edge flags as an additional parameter to the engine. The idea is to mark lines that shouldn't be drawn.

When using triangles, you can easily add hidden line removal. In the current engine, you'll always see all lines, even if they are on the back side of a 3D object. You can check whether a triangle faces back or front by computing the cross product of two of the triangle's sides and checking in which direction the result points. If a triangle faces back, you'd skip drawing it. Remember that triangles in a strip toggle between counterclockwise and clockwise winding.

Another improvement would be view frustum culling. Currently, all lines are drawn whether or not they are visible. Most of the time this is just a waste of resources, but for objects behind the camera, it's a bit more than that. Because of the underlying calculations, if you move the camera forward, the wireframe object will first vanish behind the camera just to appear again in reflected state. By clipping all objects to the view frustum, you'll avoid this behavior as well as speed up the engine.

Summary

Tackling transformations is the key to controlling what you see on the screen. In this chapter, you learned how 4-by-4 matrices are stored in `Transform` objects and transform vectors in the homogeneous coordinate system. For rotations, you can choose between axis-angle format, Euler angles, or quaternions.

Next, you saw the stages of M3G's geometry pipeline: model/view transformation, projection, perspective division, and the viewport transformation. You learned how to influence the parameters in each step so M3G renders what you want to depict. I also explained the depth buffer and how it helps you to render meshes with different distances to the camera correctly. The sample at the end of the chapter implemented an engine that mimics M3G's transformations of 3D coordinates to 2D and can draw meshes as wireframes.

After all this time that you spent with a mesh's geometry, it's now time to work on its appearance. In the next chapter, I show you how to add textures.

CHAPTER 6

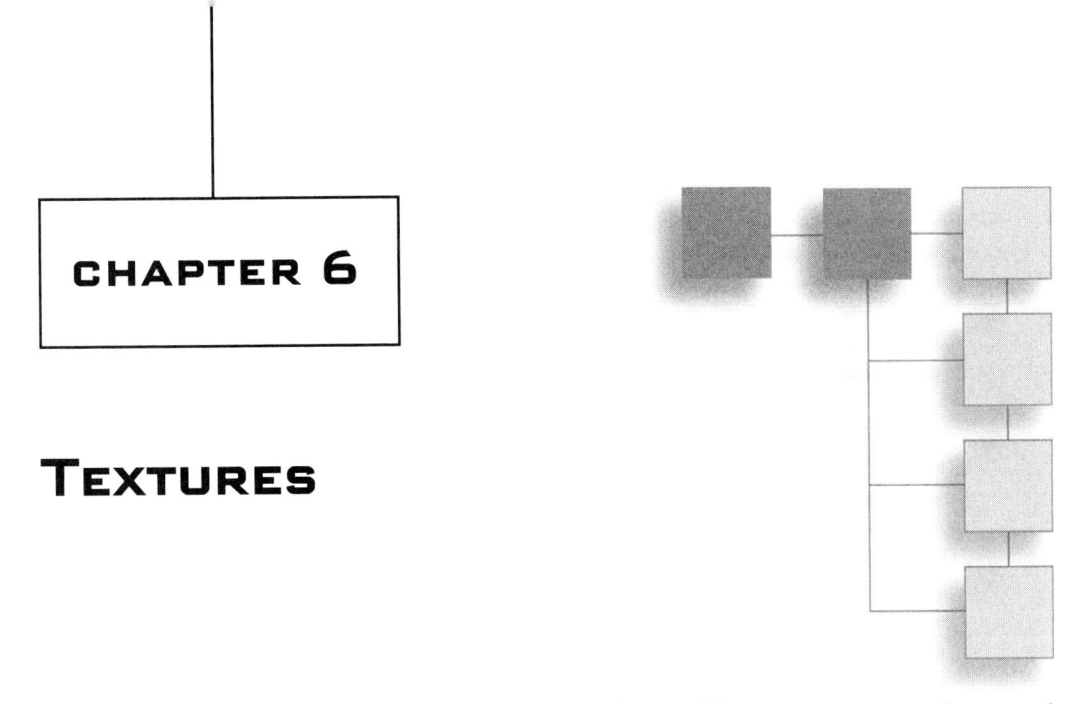

Textures

Textures are images wrapped around 3D objects like paper wrapped around a gift. You have to decide how to apply the paper to your present and choose the right design for the occasion. You must make the same decisions in 3D programming.

In this chapter, you learn:

- How to load images from PNG files.
- How to use an image as a texture.
- How to work with textures and improve their quality.
- A simpler, but faster, alternative to textures for screen-aligned images.
- An efficient way to implement environment mapping.

Image2D

In texturing, the protagonist is an image. M3G introduced its own image class, Image2D, which in contrast to MIDP's Image, distinguishes between different pixel formats.

Pixel Formats

Table 6.1 shows Image2D's interface, which is essentially a wrapper around a byte array with an associated pixel format identifier.

Table 6.1 Image2D Class Description

Method	Description
Pixel Format Specifier	
static int ALPHA	Image has alpha component only.
static int LUMINANCE	Image has luminance component only.
static int LUMINANCE_ALPHA	Image has luminance and alpha components.
static int RGB	Image has red, green, and blue components.
static int RGBA	Image has red, green, blue, and alpha components.
Construction	
Image2D(int format, int width, int height)	Constructs a mutable image.
Image2D(int format, int width, int height, byte[] image)	Constructs an immutable image from a byte array.
Image2D(int format, int width, int height, byte[] image, byte[] palette)	Constructs an immutable image from indexed image data.
Image2D(int format, java.lang.Object image)	Constructs an immutable image by copying pixels from a MIDP or AWT image.
Image Properties	
int getFormat()	Getter for image format.
int getHeight()	Getter for height.
int getWidth()	Getter for width.
boolean isMutable()	Returns true if the image can be changed.
Setting Data	
void set(int x, int y, int width, int height, byte[] image)	Updates a rectangular area in a mutable image.

Apart from telling M3G how to interpret the byte array's contents, a pixel format also determines the memory required per pixel. The following formats are available:

Pixel Format	Size per Pixel	Use in
ALPHA	1 byte	Texture2D, Sprite3D
LUMINANCE	1 byte	Texture2D, Sprite3D
LUMINANCE_ALPHA	2 bytes	Texture2D, Sprite3D
RGB	3 bytes	Texture2D, Sprite3D, Graphics.bindTarget(), Background
RGBA	4 bytes	Texture2D, Sprite3D, Graphics.bindTarget(), Background

The third column indicates a particular format's application area. All `Image2D` types can be used as textures and for `Sprite3D`s. A `Sprite3D` is an alternative to a textured plane with a restricted feature set, which is described later in this chapter.

Conversely, only RGB and RGBA formats can be used as render targets or backgrounds. Backgrounds are further restricted to have the same format as the currently bound rendering target. As you saw in Chapter 4, when using a MIDP graphics context this means you can only use RGB. However, when you bind an `Image2D` in RGBA format as render target, you can also use a background of the same type.

Creating Images

You can create either mutable or immutable images. With the constructor that creates a mutable `Image2D`, you reserve image memory at construction time and can change it later with `set()`. You can't however switch the pixel format once constructed. For example, you'd create an empty mutable image in RGBA format and initialize all pixels to opaque white with

```
Image2D image = new Image2D(Image2D.RGBA, 64, 64);
```

The remaining three constructors create immutable images. Two constructors copy an image from a `byte` array that either contains the color values itself or indices to a color palette. The fourth constructor, overloaded with an `Object` parameter, creates an `Image2D` from an existing image. The exact class you pass to this method depends on the Java profile you work with; for MIDP this is `javax.microedition.lcdui.Image`.

When creating an immutable `Image2D`, you use existing data and pass a target pixel format in the constructor. Hence, if the source doesn't match the target, M3G must convert the data. As the source format, M3G treats all mutable MIDP images as RGB and immutable ones as RGBA. Matching values are copied unchanged; for example when converting a MIDP image in RGBA format to `Image2D.ALPHA`, the alpha component is copied in. Missing components are set to 1.0 (the `byte` equivalent would be 255) or generated from existing values. When converting from RGB to `LUMINANCE` or `ALPHA`, M3G suggests (but doesn't require) that *R*, *G*, and *B* values be averaged to create the missing component.

> **Note**
>
> The rules to convert images to `Image2D` have been clarified and extended in M3G 1.1. Unfortunately, that means that you'll find older devices that have slightly different behavior. Have a look at the Pixel Format Conversion section in the package description of M3G's javadoc.

Most of the time, however, you'll probably create an `Image2D` object by loading it from a file. The only image format required by M3G is PNG.

> **Tip**
>
> Devices that comply with the Mobile Service Architecture (JSR 248) also support JPEG images, and some devices support additional image formats. However, PNG is your best bet if you want to stay compatible with a broad range of devices.

You can create a MIDP image from a PNG file and afterward convert it to `Image2D`:

```
try {
  Image image = Image.createImage("/image.png");
  Image2D image2D = new Image2D(Image2D.RGBA, image);
} catch (Exception e) {
  System.out.println("Error loading image.");
}
```

However, this creates the image data twice: once when constructing `Image` and a second time when copying the result to `Image2D`. You avoid this duplication by creating an `Image2D` object with `Loader.load()`:

```
try {
  Image2D image2D = (Image2D) Loader.load("/image.png")[0];
} catch (Exception e) {
  System.out.println("Error loading image.");
}
```

Loading images is just a subset of `Loader`—you'll see this class again in Chapter 10 and use it to import model data from binary files. `load()` returns an array of objects if several items are stored in a file. Because one PNG file contains only one image, you can directly access it at position zero of the array and cast it into an `Image2D`.

Because you can't tell `load()` what pixel format you want to use, you have to rely on your M3G implementation to determine the proper value itself. Unfortunately, the exact rules on how to do this were ambiguous until version 1.1 of M3G. If your device doesn't automatically create the right value, you have a problem because you can't change `Image2D`'s pixel format after construction. Hence, sometimes, you might have to take a detour via `Image.createImage()` to get what you want.

To anticipate an optimal result, you have to consider three items:

- **Minimal file size**. PNG knows different *color types*, which are similar to `Image2D`'s pixel formats. You can decrease the file size by storing the data in the proper format and reducing the number of colors. The file size influences the size of your application as well as determines how long it will take to read the image by your application. The PNG color type gives your implementation a hint on how to interpret the data when reading the file with `Loader`.

- **Minimal runtime memory size**. The memory size your image occupies at runtime is unrelated to the file size because the image must be decompressed before being displayed on the screen. To keep runtime memory usage to a minimum, you'll want to keep the image dimensions small and avoid copying and converting between formats. Ideally, the image ends up directly in an `Image2D` object.

- **Correct `Image2D` type**. To be useful, M3G must interpret your image correctly; this requires the pixel format identifier to be correct. The proper pixel format also ensures that an image doesn't occupy memory for more color channels than necessary.

The chain of dependencies starts with the color type of the PNG image. If `Loader` interprets the value correctly, you have a fast mechanism to load an image. Fortunately, finding out the color type of a PNG file is easy.

Reading PNG Images

A PNG file consists of several sections, called *chunks*. In the simplest case, there's an IHDR chunk for image information, an IDAT chunk for the image data itself, and an IEND chunk that signals the end of the file. Each chunk consists of a length field, a type field, the chunk data, and a checksum at the end. Figure 6.1 shows the first 33 bytes of a PNG file including the IHDR chunk, which always comes right after the eight-byte long PNG signature.

The data is encoded in network byte order (most significant byte comes first). With this in mind, you can determine that the sample PNG's image size is 240 × 320.

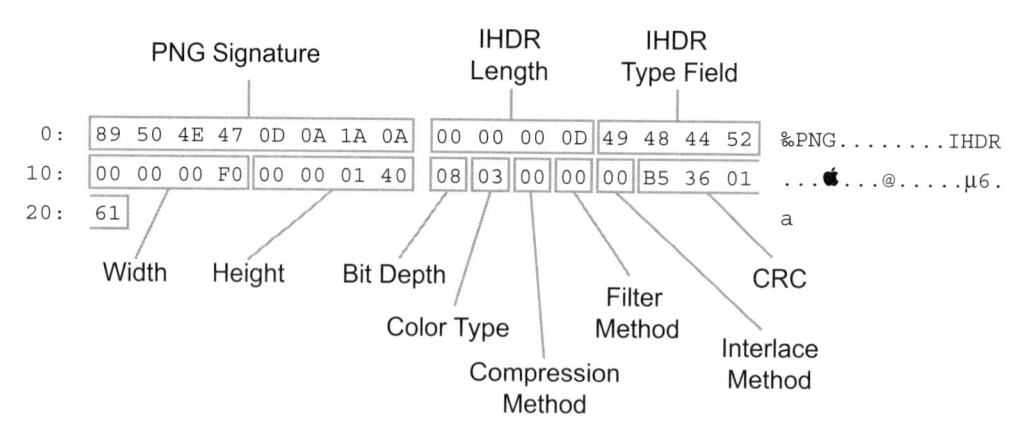

```
             PNG Signature         IHDR         IHDR
                                   Length       Type Field
                |                    |            |
  0:  | 89 50 4E 47 0D 0A 1A 0A |  | 00 00 00 0D | 49 48 44 52 |    %PNG........IHDR
 10:  | 00 00 00 F0 | 00 00 01 40 | | 08 | 03 | 00 | 00 | 00 | B5 36 01    ...........μ6.
 20:  | 61 |                                                              a
         \     \         \          \         \
        Width  Height   Bit Depth    \         \       CRC
                                   Filter       \
                          Color Type  Method
                               Compression   Interlace
                               Method        Method
```

Figure 6.1
The first 33 bytes of a PNG image file.

Inside the IHDR chunk you'll also find the bit depth of the image, the color type, compression method, filter method, and interlace method. Compression and filter are always zero because PNG defines only one method for each. The interlace method is 1 if the image can be displayed progressively—you'll see an increasingly improved version of the image as the PNG file is being decoded. This is great for Web sites, but without benefit for Java applications. Interlacing can slightly increase the file size, so this field should always be zero. The bit depth specifies the number of bits per sample or per palette index for paletted images.

The most important information for M3G is the color type, which defines how to interpret the image data. There are five color types for PNG images. Palleted images store their data as indices to a color palette with a maximum of 256 colors. Grayscale and RGB color types indicate images with one and three color channels. In addition, there are two more color types for grayscale and RGB images that include a transparency channel.

There are actually two ways to encode transparency. In case the image uses alpha blending, one of the two color types that indicate transparency is set and the transparency exists as an alpha channel encoded together with the image data. Alternatively, you can specify transparency separately from image data with the tRNS chunk, but the tRNS chunk can only define one single transparent color or, for paletted images, alpha values that are associated with palette entries. You can check for the existence of a tRNS chunk by simply looking at the file with a hex editor and searching for the string.

Tip

When working with PNG images, use a tool such as PNGGauntlet (http://brh.numbera.com/software/pnggauntlet/) to reduce the file size. To get the smallest file, save your images with as few colors as possible and then let PNGGauntlet run over the image. PNGGauntlet also lets you modify your image to have a particular PNG color type. If you can restrict your image to 256 colors, paletted images (color type three) usually create the smallest files.

Another great tool is TweakPNG (http://entropymine.com/jason/tweakpng/), which you can use to modify the internal structure of PNG files. For example, you can add a tRNS chunk.

Out of the possible permutations of color type and transparency, the PNG specification allows eight. You can distinguish each combination by looking at the color type stored in the IHDR chunk and checking whether the tRNS chunk exists. Ideally, every PNG image format should match to a well defined Image2D format when created with Loader.load(). The following table shows what Image2D format M3G 1.1 expects:

Color Type	PNG Interpretation	tRNS	Image2D Pixel Format (M3G 1.1)
0	Grayscale	No	LUMINANCE
		Yes	LUMINANCE_ALPHA
2	RGB	No	RGB
		Yes	RGBA
3	Palleted	No	RGB
		Yes	RGBA
4	Grayscale + alpha	No	LUMINANCE_ALPHA
6	RGB + alpha	No	RGBA

Unfortunately, M3G 1.0 didn't specify what happens when loading images and therefore older devices will produce implementation-specific results. M3G 1.1 clarified this issue and requires compliant devices to interpret PNG files as indicated in the right-most column.

Note

If you want to find out what Loader does on your device, you can use Image2DTypesSample.java from the CD-ROM. I created eight different PNG test images—one for each format. Image2DTypesSample loads each image with Loader.load() and displays the pixel format returned by Image2D.getFormat().

So, what do you do to achieve a specific Image2D format? Loader.load() is the fastest and most efficient way. Set the PNG image format to the type that most closely resembles your target Image2D pixel format. However, if Loader on your device doesn't interpret the image correctly, you'll have to create the image first with `Image.createImage()` and then force the pixel format when constructing `Image2D`. Constructing the image twice can't be avoided in this case.

> **Tip**
>
> In my experience, RGB images load fine with `Loader`, but images with transparency should be read with the `Image` class.

Reading JPEG Images

The Mobile Service Architecture (JSR 248) requires compliant devices to support JPEG images in addition to PNG. In contrast to PNG files, JPEG images use a lossy compression scheme. This might introduce artifacts, but decreases the file size greatly for images with many colors such as photos.

When reading JPEG files with `Loader`, JSR 248 requires implementations to return `Image2D.RGB` for color images and `LUMINANCE` for monochrome images.

> **Tip**
>
> If you use JPEG images, make sure your device supports it. Have a look in Chapter 3 for ways to find out whether your phone complies with JSR 248.

Using Textures

Once you have created an `Image2D` object, you can wrap it around a 3D object. To do this, you have to specify which part of the image maps to which part of your object. Afterward, you can adjust parameters that influence the texturing process and its quality.

Texture Mapping

The pixels inside a texture, called *texels*, are identified by texture coordinates. This is another vertex-specific attribute of a mesh. When M3G renders a textured shape, it looks up the texture coordinates for each vertex and draws the image accordingly. Figure 6.2 shows a mapping of a checkerboard texture to a quad in the *x-y* plane.

The image is a 4 × 4 checkerboard with numbers so you can easily see the image's orientation. The coordinate axes of the texture coordinate system are called *s* and *t* to distinguish them from *x* and *y* used for positions. (In literature, you'll often find the names *u* and *v*.) In accordance with Java's 2D coordinate system, the

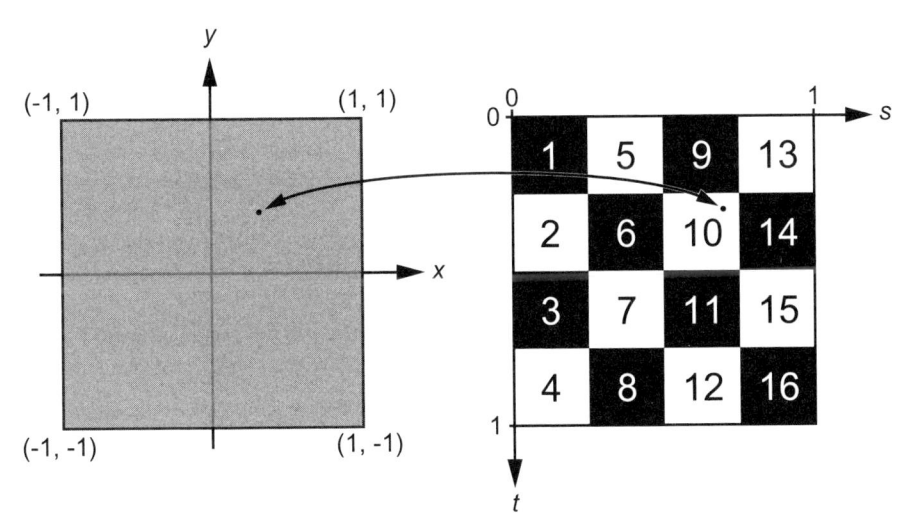

Figure 6.2
Mapping texture coordinates (s, t) to a quad.

origin is in the upper-left corner; s and t axes extend to the right and down, respectively. Note that in OpenGL, the origin is in the lower-left corner and the t axis runs upward instead.

The width and height of a texture image is restricted to powers of two—width and height may be different values though. As a minimum texture size, an implementation must support up to 256 texels in both directions. The maximum size is implementation-specific and stored in the property `maxTextureDimension` retrieved from `Graphics3D.getProperties()`.

Often, you'll create textures of different resolutions. A higher resolution improves quality, whereas a lower resolution decreases memory usage. To avoid remapping the texture, coordinates are image-size independent. That's why the origin of the image maps to the value 0 and the image width or height maps to the value 1. The coordinates (0.5, 0.5) for example will always refer to the middle of the image, no matter what size.

Once you have the texture coordinates, you can assign them to the vertices. In Figure 6.2, the texture fills the quad completely because the corners of the image are mapped to the corners of the quad. This is what the code looks like:

```
/**
 * Creates a quad with a side length of two units on the x-y plane.
 * The quad's center is at the origin (0, 0, 0).
```

```
 *
 * @param addTexCoords true to generate texture coordinates, false
 *                     otherwise.
 * @return mesh.
 */
public static Mesh createQuad(boolean addTexCoords) {
  byte[] positions = {-1, -1, 0, 1, -1, 0, -1, 1, 0, 1, 1, 0};
  int[] triangleLengths = new int[] {4};

  VertexBuffer vertexBuffer = new VertexBuffer();

  VertexArray vertexPositions
      = new VertexArray(positions.length/3, 3, 1);
  vertexPositions.set(0, positions.length/3, positions);
  vertexBuffer.setPositions(vertexPositions, 1, null);

  TriangleStripArray triangles
      = new TriangleStripArray(0, triangleLengths);

  if (addTexCoords) {
    byte[] texCoords = {0, 1, 1, 1, 0, 0, 1, 0};

    VertexArray vertexTexCoords
        = new VertexArray(texCoords.length/2, 2, 1);
    vertexTexCoords.set(0, texCoords.length/2, texCoords);
    vertexBuffer.setTexCoords(0, vertexTexCoords, 1, null);
  }

  return new Mesh(vertexBuffer, triangles, new Appearance());
}
```

No matter how you define the texture coordinates, M3G will stretch or compress the image to fit between adjacent vertices. Imagine a flexible wrapping paper that's pinned to your 3D object at the vertices.

Figure 6.3 shows the 3D shapes introduced in Chapter 4 with textures. The cube uses the same texture on each of its sides. Sphere and cylinder use the longitude as *s* coordinate and the colatitude as *t*, which generates a rectangular grid of texture coordinates on the image. Both shapes have duplicated vertices at the seam to be able to attach both ends of the texture in *s* direction. Imagine how you would wrap a paper around a can. The seam is where the paper starts and ends. For the Bézier surfaces of the teapot, *s* and *t* values of the interpolated vertices serve as texture coordinates. If you created a Bézier surface with five vertices in both directions, for example, *s* and *t* would go from zero to one in increments of 0.25.

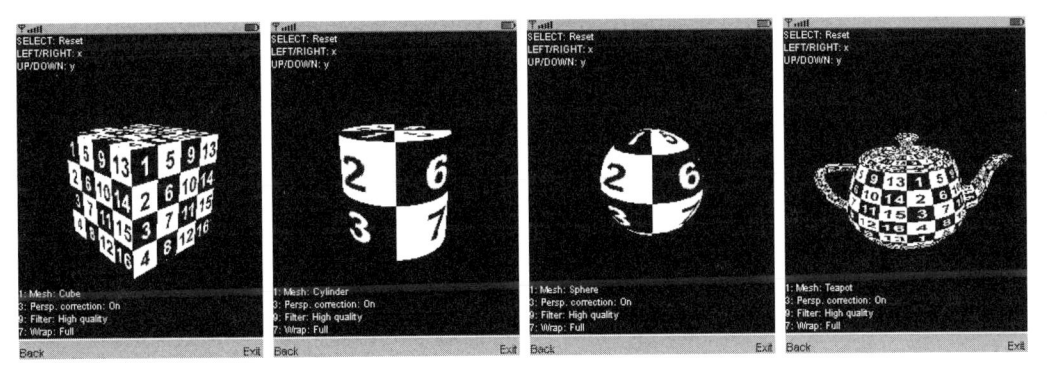

Figure 6.3
Texture mapping for cube, cylinder, sphere, and teapot.

> **Note**
>
> You'll find the implementations of these texture mappings in the classes `MeshFactory3D` and `Bezier` in the `m3g04.mesh` package.

These mappings work nicely with tiling textures, but are just examples of what you can do. How you map the texture depends on the image, the object's geometry, and the effect you want to create. For example, the sphere wastes a lot of resolution at the poles but requires more at the equator. You could draw the image so this effect is taken into account and use a different mapping algorithm.

Texturing more complex geometries, such as human models, is an artistic process that can be automated only to some extent. 3D modeling software allows you to graphically edit texture coordinates and therefore provides a high degree of freedom in finding an optimal solution. One such tool is Blender, which I use in Chapter 10 to create the texture coordinates for a monkey head.

Creating Textures

So far, you've seen the texture coordinates, but not yet how to apply the texture. `TexturingSample` implements this—the following code shows the class and its member variables.

> **Note**
>
> You can find TexturingSample.java together with a working MIDlet on the accompanying CD-ROM.

```java
/**
 * Displays different shapes with textures and allows changing
 * texture parameters interactively.
 *
 * @author Claus Hoefele
 */
public class TexturingSample extends GameCanvas implements Sample {
    /** Mesh for display. */
    private Mesh mesh;
    /** Current rotation value. */
    private float rotX, rotY;
    /** The mesh's transformation. */
    private Transform meshTransform = new Transform();
    /** The mesh's texture. */
    private Texture2D texture;

    /** Polygon mode component of appearance.*/
    private PolygonMode polygonMode;
    /** Stores whether perspective correction is enabled or not. */
    private boolean perspectiveCorrection;

    /** Cube is displayed. */
    private static final int MESH_CUBE        = 0;
    /** Sphere is displayed. */
    private static final int MESH_SPHERE      = 1;
    /** Cylinder is displayed. */
    private static final int MESH_CYLINDER    = 2;
    /** Teapot is displayed. */
    private static final int MESH_TEAPOT      = 3;
    /** Number of meshes. */
    private static final int NUMBER_OF_MESHES = 4;
    /** Current mesh. */
    private int currentMesh;

    /** 3D graphics singleton used for rendering. */
    private Graphics3D graphics3d;
    /** 2D graphics singleton used for rendering. */
    private Graphics graphics;
```

```
  /**
   * Constructor.
   */
  public TexturingSample() {
    super(false);
  }
  ...
}
```

The class contains definitions to display teapot, cube, cylinder, and sphere meshes and rotate them around the *x* and *y* axes. The processes of loading the image and creating the texture happen in `init()`:

```
  /**
   * Initializes the sample.
   */
  public void init() {
    // Get the singletons for rendering.
    graphics3d = Graphics3D.getInstance();
    graphics = getGraphics();

    try {
      // Load texture.
      Image2D image2D
          = (Image2D) Loader.load("/m3g06/checkerboard_4x4_256.png")[0];
      texture = new Texture2D(image2D);
      texture.setBlending(Texture2D.FUNC_REPLACE);
    } catch (Exception e) {
      System.out.println("Error loading texture.");
      e.printStackTrace();
    }

    // Create mesh.
    currentMesh = MESH_SPHERE;
    polygonMode = new PolygonMode();
    mesh = createMesh(currentMesh, polygonMode, texture);
    rotX = rotY = 0;

    // Create a camera with perspective projection.
    Camera camera = new Camera();
    float aspect = (float) getWidth() / (float) getHeight();
```

```
      camera.setPerspective(60, aspect, 1, 1000);
      Transform cameraTransform = new Transform();
      cameraTransform.postRotate(-20, 1, 0, 0);
      cameraTransform.postTranslate(0, 0, 5);
      graphics3d.setCamera(camera, cameraTransform);

      // Texture parameters.
      perspectiveCorrection = true;
      polygonMode.
          setPerspectiveCorrectionEnable(perspectiveCorrection);
      currentWrapping = WRAPPING_FULL;
      setWrapping(texture, currentWrapping);
      currentFilter = FILTER_HIGH;
      setFiltering(texture, currentFilter);

      render(graphics);
      flushGraphics();
  }
```

After the image is loaded, a `Texture2D` object is created by passing the image as a parameter. Table 6.2 shows `Texture2D`'s constructor and the rest of the class's interface.

Tip

You can find many great textures on the Internet. Try an image of the earth on the sphere for example. The teapot looks best if you use a tiling texture. Don't forget to resize the image so that width and height are powers of two and store the image in PNG format.

`Texture2D` has three sets of parameters: texture blending, which defines how to layer several textures over each other; wrapping, which you can use to influence how an image is distributed over a surface; and the texture filter, which influences the visual quality of texture mapping. Methods at the end of `init()` set these parameters. Except for blending, I explain them in more detail in the next sections.

Tip

Texture blending allows you to mix a texture with other textures as well as a mesh's vertex colors to create a combined effect. Because the example uses only textures, `init()` sets the texture blending mode to `Texture2D.FUNC_REPLACE` by calling `texture.setBlending()`. This blending mode overwrites any other color modifying operation and speeds up rendering because M3G doesn't have to process a blending operation. More about blending follows in Chapter 7.

Table 6.2 Texture2D Class Description

Method	Since	Description
Blending Functions		
static int FUNC_ADD		Blending function that adds colors together.
static int FUNC_BLEND		Blending function that blends colors into each other.
static int FUNC_DECAL		Blending function that blends colors depending on the transparency value.
static int FUNC_MODULATE		Blending function that multiplies colors.
static int FUNC_REPLACE		Blending function that replaces values.
Wrapping Modes		
static int WRAP_CLAMP		Clamps the texture image.
static int WRAP_REPEAT		Tiles the texture image.
Filter Modes		
static int FILTER_BASE_LEVEL		Disables mipmapping (applicable only for level filter).
static int FILTER_NEAREST		Uses nearest mipmap level (level filter) or point sampling (image filter).
static int FILTER_LINEAR		Bilinear filtering between mipmap levels (level filter) or within an image (image filter).
Texture Image		
Texture2D(Image2D image)		Creates a new texture from the given image. Defaults are as follows: wrapping is set to WRAP_REPEAT, level filter to FILTER_BASE_LEVEL, image filter to FILTER_NEAREST, blending mode to FUNC_MODULATE, and blend color to 0x00000000.
void setImage(Image2D image)		Setter for texture image.
Image2D getImage()		Getter for texture image.
Blending		
void setBlendColor(int RGB)		Sets the blending color.
int getBlendColor()		Getter for blending color.
void setBlending(int func)		Sets the blending function (constants starting with FUNC_).
int getBlending()		Getter for blending function.
Wrapping		
void setWrapping(int wrapS, int wrapT)		Setter for image wrapping mode (WRAP_CLAMP or WRAP_REPEAT).
int getWrappingS()		Getter for image wrapping in *s* direction.
int getWrappingT()		Getter for image wrapping in *t* direction.
Filter		
void setFiltering(int levelFilter, int imageFilter)		Sets the filter between mimap levels (levelFilter) and within a mimap level (imageFilter). (Constants start with FILTER_.)
int getImageFilter()	1.1	Getter for image filter.
int getLevelFilter()	1.1	Getter for level filter.

For now, let's first finish the creation of the mesh with the texture as input:

```
/**
 * Creates a mesh based on the given ID.
 *
 * @param meshId mesh ID.
 * @param polygonMode polygon mode.
 * @param texture texture image.
 * @return Mesh new mesh.
 */
private Mesh createMesh(int meshId, PolygonMode polygonMode,
    Texture2D texture) {
  Mesh mesh = null;

  switch (meshId) {
    case MESH_CUBE:
      mesh = MeshFactory3D.createCube(false, false, true);
      break;

    case MESH_SPHERE:
      mesh = MeshFactory3D.createSphere(16, 16, false, true);
      break;

    case MESH_CYLINDER:
      mesh = MeshFactory3D.createCylinder(32, false, true);
      break;

    case MESH_TEAPOT:
      mesh = Teapot.create(5, false, true);
      break;

      // no default
  }

  mesh.getAppearance(0).setTexture(0, texture);
  mesh.getAppearance(0).setPolygonMode(polygonMode);

  return mesh;
}
```

Depending on the current selection, `createMesh()` returns a mesh with texture coordinates. (This is indicated by passing `true` as the last parameter to the methods in `MeshFactory3D` and `Teapot`.) To enable texturing, you set the `Texture2D` object in the `Appearance` property of your mesh. Remember that you can have several submeshes with different appearances, but in this case there's only one mesh at position zero. You don't need to set `PolygonMode`, as is done in createMesh(), if you are happy with the defaults. However, this class lets you enable perspective correction that can greatly enhance the look of your texture. You see more of this feature in the section called "Texture Quality."

If you enable a texture, but your mesh doesn't have texture coordinates, you'll get an IllegalStateException in render(). Otherwise, rendering a mesh with a texture is no different:

```
/**
 * Renders the sample.
 *
 * @param graphics graphics context for drawing.
 */
private void render(Graphics graphics) {
  graphics3d.bindTarget(graphics);
  graphics3d.setViewport(0, 0, getWidth(), getHeight());
  graphics3d.clear(null);

  meshTransform.setIdentity();
  meshTransform.postRotate(rotX, 1, 0, 0);
  meshTransform.postRotate(rotY, 0, 1, 0);

  if (currentMesh == MESH_TEAPOT) {
    // Orient the teapot so its lid points up.
    meshTransform.postTranslate(0, -1, 0);
    meshTransform.postRotate(-90, 1, 0, 0);
    meshTransform.postScale(0.6f, 0.6f, 0.6f);
  }

  graphics3d.render(mesh, meshTransform);
  graphics3d.releaseTarget();

  drawMenu(graphics); // displays the current key assignment
}
```

Working with Texture Coordinates

After you set the texture coordinates, M3G allows you to transform coordinates with matrices. This way, you can achieve effects such as enlarging the texture or displaying it upside down without remapping the texture coordinates. You can also define what happens if texture coordinates go outside the range [0, 1]. In this case, you have the option to display the texture once or tile the image.

Transforming Texture Coordinates

Texture transformations work in a slightly different manner than mesh transformations. To transform meshes in immediate mode, you use a `Transform` object, which means that there are always two separate objects around. This becomes unwieldy if the object is part of a hierarchy, such as when `Texture2D` is part of `Appearance`. Instead, M3G's designers chose to introduce the class `Transformable`, which all objects that can be transformed inherit. `Transformable` plays an important role in Chapter 9 for scene graphs. When you put meshes in a hierarchy, you'll start using the `Transformable` class for meshes as well.

In contrast to `Transform`, `Transformable` contains four separate matrices: one each for translation, rotation, and scaling, and a generic matrix. If you name the four matrices **T**, **R**, **S**, and **M** respectively, the final transformation is created by multiplying the matrices together in the order **TRSM**.

Because you have four matrices, you'd usually use setter methods to change each component individually, such as in the following example:

```
texture.setScale(2, 2, 0);
texture.setTranslation(1, 1, 0);
texture.setOrientation(45, 0, 0, 1);
```

The combined transformation would result in texture coordinates that are first scaled, then rotated, and finally translated. Note that the order of matrix multiplications is fixed for a `Transformable` and independent of the order of method calls. The methods in `Transformable` that start with `set` overwrite previous values. `scale()`, `translate()`, `postRotate()`, and `preRotate()` on the other hand are relative to the existing values.

You might have noticed that all transformations use three parameters, although the name `Texture2D` implies that a texture is two-dimensional. 3D textures consist of a stack of images and enable you to define texture coordinates within this volume. If you take a bite out of an apple for example, the inner must be textured differently than the surface. Even though 3D textures are not supported, 3D texture coordinates are. You can set three coordinates in `VertexBuffer.setTexCoords()` and also transform texture coordinates in three dimensions. Most of the time, however, you'll use only two components for texture coordinates and ignore the third.

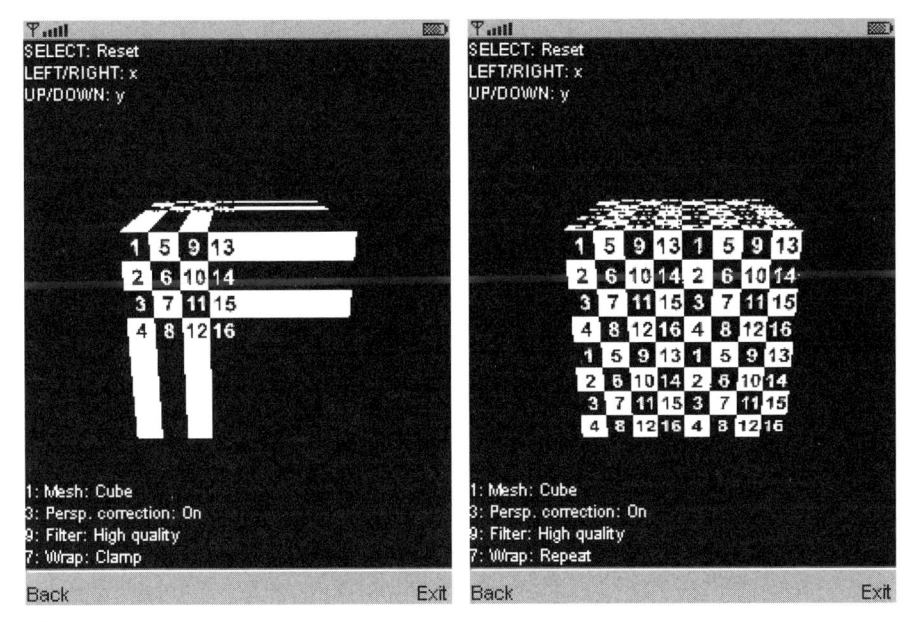

Figure 6.4
Wrapping modes `Texture2D.WRAP_CLAMP` (left picture) and `Texture2D.WRAP_REPEAT` (right picture).

Wrapping Modes

The wrapping mode defines what happens when a texture coordinate is outside the range [0, 1]. The coordinates are either wrapped around (for example, a value of 1.5 is the same as 0.5) or the values are *clamped*, which means that any value less than zero would be zero and any value greater than one would be one. Figure 6.4 shows both modes.

If a texture is clamped (`Texture2D.WRAP_CLAMP`), the border texel is repeated on the surface, which results in stripes in case of the checkerboard. If you wanted a unicolored background, you'd include a one pixel-wide frame in this color around your image. Tiling, on the other hand (`WRAP_REPEAT`), is an easy way to apply a repeating pattern over a large surface such as the stones that make up a wall.

In `TexturingSample`, you can switch between wrapping modes with the `GAME_C` key. Here are the respective settings in code form:

```
/** Texture is stretched to cover the entire surface. */
private static final int WRAPPING_FULL      = 0;
/** Texture is clamped. */
```

```
    private static final int WRAPPING_CLAMP     = 1;
    /** Texture is tiled. */
    private static final int WRAPPING_REPEAT    = 2;
    /** Number of wrapping modes. */
    private static final int NUMBER_OF_WRAPPINGS = 3;
    /** Current wrapping mode. */
    private int currentWrapping;

    /**
     * Sets the wrapping parameters of the given texture.
     *
     * @param texture texture.
     * @param wrappingMode wrapping mode.
     */
    private void setWrapping(Texture2D texture, int wrappingMode) {
      switch (wrappingMode) {
        case WRAPPING_FULL:
          texture.setScale(1, 1, 0);
          break;

        case WRAPPING_CLAMP:
          texture.setScale(2, 2, 0);
          texture.setWrapping(
              Texture2D.WRAP_CLAMP, Texture2D.WRAP_CLAMP);
          break;

        case WRAPPING_REPEAT:
          texture.setScale(2, 2, 0);
          texture.setWrapping(
              Texture2D.WRAP_REPEAT, Texture2D.WRAP_REPEAT);
          break;

          // no default
      }
    }
```

When the texture covers the entire surface, the wrapping mode isn't visible, so when clamping or tiling, `setScale(2, 2, 0)` reduces the image to a quarter of its size. The wrapping mode itself is then changed with `Texture2D.setWrapping()`. This method allows you to have different settings for the *s* and *t* directions.

Texture Quality

Texture quality improves when more sophisticated methods are employed in mapping an image to a 3D shape. Because this will usually come with a decrease in performance, you have to decide whether it's worthwhile to enable these features. In addition, not all devices support all the features M3G's interface provides.

Perspective Correction

When interpolating between vertices, artifacts can occur, which is most noticeable in textures. Perspective correction refers to any technique that helps to avoid the problem of artifacts. In Figure 6.5, you can see a cube with and without perspective correction. When it's disabled, the texture has visible artifacts at the boundary between triangles.

The problem is less obvious with textures that have an irregular pattern. It's also possible to solve the problem by adding more vertices. The teapot, for example, doesn't suffer from visible distortions because it has enough interpolation points for the texture. However, you would have to add many vertices to a flat surface to see an improvement. Enabling perspective correction is the better solution.

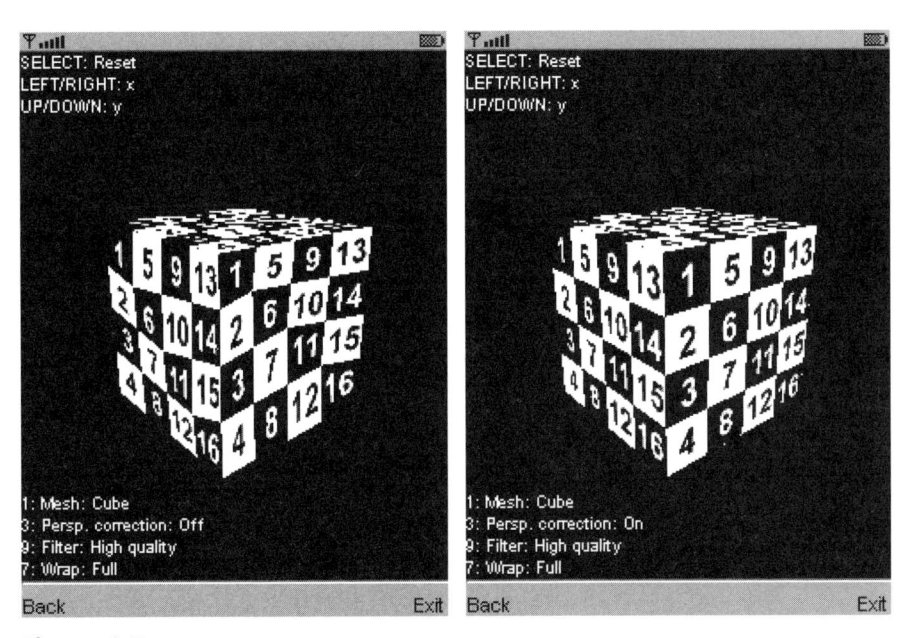

Figure 6.5
Effect of perspective correction: correction disabled (left picture) and enabled (right picture).

Perspective correction is only a hint. You can find out whether your implementation supports it by checking the supportPerspectiveCorrection property returned from Graphics3D.getProperties(). TexturingSample allows you to enable or disable perspective correction by pressing the GAME_B key:

```
/** Polygon mode component of appearance.*/
private PolygonMode polygonMode;
/** Stores whether perspective correction is enabled or not. */
private boolean perspectiveCorrection;

/**
 * Handles key presses.
 *
 * @param keyCode key code.
 */
protected void keyPressed(int keyCode) {
  switch (getGameAction(keyCode)) {
    ...
    case GAME_B:
      perspectiveCorrection = !perspectiveCorrection;
      polygonMode.
          setPerspectiveCorrectionEnable(perspectiveCorrection);
      break;
    ...
  }

  render(graphics);
  flushGraphics();
}
```

Filtering

Most of the time, a texture won't exactly fit and must be either stretched or compressed. A *texture filter* determines how pixels on the screen are retrieved from a texture. More sophisticated algorithms improve quality at the expense of performance.

In the simplest case, the filter just returns the nearest pixel in the texture (Texture2D.FILTER_NEAREST). For example, if a quad on the screen is double the size of the texture, every pixel in the image is duplicated. Higher quality methods involve linearly interpolating between neighboring texels (FILTER_LINEAR).

Another possibility for improving filtering is the introduction of *mipmaps*. These are copies of the original texture, repeatedly reduced to half the size, until the result is a single pixel. If you have a texture 16 by 16 pixels, for example, the mipmap images would be 8×8, 4×4, 2×2, and 1×1. If supported, the M3G implementation creates these images automatically ahead of render time. When the model moves farther away from the camera and the displayed texture becomes smaller, M3G replaces the original texture with a better, downsized image or even interpolates between neighboring mipmap levels. When setting the filter, `FILTER_BASE_LEVEL` disables mipmapping, `FILTER_NEAREST` takes the closest level, and `FILTER_LINEAR` interpolates linearly between mipmap levels.

M3G lets you set the image filter (filter within a mipmap level) and the level filter (filter between mipmap levels) separately. Don't get your hopes up too high though. An implementation is required only to support `FILTER_NEAREST` for the image filter and `FILTER_BASE_LEVEL` for the level filter. Except for devices with a 3D hardware accelerator, high-quality filtering isn't widespread because it's expensive to implement in software. You get to know whether mipmaps are supported by retrieving the `supportMipMap` property from `Graphics3D.getProperties()`.

Here's how to change the texture filter. You can switch between texture filters with the `GAME_D` key.

```
/** Texture filter with low quality. */
private static final int FILTER_LOW           = 0;
/** Texture filter with high quality. */
private static final int FILTER_HIGH          = 1;
/** Number of filter modes. */
private static final int NUMBER_OF_FILTERS    = 2;
/** Current filter mode. */
private int currentFilter;

/**
 * Sets the filter parameters of the given texture.
 *
 * @param texture texture.
 * @param filterMode filter mode.
 */
private void setFiltering(Texture2D texture, int filterMode) {
  switch (filterMode) {
    case FILTER_LOW:
```

```
            texture.setFiltering(
                Texture2D.FILTER_BASE_LEVEL, Texture2D.FILTER_NEAREST);
            break;

        case FILTER_HIGH:
            texture.setFiltering(
                Texture2D.FILTER_LINEAR, Texture2D.FILTER_LINEAR);
            break;

            // no default
    }
}
```

To simplify the implementation, there's only a low- and a high-quality setting. `FILTER_LOW` disables mipmapping and uses nearest neighbor interpolation for the image filter. `FILTER_HIGH` uses linear filtering for both level and image filter. If not supported, a device can silently ignore the setting and choose a different filter.

Sprite3D

Sprite3D is a simplified alternative to a textured quad. It consists of an image that's centered at a position and oriented in a way that it always faces the screen. The latter means that a Sprite3D has a constant depth. Because of the reduced features, an implementation can display Sprite3Ds much faster than comparable geometry.

> **Note**
>
> If Sprite3D isn't flexible enough for your needs, you can achieve a similar effect with a textured quad aligned to a target. In the section called "Billboards" in Chapter 9, you can see a code example for both Sprite3D and an alternative implementation with aligned, textured quads.

The first decision you have to make when constructing a Sprite3D is whether or not it is scaled. Table 6.3 shows the constructor, whose first parameter is a boolean variable that determines the scaling mode. When using an unscaled Sprite3D, the image is copied verbatim to the screen. This mode is attractive if you want to display images without any loss of quality. Conversely, a scaled Sprite3D changes its size depending on the depth. The filter method to produce the scaled image, and thus the quality, depends on the implementation.

Table 6.3 Sprite3D Class Description

Method	Description
Construction	
Sprite3D(boolean scaled, Image2D image, Appearance appearance)	Constructs a new Sprite3D with the given parameters. The crop rectangle is set to the same size as the image or the maximum crop rectangle size supported by the implementation, whatever is smaller.
General Functionality	
boolean isScaled()	Getter for scaling mode.
void setImage(Image2D image)	Sets a new image.
Image2D getImage()	Getter for image. Resets the cropping rectangle.
void setAppearance(Appearance appearance)	Sets appearance. Attributes other than CompositingMode and Fog are ignored.
Appearance getAppearance()	Getter for appearance.
Cropping	
void setCrop(int cropX, int cropY, int width, int height)	Sets the cropping rectangle.
int getCropX()	Getter for the cropping rectangle's *x* position.
int getCropY()	Getter for the cropping rectangle's *y* position.
int getCropWidth()	Getter for the cropping rectangle's width.
int getCropHeight()	Getter for the cropping rectangle's height.

In the constructor, you also set the image and the appearance. Unlike the scaling mode, which is fixed for the lifetime of the object, you can change these two properties later with the respective setter methods.

A major difference between textures and Sprite3Ds is that the image isn't restricted to power-of-two dimensions, but only by the maximum size that's allowed by your implementation. The property maxSpriteCropDimension, which you can acquire with Graphics.getProperties(), contains the respective value—the minimum is 256 pixels. For the Appearance parameter, only CompositingMode and Fog properties can be used. The rest, notably lighting, are ignored.

After construction, you have the possibility to crop a large image with Sprite3D.setCrop(), similar to Background's image discussed in Chapter 4. However, negative values for width and height of the cropping rectangle are allowed and enable you to mirror the image.

Cheap Environment Mapping

There are other interesting effects you can achieve with texture coordinates. One application is *environment mapping*, where an image of the environment is mirrored on the surface of a mesh.

The Real Thing

To clarify what cheap environment mapping is, let's have a look at why environment mapping is expensive.

The most common technique for environment mapping is cube mapping. In cube mapping, a vector from the camera position to each of a model's vertices is reflected off the surface. The reflected ray is then looked up in a cube map, which works like a textured cube that surrounds the object. The s and t coordinates where the reflected ray intercepts the cube are taken as texture coordinates. Figure 6.6 illustrates this technique with a sphere as the model.

Cube mapping needs six images, one for each side of the cube. You can obtain these images by placing a camera in the middle of a room and taking an image in each direction.

An alternative technique for environment mapping is sphere mapping. It works similar to cube mapping except that the reflected ray is mapped into a single image instead of six. You must distort the image appropriately for this to work. One approach to get such an image is to take a photo of a small chrome sphere in a large room. The image reflected on the sphere is the distorted image that you need.

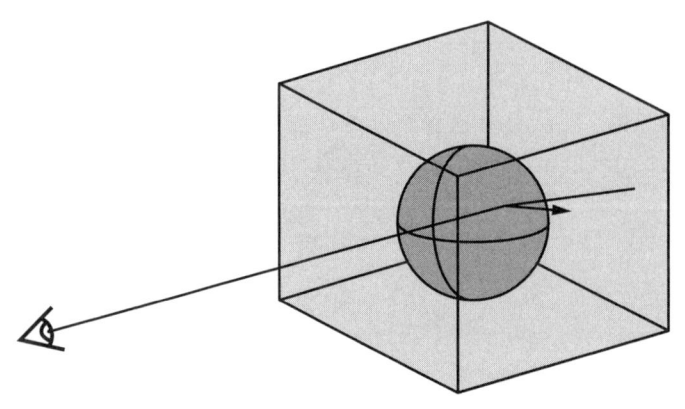

Figure 6.6
Environment mapping with a cube map.

Alternatively, you can also take a photo with a fish-eye lens, which has a similar effect.

Compared to sphere mapping, cube mapping results in better quality because of the larger available texture. Another disadvantage of sphere mapping is that the texture image is view-dependent. That means that you create the distorted image based on one camera position, which isn't necessarily the same as the one you need when applying the environment map. In both cases, you have to calculate a reflection vector at every vertex and do additional calculations to get a texture coordinate. The texture coordinates must be recalculated each time the camera or the object moves.

A Fast Alternative

The truth is that realistic reflections, especially for moving objects, are not that important to achieve pleasing results. The simplest form of environment mapping takes the *x* and *y* coordinates of the object's normals as texture coordinates.

> **Note**
> A *normal* is a vector perpendicular to a surface or perpendicular to the tangent plane of a vertex. For example, the normals of a sphere point from the center outward; the normals of a cube are perpendicular to each of the sides. Normals are also used for lighting. Chapter 8 further explains how to define normals.

This simplifies the complexity drastically: instead of computing a reflection vector, you reuse existing values and, instead of a cube map, you have one single texture. Figure 6.7 shows how different meshes look with this kind of environment mapping applied.

You can see the same image used for environment mapping also in the background. It is resized to 256 × 256, however, so it can serve as a texture map.

This technique works best with objects that have normals pointing in different directions across its surface, such as sphere and teapot. Otherwise, the mapping will create the same texture coordinate for vertices with the same normal. That's why the cylinder displays stripes on its body and a single color on the lids. Still, it creates a nice chrome-like effect.

The class `EnvironmentMap` handles the transformation of normals into texture coordinates.

178 Chapter 6 ■ Textures

Figure 6.7
Fast environment mapping.

Note

You can find this example in EnvironmentMap.java and EnvironmentMappingSample.java on the accompanying CD-ROM.

```
/**
 * Calculates environment mapping coordinates by using a mesh's
 * normals as texture coordinates.
 *
 * @author Claus Hoefele
 * @see EnvironmentMappingSample
 */
public class EnvironmentMap {
  /** Reference to mesh that has environment mapping applied. */
  private Mesh mesh;
  /** Current generic texture transformation. */
  private Transform textureTransform = new Transform();

  /**
   * Constructs a new environment map for the given mesh with
   * normalization enabled.
   *
   * @param mesh mesh for environment mapping.
   * @see #EnvironmentMap(Mesh, boolean, float)
   */
  public EnvironmentMap(Mesh mesh) {
```

```java
    this(mesh, true, Short.MAX_VALUE);
}

/**
 * Constructs a new environment map for the given mesh.
 *
 * If normalization is enabled, the mesh's normals are scaled to
 * unit length. This works for all meshes, but has a performance
 * impact. If the mesh's normals are already unit length,
 * normalization can be switched off.
 *
 * @param mesh mesh for environment mapping.
 * @param normalize enables/disables normalization.
 * @param scale scale of mesh normals.
 */
public EnvironmentMap(Mesh mesh, boolean normalize,
        float scale) {
    if (mesh == null) {
        throw new NullPointerException("Mesh must not be null.");
    }

    if (mesh.getVertexBuffer().getNormals() == null) {
        throw new IllegalArgumentException("Mesh lacks normals.");
    }

    this.mesh = mesh;

    if (normalize) {
        // Create unit length normals vectors before using them as
        // texture coordinates.
        int numVertices = mesh.getVertexBuffer().getVertexCount();
        short[] texCoords = new short[numVertices * 3];   // s, t, r
        float[] normals = new float[numVertices * 4];     // x, y, z, w
        new Transform().transform(mesh.getVertexBuffer().getNormals(),
                normals, false);

        for (int i=0; i<numVertices; i++) {
            float x = normals[i*4 + 0];
            float y = normals[i*4 + 1];
            float z = normals[i*4 + 2];

            double length = scale / Math.sqrt(x*x + y*y + z*z);
            texCoords[i*3 + 0] = (short) (x * length);
```

```
            texCoords[i*3 + 1] = (short) (y * length);
            texCoords[i*3 + 2] = (short) (z * length);
        }

        VertexArray vertexTexCoords
            = new VertexArray(texCoords.length / 3, 3, 2);
        vertexTexCoords.set(0, texCoords.length / 3, texCoords);
        mesh.getVertexBuffer().setTexCoords(0, vertexTexCoords, 1,null);
    } else {
        // Reuse normals as texture coordinates by using the same
        // VertexArray.
        mesh.getVertexBuffer().setTexCoords(0,
            mesh.getVertexBuffer().getNormals(), 1, null);
    }

    // Scale texture coordinates [0, 1]. The y coordinate must be
    // reflected because MIDP's 2D origin is in the upper left corner.
    Texture2D texture = mesh.getAppearance(0).getTexture(0);
    texture.setTranslation(0.5f, 0.5f, 0.5f);
    texture.setScale(1.0f/(scale * 2), -1.0f/(scale * 2),
        1.0f/(scale * 2));
    }
    ...
}
```

Before using normals for environment mapping, they have to be unit length. However, this is not required for normals used for lighting. For this reason, if you set the boolean parameter in the constructor to true, EnvironmentMap will loop through the normals, divide them by their length, and create a new VertexArray with the resulting values. This VertexArray is then used for the texture coordinates.

The alternative is much simpler. If the normals are already unit length, you can use the same VertexArray with the normals as texture coordinates. This elegant solution is possible because M3G allows you to have 3D texture coordinates although textures are only 2D.

The only thing that's left is to adjust the texture coordinates to be in the correct range. First of all, you have to divide them by the scale parameter to get the texture coordinates in the range [−1, 1]. This is the same scale that you used when creating the normals. For example, if you scaled your normals with Short.MAX_VALUE, this is what you'd set.

Next, you put the coordinates in the [0, 1] range by halving them and adding a bias of 0.5 to the *x*, *y*, and *z* coordinates. The *y* coordinate has to be negated because the texture image has its positive *t* axis run downward, whereas the positive *y* axis for the normals goes upward.

This creates the environment mapping effect, but you also have to take mesh and camera movements into account. Even if the mesh moves, the environment doesn't—so you have to adjust the texture coordinates each time. To do this, EnvironmentMap implements transform(), which a client must call to update the texture coordinates.

```
/**
 * Updates the texture coordinates. Rotation matrices for camera
 * and model are built in the order Rx*Ry*Rz.
 *
 * @param cameraX camera rotation around the x axis.
 * @param cameraY camera rotation around the y axis.
 * @param cameraZ camera rotation around the z axis.
 * @param modelX model rotation around the x axis.
 * @param modelY model rotation around the y axis.
 * @param modelZ model rotation around the z axis.
 */
public void transform(float cameraX, float cameraY, float cameraZ,
    float modelX, float modelY, float modelZ) {
  textureTransform.setIdentity();
  textureTransform.postRotate(-cameraX, 1, 0, 0);
  textureTransform.postRotate(-cameraY, 0, 1, 0);
  textureTransform.postRotate(-cameraZ, 0, 0, 1);
  textureTransform.postRotate(modelX, 1, 0, 0);
  textureTransform.postRotate(modelY, 0, 1, 0);
  textureTransform.postRotate(modelZ, 0, 0, 1);
  mesh.getAppearance(0).getTexture(0).setTransform(textureTransform);
}
```

Only rotations matter—scaling and translation values would mess up the range of the texture coordinates set in EnvironmentMap's constructor. transform() inverts the camera rotations because it must transform the texture coordinates in the model's local coordinate system.

Applying Environment Mapping to Meshes

Using `EnvironmentMap` is straightforward—all you have to do is create a mesh, assign it to `EnviromentMap`, and regularly update the texture coordinates.

```
/**
 * Demonstrates environment mapping.
 *
 * @author Claus Hoefele
 * @see EnvironmentMap
 */
public class EnvironmentMappingSample extends GameCanvas
    implements Sample {
  /** Calculates environment mapping coordinates. */
  private EnvironmentMap environmentMap;

  /** Mesh for display. */
  private Mesh mesh;
  /** The mesh's transformation. */
  private Transform meshTransform = new Transform();
  /** The model's current rotation value. */
  private float modelX, modelZ;
  /** The camera's current rotation value. */
  private float cameraX;
  /** The mesh's texture. */
  private Texture2D texture;
  /** Background image. */
  private Background background;

  /** Sphere is displayed. */
  private static final int MESH_SPHERE = 0;
  /** Cylinder is displayed. */
  private static final int MESH_CYLINDER = 1;
  /** Teapot is displayed. */
  private static final int MESH_TEAPOT = 2;
  /** Number of meshes. */
  private static final int NUMBER_OF_MESHES = 3;
  /** Current mesh. */
  private int currentMesh;

  /** 3D graphics singleton used for rendering. */
  private Graphics3D graphics3d;
  /** 2D graphics singleton used for rendering. */
```

```java
  private Graphics graphics;

  /**
   * Constructor.
   */
  public EnvironmentMappingSample() {
    super(false);
  }

  /**
   * Initializes the sample.
   */
  public void init() {
    // Get the singletons for rendering.
    graphics3d = Graphics3D.getInstance();
    graphics = getGraphics();

    try {
      // Image is used for both the texture and the background.
      Image2D image2D
          = (Image2D) Loader.load("/m3g06/background.png")[0];

      texture = new Texture2D(image2D);
      texture.setBlending(Texture2D.FUNC_REPLACE);
      texture.setFiltering(
          Texture2D.FILTER_LINEAR, Texture2D.FILTER_LINEAR);

      background = new Background();
      background.setImage(image2D);
    } catch (Exception e) {
      System.out.println("Error loading image.");
      e.printStackTrace();
    }

    // Create mesh.
    currentMesh = MESH_TEAPOT;
    mesh = createMesh(currentMesh, texture);
    modelX = modelZ = 0;

    // Create a camera with perspective projection.
    Camera camera = new Camera();
    float aspect = (float) getWidth() / (float) getHeight();
    camera.setPerspective(60, aspect, 1, 1000);
```

```
      Transform cameraTransform = new Transform();
      cameraX = -20;
      cameraTransform.postRotate(cameraX, 1, 0, 0);
      cameraTransform.postTranslate(0, 0, 5);

      graphics3d.setCamera(camera, cameraTransform);

      render(graphics);
      flushGraphics();
   }
   ...
}
```

`init()` sets up the same image for environment mapping and the background. This causes slight distortions in the background image because the square image doesn't have the same aspect ratio as the screen.

```
  /**
   * Creates a mesh based on the given ID.
   *
   * @param meshId mesh ID.
   * @param texture texture data.
   * @return Mesh new mesh.
   */
  private Mesh createMesh(int meshId, Texture2D texture) {
    Mesh mesh = null;

    switch (meshId) {
      case MESH_SPHERE:
        mesh = MeshFactory3D.createSphere(16, 16, true, false);
        mesh.getAppearance(0).setTexture(0, texture);
        environmentMap
            = new EnvironmentMap(mesh, false, Short.MAX_VALUE);
        break;

      case MESH_CYLINDER:
        mesh = MeshFactory3D.createCylinder(32, true, false);
        mesh.getAppearance(0).setTexture(0, texture);
        environmentMap
            = new EnvironmentMap(mesh, false, Short.MAX_VALUE);
        break;
```

```
    case MESH_TEAPOT:
      mesh = Teapot.create(5, true, false);
      mesh.getAppearance(0).setTexture(0, texture);
      environmentMap = new EnvironmentMap(mesh);
      break;

      // no default
  }

  PolygonMode polygonMode = new PolygonMode();
  polygonMode.setPerspectiveCorrectionEnable(true);
  mesh.getAppearance(0).setPolygonMode(polygonMode);

  return mesh;
}
```

createMesh() constructs the currently selected mesh. You can choose between sphere, cylinder, and teapot. When calling MeshFactory3D, the boolean parameter that's set to true causes the class to generate normals for the shapes. Afterward, the code constructs a new EnvironmentMap object and assigns the mesh to it. Sphere and cylinder already have unit length normals, so they disable normalization. You can look up the scale in MeshFactory3D; the same value is used when constructing the normals. The teapot, on the other hand, needs normalization and implicitly enables the feature by calling the non-argument constructor.

```
/**
 * Renders the sample.
 *
 * @param graphics graphics context for drawing.
 */
private void render(Graphics graphics) {
  graphics3d.bindTarget(graphics);
  graphics3d.setViewport(0, 0, getWidth(), getHeight());
  graphics3d.clear(background);

  meshTransform.setIdentity();
  float x = modelX;
  if (currentMesh == MESH_TEAPOT) {
    // Orient teapot so its lid points up.
    meshTransform.postTranslate(0, -1, -1);
    meshTransform.postScale(0.6f, 0.6f, 0.6f);
    x -= 90;
  }
```

```
        // The rotations must be executed in the same order as in
        // EnvironmentMap.
        meshTransform.postRotate(x, 1, 0, 0);
        meshTransform.postRotate(modelZ, 0, 0, 1);
        environmentMap.transform(cameraX, 0, 0, x, 0, modelZ);

        graphics3d.render(mesh, meshTransform);
        graphics3d.releaseTarget();

        drawMenu(graphics); // displays the current key assignment
    }
```

Before rendering, you have to call `environmentMap.transform()` to update the latest transformation. This call will adjust the texture coordinates for the mesh and you can render it on the screen.

Summary

In this chapter, you learned how to load an image with `Loader.load()`, which is the most efficient way, and with `Image.createImage()`, which you have to use if your implementation produces the wrong `Image2D` type.

After loading the image, you saw how to use it as a texture. You have to generate texture coordinates that specify how to map the image to the vertices of your mesh. These coordinates can be transformed with matrix multiplications. This way, you can easily scale your texture, for example. Tiling is achieved by setting the respective wrapping mode.

Two parameters change the texture quality: perspective correction and the texture filter. Especially large quads benefit from perspective correction. A better texture filter improves the look of your mesh, but for performance reasons only a few software renderers support high-quality filters.

A `Sprite3D` has fewer features than a textured geometry. However, with this reduced functionality comes an increase in performance, if screen-aligned images are what you need. At the end of the chapter, you saw an interesting effect that uses a texture for environment mapping.

Texturing dramatically increases the realism of your 3D objects—it's the key to creating aesthetically pleasing content. But this is not the end to what you can do with images. In the next chapter, you get to know multi-texturing, where you combine several textures. I discuss multi-texturing in the context of blending and transparency.

CHAPTER 7

BLENDING AND TRANSPARENCY

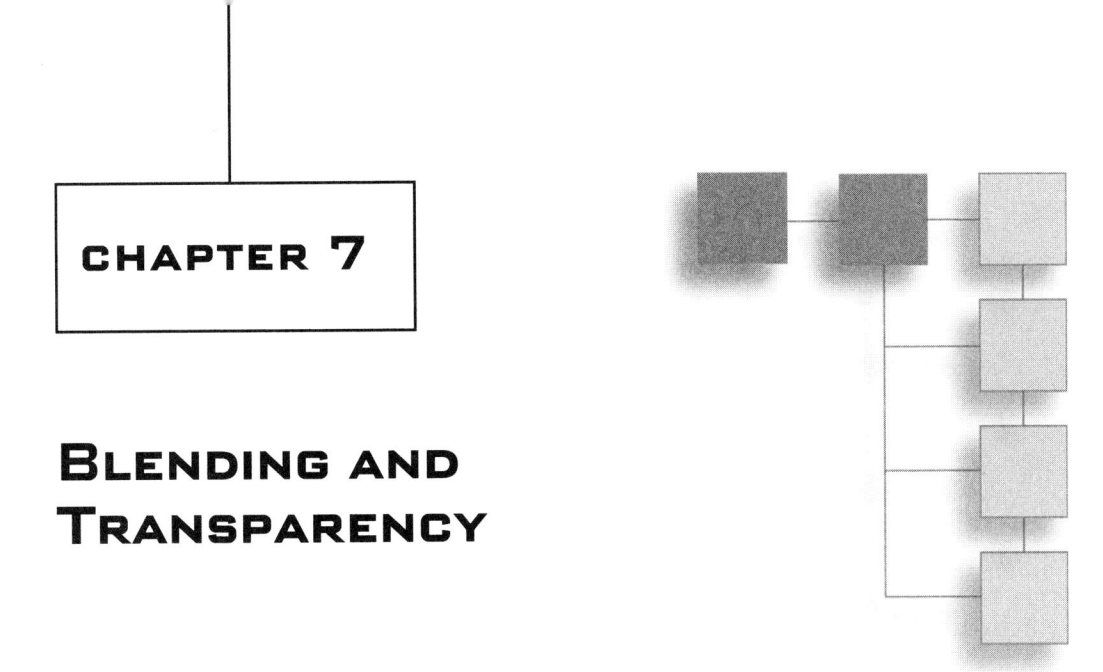

So far, you have seen how to change one visual aspect of an object in isolation. With blending, you can create additional effects by combining different sources. Blending operations can be as simple as replacing one value with another. More complicated methods take two pixel values into account or blend colors using transparency. In this chapter, you learn how M3G combines pixel values and how you can influence the blending operations.

You learn how:

- Compositing blends pixel values with the contents of the color buffer.
- A mesh can own multiple textures layered on top of each other.
- Fog fades out a mesh into the fog color.
- Compositing and multi-texturing create an embossing effect.

Compositing

After M3G has applied all transformations and appearance attributes, but before the rendered 3D image is written into the color buffer, you have one last opportunity to influence the result: you can define how separate meshes and the background build a composite image.

Fragment Tests

The ultimate goal of rendering is to have an image in the color buffer that can subsequently be displayed on the screen. To make this possible, triangles are rasterized into fragments, which have an associated screen coordinate and are destined to become pixels in the color buffer. However, before written into the color buffer, a fragment must pass a series of tests. If it passes, it's blended together with the existing value in the color buffer. Figure 7.1 shows this process.

One such test includes the depth buffer introduced in Chapter 5, which helps with removing occluded objects: only fragments closer to the viewer than previous fragments end up in the color buffer. In addition, you have the alpha test: only fragments with an alpha value greater than or equal to a threshold will pass. Table 7.1 shows the interface to change the respective settings in `CompositingMode`.

You can initialize color and depth buffer with the settings in `Background` by calling `Graphics3D.clear()`. At this point, you can draw an image or a background color into the color buffer and reset the depth buffer values.

You can disable the depth buffer completely when calling `Graphics3D.bindTarget()` with `false` as the second parameter. Otherwise, you can also enable it for each mesh individually as part of `CompositingMode.setDepthTestEnabled()`. The alpha test is enabled indirectly by setting the threshold.

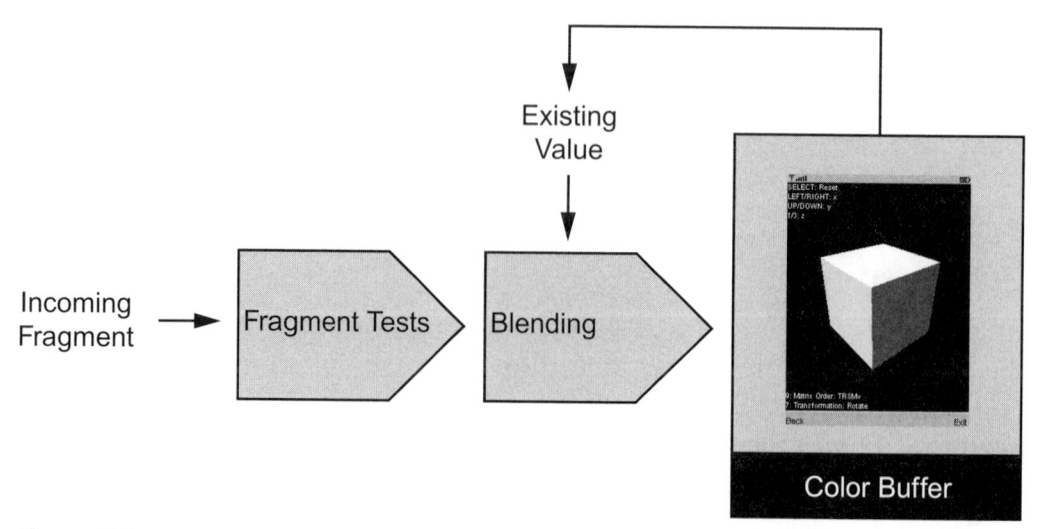

Figure 7.1
Fragment tests and blending.

Table 7.1 CompositingMode Class Description

Method	Description
Blending Modes	
static int ALPHA	Blends between colors by averaging source and destination values weighted by the transparency.
static int ALPHA_ADD	Adds the destination value to the source value, depending on the source's transparency.
static int MODULATE	Multiplies source and destination color.
static int MODULATE_X2	Same as MODULATE, but scaled by factor 2.
static int REPLACE	Overwrites the destination value with the source color.
Construction	
CompositingMode()	Default values are blending mode set to REPLACE; alpha threshold and depth offset values set to 0.0; depth test, depth write, color write, and alpha write enabled.
Depth Buffer	
void setDepthOffset(float factor, float units)	Sets the depth offset.
float getDepthOffsetFactor()	Getter for offset factor.
float getDepthOffsetUnits()	Getter for offset units.
void setDepthWriteEnable(boolean enable)	Enables writing into the depth buffer.
boolean isDepthWriteEnabled()	Checks whether writing in the depth buffer is enabled.
void setDepthTestEnable(boolean enable)	Enables depth buffer testing.
boolean isDepthTestEnabled()	Checks whether depth buffer testing is enabled.
Color Buffer	
void setColorWriteEnable(boolean enable)	Enables writing in the color buffer.
boolean isColorWriteEnabled()	Checks whether writing in the color buffer is enabled.
void setAlphaWriteEnable(boolean enable)	Enables writing transparency values into the color buffer.
boolean isAlphaWriteEnabled()	Checks whether writing transparency values is enabled.
void setAlphaThreshold(float threshold)	Sets the value for alpha testing.
float getAlphaThreshold()	Getter for alpha threshold.
Blending	
void setBlending(int mode)	Sets the blending mode (ALPHA, ALPHA_ADD, MODULATE, MODULATE_X2, or REPLACE).
int getBlending()	Getter for blending mode.

Setting the value zero with `setAlphaThreshold()` will cause all fragments to pass; other values require a minimum value in the alpha component.

A passing fragment changes the current contents of the buffers and therefore influences subsequent tests. If you want to perform the tests without updating the frame buffer, you can disable writing alpha, color, and depth values by calling the respective setter function. For example, you disable writing depth values with `setDepthWriteEnabled(false)`. In Chapter 5, you saw an example where doing this helps rendering transparent meshes correctly.

Blending Modes

Once a fragment passes all tests, it's ready to be written into the color buffer. By default, the incoming fragment overwrites the existing value, but you can also instruct M3G to blend them together. The value passed to `CompositingMode.setBlending()` decides how that is done.

As an example, `CompositingSample` demonstrates the difference between blending modes with two overlapping quads, as shown in Figure 7.2. The upper-left quad is gray (0x808080) and the background black (0x000000). Because the sample uses a MIDP graphics context, the color buffer contains RGB values and transparency information is discarded. Together with the fact that the default mode for meshes overwrites values in the color buffer, you can ignore the transparency values for the background and the upper-left quad.

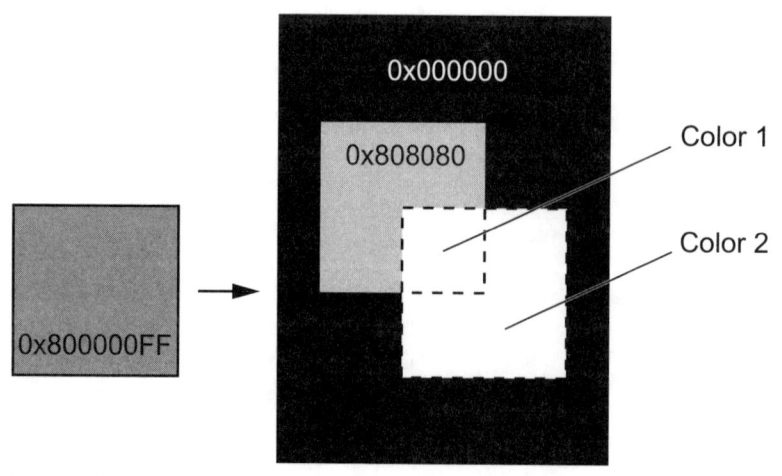

Figure 7.2
Blending modes.

Note

CompositingSample sets the colors of the quads with VertexBuffer.setDefaultColor(). This method takes the color as an `int` argument in the format 0xAARRGGBB. If you don't need transparency, you can ignore the alpha value.

However, transparency is used for blending an incoming fragment with the existing value at that position. CompositingSample answers the question, what happens if you render a blue quad with 50% transparency (0x800000FF) on top of the background and the upper-left quad. The GAME_A key switches among the blending modes.

The following table lists the different modes, where C_s is the incoming fragment, or source color, and C_d the destination color. Color 1 is the value where the quads overlap; Color 2 where the lower-right quad blends with the background.

Blending Mode	Definition	Color 1	Color 2
ALPHA	$C_d = C_s A_s + C_d(1 - A_s)$	0x4040C0	0x000080
ALPHA_ADD	$C_d = C_s A_s + C_d$	0x8080FF	0x000080
MODULATE	$C_d = C_s C_d$	0x000080	0x000000
MODULATE_X2	$C_d = 2 C_s C_d$	0x0000FF	0x000000
REPLACE	$C_d = C_s$	0x0000FF	0x0000FF

When computing with colors, it's best to use fractional numbers, where a value of 0.0 corresponds to 0 (0x00) and 1.0 to 255 (0xFF). In this notation, the lower-right quad has the color (0.0, 0.0, 1.0) with an alpha value of 0.5 and the upper-left quad the color (0.5, 0.5, 0.5). For example, using the color values of the lower-right quad as C_s, its transparency value as A_s, and the color values of the upper-left quad as C_d in the formula for the blending mode ALPHA yields (0.25, 0.25, 0.75). This value is noted as 0x4040C0 in the preceding table for color 1.

Here's how CompositingSample implements blending:

```
/**
 *  Demonstrates compositing with different blending modes.
 *
 * @author Claus Hoefele
 */
public class CompositingSample extends GameCanvas implements Sample {
    /** First mesh for display. */
```

Chapter 7 ■ Blending and Transparency

```java
private Mesh mesh1 = MeshFactory2D.createQuad(false);
/** Second mesh for display. */
private Mesh mesh2 = MeshFactory2D.createQuad(false);
/** The mesh's transformation. */
private Transform meshTransform = new Transform();

/** The second mesh's compositing attributes. */
private CompositingMode compositingMode;
...

/** 3D graphics singleton used for rendering. */
private Graphics3D graphics3d;
/** 2D graphics singleton used for rendering. */
private Graphics graphics;

/**
 * Constructor.
 */
public CompositingSample() {
  super(false);
}

/**
 * Initializes the sample.
 */
public void init() {
  // Get the singletons for rendering.
  graphics3d = Graphics3D.getInstance();
  graphics = getGraphics();

  // The first mesh is gray. The default blending mode is REPLACE,
  // which means that the transparency value is ignored and the
  // color is considered fully opaque.
  mesh1.getVertexBuffer().setDefaultColor(0x808080);

  // The second mesh is blue with 50% transparency; its
  // CompositingMode defines how this color is blended.
  mesh2.getVertexBuffer().setDefaultColor(0x800000FF);
  compositingMode = new CompositingMode();
  currentBlending = BLENDING_ALPHA;
  mesh2.getAppearance(0).setCompositingMode(compositingMode);
  setBlending(compositingMode, currentBlending);

  // Create a camera with perspective projection.
```

```
    Camera camera = new Camera();
    float aspect = (float) getWidth() / (float) getHeight();
    camera.setPerspective(60, aspect, 1, 1000);
    Transform cameraTransform = new Transform();
    cameraTransform.postTranslate(0, 0, 4);
    graphics3d.setCamera(camera, cameraTransform);

    render(graphics);
    flushGraphics();
  }
  ...
}
```

CompositingSample owns two meshes: the overlapping quads that become initialized in init(). To make the second quad blend into the first and the background, you have to construct a new CompositingMode object and set it in the Appearance node of your mesh.

Initially, CompositingMode uses REPLACE as blending mode, which you change with a call to setBlending():

```
/** Identifier representing blending mode ALPHA. */
private static final int BLENDING_ALPHA                 = 0;
/** Identifier representing blending mode ALPHA_ADD. */
private static final int BLENDING_ALPHA_ADD             = 1;
/** Identifier representing blending mode MODULATE. */
private static final int BLENDING_MODULATE              = 2;
/** Identifier representing blending mode MODULATE_X2. */
private static final int BLENDING_MODULATE_X2           = 3;
/** Identifier representing blending mode REPLACE. */
private static final int BLENDING_REPLACE               = 4;
/** Number of blending modes. */
private static final int NUMBER_OF_BLENDINGS            = 5;

/** Current blending mode. */
private int currentBlending;

/**
 * Sets the current blending mode.
 *
 * @param compositingMode compositing attributes.
 * @param mode blending mode.
 */
```

Chapter 7 ■ Blending and Transparency

```
private void setBlending(CompositingMode compositingMode, int mode){
  switch (mode) {
    case BLENDING_ALPHA:
      compositingMode.setBlending(CompositingMode.ALPHA);
      break;

    case BLENDING_ALPHA_ADD:
      compositingMode.setBlending(CompositingMode.ALPHA_ADD);
      break;

    case BLENDING_MODULATE:
      compositingMode.setBlending(CompositingMode.MODULATE);
      break;

    case BLENDING_MODULATE_X2:
      compositingMode.setBlending(CompositingMode.MODULATE_X2);
      break;

    case BLENDING_REPLACE:
      compositingMode.setBlending(CompositingMode.REPLACE);
      break;

    // no default
  }
}
```

`render()` displaces the two quads so they overlap:

```
/**
 * Renders the sample.
 *
 * @param graphics graphics context for rendering.
 */
private void render(Graphics graphics) {
  graphics3d.bindTarget(graphics);
  graphics3d.setViewport(0, 0, getWidth(), getHeight());
  graphics3d.clear(null);

  meshTransform.setIdentity();
  meshTransform.postTranslate(-0.5f, 0.5f, 0);
  graphics3d.render(mesh1, meshTransform);
```

```
    meshTransform.setIdentity();
    meshTransform.postTranslate(0.5f, -0.5f, 0);
    graphics3d.render(mesh2, meshTransform);

    graphics3d.releaseTarget();

    drawMenu(graphics); // displays the current key assignment
}

/**
 * Handles key presses.
 *
 * @param keyCode key code.
 */
protected void keyPressed(int keyCode) {
    switch (getGameAction(keyCode)) {
      case GAME_A:
        currentBlending++;
        currentBlending %= NUMBER_OF_BLENDINGS;
        setBlending(compositingMode, currentBlending);
        break;

      case FIRE:
        init();
        break;

        // no default
    }

    render(graphics);
    flushGraphics();
}
```

Multi-Texturing

Multi-texturing does for textures what compositing does for fragments: it allows you to blend several textures. By combining textures, you can, for example, apply a decal to a mesh or vary an otherwise repetitive texture.

Texture Blending

You can visualize multi-texturing as a stack of layers as Figure 7.3 depicts. Layers are blended together starting from the bottom, working upward.

The lowest layer contains the mesh's vertex colors. It is the result of any color modifying operation such as the default color, vertex colors, and lighting. Next in the stack are the texture units. An implementation must have a minimum of one texture unit, up to a maximum reported in the property `numTextureUnits` obtained from `Graphics3D.getProperties()`.

For every texture unit you are using, you also have to supply a set of texture coordinates—of course, you can share the same `VertexArray` if both units should have the same values. As an example, the following code sets the texture coordinates of unit zero and one:

```
byte[] texCoords = {0, 1,    1, 1,    0, 0,    1, 0};

VertexArray vertexTexCoords
  = new VertexArray(texCoords.length / 2, 2, 1);
vertexTexCoords.set(0, texCoords.length / 2, texCoords);

vertexBuffer.setTexCoords(0, vertexTexCoords, 1, null);
vertexBuffer.setTexCoords(1, vertexTexCoords, 1, null);
```

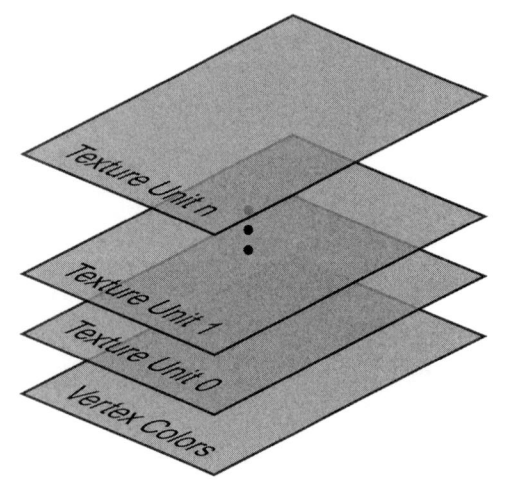

Figure 7.3
Texture blending.

Afterward, you can set two textures in your mesh's appearance:

```
appearance.setTexture(0, new Texture2D(image1));
appearance.setTexture(1, new Texture2D(image2));
```

After finishing these preparations, `Texture2D.setBlending()` defines how the layers are merged.

Blending Modes

Texture unit zero's blending mode determines how to merge unit zero with vertex colors, texture unit one's blending mode determines how to merge unit one with unit zero, and so forth, until all layers are merged.

When two layers are blended:

- C_f and A_f are the color and transparency values of the lower layer.
- C_t and A_t are the color and transparency values of the upper layer.
- C_c is the blending color set with `Texture2D.setBlendColor()`.
- C_v and A_v are the results of the blending operation.

Using these definitions, you can look up the result of the blending in the following table. Apart from the blending mode in `Texture2D`, the pixel format of the `Image2D` object used as the texture also plays a role in determining the result.

Tip

`Texture2D`'s default blending mode is FUNC_MODULATE. Whenever you don't need vertex colors, use FUNC_REPLACE by calling `texture.setBlending()`. This speeds up rendering because M3G doesn't have to process a blending operation.

Texture Format	Blending Mode				
	FUNC_REPLACE	FUNC_MODULATE	FUNC_DECAL	FUNC_BLEND	FUNC_ADD
ALPHA	$C_v = C_f$ $A_v = A_t$	$C_v = C_f$ $A_v = A_f A_t$	undefined	$C_v = C_f$ $A_v = A_f A_t$	$C_v = C_f$ $A_v = A_f A_t$
LUMINANCE	$C_v = C_t$ $A_v = A_f$	$C_v = C_f C_t$ $A_v = A_f$	undefined	$C_v = C_f(1-C_t) + C_c C_t$ $A_v = A_f$	$C_v = C_f + C_t$ $A_v = A_f$

(Continued)

Texture Format	Blending Mode				
	FUNC_REPLACE	FUNC_MODULATE	FUNC_DECAL	FUNC_BLEND	FUNC_ADD
LUMINANCE_ALPHA	$C_v = C_t$	$C_v = C_f C_t$	undefined	$C_v = C_f(1-C_t) + C_c C_t$	$C_v = C_f + C_t$
	$A_v = A_t$	$A_v = A_f A_t$		$A_v = A_f A_t$	$A_v = A_f A_t$
RGB	$C_v = C_t$	$C_v = C_f C_t$	$C_v = C_t$	$C_v = C_f(1-C_t) + C_c C_t$	$C_v = C_f + C_t$
	$A_v = A_f$	$A_v = A_f$	$A_v = A_f$	$A_v = A_f$	$A_v = A_f$
RGBA	$C_v = C_t$	$C_v = C_f C_t$	$C_v = C_f(1-A_t) + C_t A_t$	$C_v = C_f(1-C_t) + C_c C_t$	$C_v = C_f + C_t$
	$A_v = A_t$	$A_v = A_f A_t$	$A_v = A_f$	$A_v = A_f A_t$	$A_v = A_f A_t$

Some blending operations are the same as for `CompositingMode`, others are exclusive to `Texture2D`. For identical blending operations, you can replace multi-texturing with compositing by drawing the same mesh geometry with different textures and blending the meshes with `CompositeMode` settings. That way, you can achieve multi-texturing even if your M3G implementation has only one texture unit.

Note

At the end of this chapter, you'll see an example of this technique.

Adding Fog for Realism

Be it pollution or haze, the visibility when you look at the horizon is limited. Fog is often added to make outside scenes more realistic by simulating this effect and fading 3D objects into the fog color. Fog is a per-object property and can be easily enabled by adding it to the object's appearance.

Creating Fog

In `FogSample`, you see disc-shaped objects placed at increasing distance to the camera. Figure 7.4 shows how fog changes their color.

Without fog, the shapes merge into one blob because they all have the same color. With fog applied, the shapes change from white (the shape's color) to black (the fog's color). Linear and exponential fog modes decide how quickly one color blends into the other.

Tip

Fog is a simple way to add depth to a scene without the use of lighting.

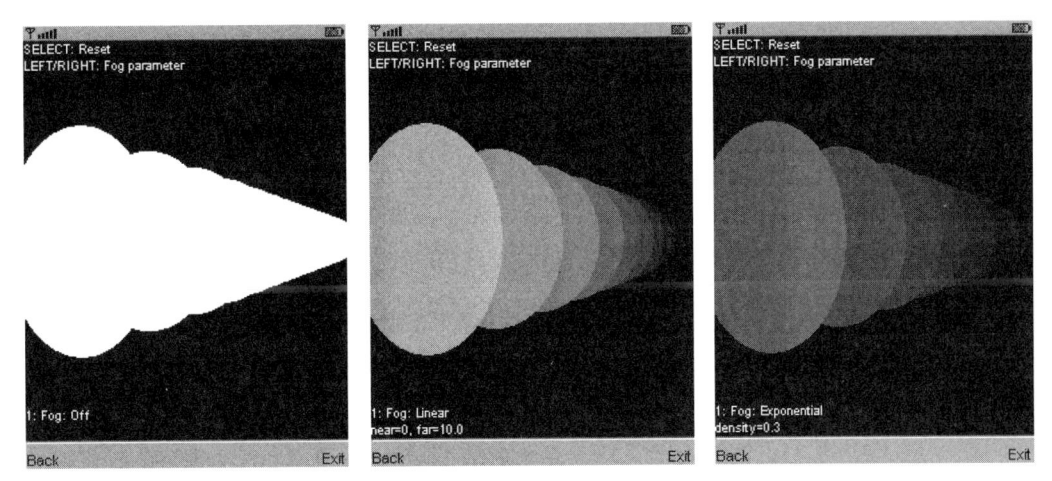

Figure 7.4
Discs rendered in increasing distance to the camera. Left picture is without fog, middle picture is with linear fog, and the right picture is with exponential fog.

`FogSample` contains a member of type `Fog` that contains the fog properties. `init()` instantiates the object as shown in the following code:

```
/**
 * Sample demonstrating fog.
 *
 * @author Claus Hoefele
 */
public class FogSample extends GameCanvas implements Sample {
  /** Mesh for display. */
  private Mesh mesh = MeshFactory2D.createDisc(32);
  /** The mesh's transformation. */
  private Transform meshTransform = new Transform();
  ...

  /** 3D graphics singleton used for rendering. */
  private Graphics3D graphics3d;
  /** 2D graphics singleton used for rendering. */
  private Graphics graphics;

  /**
   * Constructor.
   */
  public FogSample() {
    super(false);
  }
```

Chapter 7 ■ Blending and Transparency

```java
/**
 * Initializes the sample.
 */
public void init() {
  // Get the singletons for rendering.
  graphics3d = Graphics3D.getInstance();
  graphics = getGraphics();

  // Initialize fog.
  mesh.getVertexBuffer().setDefaultColor(0xFFFFFF); // white
  fog = new Fog();
  currentFogMode = FOG_MODE_LINEAR;
  fogParam = FOG_PARAM_FAR;
  setFogMode(mesh, fog, currentFogMode, fogParam);

  // Create a camera with perspective projection.
  Camera camera = new Camera();
  float aspect = (float) getWidth() / (float) getHeight();
  camera.setPerspective(60, aspect, 1, 1000);
  Transform cameraTransform = new Transform();
  cameraTransform.postTranslate(2.5f, 0, 2);
  cameraTransform.postRotate(32, 0, 1, 0);
  graphics3d.setCamera(camera, cameraTransform);

  render(graphics);
  flushGraphics();
  }
  ...
}
```

The interesting part happens in `setFogMode()`, which sets the fog parameters. Let's first finish the rendering.

```java
/**
 * Renders the sample.
 *
 * @param graphics graphics context for rendering.
 */
private void render(Graphics graphics) {
  graphics3d.bindTarget(graphics);
  graphics3d.setViewport(0, 0, getWidth(), getHeight());
  graphics3d.clear(null);
```

```
  // Draw 15 discs in a row.
  for (int i=0; i<15; i++) {
    meshTransform.setIdentity();
    meshTransform.postTranslate(0, 0, -i);
    graphics3d.render(mesh, meshTransform);
  }

  graphics3d.releaseTarget();
  drawMenu(graphics); // displays the current key assignment
}
```

`init()` already moved the camera to the side so you can see the meshes behind each other with a decreasing *z* value. Each mesh is one unit apart, so it gives you a good idea of the distance to the camera.

Coming back to the fog parameters, Table 7.2 shows the interface to `Fog`. When instantiated, you can set the destination color of the blending operation with `setColor()`.

Table 7.2 Fog Class Description

Method	Description
Fog Modes	
`static int EXPONENTIAL`	Fog increases exponentially with distance to the camera.
`static int LINEAR`	Fog increases linearly with distance to the camera.
Construction	
`Fog()`	Default values are linear fog mode, density set to 1.0, near distance 0.0, far distance 1.0, and color 0x00000000.
General Methods	
`void setColor(int RGB)`	Changes the fog blending color.
`int getColor()`	Getter for fog color.
`void setMode(int mode)`	Changes the fog mode (LINEAR or EXPONENTIAL).
`int getMode()`	Getter for fog mode.
Linear Fog	
`void setLinear(float near, float far)`	Sets near and far distances for linear fog mode.
`float getFarDistance()`	Getter for far distance.
`float getNearDistance()`	Getter for near distance.
Exponential Fog	
`void setDensity(float density)`	Sets density value for exponential fog.
`float getDensity()`	Getter for density.

The source color depends on what method you used to create the look of your mesh. M3G applies fog after determining the final color of your mesh; vertex colors, lighting, or texturing are taken into account. `FogSample` sets the mesh's default color in `VertexBuffer` to white and the fog color to black. Because the background is black as well, this will make the disc shapes invisible with increasing distance.

Fog Modes

When calculating the final color of a fogged object, the source color is blended with the fog color depending on a blending factor. This factor is clamped to the range of [0, 1]. If it's one, the source color remains unchanged; if it's zero, the fog color takes over completely. Any value in between is a linear interpolation of both colors.

The blending factor changes with the distance to the camera using either a linear or an exponential equation. For linear fog, this is given as

$$f = \frac{far - z}{far - near}$$

where *far* and *near* are the values set with `Fog.setLinear()` and z is the camera's distance to the fragment.

In contrast, the blending factor for exponential fog is computed by

$$f = e^{-density \cdot z}$$

This function depends on the *density* parameter passed to `setDensity()`. Figure 7.5 shows plots of the fog blending factor *f* in relation to the distance *z* of a fragment to the camera.

Linear fog results in a straight line. With exponential fog, the blending factor decreases quickly and then approaches zero slowly. Higher values for the density cause the slope to increase.

Adding Fog for Realism

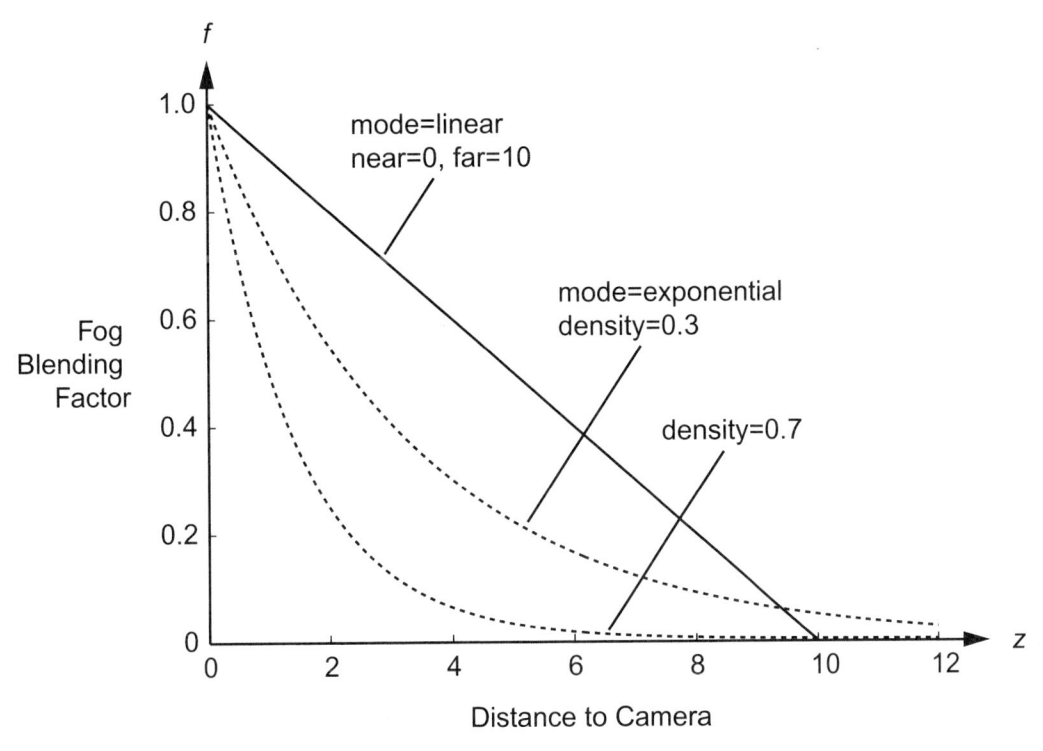

Figure 7.5
Linear and exponential fog.

The following code snippet shows how to switch between fog modes and adjust the parameters:

```
/** Initial value for far distance of linear fog. */
private static final float FOG_PARAM_FAR            = 10;
/** Initial value for density of exponential fog. */
private static final float FOG_PARAM_DENSITY        = 0.3f;
/** Fog object. */
private Fog fog;
/** The current fog parameter. Stores the far distance for linear
  * fog; density for exponential fog. */
private float fogParam;

/** Identifier representing linear fog. */
private static final int FOG_MODE_LINEAR            = 0;
/** Identifier representing exponential fog. */
private static final int FOG_MODE_EXPONENTIAL       = 1;
/** Identifier representing disabled fog. */
```

```
    private static final int FOG_MODE_OFF                    = 2;
    /** Number of fog mode identifiers. */
    private static final int NUMBER_OF_FOG_MODES             = 3;

    /** Current fog mode. */
    private int currentFogMode;

    /**
     * Sets the current fog parameters.
     *
     * @param mesh target of fog.
     * @param fog Fog object.
     * @param mode fog mode.
     * @param param far distance for linear fog, density for exponential
     *              fog, otherwise ignored.
     */
    private void setFogMode(Mesh mesh, Fog fog, int mode, float param) {
      switch (mode) {
        case FOG_MODE_EXPONENTIAL:
          fog.setDensity(param);
          fog.setMode(Fog.EXPONENTIAL);
          mesh.getAppearance(0).setFog(fog);
          break;

        case FOG_MODE_LINEAR:
          fog.setLinear(0, param);
          fog.setMode(Fog.LINEAR);
          mesh.getAppearance(0).setFog(fog);
          break;

        case FOG_MODE_OFF:
          mesh.getAppearance(0).setFog(null);
          break;

          // no default
      }
    }
```

`param` either contains the far distance value for linear fog or the density for exponential fog. In `FogSample`, you can change the value by pressing the left and right keys. Switching between modes happens with the `GAME_A` key. Apart from linear and exponential fog, you can also disable fog by setting the property in `Appearance` to `null`. The following code shows the key handler.

```java
/**
 *  Handles key presses.
 *
 * @param keyCode key code.
 */
protected void keyPressed(int keyCode) {
  switch (getGameAction(keyCode)) {
    case GAME_A:
      currentFogMode++;
      currentFogMode %= NUMBER_OF_FOG_MODES;
      if (currentFogMode == FOG_MODE_LINEAR) {
        fogParam = FOG_PARAM_FAR;
      } else {
        fogParam = FOG_PARAM_DENSITY;
      }
      setFogMode(mesh, fog, currentFogMode, fogParam);
      break;

    case LEFT:
      if (currentFogMode == FOG_MODE_LINEAR) {
        fogParam -= 1;
      } else {
        fogParam *= 1.3f;
      }
      setFogMode(mesh, fog, currentFogMode, fogParam);
      break;

    case RIGHT:
      if (currentFogMode == FOG_MODE_LINEAR) {
        fogParam += 1;
      } else {
        fogParam *= 0.7f;
      }
      setFogMode(mesh, fog, currentFogMode, fogParam);
      break;

    case FIRE:
      init();
      break;

    // no default
  }

  render(graphics);
  flushGraphics();
}
```

Creating an Emboss Effect

Embossing is an effect you can achieve with blending. The same technique is used in computer interfaces to indicate that a button is pressed. You can see when a button is down because its shading is different from the up state. Using embossing, you can show cracks and scratches in a wall or simulate ripples in water without adding geometry.

Creating the Emboss Image

Embossing needs a grayscale image that encodes the shading information. You create this image from two base images. The first one has a background color of 50% gray (0.5, 0.5, 0.5), which is exactly half the value between black (0.0, 0.0, 0.0) and white (1.0, 1.0, 1.0). From this background, you carve out the shape you want to create with any gray tone between 50% gray and black. The second image is the same image as the first one; except it is inverted. Figure 7.6 shows these two images. The first one displays the word "Emboss" in black on a gray background.

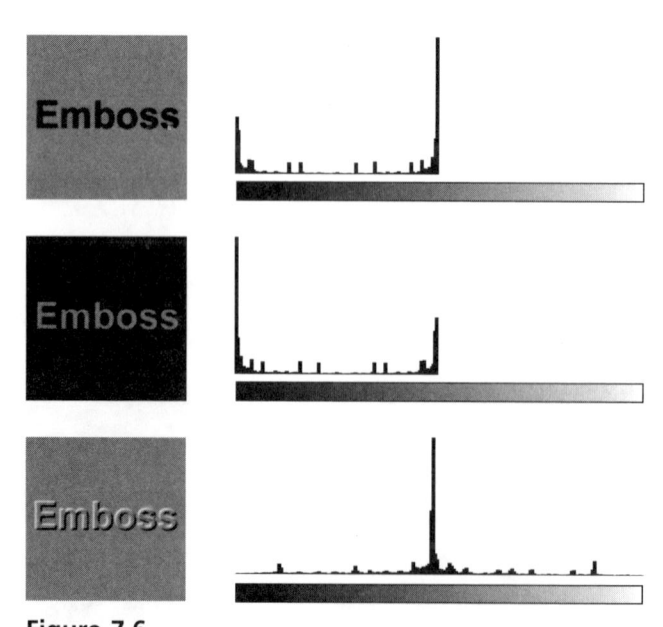

Figure 7.6
Histograms of images used for embossing. The upper image is the original grayscale image, the middle image is the inverted version of the same image, and the lower image is the overlaid result.

The inverted image shows a gray "Emboss" on a black background. To smooth out the hard transitions between colors, the images are slightly blurred.

It's important that both images use only the lower half of the spectrum of gray colors, because in the next step you slightly move both images against each other, say two pixels in x and y direction, and add the color values together. This creates white where two 50% gray colors overlap, gray where black and gray colors meet, and black where both colors are black. The added image thus uses the full spectrum again. In Figure 7.6, you can follow this operation by looking at the distribution of gray colors in the histograms next to the images. The bottom image is the result after adding the first to the second image.

All that's left is to modulate the appearance of a mesh with the emboss images you have just created. You could use the composite image to do this. However, adding the base images together manually with M3G's texture-combine function allows you to vary the amount of gap between the images. The gap determines the strength of the effect and enables you to choose between creating a dent or a bulge. The disadvantage is that each image occupies memory and a separate texture unit.

Embossing a Texture

A grayscale image darkens another image by multiplication. In the case of the emboss image, you want to darken and lighten the other image at the same time. The `CompositingMode.MODULATE_X2` operator achieves this by multiplying two colors and multiplying the result by two; this effectively cancels out the gray. Figure 7.7 shows the result.

`Texture2D` only offers `FUNC_MODULATE`. If you wanted to create the effect with multi-texturing alone, you could add the wood texture twice, but that would

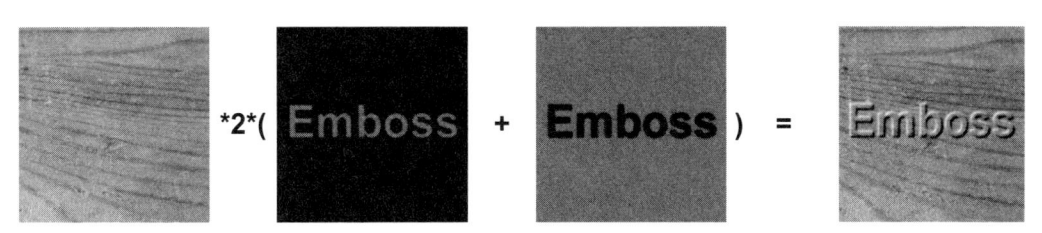

Figure 7.7
Multiplying the base texture with the emboss images creates the final effect.

require four texture units (twice the wood texture plus the two emboss images). With compositing, on the other hand, you render your mesh in two passes: first the original mesh with the wood texture and, second, the same mesh with the two emboss textures and `CompositingMode.MODULATE_X2` applied. This requires only two texture units, which is much more likely to be supported by real devices. Texturing happens before compositing in the order of the render pipeline; hence the emboss images are blended first and the result modulated with the wood texture. The following code creates this setup:

Note

This sample is implemented in EmbossEffect.java and EmbossingSample.java, which you can find on the accompanying CD-ROM.

```
/**
 * Blends images to achieve an emboss effect.
 *
 * @author Claus Hoefele
 * @see EmbossingSample
 */
public class EmbossEffect {
  /** Mesh for the emboss effect. */
  private Mesh mesh;
  ...

  /**
   * Applies an emboss effect to a mesh. The mesh must have texture
   * coordinates set in texture unit 0.
   *
   * @param mesh mesh for the emboss effect.
   * @param embossMap1 emboss map.
   * @param embossMap2 inverted version of embossMap1.
   */
  public EmbossEffect(Mesh mesh,
      Image2D embossMap1, Image2D embossMap2) {
    if (mesh.getVertexBuffer().getTexCoords(0, null) == null) {
      throw new IllegalArgumentException("Mesh must have" +
          "texture coordinates set.");
    }

    // Create the appearance for the second pass. The compositing mode
    // influences how first and second pass blend.
```

```java
        CompositingMode compositingMode = new CompositingMode();
        compositingMode.setBlending(CompositingMode.MODULATE_X2);
        Appearance appearance = new Appearance();
        appearance.setCompositingMode(compositingMode);

        // Force second pass to render after first pass. This function
        // throws an exception if the original mesh's layer > 62.
        appearance.setLayer(mesh.getAppearance(0).getLayer() + 1);

        // Copy texture coordinates from texture unit 0 to unit 1 because
        // second pass has two textures.
        float[] scaleBias = new float[4];
        float[] bias = new float[3];
        VertexBuffer vertexBuffer = mesh.getVertexBuffer();
        VertexArray texCoords = vertexBuffer.getTexCoords(0, scaleBias);
        System.arraycopy(scaleBias, 1, bias, 0, 3);
        vertexBuffer.setTexCoords(1, texCoords, scaleBias[0], bias);

        // Set the two emboss textures with FUNC_ADD operator.
        Texture2D texture1 = new Texture2D(embossMap1);
        texture1.setBlending(Texture2D.FUNC_REPLACE);
        appearance.setTexture(0, texture1);
        Texture2D texture2 = new Texture2D(embossMap2);
        texture2.setBlending(Texture2D.FUNC_ADD);
        appearance.setTexture(1, texture2);

        // Create new mesh with two submeshes; one for each render pass.
        this.mesh = new Mesh(mesh.getVertexBuffer(),
            new IndexBuffer[] {
                mesh.getIndexBuffer(0), mesh.getIndexBuffer(0)},
            new Appearance[] {mesh.getAppearance(0), appearance});

        // Initial strength of embossing effect.
        setGap(0.005f);
    }
    ...
}
```

You need two `Appearance` objects for the two-pass technique; one with the wood texture and one with the emboss images. Because both are applied to the same mesh geometry, you can create a `Mesh` object with two submeshes. The submeshes have the same `IndexBuffer` but different `Appearance` objects. You can enforce the correct render order of the submeshes by setting the layer of the second appearance to a higher value than the layer of the first.

For the first pass, the constructor keeps the original appearance unmodified. This leaves the look of the mesh up to the client of `EmbossEffect`. In `EmbossingSample`, the mesh has a wood texture set.

The second pass requires an `Appearance` with the emboss images and `CompositingMode.MODULATE_X2` set. For the two textures, the constructor creates the texture coordinates and sets the `Texture2D.FUNC_ADD` blending mode for texture unit 1. Texture unit 0 can be set to `FUNC_REPLACE` because the second pass doesn't require vertex colors.

To see any effect, you have to move one emboss image slightly with `setGap()`. You see the contents of this function here:

```
/** Strength of embossing effect. */
private float gap;

/**
 * Sets the strength of the embossing effect. A positive value will
 * create an bulge; a negative value a dent.
 *
 * @param gap distance between emboss images.
 */
public void setGap(float gap) {
  this.gap = gap;
  Texture2D texture = mesh.getAppearance(1).getTexture(1);
  texture.setTranslation(gap, gap, 0);
}

/**
 *  Getter for gap.
 *
 * @return distance between emboss images.
 */
public float getGap() {
  return gap;
}

/**
 *  Inverts the distance between emboss images, thus switching
 *  between creating a bulge or a dent.
```

```
  */
  public void invertGap() {
    setGap(-getGap());
  }
  /**
   * Renders the mesh with emboss effect.
   *
   * @param graphics graphics context.
   * @param transform mesh transformation.
   */
  public void render(Graphics3D graphics, Transform transform) {
    graphics.render(mesh, transform);
  }
```

`setGap()` translates the second texture of the second pass, which will create an overlap and thus the emboss effect. Larger values will strengthen the effect; a negative value will create the impression of a dent rather than a bulge. Because `EmbossEffect`'s `mesh` member stores all compositing and texture information, all you have to do at render time is draw the mesh.

Using the Emboss Effect

`EmbossingSample` is the canvas that loads the images and renders the embossed mesh:

```
/**
 * Demonstrates embossing.
 *
 * @author Claus Hoefele
 * @see EmbossEffect
 */
public class EmbossingSample extends GameCanvas implements Sample {
  /** Instance of the emboss effect. */
  private EmbossEffect embossEffect;

  /** 3D graphics singleton used for rendering. */
  private Graphics3D graphics3d;
  /** 2D graphics singleton used for rendering. */
  private Graphics graphics;

  /** Creates a new instance of EmbossSample */
  public EmbossingSample() {
```

```
    super(false);
  }

  /**
   * Initializes the sample.
   */
  public void init() {
    graphics3d = Graphics3D.getInstance();
    graphics = getGraphics();

    try {
      Image2D baseTexture
          = (Image2D) Loader.load("/m3g07/wood.png")[0];
      Image2D embossMap
          = (Image2D) Loader.load("/m3g07/text_bump.png")[0];
      Image2D embossMapInv
          = (Image2D) Loader.load("/m3g07/text_bump_inv.png")[0];

      Mesh mesh = MeshFactory2D.createQuad(true);
      Texture2D texture = new Texture2D(baseTexture);
      texture.setBlending(Texture2D.FUNC_REPLACE);
      mesh.getAppearance(0).setTexture(0, texture);
      embossEffect = new EmbossEffect(mesh, embossMap, embossMapInv);
    } catch (Exception e) {
      e.printStackTrace();
    }

    // Create a camera with perspective projection.
    Camera camera = new Camera();
    float aspect = (float) getWidth() / (float) getHeight();
    camera.setPerspective(60, aspect, 1, 1000);
    Transform cameraTransform = new Transform();
    cameraTransform.postTranslate(0, 0, 3);
    graphics3d.setCamera(camera, cameraTransform);

    render(graphics);
    flushGraphics();
  }

  /**
   * Renders the sample.
   *
   * @param graphics graphics context for rendering.
   */
```

```java
  private void render(Graphics graphics) {
    graphics3d.bindTarget(graphics);
    graphics3d.setViewport(0, 0, getWidth(), getHeight());
    graphics3d.clear(null);
    embossEffect.render(graphics3d, null);
    graphics3d.releaseTarget();

    drawMenu(graphics); // displays the current key assignment
  }

  /**
   * Handles key presses.
   *
   * @param keyCode key code.
   */
  protected void keyPressed(int keyCode) {
    switch (getGameAction(keyCode)) {
      case GAME_A:
        embossEffect.invertGap();
        break;

      case LEFT:
        embossEffect.setGap(embossEffect.getGap() - 0.001f);
        break;

      case RIGHT:
        embossEffect.setGap(embossEffect.getGap() + 0.001f);
        break;

      case FIRE:
        init();
        break;

        // no default
    }

    render(graphics);
    flushGraphics();
  }
  ...
}
```

You can decrease the resolution of the emboss images; their quality is not that important for the effect. As already mentioned, another way of saving memory is to composite the emboss images beforehand. On the other hand, keeping the images separately enables you to simulate a moving light by changing the distance between images according to the light source's position. You can also dynamically change the emboss effect to simulate moving ripples in water.

You could also automatically generate the second emboss image from the first. To do this, load the first image with `Image.createImage()` and read the contents with `Image.getRGB()`. Because you are dealing with a grayscale image, all color channels will have the same value. Then, for every pixel, build the difference between 128 and the value in one of the color channels at this position. This will give you the inverted image because the emboss image uses gray colors with a maximum value of 128.

If your device doesn't have two texture units, you can change the code to a three-pass algorithm. Instead of `Texture2D.FUNC_ADD`, you would then use `Compositing.ALPHA_ADD`. Multi-texturing is faster than compositing though.

Summary

Blending and transparency are powerful tools for achieving effects. In this chapter, you saw how to composite fragments, use multi-texturing, and create fog.

Fog is easy to add to your meshes and works with exponential or linear equations. You use it to blend your scene into the fog color.

Compositing and multi-texturing work with blending modes that define how two colors are merged. Depending on the effect you want to achieve, you can replace one with the other. If you have the choice, you should use multi-texturing rather than compositing for performance reasons. Be aware, though, that an M3G implementation isn't required to support more than one texture unit. At the end of the chapter, you saw compositing and multi-texturing together to create an emboss effect.

CHAPTER 8

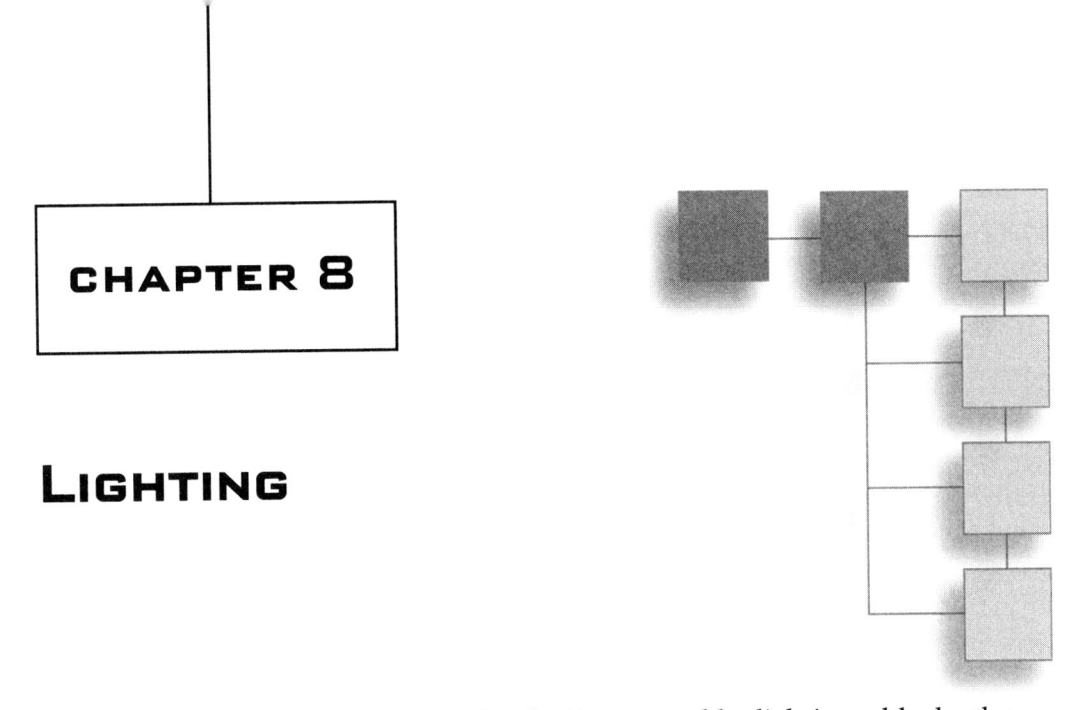

Lighting

Without light, surfaces look flat. The shading caused by lighting adds depth to a scene. To simulate lighting, M3G offers different light types that you can use to illuminate your scene. On the receiving side, an object reflects this light according to material characteristics.

This chapter shows you:

- What normals are and how to define them.
- The types of light sources M3G offers.
- How to change material properties.
- Alternatives to dynamic lighting.

Lighting in M3G

Because of the complex nature of the involved physics, it's especially difficult and computationally expensive to simulate light in 3D graphics. In M3G's model, you need three items to make lighting work: a light source that defines the type of light, material properties that describe how light is reflected from an object, and a normal vector that influences the direction of the reflected light.

M3G's Lighting Model

Light comes in various forms: light bulbs, the sun, and a flashlight, among others. Their counterparts in M3G are omnidirectional, directional, and spot light. Each type has different properties such as location or direction.

Light also bounces off objects and illuminates other objects nearby. If you switch on your bedroom light, some light will reach under the bed even if the light doesn't have a direct path to it. To achieve interactive frame rates, M3G uses a simpler alternative to realistic reflections: ambient light. Ambient light illuminates objects from every direction at a constant rate. You could model the bed scene with an ambient light to lighten up all objects to some degree and create an additional omnidirectional light. `Light` is M3G's representation of light properties.

Material is the light's antagonist and defines how a surface reflects light. In M3G's lighting model, four components contribute to the final shading color:

- **Emission**. An object can send out light to imitate glowing objects.
- **Ambient reflection**. The light reflected from an ambient light source.
- **Diffuse reflection**. The reflected light is scattered equally in all directions.
- **Specular reflection**. The light reflected from objects with a shiny surface.

In contrast to OpenGL, which allows you to specify these four components for both light and material separately, M3G retrieves the attributes from the object's material exclusively. Combinations of these properties are stored in `Material`. For example, a chrome ball's diffuse color would be silver and its specular component white. A neon sign on the other hand would have a large emissive component.

Finding Normals

If you point a flashlight to a mirror that is facing you, the light will reflect back to you. If the mirror is tilted, the light will reflect at an angle. The general idea is that you need a direction vector that defines the orientation of a surface and influences the path of the reflected light. This vector is called a *normal vector,* or *normal* for short. M3G calculates the shading based on the normal, the light and material properties, and the camera's location. Normals are vertex attributes. Figure 8.1 displays two different ways to define normals for a cube.

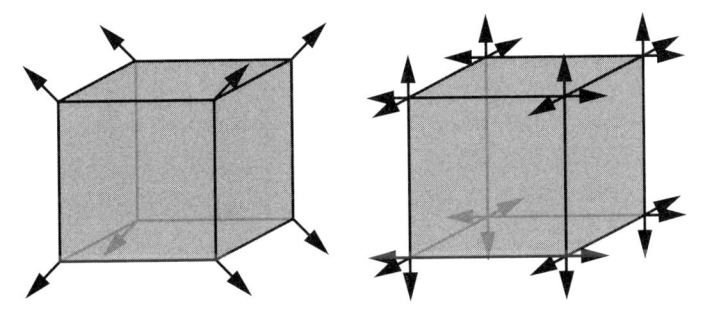

Figure 8.1
Two ways to define cube normals.

In the simplest case, you can define a cube from eight vertices. However, this would result in an incorrectly shaded cube because you can specify only one normal per vertex. If you averaged the surface normals of each side and assigned the result to a vertex, the normals would appear as shown for the left cube in Figure 8.1. The corners acquire a round look because the shading color is shared. No matter how you defined the normal for one vertex, it wouldn't be correct for all of the three adjacent surfaces. Hence, to create a hard edge, you must duplicate vertices, which is shown for the right cube in Figure 8.1.

This is the definition of the cube's normals with four vertices for each side:

```
public static Mesh createCube(boolean addColors, boolean addNormals,
    boolean addTexCoords) {
  VertexBuffer vertexBuffer = new VertexBuffer();

  ////
  //// Vertex positions.
  ////
  byte[] positions = {
    -1, -1,  1,  1, -1,  1, -1,  1,  1,  1,  1,  1, // front
     1, -1, -1, -1, -1, -1,  1,  1, -1, -1,  1, -1, // back
     1, -1,  1,  1, -1, -1,  1,  1,  1,  1,  1, -1, // right
    -1, -1, -1, -1, -1,  1, -1,  1, -1, -1,  1,  1, // left
    -1,  1,  1,  1,  1,  1, -1,  1, -1,  1,  1, -1, // top
    -1, -1, -1,  1, -1, -1, -1, -1,  1,  1, -1,  1  // bottom
  };

  VertexArray vertexPositions
      = new VertexArray(positions.length/3, 3, 1);
```

```
      vertexPositions.set(0, positions.length/3, positions);
      vertexBuffer.setPositions(vertexPositions, 1, null);

      ////
      //// Triangles.
      ////
      int[] triangleLengths = {4, 4, 4, 4, 4, 4};
      TriangleStripArray triangles
          = new TriangleStripArray(0, triangleLengths);

      ////
      //// Normals.
      ////
      if (addNormals) {
        byte max = Byte.MAX_VALUE;
        byte min = Byte.MIN_VALUE;
        byte[] normals = {
          0, 0, max,   0, 0, max,   0, 0, max,   0, 0, max,   // front
          0, 0, min,   0, 0, min,   0, 0, min,   0, 0, min,   // back
          max, 0, 0,   max, 0, 0,   max, 0, 0,   max, 0, 0,   // right
          min, 0, 0,   min, 0, 0,   min, 0, 0,   min, 0, 0,   // left
          0, max, 0,   0, max, 0,   0, max, 0,   0, max, 0,   // top
          0, min, 0,   0, min, 0,   0, min, 0,   0, min, 0,   // bottom
        };

        VertexArray vertexNormals
            = new VertexArray(normals.length/3, 3, 1);
        vertexNormals.set(0, normals.length/3, normals);
        vertexBuffer.setNormals(vertexNormals);
      }

      return new Mesh(vertexBuffer, triangles, new Appearance());
    }
```

Note

The normals described in this section are implemented in m3g04\mesh\MeshFactory3D.java.

The lighting computations require the normal vector's length to equal 1. When calling VertexBuffer.setNormals(), M3G interprets a maximum positive integer value in the VertexArray as +1 and a maximum negative integer value as −1. The example uses bytes, which means that Byte.MAX_VALUE (127) maps to +1 and Byte.MIN_VALUE (−128) to −1. If you used short values, this would be

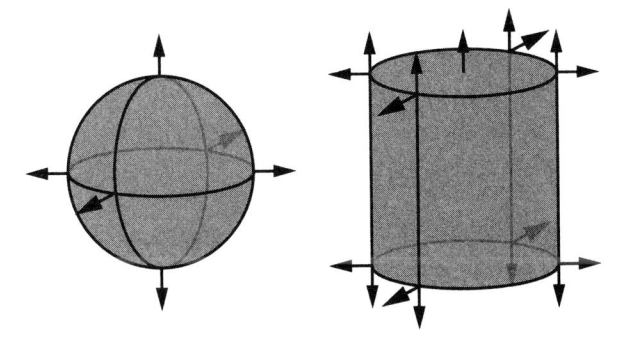

Figure 8.2
Normals for a sphere and cylinder.

`Short.MAX_VALUE` (32767) and `Short.MIN_VALUE` (–32768), respectively. In the previous code example, the normals are already unit length, but M3G will normalize them automatically before using them if they are not.

Figure 8.2 shows two more examples how to define normals. Because a sphere doesn't have any hard edges, getting the normals is very simple—you can just reuse the vertex positions. They already point in the right direction, so you avoid additional memory for normals by passing the same `VertexArray` that you created for the vertex positions to `VertexBuffer.setNormals()`.

Tip
> When passing an array to `VertexArray.set()`, the values are copied in. `VertexArrays`, on the other hand, are stored in a `VertexBuffer` as a reference. If you want to save memory, reuse the same `VertexArray` object and not the array with the vertex values themselves.

The cylinder is a combination of a round surface at the body and hard edges at the top and the bottom cap. You can have a look at the class `MeshFactory3D` to see how to define its normals.

Computing Normals

For less regular shapes, such as the teapot, it's not as easy to find normals. The most generic algorithm used to compute normals is to take the normal of each surface adjacent to a vertex, add all normals, and average the result. If you defined a rectangular grid of triangle strips for example, one vertex in the middle of the grid is surrounded by six triangles. To get the six normals, you build the cross product of two edges of each triangle. Then, you have to make each normal unit length, otherwise large triangles will influence the result more than smaller ones. To get the average, you just add all normals together and divide them by six.

If you have a mathematical description of the surface, such as in the case of the Bézier curve, you can work with the first derivative of the equation. When using cubic Bézier curves, the derivative is a quadratic function, which describes the tangents at each point. For a Bézier patch, you need two tangents: one in s direction and one in t direction. The cross product of these vectors is the normal.

> **Note**
>
> You can find the implementation of the normal calculation in m3g04\mesh\Bezier.java. As with the cubic function in Chapter 4, the quadratic function is evaluated with forward differencing.

Lighting Quality

The correct placement of normals is essential to good lighting, but several other factors contribute to the quality as well.

First of all, you can decide how the shading color is distributed over the triangle. Similar to vertex colors, `PolygonMode.SHADE_FLAT` will take the third vertex's lighting color and fill the whole triangle with it. `PolygonMode.SHADE_SMOOTH`, on the other hand, will produce a different shading color for each pixel. An implementation is free to decide how this is exactly done, but realistically, it will compute the lighting color at each vertex and interpolate the result inside the triangle (called *Gouraud shading*). Per-pixel shading (called *Phong shading*), as is available on state-of-the-art graphics hardware for desktop computers, is not yet commonplace for mobile devices.

You can improve lighting by increasing the number of vertices. More vertices mean less distance between them and fewer errors through interpolation. Gouraud shading is especially prone to errors because it evaluates the lighting model at the vertices only. If you point a spot light on a large polygon and the cone doesn't illuminate the vertices, the light will be missed altogether. In this case, you might want to add more vertices just for the sake of lighting and weigh up performance versus quality. Once you determine the number of vertices, it's also important that your device supports a high color resolution because lighting produces finely graded colors.

> **Note**
>
> Most of the screenshots in this book are taken with the Wireless Toolkit emulator's DefaultColorPhone device. This device specifies a color resolution of 12 bits, which doesn't look very good for lighting. To get better pictures, I took the screenshots with the emulator set to a resolution of 16 bits.

The color resolution of a device in the WTK is defined in a file called <device name>.properties. You can find it in the WTK installation directory in wtklib\devices\<device name>. Inside the file, look for the `colorCount` property. To determine what color resolution your hardware supports, you can use the MIDlet introduced in Chapter 3, which reads the information from `Display.numColors()`.

Light Sources

M3G defines four different types of light: an *ambient* light illuminates objects from every direction at a constant rate; a *directional* light emits parallel rays in one direction; an *omnidirectional* light originates in one point and shines equally in all directions; and a *spot light* casts a cone shape and illuminates objects where the cone meets with the surface. Figure 8.3 shows how the rays from these light sources hit a round object.

Depending on the light source, you work with different properties. For example, an omnidirectional light has a position and a directional light a direction, but an ambient light has neither. With an increasing number of constraints comes additional computational complexity. An ambient light is less to compute than a directional light; a directional less than an omnidirectional; and an omnidirectional less than a spot light.

Creating Lights

After instantiating a `Light`, you set the light type with `setMode()`. The parameter can be `AMBIENT`, `DIRECTIONAL`, `OMNI`, or `SPOT`. Have a look at Table 8.1 for the class's interface.

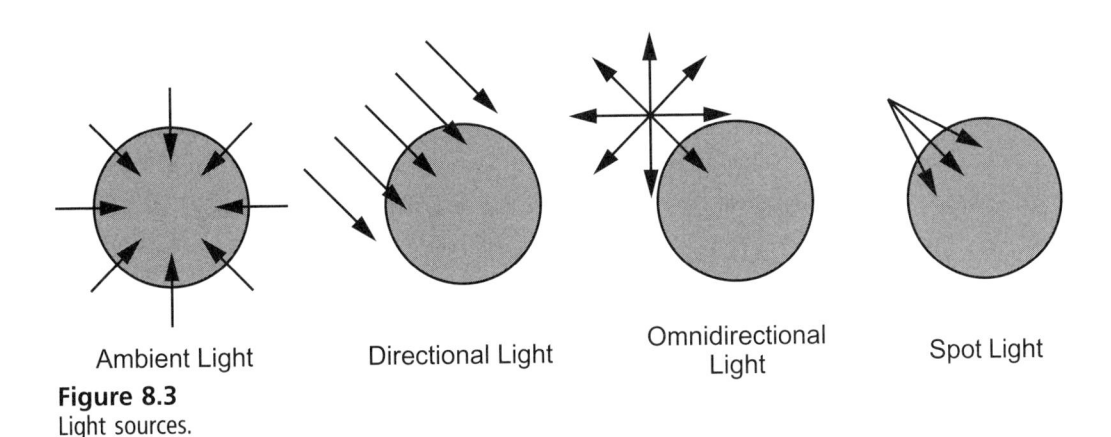

Figure 8.3
Light sources.

Table 8.1 Light Class Description

Method	Description
Light Types	
static int AMBIENT	Light comes from all directions.
static int DIRECTIONAL	Parallel light from one direction (similar to sunlight).
static int OMNI	Light from a point source (similar to a light bulb).
static int SPOT	Light that casts a cone (similar to a spot light).
Construction	
Light()	Default values are DIRECTIONAL light, color set to (1.0, 1.0, 1.0), intensity to 1.0, attenuation to (1, 0, 0), spot angle to 45 degrees, and spot exponent to 0.0.
General Properties	
void setMode(int mode)	Sets the light mode (AMBIENT, DIRECTIONAL, OMNI, or SPOT).
int getMode()	Getter for light mode.
void setColor(int RGB)	Sets the light's color.
int getColor()	Getter for light color.
void setIntensity(float intensity)	Sets the light's intensity.
float getIntensity()	Getter for intensity.
Attenuation (Omni and Spot Lights)	
void setAttenuation (float constant, float linear, float quadratic)	Defines how the distance of the light to the object affects the light's intensity.
float getConstantAttenuation()	Getter for constant component of attenuation.
float getLinearAttenuation()	Getter for linear component of attenuation.
float getQuadraticAttenuation()	Getter for quadratic component of attenuation.
Spot Light Properties	
void setSpotAngle (float angle)	Sets the size of the spot.
float getSpotAngle()	Getter for spot angle.
void setSpotExponent (float exponent)	Affects the distribution of the light. Valid values go from 0.0 to 128.0; larger values produce a more concentrated cone.
float getSpotExponent()	Getter for spot exponent.

> **Note**
>
> The sample is implemented in LightingSample.java, which you can find together with a working MIDlet on the accompanying CD-ROM.

Here is a snippet from `LightingSample` that shows how to create a light:

```java
/**
 * A sphere lit with different light sources.
 *
 * @author Claus Hoefele
 */
public class LightingSample extends GameCanvas implements Sample {
  /** Mesh for display. */
  private Mesh mesh = MeshFactory3D.createSphere(32, 32, true, false);
  /** The mesh's transformation. */
  private Transform meshTransform;

  /** Light for the scene. */
  private Light light;
  /** The light's transformation. */
  private Transform lightTransform = new Transform();
  /** Current rotation value. */
  private float lightRotY;

  ...

  /** 3D graphics singleton used for rendering. */
  private Graphics3D graphics3d;
  /** 2D graphics singleton used for rendering. */
  private Graphics graphics;

  /**
   * Constructor.
   */
  public LightingSample() {
    super(false);
  }

  /**
   * Initializes the sample.
   */
  public void init() {
    // Get the singletons for rendering.
```

```
        graphics3d = Graphics3D.getInstance();
        graphics = getGraphics();

        // Create a camera with perspective projection.
        Camera camera = new Camera();
        float aspect = (float) getWidth() / (float) getHeight();
        camera.setPerspective(60, aspect, 1, 1000);
        graphics3d.setCamera(camera, null);

        // Use default material and position mesh.
        mesh.getAppearance(0).setMaterial(new Material());
        meshTransform = new Transform();
        meshTransform.postTranslate(0, 0, -3);

        // Create light.
        light = new Light();
        lightMode = LIGHT_DIRECTIONAL;
        setLightMode(light, lightMode);
        lightRotY = 30;
        setLight(lightTransform, lightRotY);

        render(graphics);
        flushGraphics();
    }
    ...
}
```

For lighting to work, you need to set a material in the Appearance property of your mesh. More details about materials follow in the next section; at the moment, the default constructor for Material is sufficient. The mesh also needs normals, which are generated by passing true as the third parameter to MeshFactory3D.createSphere().

Setting the light parameters happens in setLightMode(). Apart from within the init() method, this method is also called when pressing the GAME_A key to switch between different modes. Here is what setLightMode() looks like:

```
/** Light mode ambient. */
private static final int LIGHT_AMBIENT          = 0;
/** Light mode directional. */
private static final int LIGHT_DIRECTIONAL      = 1;
/** Light mode omni. */
```

```java
    private static final int LIGHT_OMNI        = 2;
    /** Light mode spot. */
    private static final int LIGHT_SPOT        = 3;
    /** Number of light sources. */
    private static final int NUMBER_OF_LIGHTS  = 4;
    /** Current light mode. */
    private int lightMode;

    /**
     * Sets the light mode.
     *
     * @param light light to be modified.
     * @param mode light mode.
     */
    private void setLightMode(Light light, int mode) {
      switch (mode) {
        case LIGHT_AMBIENT:
          light.setMode(Light.AMBIENT);
          light.setIntensity(2.0f);
          break;

        case LIGHT_DIRECTIONAL:
          light.setMode(Light.DIRECTIONAL);
          light.setIntensity(0.8f);
          break;

        case LIGHT_OMNI:
          light.setMode(Light.OMNI);
          light.setIntensity(2.0f);
          light.setAttenuation(1, 0, 0.5f);
          break;

        case LIGHT_SPOT:
          light.setMode(Light.SPOT);
          light.setIntensity(1);
          light.setAttenuation(1, 0, 0);
          light.setSpotAngle(15.0f);
          break;

          // no default
      }
    }
```

Apart from the mode, common properties for all lights are the color and intensity. The color determines what light a material can reflect. If you point a white light at a red sphere, it will appear red because it absorbs all green and blue color components. On the other hand, if you point a blue light at the same red sphere, there's no red light it can reflect and it will appear black.

The light's color is multiplied by its intensity, which regulates the power of the light source. Extreme intensity values might make sense in the calculation of the lighting model. For example, negative intensities darken an object and large values can be attenuated with the distance.

Other attributes that concern lighting are stored in PolygonMode, which Chapter 4 introduced. With PolygonMode.setLocalCameraLightingEnable(), you can tell M3G to calculate specular highlights based on the real camera position. Otherwise, this position is approximated with (0, 0, –1). Supporting local camera lighting is optional, and you can find out about your implementation with a call to Graphics3D.getProperties(). PolygonMode.setTwoSidedLightingEnable() defines whether the same color is used for both the front and back faces. If you enable two-sided lighting, M3G will calculate a separate color, taking the surface orientation into account.

Once you set up the light, you are ready to enable it in Graphics3D.

```
/**
 * Transforms the light and adds it to the Graphics3D context.
 *
 * @param lightTransform transform object to modify.
 * @param lightRotY rotation value around the y axis.
 */
private void setLight(Transform lightTransform, float lightRotY) {
  lightTransform.setIdentity();
  lightTransform.postTranslate(0, 0, -3);
  lightTransform.postRotate(lightRotY, 0, 1, 0);
  lightTransform.postTranslate(0, 1.5f, 1.5f);
  lightTransform.postRotate(-50, 1, 0, 0);

  graphics3d.resetLights();
  graphics3d.addLight(light, lightTransform);
}
```

addLight() takes a Transform object that defines the light's position and orientation. It depends on the light type whether position and orientation plays a role, but if it does, it works analogous to camera transformation. A light is initially positioned at the origin (0, 0, 0) and oriented toward the negative z axis (0, 0, –1).

The following sections show screenshots of the different light sources. In each case the light illuminates a sphere with 32 slices and 32 stacks from above. You can rotate the light source around the y axis, and the sample constrains the orientation so the light always points toward the sphere.

Ambient Light

The simplest of all lights is ambient light, which adds a constant offset to the shading color of an object; see Figure 8.4. M3G uses a local lighting model, which means that light rays that bounce off other objects aren't taken into account. Ambient light is a work-around to simulate global lighting. It's completely independent of the position and orientation of the light; only the intensity and color can be changed.

Directional Light

This light type takes the direction into account and casts parallel rays onto the sphere as Figure 8.5 shows. Because of the directionality of the light, only half of the sphere is illuminated. The light is strongest at the point nearest to the light and slowly fades out to the sides.

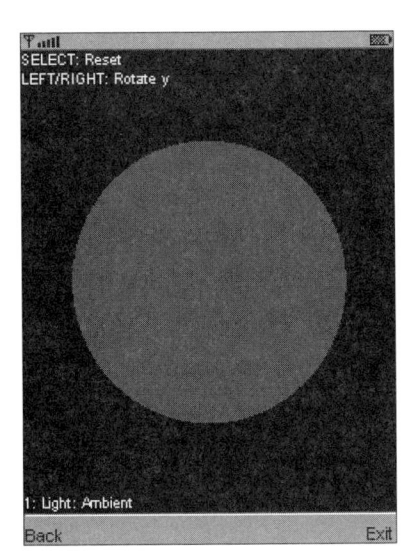

Figure 8.4
Sphere in ambient light.

Figure 8.5
Sphere in directional light.

The color gradient exists because the sphere consists of small triangles with differently oriented normals. If you use an object with a flat surface such as a cube, one side will have the same shading color all over.

Omnidirectional Light

An omnidirectional light, as seen in Figure 8.6, looks similar to a directional light. In this case, however, the position of the light determines where the light rays come from. Its rays extend in a radial manner from the center and illuminate all objects that surround it.

For position-based light sources (omnidirectional and spot), the attenuation regulates how much the distance between the light and the illuminated object plays a role. The settings determine the amount of light that reaches the object as well as how quickly the light falls off with increasing distance. The attenuation factor works together with the intensity and is multiplied with the light's color; however, negative values and zero are not allowed. The attenuation factor f is calculated with the following formula where d is the distance to the light and c, l, and q are the constant, linear, and quadratic parameters passed in `setAttenuation()`.

$$f = \frac{1}{c + ld + qd^2}$$

Figure 8.6
Sphere in omnidirectional light.

You can see plots of sample values in Figure 8.7. By default, (c, l, q) are set to $(1, 0, 0)$; that means no attenuation. The constant factor c determines the start value at the light source $(d=0)$—it works like the reciprocal of the intensity. With l and q, you can define how quickly the light falls off with increasing distance. The linear function causes the attenuation to approach zero slower than the quadratic function.

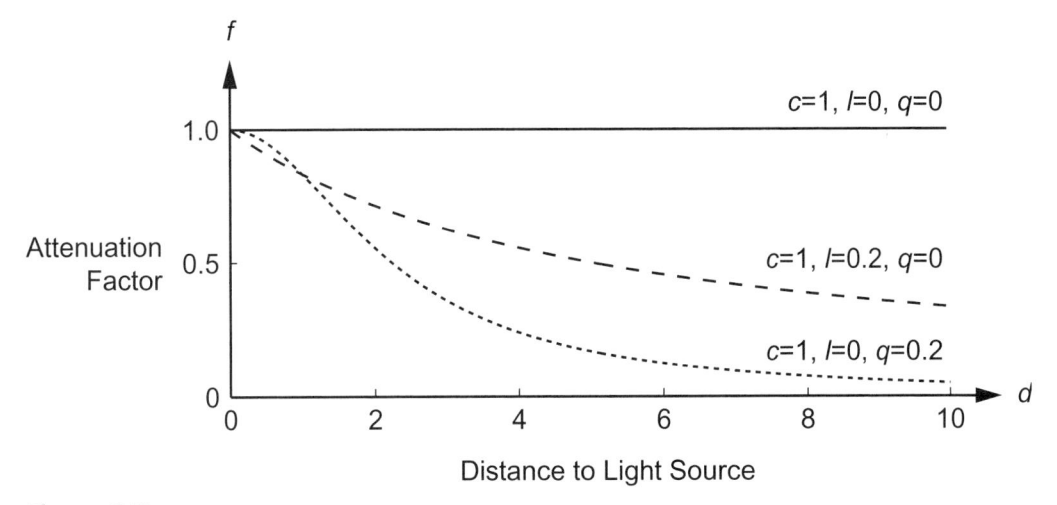

Figure 8.7
Attenuation as it's related to distance to the light source.

Figure 8.8
Sphere in spot light.

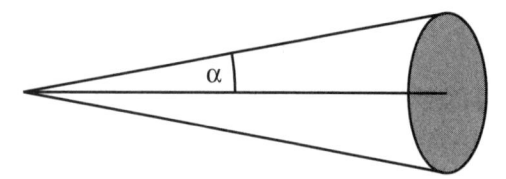

Figure 8.9
Spot angle α.

Spot Light

A spot light not only has a position and a direction, but you can also restrict the angle of the cone that the light emits. Figure 8.8 shows a spot light with a cone angle of 15 degrees.

With a sphere that has 32 subdivisions, the cone of the spot creates a circle with jagged edges on the surface. You'll see a better circle when subdividing the sphere with a higher number of triangles.

Figure 8.9 depicts the spot angle. It's restricted to a value between 0 and 90 degrees and defines the cone's extension to the sides; you can set it with `Light.setSpotAngle()`. Another attribute of the spot is its exponent, which changes the distribution of the light inside the cone. The default value of zero causes a uniform distribution of the light, whereas larger values will make the spot more concentrated in the cone's center. You pass the exponent value to `setSpotExponent()`; the maximum is 128.

Materials

A material has four characteristics, which you can see in Figure 8.10. With *emissive* material, an object can send out light to imitate glowing objects; *ambient* reflection defines the light that is reflected by an ambient light source; with *diffuse* reflection, the reflected light is scattered equally in all directions; and *specular* reflection describes the light that reflects off objects with a shiny surface.

Each material characteristic has an associated color, which is used by the lighting calculation to yield the final shading color. For a point on an object's surface, M3G computes the ambient, diffuse, and specular contributions from each light source and adds them together. Depending on the reflection type, this can involve the vertex normal, light properties such as color, intensity, and position, and the camera's position. The contributions from all light sources are summed up and, at the end, the material emission is added.

Compared to OpenGL, M3G's lighting model is simplified; for example there is no global ambient light. For the features that are supported, however, the OpenGL documentation specifies the exact formula for how each component is calculated. Each color channel is calculated separately and the resulting shading color is clamped to the interval [0, 1].

Creating Materials

Material's interface, shown in Table 8.2, consists of a default constructor and setter and getter for the properties.

In contrast to LightingSample, MaterialsSample changes the default material to something more interesting.

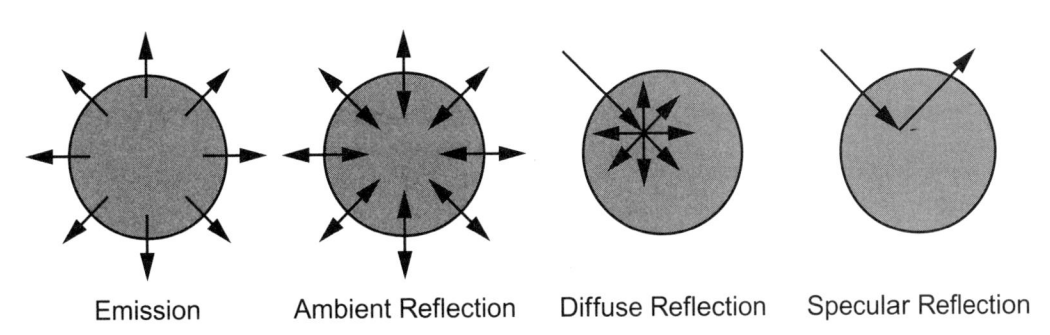

Figure 8.10
Material types.

Table 8.2 Material Class Description

Method	Description
Light Types	
static int AMBIENT	Light reflected from ambient light source.
static int DIFFUSE	Light reflected in all directions.
static int EMISSIVE	Light that emanates from the object.
static int SPECULAR	Light reflected in the direction of the viewer.
Construction	
Material()	Default values are vertex color tracking disabled, shininess is set to 0.0, ambient color to (0.2, 0.2, 0.2, 0.0), diffuse color to (0.8, 0.8, 0.8, 1.0), and emissive and specular color to (0.0, 0.0, 0.0, 0.0).
Material Properties	
void setColor(int target, int ARGB)	Sets the given color component (AMBIENT, DIFFUSE, EMISSIVE, SPECULAR, or a bitmask of several values) in ARGB format. Transparency is supported only for the diffuse component.
int getColor(int target)	Getter for material color.
void setVertexColorTrackingEnable(boolean enable)	When enabled, diffuse and ambient colors are taken from the vertex colors instead of the material settings.
boolean isVertexColorTrackingEnabled()	Getter for vertex color tracking.
void setShininess(float shininess)	Determines the spread of specular highlights. Valid values go from 0.0 to 128.0; smaller values will make the highlights more concentrated.
float getShininess()	Getter for shininess.

> **Note**
>
> The sample is implemented in MaterialsSample.java, which you can find together with a working MIDlet on the accompanying CD-ROM.

```
/**
 * Demonstrates how different materials change the look of a mesh.
 *
 * @author Claus Hoefele
 */
public class MaterialsSample extends GameCanvas implements Sample {
  /** The mesh for display. */
  private Mesh mesh = Teapot.create(5, true, false);
  /** The mesh's transformation. */
```

```java
  private Transform meshTransform = new Transform();

  /** First light for the scene. */
  private Light light;
  /** The first light's transformation. */
  private Transform lightTransform = new Transform();
  /** Ambient light for the scene. */
  private Light ambientLight;
  /** Current rotation value. */
  private float lightRotY;
  /** Current material. */
  private Material material;
  ...

  /** 3D graphics singleton used for rendering. */
  private Graphics3D graphics3d;
  /** 2D graphics singleton used for rendering. */
  private Graphics graphics;

  /**
   * Constructor.
   */
  public MaterialsSample() {
    super(false);
  }

  /**
   * Initializes the sample.
   */
  public void init() {
    // Get the singletons for rendering.
    graphics3d = Graphics3D.getInstance();
    graphics = getGraphics();

    // Create material.
    mesh.getVertexBuffer().setDefaultColor(0x000055); // blue
    material = new Material();
    isVertexTrackingEnabled = false;
    material.setVertexColorTrackingEnable(isVertexTrackingEnabled);
    colorTarget = COLOR_ALL;
    setMaterial(mesh, material, colorTarget);

    // Create light.
```

```
      light = new Light();
      light.setMode(Light.OMNI);
      light.setIntensity(0.5f);
      lightRotY = 30;
      ambientLight = new Light();
      ambientLight.setMode(Light.AMBIENT);
      setLight(light, ambientLight, lightTransform, lightRotY);

      // Create a camera with perspective projection.
      Camera camera = new Camera();
      float aspect = (float) getWidth() / (float) getHeight();
      camera.setPerspective(60, aspect, 1, 1000);
      graphics3d.setCamera(camera, null);

      render(graphics);
      flushGraphics();
   }
   ...
}
```

init() defines two lights: one omnidirectional and one ambient light. setMaterial() defines the material settings with calls to Material.setColor(), as implemented in the following code:

```
/** Material color for ambient reflection. */
private static final int AMBIENT = 0x333333;          // gray
/** Material color for diffuse reflection. */
private static final int DIFFUSE = 0xFFFFFF;          // white
/** Material color for specular reflection. */
private static final int SPECULAR = 0xFFFFFF;         // white
/** Material color for emission. */
private static final int EMISSIVE = 0x333333;         // gray
/** Shininess constant for specular reflection. */
private static final float SHININESS = 15;

/**
 * Sets the mesh's material.
 *
 * @param mesh mesh.
 * @param material Material object.
 * @param colorTarget color target that will be enabled in the mesh.
 */
```

```
private void setMaterial(Mesh mesh, Material material,
    int colorTarget) {
  int ambient = 0, diffuse = 0, specular = 0, emissive = 0;
  float shininess = 0;

  switch (colorTarget) {
    case COLOR_AMBIENT:
      ambient = AMBIENT;
      break;

    case COLOR_DIFFUSE:
      diffuse = DIFFUSE;
      break;

    case COLOR_EMISSIVE:
      emissive = EMISSIVE;
      break;

    case COLOR_SPECULAR:
      specular = SPECULAR;
      shininess = SHININESS;
      break;

    case COLOR_ALL:
      ambient = AMBIENT;
      diffuse = DIFFUSE;
      emissive = EMISSIVE;
      specular = SPECULAR;
      shininess = SHININESS;
      break;
  }

  material.setColor(Material.AMBIENT, ambient);
  material.setColor(Material.DIFFUSE, diffuse);
  material.setColor(Material.SPECULAR, specular);
  material.setColor(Material.EMISSIVE, emissive);
  material.setShininess(shininess);

  mesh.getAppearance(0).setMaterial(material);
}
```

In the call to setColor(), you can either set a single color component one after each other or set several components to the same value by combining color identifiers with the bitwise OR (|) operator.

To see what emission, ambient, diffuse, and specular color components add to an object's appearance, you can switch on each of them separately and circle through the settings with the GAME_A button. As you can see in the following code, you can also rotate the light and enable vertex color tracking. Vertex colors play a role in diffuse reflection.

```
/** Flag whether vertex tracking is enabled. */
private boolean isVertexTrackingEnabled;

/**
 * Handles key presses.
 *
 * @param keyCode key code.
 */
protected void keyPressed(int keyCode) {
  switch (getGameAction(keyCode)) {
    case LEFT:
      lightRotY -= 10;
      setLight(light, ambientLight, lightTransform, lightRotY);
      break;

    case RIGHT:
      lightRotY += 10;
      setLight(light, ambientLight, lightTransform, lightRotY);
      break;

    case FIRE:
      init();
      break;

    case GAME_A:
      colorTarget++;
      colorTarget %= NUMBER_OF_COLOR_TARGETS;
      setMaterial(mesh, material, colorTarget);
      break;

    case GAME_B:
      isVertexTrackingEnabled = !isVertexTrackingEnabled;
```

```
    material
        .setVertexColorTrackingEnable(isVertexTrackingEnabled);
    break;

    // no default
  }

  render(graphics);
  flushGraphics();
}

/**
 * Transforms the light and adds it to the Graphics3D context.
 *
 * @param light light one.
 * @param ambientLight light two.
 * @param lightTransform transform object for light one.
 * @param lightRotY rotation value around the y axis.
 */
private void setLight(Light light, Light ambientLight,
    Transform lightTransform, float lightRotY) {
  lightTransform.setIdentity();
  lightTransform.postTranslate(0, 0, -10);
  lightTransform.postRotate(lightRotY, 0, 1, 0);
  lightTransform.postRotate(-20, 1, 0, 0);
  lightTransform.postTranslate(0, 0, 10);

  graphics3d.resetLights();
  graphics3d.addLight(light, lightTransform);
  graphics3d.addLight(ambientLight, null);
}
```

Defining Material Properties

Figure 8.11 shows how individual material settings create a lit teapot.

Emission

Emission is the simplest of all material properties—it just adds a constant value to the shading color.

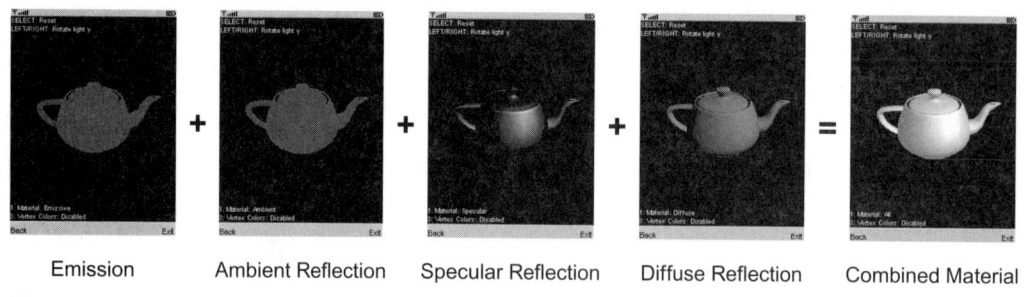

Figure 8.11
Rendered teapot broken down into individual material components.

Ambient Reflection

Ambient reflection is similar to emission, except that it's dependent on an ambient light source (`Light.AMBIENT`). Compared with emission, this has the advantage that you can define the strength of the ambient characteristic for several objects at the same time by changing the light's intensity. Once you determine the general ambient light, you can give an object an individual offset with the emission parameter. The disadvantage is that you need a separate `Light` object to activate the ambient material. That's the reason `MaterialsSample` has two lights: one for ambient material and another for diffuse and specular material properties. In Figure 8.11, ambient reflection looks exactly the same as emission because both material properties have equal color values.

Diffuse Reflection

The diffuse reflection has the biggest impact on the sphere's color. Most likely, the diffuse color will be the same as the ambient color, which will create a smooth color ramp from the point where the light hits the surface to the outskirts of the teapot. Instead of setting the color with `Material.setColor()`, you also have the choice of using the vertex colors or, if they are not defined, the default color stored in `VertexBuffer`. Vertex colors only work for ambient and diffuse reflection. To switch between modes, call `setVertexColorTrackingEnabled()`.

Specular Reflection

The specular reflection adds highlights on an object's surface. Most likely, you'll set the color to white. In contrast to diffuse reflection, specular reflection depends on the viewer's position. As already mentioned in the section about light, the value set in `PolygonMode.setLocalCameraLightingEnable()` determines whether this is the true camera position or an approximation. Furthermore, `Material.setShininess()` changes the effect of the specular component. The shininess value that you pass to this method goes from 0 to 128. Small values cause the reflection to spread out more, whereas large values create a more concentrated highlight.

Emulating Light

Now that you learned about M3G's lighting model, you might wonder why you need a way to emulate it. Lighting is computationally expensive—sometimes too expensive to keep up with interactive frame rates. One way to solve the problem is to keep the number of lights down and use simple light types. For example, a directional light is faster than an omnidirectional or spot light. This will restrict what you can do with lighting.

Lighting is not only expensive, but the predominant Gouraud shading also has problems with visual quality. As the distances between vertices become larger, the interpolation of light at the vertices falls short of reality.

In this section, you read about some alternative techniques that keep up visual quality without the computational overhead of dynamic lighting.

Texture Baking

The simplest way to avoid lighting is to include the shading information in the texture. The light is *baked* into the texture like the ingredients of a cake. This is done offline, so it doesn't matter how long it takes to compute the lighting. For example, you can employ a ray tracing algorithm to compute realistic light and reflections. Another advantage is that texturing works on a pixel level. This makes lighting quality less dependent on the number of vertices. You only have to be careful that your texture isn't distorted too much.

The disadvantage is that light baked into the texture is fixed—you can't change it if the light source or the object moves. This is no problem for large static walls, for example. However, when applying texture baking to walls, you lose the ability to tile a small texture over the surface. If the lighting is included in the texture, the texture image must be different at each place.

Vertex Colors   **Texture**   **Combined Result**

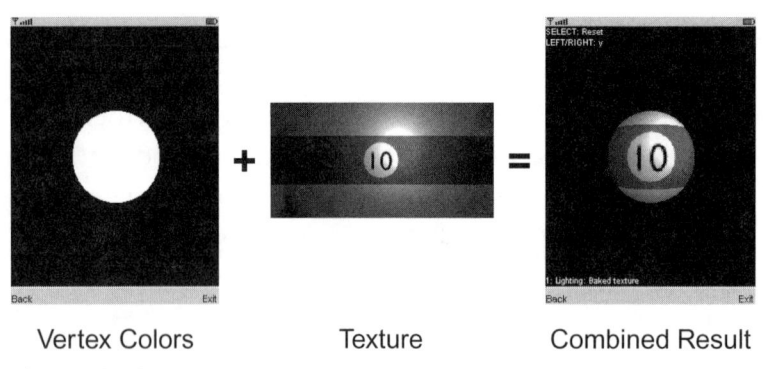

Figure 8.12
Emulating light with texture baking.

Baking light into the texture needs tool support. This is true for all of the mentioned alternatives to lighting. You'd usually create your objects in a 3D modeling software and pick a tool that can calculate lighting and transfer this information to a texture. Figure 8.12 shows the texture of a billiard ball with lighting information baked into the image.

Tip

I created the shading of the texture with Photoshop's Lighting Effects plug-in.

Creating a mesh with lighting baked into a texture is nothing more than applying a texture:

Note

The sample is implemented in EmulatingLightSample.java, which you can find together with a working MIDlet on the accompanying CD-ROM.

```
/**
 * Creates a new mesh with lighting baked into the texture.
 *
 * @return mesh mesh.
 */
private Mesh bakedTexture() {
  Mesh mesh = MeshFactory3D.createSphere(16, 16, false, true);

  try {
    Image2D image
        = (Image2D) Loader.load("/m3g08/billiard_baked.png")[0];
    Texture2D texture = new Texture2D(image);
```

```
      texture.setBlending(Texture2D.FUNC_REPLACE);
      mesh.getAppearance(0).setTexture(0, texture);
   } catch (Exception e) {
      System.out.println("Error loading texture.");
      e.printStackTrace();
   }

   return mesh;
}
```

Texture baking works best with objects that have a complex surface, such as an airplane. Although it's not possible to update the lighting because the information is included in the texture, the static shading still adds depth to the model.

Vertex Colors

The main problem of texture baking is that it prevents tiling. You can solve this problem by separating the lighting information from the base texture. One way to do this is to include the lighting information in the vertex colors and blend them with the texture of the mesh. The additional memory you need for this method depends on the number of vertices. The more vertices, the more vertex colors you have to store. Figure 8.13 shows the components of a mesh with lighting information stored in the vertex colors.

Usually, the vertex colors are grayscale values representing luminance, although you can use RGB for colored lights as well. You blend the vertex colors with a texture using the `Texture2D.MODULATE` operator. Because this operator can only darken an image, the base texture has to be taken with maximum brightness.

Vertex Colors   Texture   Combined Result

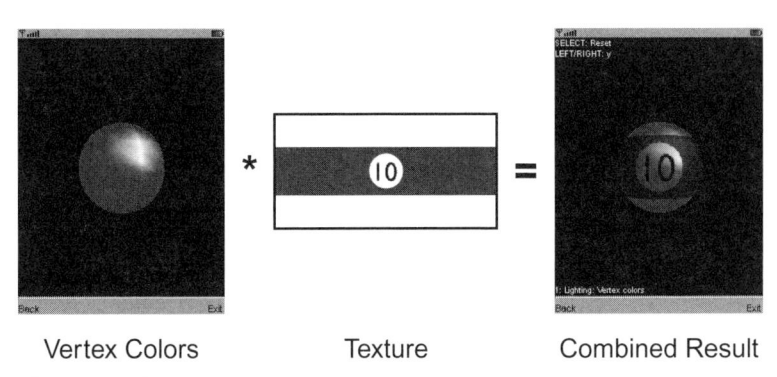

Figure 8.13
Emulating light with vertex colors.

A black vertex color would create a black spot, a white vertex color a white one. Gray vertex colors create different levels of shading. This is what it looks like in code:

```java
/**
 * Creates a new mesh with lighting information in the vertex
 * colors.
 *
 * @return mesh mesh with vertex colors.
 */
private Mesh vertexColors() {
  Mesh mesh = MeshFactory3D.createSphere(16, 16, false, true);

  try {
    // Default texture blending is Texture2D.FUNC_MODULATE.
    Image2D image
        = (Image2D) Loader.load("/m3g08/billiard_base.png")[0];
    Texture2D texture = new Texture2D(image);
    mesh.getAppearance(0).setTexture(0, texture);
  } catch (Exception e) {
    System.out.println("Error loading texture.");
    e.printStackTrace();
  }

  VertexArray vertexColors =
      new VertexArray(VERTEX_COLORS.length/3, 3, 1);
  vertexColors.set(0, VERTEX_COLORS.length/3, VERTEX_COLORS);
  mesh.getVertexBuffer().setColors(vertexColors);

  return mesh;
}
```

This code depends on `VERTEX_COLORS`, which is a `byte` array that stores the precomputed vertex colors. A texture's default blending mode is `FUNC_MODULATE`, so you don't have to set it explicitly.

Tip

To get the vertex colors, I calculated them manually according to a simplified version of OpenGL's lighting equation. This produces the same vertex colors as you would get with dynamic lighting. Have a look at `computeVertexColors()` in EmulatingLightSample.java.

Again, you have the advantage that you can employ any kind of expensive lighting and pre-compute the values. However, in contrast to texture baking, the quality is worse because the lighting is computed at the vertices only. You can see the result of using vertex colors in Figure 8.13; this is the same quality as you would get with Gouraud shading. Although Gouraud shading is often sufficient, it might be a problem with large walls, for example.

Adapting the light dynamically, although not impossible, is difficult. You would have to change the vertex color information depending on the light position. This would cause expensive array copying in and out of the `VertexBuffer`.

The main advantage of including light information in vertex colors is that it works on all devices. This is in contrast to the next solution, which uses two texture units, an optional feature that not all M3G implementations support.

Light Maps

The most flexible way to emulate lighting is to use light maps. As with the vertex color technique, light maps separate lighting information from the appearance of the mesh. A light map stores the lighting information in a texture that is blended with the base texture. Just as with vertex colors, a light map usually contains luminance values.

There are basically two ways to use a light map: use a different light map for each part of the object or generate a generic light map for a specific light type and apply it to your mesh. Using a different light map is similar to texture baking. With your 3D modeling software, you calculate the lighting information and transfer this to a texture. Except in this case, the lighting information is not combined with the base texture, but creates a new texture layer with luminance information. This takes the most amount of memory but also looks very realistic. Figure 8.14 shows how this process looks for a sphere.

Alternatively, you can create a generic light map. For a spot light, for example, you'd create a white circle and use this map wherever you want to place a spot. This has the advantage that you can also move and scale the spot with texture coordinate transformations. In a similar manner, you can create a gradient luminance ramp for directional lights. When using light maps, you have to watch the additional texture budget; a generic light map uses much less memory. To decrease memory, you can also test the look of different light map resolutions.

244   Chapter 8 ■ Lighting

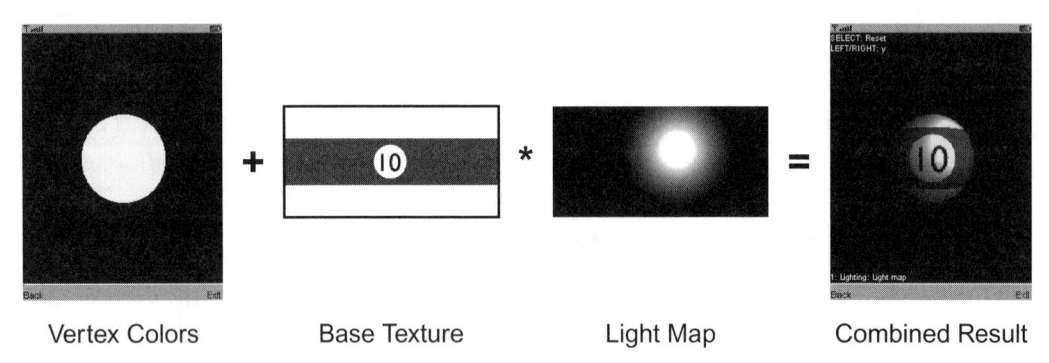

Vertex Colors **Base Texture** **Light Map** **Combined Result**

Figure 8.14
Emulating light with a light map.

To use a light map, you have to load two texture images and apply them to the mesh, such as in the following code:

```
/**
 * Creates a new mesh with a light map applied.
 *
 * @return mesh mesh with light map.
 */
private Mesh lightMap() {
  Mesh mesh = MeshFactory3D.createSphere(16, 16, false, true);

  // Copy texture coordinates from unit 0 to 1 because the mesh
  // requires two textures.
  MeshUtils.copyTexCoords(mesh, 0, 1);

  try {
    Image2D image
        = (Image2D) Loader.load("/m3g08/billiard_base.png")[0];
    Texture2D texture1 = new Texture2D(image);
    texture1.setBlending(Texture2D.FUNC_REPLACE);
    mesh.getAppearance(0).setTexture(0, texture1);

    // Default texture blending is Texture2D.FUNC_MODULATE.
    image
        = (Image2D) Loader.load("/m3g08/billiard_lightmap.png")[0];
    Texture2D texture2 = new Texture2D(image);
    mesh.getAppearance(0).setTexture(1, texture2);
  } catch (Exception e) {
```

```
        System.out.println("Error loading texture.");
        e.printStackTrace();
    }

    return mesh;
}
```

Light maps have the most advantages, but need two texture units. If your device doesn't support two texture units, you can either revert to vertex colors or use a two-pass rendering algorithm and compositing. This would work similar to the embossing effect introduced in Chapter 7.

Summary

Lighting adds important realism to your scene. M3G models lighting with the Light class that represents a light source, and with Material, which defines how light is reflected from an object. Light and materials combined determine the shading.

Because lighting is computationally expensive, you have to consider using few and simple light types. You have also seen three alternatives to lighting: texture baking is simple, but inflexible; lighting information included in vertex colors works on every device, but has the same quality problem as Gouraud shading; and light maps, which are flexible, also use a lot of texture memory and need two texture units.

PART III

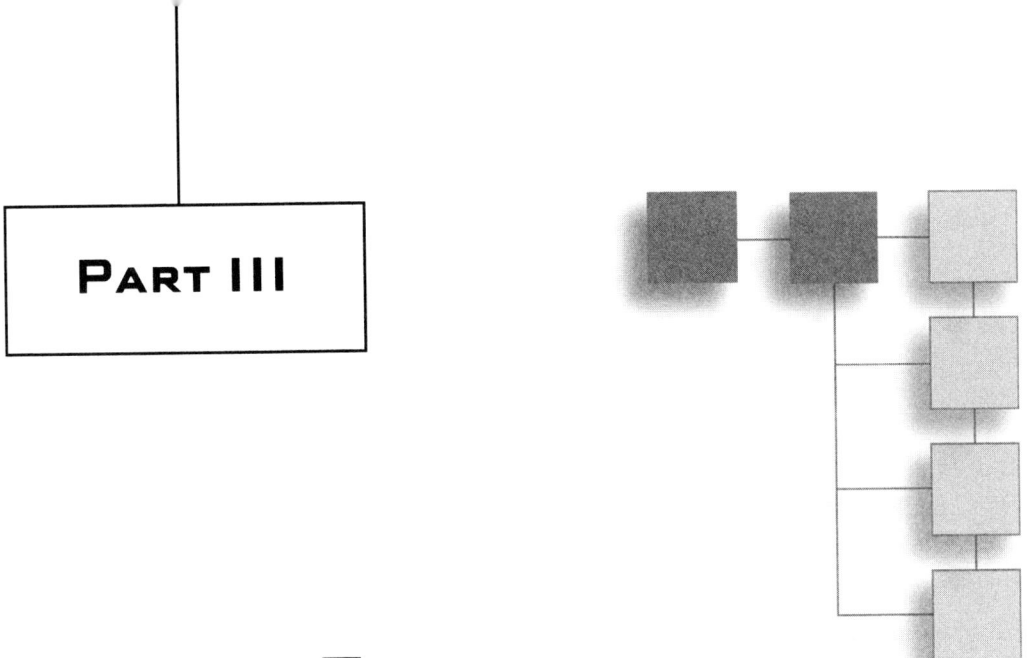

ADVANCED TOPICS

CHAPTER 9

SCENE GRAPHS

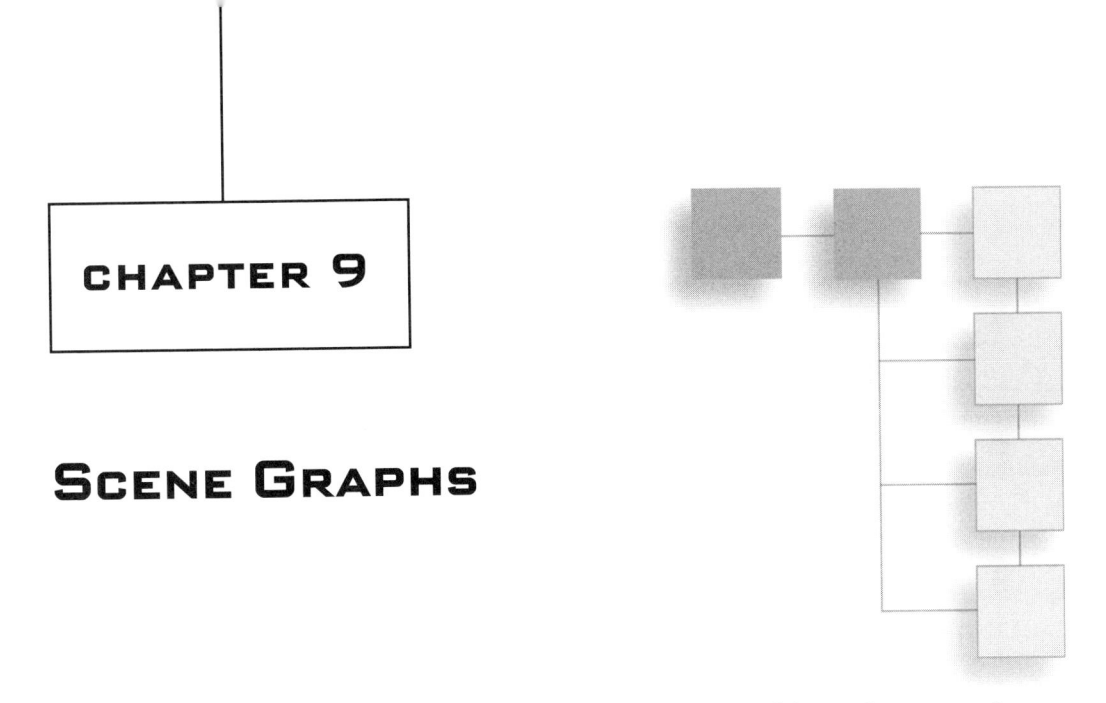

A scene graph is a data structure used to organize scene objects. Scene graphs are closely related to an alternate rendering technique that I'll introduce in this chapter: retained mode. Up until now, you added camera and lighting settings to `Graphics3D` and rendered individual meshes in immediate mode. M3G operates in retained mode when rendering a complete scene graph representation of your 3D world, including all scene parameters.

This chapter shows you:

- How to build and render a scene graph.
- The difference between immediate and retained mode.
- Various methods of selecting a node in a scene graph.
- How to fake geometry using billboards.

Retained Mode

M3G's specification defines retained mode based on the type of `render()` call in `Graphics3D` that you use for drawing. If you render a `World` object including all mesh, camera, and lighting information, the API is said to operate in retained mode.

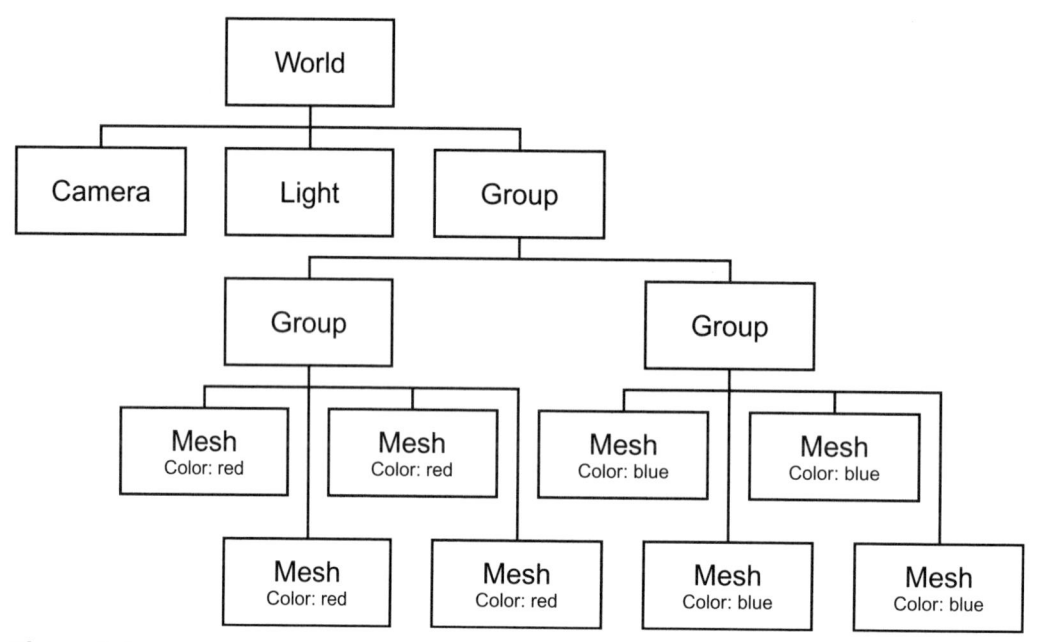

Figure 9.1
A scene graph organizes scene objects in a tree structure.

Creating a Scene Graph

`World` represents the root of a scene graph whose children are organized in a tree structure. You create branches with `Group` objects and the leaves comprise objects such as `Light`, `Camera`, and `Mesh`. You can see a sample graph in Figure 9.1.

The sample scene graph contains a light and a camera. In addition, two groups contain four meshes each; one group contains blue meshes, the other red meshes. Another group is the container for both the blue and red group. The tree structure forbids cycles and requires that each node have exactly one parent.

The following example implements the code necessary to produce this scene graph:

> **Note**
>
> You can find this code in SceneGraphSample.java on the CD-ROM.

```
/** Object that represents the scene graph. */
private World world;
/** Group with all meshes. */
```

```
  private Group allMeshes;
  /** Group with blue meshes. */
  private Group blueMeshes;
  /** Group with red meshes. */
  private Group redMeshes;

  /**
   * Resets the sample's state.
   */
  private void reset() {
    graphics3d = Graphics3D.getInstance();
    graphics = getGraphics();
    world = new World();

    // Create a camera with perspective projection.
    Camera camera = new Camera();
    float aspect = (float) getWidth() / (float) getHeight();
    camera.setPerspective(30, aspect, 1, 1000);
    camera.setTranslation(0, 0, 10);
    world.addChild(camera);
    world.setActiveCamera(camera);

    // Create light.
    Light light = new Light();
    light.setMode(Light.OMNI);
    light.setTranslation(0, 0, 3);
    world.addChild(light);

    // Organize groups.
    allMeshes = new Group();
    blueMeshes = new Group();
    redMeshes = new Group();
    world.addChild(allMeshes);
    allMeshes.addChild(blueMeshes);
    allMeshes.addChild(redMeshes);

    // Create meshes that serve as stencils for blue and red cubes.
    Mesh blueStencil = MeshFactory3D.createCube(false, true, false);
    blueStencil.getVertexBuffer().setDefaultColor(0x0000FF); // blue
    Material material = new Material();
    material.setVertexColorTrackingEnable(true);
    blueStencil.getAppearance(0).setMaterial(material);
```

```
    Mesh redStencil = new Mesh(
        (VertexBuffer) blueStencil.getVertexBuffer().duplicate(),
         blueStencil.getIndexBuffer(0), blueStencil.getAppearance(0));
    redStencil.getVertexBuffer().setDefaultColor(0xFF0000);    // red

    // Place eight cubes in a circle.
    for (int i=0; i<8; i++) {
      Mesh cubeMesh = null;

      if ((i%2) == 0) {
        cubeMesh = (Mesh) blueStencil.duplicate();
        blueMeshes.addChild(cubeMesh);
      } else {
        cubeMesh = (Mesh) redStencil.duplicate();
        redMeshes.addChild(cubeMesh);
      }

      cubeMesh.setTranslation(1.5f*(float) Math.cos(i*Math.PI/4),
          1.5f*(float) Math.sin(i*Math.PI/4), 0);
      cubeMesh.setScale(0.4f, 0.4f, 0.4f);
    }
}
```

The initialization of light and camera parameters works the same as in immediate mode. However, instead of using `Graphics3D.addLight()` and `setCamera()`, `Camera` and `Light` objects are added to the scene graph with `World.addChild()`. Cameras and lights in `Graphics3D` are ignored in retained mode.

The location of cameras and lights in the scene graph has no effect on their function. In addition, the number of objects in a scene graph is limited only by memory. However, you can have only one currently active camera and the `maxLights` property retrieved from `Graphics3D.getProperties()` determines the maximum number of concurrent lights that contribute to the shading of a mesh. If the number of lights exceeds this limit, the implementation can pick which ones it uses, but must be deterministic in its choice. Keep in mind that the number of lights also negatively influences the rendering time.

Apart from `Light` and `Camera` nodes, `SceneGraphSample` also creates eight cubes in a circle and groups them by color. Every even-numbered mesh is added to the blue group; every odd one is added to the red group. `Group`, whose interface is shown in Table 9.1, serves as the container for other nodes so you can handle them as if they were one entity.

Table 9.1 Group Class Description

Method	Description
Constructor	
Group()	Creates an empty group.
Node Management	
void addChild(Node child)	Adds a child to the group.
Node getChild(int index)	Getter for children.
int getChildCount()	Returns the number of children.
void removeChild(Node child)	Removes a child.
Picking	
boolean pick(int scope, float x, float y, Camera camera, RayIntersection ri)	Picks a Mesh or scaled Sprite3D based on viewport coordinates.
boolean pick(int scope, float ox, float oy, float oz, float dx, float dy, float dz, RayIntersection ri)	Picks a Mesh based on the given pick ray.

Table 9.2 World Class Description

Method	Description
Constructor	
World()	Creates an empty world.
General Functionality	
void setActiveCamera(Camera camera)	Sets the active camera used for rendering.
Camera getActiveCamera()	Getter for active camera.
void setBackground(Background background)	Sets the background.
Background getBackground()	Getter for background.

Tip

You can't use the same Node instance more than once in a scene graph, but you can reuse the references inside the object such as its VertexArrays. Object3D.duplicate() comes in handy to create a shallow copy of an object.

World derives from Group and includes additional behavior to act as the root node of a scene graph. If you look at its interfaces in Table 9.2, you'll see that World only adds two properties: an active camera and a background. setActiveCamera() selects one camera as the current view of the 3D scene. The scene graph must already contain this camera as a node. `setBackground()` replaces `Graphics3D.clear()` in retained mode and sets the background color or image of a scene. If a `World`'s `Background` property is `null`, M3G clears the color buffer to transparent black and the depth buffer to maximum depth.

Node Transformations

You might have noticed that the initialization of the scene graph didn't require any `Transform` objects. Instead, you transform nodes in a scene graph with methods inherited from `Transformable`. You have already seen this class in Chapter 6, where it was used to transform the texture coordinates of a `Texture2D` object. Table 9.3 shows `Transformable`'s interface.

Table 9.3 Transformable Class Description

Method	Description
Transformation Result	
void getCompositeTransform(Transform transform)	Returns the concatenation of all matrices.
Translation	
void setTranslation(float tx, float ty, float tz)	Sets the translation matrix.
void getTranslation(float[] xyz)	Getter for translation matrix.
void translate(float tx, float ty, float tz)	Sets the translation matrix relative to the existing values.
Rotation	
void setOrientation(float angle, float ax, float ay, float az)	Sets the orientation matrix.
void getOrientation(float[] angleAxis)	Getter for orientation matrix.
void postRotate(float angle, float ax, float ay, float az)	Sets the orientation matrix relative to the existing values by post-multiplication.
void preRotate(float angle, float ax, float ay, float az)	Sets the orientation matrix relative to the existing values by pre-multiplication.
Scale	
void setScale(float sx, float sy, float sz)	Sets the scale matrix.
void getScale(float[] xyz)	Getter for scale matrix.
void scale(float sx, float sy, float sz)	Sets the scale matrix relative to the existing values.
Generic Matrix	
void setTransform(Transform transform)	Sets the generic matrix.
void getTransform(Transform transform)	Getter for generic matrix.

`Transformable` features four transformation components: translation (**T**), rotation (**R**), scale (**S**), and a generic 4 × 4 matrix (**M**). All four components can be set at the same time. The composite result **C** is obtained by calculating:

$$C = TRSM$$

The order of the matrix multiplication is fixed and reflects the most common use case: first comes scaling without previous transformation, and then rotation around the object's origin, and finally a translation.

In case you need a different order of matrix multiplications, you can either use the generic matrix or insert an extra `Group` node in your scene graph. If you want to rotate a mesh around an arbitrary pivot point, for example, you can place a `Group` node at this point and add the object to be transformed as a child. Children of a group are always transformed relative to the parent node.

Two peculiarities exist: Although `World` inherits from `Transformable`, M3G ignores its transformation when rendering. If you want to transform a complete scene graph, you have to add a `Group` as the first child and add all other nodes below. Second, the bottom row of the `Transformable`'s generic 4 × 4 matrix must be 0 0 0 1 if the class derives from `Node`. Projective transformations are not supported to increase performance and reduce memory consumption of a scene graph. `Texture2D`, because it's not a `Node`, does not have this restriction.

Rendering a World

Rendering becomes very simple: you just have to call `Graphics3D.render()` with the `World` object as a parameter. Because `World` also stores the background properties, there's no need to call `clear()` any more. However, you still have to set the viewport parameters with `Graphics3D.setViewport()`.

To make things a bit more interesting, `SceneGraphSample` animates the cubes with two separate transformations. One transformation causes all cubes to rotate around the *z* axis, whereas the other transformation gives odd-numbered cubes (red) a different scale than even-numbered cubes (blue). This is made easy because the previous code in `SceneGraphSample.reset()` sorted the cubes by color in `Group` objects called `blueMeshes` and `redMeshes` and created another group with all cubes in it called `allMeshes`. Figure 9.2 shows the rendering result.

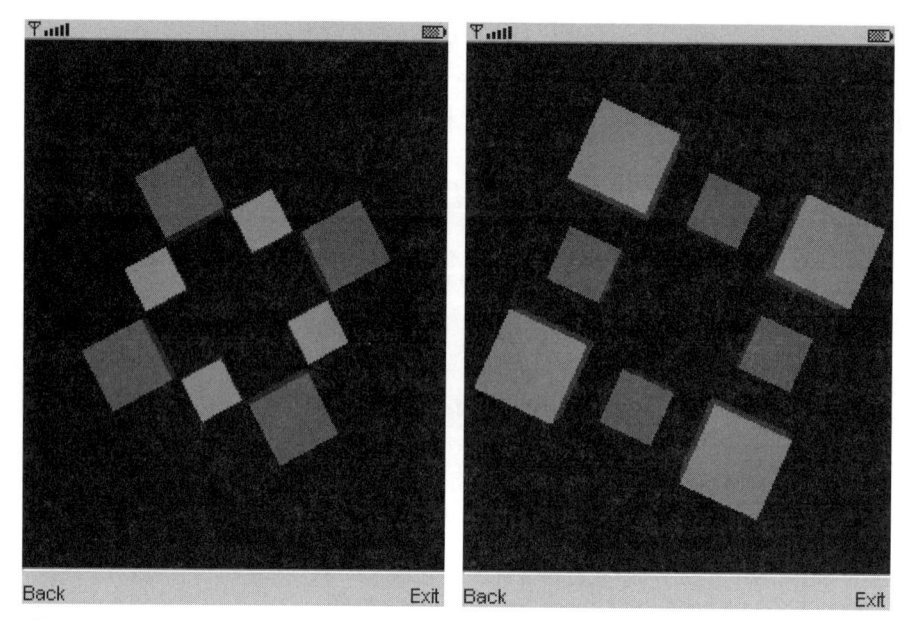

Figure 9.2
Rendered scene graph.

The cubes alternate between big and small, according to the group to which they belong.

```java
/**
 * Uses a scene graph tree to structure a hierarchy of 3D objects.
 *
 * @author Claus Hoefele
 */
public class SceneGraphSample extends GameCanvas
    implements Sample, Runnable {
  /** Flag whether thread is running. */
  private boolean isRunning;
  ...

  /**
   * Constructor.
   */
  public SceneGraphSample() {
    super(true);
  }

  /**
   * Initializes the sample.
```

```java
 */
public void init() {
  reset();

  Thread thread = new Thread(this);
  isRunning = true;
  thread.start();
}
...

/**
 * Destroys the sample.
 */
public void destroy() {
  isRunning = false;
}

/**
 * Animation loop.
 */
public void run() {
  int counter = 10;

  // Animate and render meshes.
  while(isRunning) {
    counter++;
    float scale = (float) Math.sin((float) counter / 10.0f) * 0.2f;
    blueMeshes.setScale(1 + scale, 1 + scale, 1 + scale);
    redMeshes.setScale(1 - scale, 1 - scale, 1 - scale);
    allMeshes.postRotate(2, 0, 0, 1);

    render(graphics);
    flushGraphics();

    try {
      Thread.sleep(20);       // max 50 FPS
    } catch (Exception e) {}
  }
}

/**
 * Renders the sample.
 *
```

```
   * @param graphics graphics context for drawing.
   */
  private void render(Graphics graphics) {
    graphics3d.bindTarget(graphics);
    graphics3d.setViewport(0, 0, getWidth(), getHeight());
    graphics3d.render(world);              // retained mode
    graphics3d.releaseTarget();
  }
}
```

Retained versus Immediate Mode

If you reconsider the `render()` methods in `Graphics3D`, you now have two choices: In retained mode, you render a complete scene graph represented by a `World` object. In immediate mode, you render individual nodes in `Sprite3D` or `Mesh` objects, branches of a scene graph in a `Group` object, or individual submeshes stored in a `VertexBuffer`.

Although scene graphs are closely related to retained mode, this is by no means an exclusive partnership. To render a `World` in immediate mode, transfer the active camera and all lights from the scene graph to `Graphics3D`. You can retrieve the retained mode transformation of these objects with `getCompositeTransform()` and pass this matrix to the respective immediate mode method such as `setCamera()`.

When rendering, clear the color buffer with the `Background` object stored in `World` and render the graph in immediate mode with the `render()` method that takes a `Node` and a `Transform` parameter. Because `World` inherits from `Node`, you can pass your scene graph directly to this method as the first parameter. In this case, the `World` object is rendered as if it were a `Group` object, including all its children. You can set the second parameter to `null` because a `World`'s transformation is ignored in retained mode. Conversely, to switch from immediate mode to retained mode, put all objects into a `World` object and render the scene graph with the `render()` method that takes a `World` object.

Immediate and retained modes also mix well. After using `Graphics3D.render(World)`, the active camera and the lights of the rendered world automatically replace `Graphics3D`'s current camera and lights. This way, subsequent immediate mode rendering can use the same parameters.

The reason to use a scene graph stems from the need to structure your scene data. It's often more convenient to set up a scene graph instead of dealing with individual objects. By grouping your scene data in `World` and `Group` objects, you also minimize the number of calls to the M3G API, which can improve performance. If you do this, it's often more convenient to render the complete graph in retained mode. In the end, it doesn't really matter which render mode you prefer as long as you use the right set of methods. Table 9.4 should help you distinguish between immediate and retained mode APIs.

Table 9.4 API Calls to Use in Immediate and Retained Mode

Call	Immediate Mode	Retained Mode
Camera	Set the current camera in `Graphics3D` before render call. `Graphics3D.setCamera(Camera camera, Transform transform)`	Add one or more cameras to the world as children and activate one of them. `World.addChild(Node child)` `World.setActiveCamera(Camera camera)`
Light	Add lights to `Graphics3D` before render call. `Graphics3D.addLight(Light light, Transform transform)` `Graphics3D.setLight(int index, Light light, Transform transform)` `Graphics3D.resetLights()`	Add lights to the world as children. `World.addChild(Node child)`
Transformation	Pass `Transform` object in API call, for example: `Graphics3D.render(Node node, Transform transform)`	Use methods inherited from `Transformable`, for example: `Transformable.setTransform (Transform transform)`
Background	Set background with `Graphics3D.clear()`. `Graphics3D.clear(Background background)`	Set background in `World` object. If not set, the background is cleared to black automatically. `World.setBackground(Background background)`
Rendering	Render scene graph nodes (`Sprite3D`, `Mesh`, `Group`, and their subclasses) or submeshes (`VertexBuffer`). `Graphics3D.render(Node node, Transform transform)` `Graphics3D.render(VertexBuffer vertices, IndexBuffer triangles, Appearance appearance, Transform transform, int scope)` `Graphics3D.render(VertexBuffer vertices, IndexBuffer triangles, Appearance appearance, Transform transform)`	Render complete world. `Graphics3D.render(World world)`

Node Properties

All elements in a scene graph have Node as a common superclass. Although you will most often work with classes derived from it, Node contains generally useful parameters. Table 9.5 shows its interface.

The alpha factor blends nodes in and out. To determine the final alpha value, the node's value is first multiplied with the values of all its ancestors. This alpha factor is then multiplied by a mesh's alpha component.

Table 9.5 Node Class Description

Method	Description
Alignment Targets	
static int NONE	Disables alignment.
static int ORIGIN	Uses origin as reference.
static int X_AXIS	Uses *x* axis as reference.
static int Y_AXIS	Uses *y* axis as reference.
static int Z_AXIS	Uses *z* axis as reference.
Alignment	
void setAlignment(Node zRef, int zTarget, Node yRef, int yTarget)	Sets the alignment references and targets for *y* and *z* axis.
Node getAlignmentReference(int axis)	Getter for alignment reference. (Since 1.1.)
int getAlignmentTarget(int axis)	Getter for alignment target. (Since 1.1.)
void align(Node reference)	Executes the alignment set in setAlignment().
Inherited Properties	
void setAlphaFactor(float alphaFactor)	Sets transparency.
float getAlphaFactor()	Getter for transparency.
void setPickingEnable(boolean enable)	Enables or disables picking.
boolean isPickingEnabled()	Getter for picking state.
void setRenderingEnable(boolean enable)	Enables or disables rendering.
boolean isRenderingEnabled()	Getter for rendering state.
Other Functionality	
void setScope(int scope)	Sets the scope for lighting, picking, and visibility.
int getScope()	Getter for scope.
boolean getTransformTo(Node target, Transform transform)	Computes the accumulated transformation from this node to another.
Node getParent()	Returns the parent of this node.

Depending how you set up the mesh, this could be the mesh's diffuse color, vertex colors, or the default color. To enable blending, you still have to enable appropriate blending values in `CompositingMode` and `Texture2D`. In M3G 1.0, the alpha factor only applied to `Mesh` objects. In version 1.1, this was extended to affect `Sprite3D`s as well. In this case, the alpha factor is multiplied by the image's alpha channel.

As with the alpha factor, the flags for rendering and picking take a `Node`'s ancestor into account. A flag is enabled only if all ancestors are enabled too. There are two flags: the rendering enabled flag, which determines visibility, and the picking enabled flag. Picking, along with aligning and scoping, deserves its own section in the remainder of this chapter.

Selecting Nodes

When creating scene graphs, you often want to access an object in the hierarchy. The easiest way is to keep a reference to the original object, but this approach works only if you created the scene graph yourself and know what objects you need.

Traversing a Scene Graph

The most generic method to get all descendents of an `Object3D` is to call `getReferences()` on it. This will return all direct references; the only exception is the parent node and the alignment reference of a `Node` object. Table 9.6 shows `Object3D`'s interface.

Nearly all classes in M3G's API inherit from `Object3D` and can be queried. For example, depending on what you stored in a `Mesh`, the method will return the `VertexBuffer`, one or several `IndexBuffer`s, and zero or more `Appearance` objects. To receive all data, you first call `getReferences()` with a `null` parameter to get the number of references and call the method a second time with an array that can hold the same amount of elements. Note that if you share objects between nodes, for example the same `VertexArray` for several `Mesh`es, you'll receive duplicate references.

Most of the time, this is too much information. What you usually want are the members of a group or world. To do this, you can use `Group.getChildCount()` and `getChild()`. This will restrict the data to `Node` objects such as `Camera`, `Mesh`, or `Group`.

Table 9.6 Object3D Class Description

Method	Description
Animation	
void addAnimationTrack(AnimationTrack animationTrack)	Adds a new animation track.
void removeAnimationTrack(AnimationTrack animationTrack)	Removes an animation track.
AnimationTrack getAnimationTrack(int index)	Getter for animation tracks.
int getAnimationTrackCount()	Returns the number of animation tracks for this Object3D.
int animate(int time)	Executes an animation.
User Data	
void setUserID(int userID)	Sets a user ID.
int getUserID()	Getter for user ID.
Object3D find(int userID)	Finds a user ID.
void setUserObject(java.lang.Object userObject)	Sets user-specific data.
java.lang.Object getUserObject()	Getter for user data.
General Functionality	
Object3D duplicate()	Clones an Object3D.
int getReferences(Object3D[] references)	Returns all references in this Object3D.

User IDs

When traversing the scene graph, you can identify your target object with the `instanceof` operator or select it depending on the traversal depth. This will produce runtime errors if you decide to change the scene graph structure. A better alternative is a user ID.

Every `Object3D` can have an application specific number assigned with `setUserID()`. You search for a specific `Object3D` by calling `Object3D.find()`. This method traverses all objects that can be obtained by recursively calling `getReferences()` and returns the object that matches the given user ID. You can use the same ID for several objects, but `find()` will return only one of them; which one is undefined.

Apart from the ID, you can also attach an arbitrary object to an `Object3D` by calling `setUserObject()`. This might come in handy if you want to store metadata about a node in your scene graph. You can, for example, store the hit count of an enemy in its mesh node.

Picking

Picking selects objects based on their position. Picking casts a ray. If that ray intersects with a mesh, the method reports the struck object. Applications include collision detection and selecting a 3D object based on user input.

General Method

Picking works on `Group` objects and by extension also on a `World`. The more general way of picking casts a ray described by an origin and a direction. These values are passed to `Group.pick()`, which returns `true` if the pick ray hit an object. You can exclude individual objects from picking by setting `Node.setPickingEnabled()` to `false`.

The result of the intersection test is written into a `RayIntersection` object, whose interface is summarized in Table 9.7. `getIntersected()` returns the first `Mesh` in the group that was hit by the ray. You also get the distance between the ray origin and the intersection point, the index of the submesh of the intersected mesh, and the normal and texture coordinates of the struck mesh at the intersection point.

The distance is interesting for collision detection. You could, for example, measure how far away your player character is from objects in the walking direction to determine whether you can move farther.

Table 9.7 RayIntersection Class Description

Method	Description
Constructor	
RayIntersection()	Creates a new object with default values.
Pick Ray	
void getRay(float[] ray)	Getter for origin and direction of pick ray used for intersection.
Intersection Result	
Node getIntersected()	Getter for intersected object.
float getDistance()	Distance between the pick ray's origin and the picked object.
float getNormalX()	x value of the normal at the intersection point.
float getNormalY()	y value of the normal at the intersection point.
float getNormalZ()	z value of the normal at the intersection point.
int getSubmeshIndex()	Submesh index of an intersected `Mesh`.
float getTextureS(int index)	s value of the texture coordinate at the intersection point.
float getTextureT(int index)	t value of the texture coordinate at the intersection point.

Because the distance is scaled with the pick ray's length, you should normalize the ray direction if you want the exact distance.

The general `pick()` method that uses an arbitrary pick ray will only report `Mesh` objects. That's because the method has no access to the projection matrix of the camera, which is needed to calculate the dimensions of a `Sprite3D`. Alternatively, there's a second `pick()` variant that picks objects in viewport coordinates, which takes a `Camera` parameter. This method then allows you to select scaled `Sprite3D`s as well.

Picking in Viewport Coordinates

When picking in viewport coordinates, the direction of the pick ray is aligned with the camera's orientation. This is commonly used in first-person shooters to check whether the gun points at the enemy.

The viewport coordinates are two-dimensional because they describe a position on the near and far clipping planes of the viewing volume. The intersection ray is created with the origin on the near plane and the direction of the corresponding point on the far plane. This means that the distance returned by `RayIntersection` is measured from the near plane rather than the camera's position. Figure 9.3 shows an example.

As the viewing volume is defined by the camera, you have to pass a `Camera` object to `pick()` as well. The interface requires that the camera and the group used for picking be in the same scene graph. Having the camera parameters available also

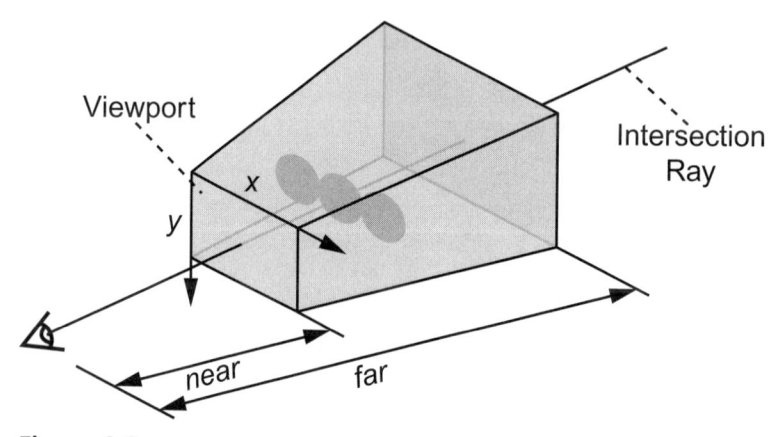

Figure 9.3
Picking in viewport coordinates.

enables you to pick scaled `Sprite3D`s in addition to `Mesh` objects. Unscaled `Sprite3D`s are still not selectable because this would require information about the viewport transformation.

Viewport coordinates have their origin in the upper-left corner of the viewing volume; the positive *x* axis extends to the right and the positive *y* axis extends down. The visible part of the near and far clipping plane corresponds to viewport coordinates in the range of [0, 1]. It's not a requirement to stay in this range though, which enables you to pick invisible objects as well.

`PickingSample` demonstrates how to select a mesh in your scene based on user input:

```
/**
 * Picks meshes in viewport coordinates.
 *
 * @author Claus Hoefele
 */
public class PickingSample extends GameCanvas implements Sample {
  /** Image object for crosshair.*/
  private Image crosshair;


  /** Object that represents the 3D world. */
  private World world;

  /** 3D graphics singleton used for rendering. */
  private Graphics3D graphics3d;
  /** 2D graphics singleton used for rendering. */
  private Graphics graphics;

  /**
   * Constructor.
   */
  public PickingSample() {
    super(false);
  }

  /**
   * Initializes the sample.
   */
  public void init() {
    graphics3d = Graphics3D.getInstance();
```

266 Chapter 9 ▪ Scene Graphs

```java
    graphics = getGraphics();
    world = new World();

    // Load crosshair image.
    try {
      crosshair = Image.createImage("/m3g09/crosshair.png");
    } catch (Exception e) {
      e.printStackTrace();
    }

    // Create grid of discs.
    Mesh stencil = MeshFactory2D.createDisc(32);
    for (int i=0; i<4; i++) {
      for (int j=0; j<4; j++) {
        // Duplicate disc so each mesh can have a different default
        // color.
        Mesh disc = new Mesh(
            (VertexBuffer) stencil.getVertexBuffer().duplicate(),
            stencil.getIndexBuffer(0), stencil.getAppearance(0));
        disc.setTranslation(i-1.5f, j-1.5f, 0);
        disc.setScale(0.5f, 0.5f, 1);
        disc.getVertexBuffer().setDefaultColor(0x0000FF);        // blue
        world.addChild(disc);
      }
    }

    // Create a camera with parallel projection.
    Camera camera = new Camera();
    float aspect = (float) getWidth() / (float) getHeight();
    camera.setParallel(6, aspect, 1, 1000);
    camera.setTranslation(0, 0, 10);
    world.addChild(camera);
    world.setActiveCamera(camera);

    render(graphics);
    flushGraphics();
  }

  /**
   * Renders the sample.
   *
   * @param graphics graphics context for rendering.
   */
```

```
  private void render(Graphics graphics) {
    graphics3d.bindTarget(graphics);
    graphics3d.setViewport(0, 0, getWidth(), getHeight());
    graphics3d.render(world);
    graphics3d.releaseTarget();
    graphics.drawImage(crosshair, getWidth()/2, getHeight()/2,
        Graphics.VCENTER | Graphics.HCENTER);

    drawMenu(graphics);
  }
  ...
}
```

`init()` creates a grid of blue discs. Each can have an individual default color, which requires separate `VertexBuffers` for all meshes.

`init()` also loads a crosshair image that `render()` draws in the middle of the screen. This serves as a reference point for the picking ray. All you have to do to select a mesh in the direction of the camera is supply the camera and the correct viewport coordinates:

```
  /**
   * Handles key presses.
   *
   * @param keyCode key code.
   */
  protected void keyPressed(int keyCode) {
    switch (getGameAction(keyCode)) {
      case LEFT:
        world.getActiveCamera().translate(-0.1f, 0, 0);
        break;

      case RIGHT:
        world.getActiveCamera().translate(0.1f, 0, 0);
        break;

      case UP:
        world.getActiveCamera().translate(0, 0.1f, 0);
        break;

      case DOWN:
        world.getActiveCamera().translate(0, -0.1f, 0);
        break;
```

```
        case FIRE:
          init();
          break;

        // no default
      }

      // Check whether ray cast by crosshair intersects.
      checkHit();

      render(graphics);
      flushGraphics();
    }

    /**
     * Checks whether a ray that originates in the middle of the
     * viewport and has the same direction as the active camera
     * intersects with a mesh. If there's a hit, the mesh is colored
     * red.
     */
    private void checkHit() {
      RayIntersection rayIntersection = new RayIntersection();

      if (world.pick(-1, 0.5f, 0.5f, world.getActiveCamera(),
          rayIntersection)) {
        Mesh mesh = (Mesh) rayIntersection.getIntersected();
        mesh.getVertexBuffer().setDefaultColor(0xFF0000); // red
      }
    }
```

Each time a key input moves the camera, checkHit() checks whether the crosshair points at a disc. If so, the corresponding mesh's color is changed to red. To coordinate the picking with the crosshair position, the intersection ray starts from the middle of the screen. This corresponds to the viewport coordinates (0.5, 0.5). Figure 9.4 shows the initial screen as well as the crosshair moved to the side.

Picking, whether in viewport coordinates or with the more general method, is rather slow. Because the performance depends on the complexity of your meshes, you might consider using invisible meshes that approximate the real volume for the intersection tests instead.

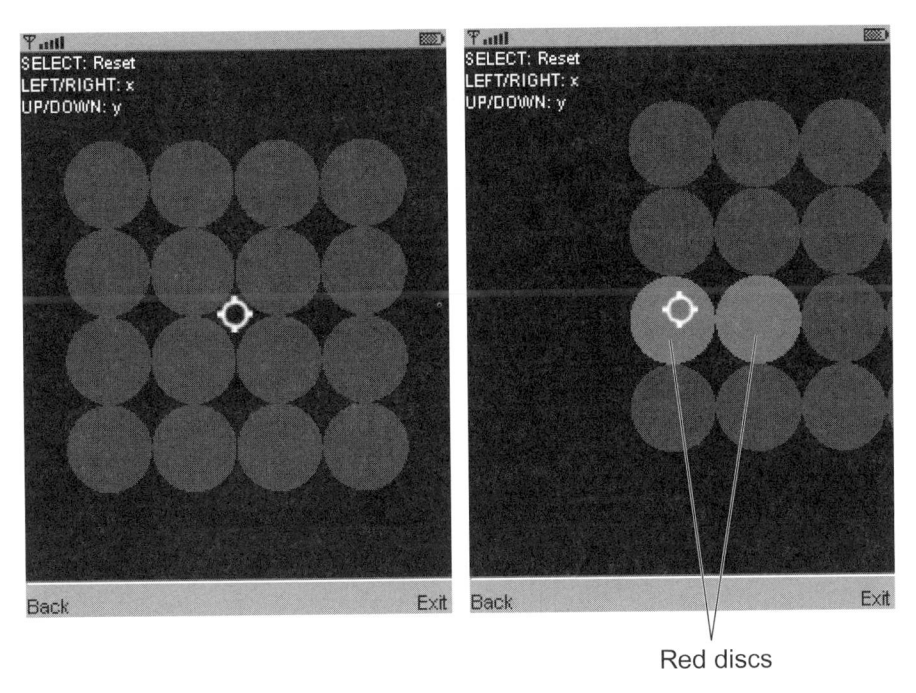

Figure 9.4
Picking meshes.

Scoping

If you want to group nodes without direct object relationships, you can use scoping. Two objects are in the same scope if the bitwise AND (&) of their respective scope values is nonzero. The scope value of an object is set with `Node.setScope()`.

Scoping is used for the following:

- **Rendering**. A `Node` is visible only if it's in the same scope as the camera. This is similar to `Node.setRenderingEnabled()` except that it works for several objects.

- **Lighting**. A `Mesh` is affected by a light only if their scope values match.

- **Picking**. A `Node` can be picked only if its scope matches the value passed when calling `Group.pick()`. Picking is enabled analogous to `setPicking Enable()`.

Aligning Nodes

If you were to tee off in a televised golf game, you'd want the camera to show the ball in the middle of the screen on its way to the green. Node alignment automatically orients a source, such as the camera, to a reference, such as the ball.

In Chapter 6, you saw a related feature: Sprite3D. Sprite3Ds are restricted to screen-aligned images. Node alignment, on the other hand, works with any class derived from Node, and you can freely choose the alignment axes.

> **Note**
>
> The sample at the end of this chapter demonstrates billboards with node alignment and compares it with an approach using Sprite3D.

To align a node, you define one reference node and one target axis for each of the source's *z* and *y* axes. These are the values you pass to setAlignment(Node zRef, int zTarget, Node yRef, int yTarget). As a target, you can choose between the *x* (X_AXIS), *y* (Y_AXIS), and *z* (Z_AXIS) axes as well as the origin of the reference node (ORIGIN); NONE disables alignment.

In the example in Figure 9.5, I selected the parameters so both the *z* and *y* axes of the source align to the same axes of the reference. The respective method call is:

```
source.setAlignment(reference, Node.Z_AXIS, reference, Node.Y_AXIS)
```

Alignment is a two step process: First, the implementation finds the smallest rotation that aligns the source's *z* axis with the reference. The rotation axis is the cross product of the source's *z* axis and the target axis. Then, the source's *y* axis is aligned by rotating it around the reference's *z* axis. The execution order means

Alignment Source   z Axis Alignment   y Axis Alignment   Alignment Reference

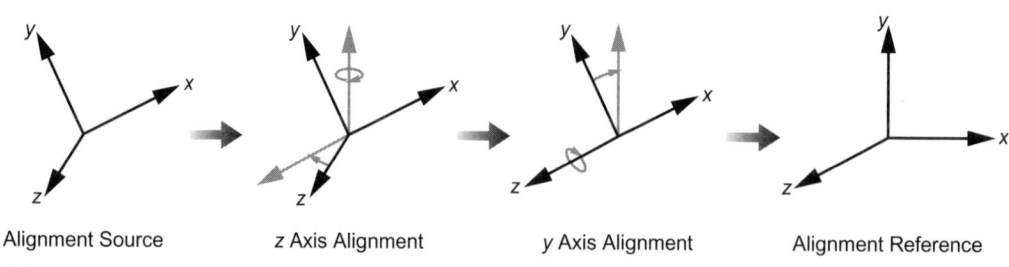

Figure 9.5
Alignment orients a node so its coordinate system matches the reference's.

that if an alignment target is set for both the source's axes, the z alignment constraints the y alignment.

The actual alignment isn't executed until you call `Node.align()`. You would usually call this method each frame before you render the scene to the screen. `align()` works down the hierarchy of a scene graph too. To align several objects at once, you can call it on the `World` or a parent `Group` object. Alignment only affects the rotation component in the `Transformable` of a node. Other transformation components such as translation and scaling are left untouched.

When setting the parameters in `setAlignment()`, the reference node is optional. If you pass `null`, the node is determined from the parameter to the `align()` method. This is handy if you have a reference node that can change over time, such as the currently active camera.

Billboards

An application of node alignment is a billboard: an image that's glued to a rectangular area like a poster. To avoid making it obvious that you are dealing with flat images, you have to make sure that the image orients toward the camera. This works nicely with stationary objects that look similar from all sides, such as trees. You can also create fake monsters that always move toward the player in a first-person shooter using billboards. As long as you don't need to see an object's backside, billboards provide the illusion of 3D without the computational overhead of geometry.

Screen-Aligned Billboards

One possible implementation of billboards uses `Sprite3D`s, which Chapter 6 introduced. They provide a convenient means to display screen-aligned images. The following code produces a number of `Sprite3D`s to display flowers:

Note

You can find this code in BillboardSample.java on the CD-ROM.

```
/**
 * Creates a number of billboards using screen-aligned
 * <code>Sprite3D</code>s.
 *
 * @param number number of billboards to create.
```

```
 * @return <code>Group</code> node with billboards as children.
 */
private Group createSprite3D(int number) {
  Group group = new Group();

  try {
    // Load via Image because on some devices, Loader sets the wrong
    // Image2D format when reading images that include transparency.
    Image image = Image.createImage("/m3g09/daisy.png");
    Image2D daisy = new Image2D(Image2D.RGBA, image);
    image = Image.createImage("/m3g09/knotweed.png");
    Image2D knotweed = new Image2D(Image2D.RGBA, image);

    CompositingMode compositingMode = new CompositingMode();
    compositingMode.setBlending(CompositingMode.ALPHA);
    Appearance appearance = new Appearance();
    appearance.setCompositingMode(compositingMode);

    // Create the Sprite3Ds. A Sprite3D has a length of 1 unit and
    // its origin at the center.
    for (int i=0; i<number; i++) {
      Image2D flower = (i%2 == 0 ? daisy : knotweed);
      Sprite3D sprite = new Sprite3D(true, flower, appearance);
      sprite.setScale(0.5f, 0.5f, 0.5f);
      group.addChild(sprite);
    }
  } catch (Exception e) {
    System.out.println("Error creating Sprite3D.");
    e.printStackTrace();
  }

  return group;
}
```

The screen-aligned Sprite3Ds work nicely as long as you position the camera at about the same height as the flowers and the camera only pans around the *y* axis. However, they look rather silly as soon as you look down on them. As depicted in Figure 9.6, the flowers will follow the camera's orientation and eventually lie flat on the ground. Hence, although Sprite3Ds are convenient in certain situations, it depends on the camera movements whether they are useful.

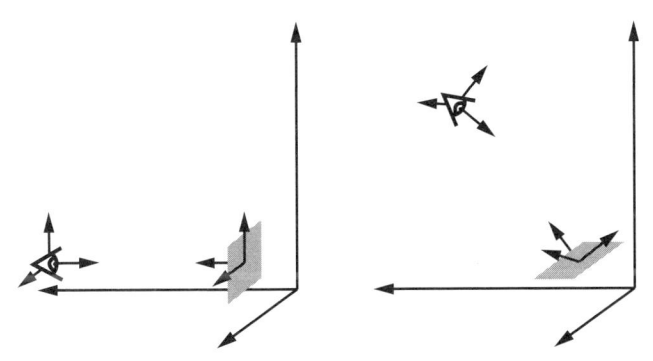

Figure 9.6
A screen-aligned Sprite3D will lie flat on the ground when the camera hovers over it.

Axis-Aligned Billboards

Node alignment, introduced in this chapter, provides an alternative to Sprite3Ds. Although it's more complicated to set up, node alignment provides the possibility to align the billboard toward arbitrary axes instead of the screen.

The following code replaces Sprite3Ds with axis-aligned, textured quads. createTexturedQuad() is very similar to createSprite3D(), except for the call to setAlignment().

```
/**
 * Creates a number of billboards using axis-aligned, textured
 * quads.
 *
 * @param number number of billboards to create.
 * @return <code>Group</code> node with billboards as children.
 */
private Group createTexturedQuad(int number) {
  Group group = new Group();

  try {
    Image image = Image.createImage("/m3g09/iris.png");
    Image2D image2D = new Image2D(Image2D.RGBA, image);
    Texture2D iris = new Texture2D(image2D);
    image = Image.createImage("/m3g09/tulip.png");
    image2D = new Image2D(Image2D.RGBA, image);
    Texture2D tulip = new Texture2D(image2D);
```

```
      Mesh quad = MeshFactory2D.createQuad(true);
      CompositingMode compositingMode = new CompositingMode();
      compositingMode.setBlending(CompositingMode.ALPHA);
      PolygonMode polygonMode = new PolygonMode();
      polygonMode.setCulling(PolygonMode.CULL_NONE);

      // Create the textured quads. A quad is 2 units long, has its
      // origin at the center, and is parallel to the x-y plane.
      for (int i=0; i<number; i++) {
        Mesh mesh = (Mesh) quad.duplicate();
        Appearance appearance = new Appearance();
        appearance.setCompositingMode(compositingMode);
        appearance.setPolygonMode(polygonMode);
        Texture2D flower = (i%2 == 0 ? iris : tulip);
        flower.setBlending(Texture2D.FUNC_REPLACE);
        appearance.setTexture(0, flower);
        mesh.setAppearance(0, appearance);
        mesh.setScale(0.25f, 0.25f, 0.25f);
        group.addChild(mesh);

        mesh.setAlignment(alignNode, Node.Z_AXIS, null, Node.NONE);
      }
    } catch (Exception e) {
      System.out.println("Error loading image.");
      e.printStackTrace();
    }

    return group;
  }
```

To create the billboard, you need its z axis aligned with the camera's z axis; the y axis of the billboard shouldn't move at all. There's a catch when aligning a billboard to the camera though: the camera points toward the negative z axis when initialized—the opposite direction than what you need. To solve the problem, you could align the z axis with the camera's origin (using `Node.ORIGIN`), lock the y axis onto the `World`'s y axis, and constrain this z axis by the y axis. Unfortunately, the execution order of the alignment rotations constrains the y axis by the z axis and not the other way around. This means you'd have to construct the billboards in a local coordinate system that reverses these constraints.

In the end, the easiest solution is to use an additional `Group` node as the alignment target. `createTexturedQuad()` refers to this node as `alignNode` in the call to `setAlignment()`. Here's the initialization of the groups:

```
/** Root node of world. */
private World world;
/** Group that contains camera. */
private Group cameraGroup;
/** Group used for alignment. */
private Group alignNode;

/**
 * Initializes the sample.
 */
public void init() {
  graphics3d = Graphics3D.getInstance();
  graphics = getGraphics();
  world = new World();

  // Create a camera with perspective projection.
  Camera camera = new Camera();
  float aspect = (float) getWidth() / (float) getHeight();
  camera.setPerspective(60, aspect, 1, 1000);
  camera.setTranslation(0, 0, 4);
  world.setActiveCamera(camera);

  // Camera groups.
  cameraGroup = new Group();
  cameraGroup.addChild(camera);
  cameraGroup.postRotate(-15, 1, 0, 0);
  alignNode = new Group();
  alignNode.addChild(cameraGroup);
  world.addChild(alignNode);

  // Billboards.
  world.addChild(createGrass());
  world.addChild(distribute(createSprite3D(10)));
  world.addChild(distribute(createTexturedQuad(10)));

  render(graphics);
  flushGraphics();
}
```

```java
/**
 * Handles key presses.
 *
 * @param keyCode key code.
 */
protected void keyPressed(int keyCode) {
  switch (getGameAction(keyCode)) {
    case LEFT:
      alignNode.postRotate(5, 0, 1, 0);
      break;

    case RIGHT:
      alignNode.postRotate(-5, 0, 1, 0);
      break;

    case UP:
      cameraGroup.postRotate(-10, 1, 0, 0);
      break;

    case DOWN:
      cameraGroup.postRotate(10, 1, 0, 0);
      break;

    case FIRE:
      init();
      break;

    // no default
  }

  render(graphics);
  flushGraphics();
}
...
}
```

`init()` creates a hierarchy of nodes for the camera with two additional `Group`s: `cameraGroup` for the *x* axis rotations and `alignNode` for the *y* axis rotations. Both nodes stay at the origin while the camera moves to its location, away from the flowers. Hence, when rotating either node, the camera orbits over the flowers. Splitting the rotation into *x* and *y* axis is the reason you can use `alignNode` as the alignment target—the *y* axis rotations are what's needed to properly align the billboard.

To actually do the rotation, call `align()` before rendering:

```
/**
 * Renders the sample.
 *
 * @param graphics graphics context for drawing.
 */
private void render(Graphics graphics) {
  graphics3d.bindTarget(graphics);
  graphics3d.setViewport(0, 0, getWidth(), getHeight());
  world.align(null);
  graphics3d.render(world);
  graphics3d.releaseTarget();
  drawMenu(graphics);         // displays the current key assignments
}
```

Figure 9.7 shows the result of `BillboardSample` that ties together the previously mentioned code: it draws a patch of grass with flowers using both billboard techniques. Daisy and knotweed flowers are implemented as `Sprite3D`s and will end up flat on the ground when the camera flies over them. Irises and tulips, on the other hand, use aligned quads and will stay upright.

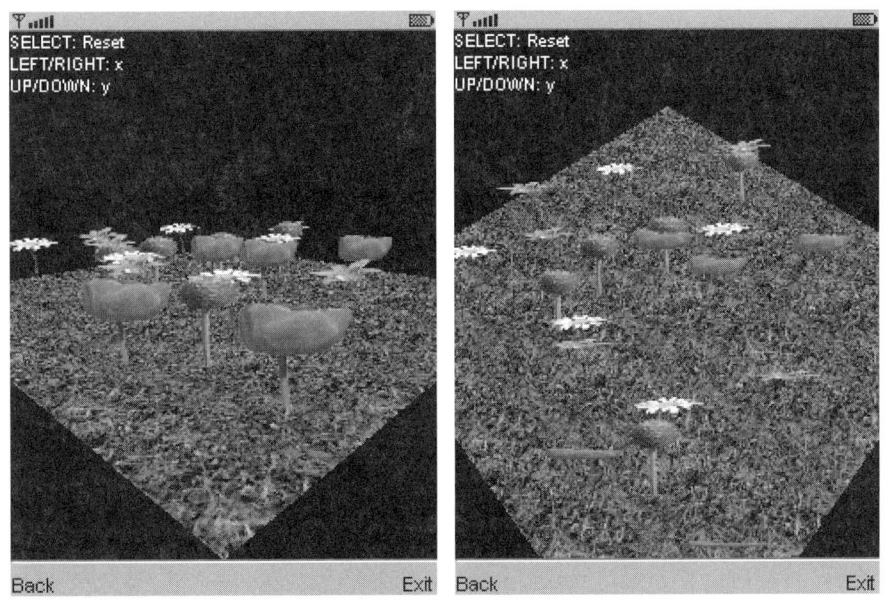

Figure 9.7
An axis-aligned quad will keep staying upright when the camera flies over it.

Aligned, textured quads are a good alternative to Sprite3Ds if you need the flexibility. If not, the simplified features of Sprite3D will provide faster rendering. Another crucial factor can be lighting, which affects textured quads but not Sprite3Ds.

```java
/**
 * This sample displays a field of flowers to demonstrate two
 * alternative billboard techniques: daisies and knotweeds use
 * screen-aligned <code>Sprite3D</code>s; tulips and irises use
 * axis-aligned, textured quads.
 *
 * @author Claus Hoefele
 */
public class BillboardSample extends GameCanvas implements Sample {
  ...

  /** 3D graphics singleton used for rendering. */
  private Graphics3D graphics3d;
  /** 2D graphics singleton used for rendering. */
  private Graphics graphics;

  /**
   * Constructor.
   */
  public BillboardSample() {
    super(false);
  }

  /**
   * Creates a patch of grass for the flower field.
   *
   * @return grass field.
   */
  private Node createGrass() {
    Mesh grass = MeshFactory2D.createQuad(true);
    grass.setOrientation(-90, 1, 0, 0);
    grass.setScale(2, 2, 1);

    PolygonMode polygonMode = new PolygonMode();
    polygonMode.setPerspectiveCorrectionEnable(true);
    polygonMode.setCulling(PolygonMode.CULL_NONE);
    grass.getAppearance(0).setPolygonMode(polygonMode);
```

```
    try {
      Image2D image2D = (Image2D) Loader.load("/m3g09/grass.png")[0];
      Texture2D texture = new Texture2D(image2D);
      texture.setBlending(Texture2D.FUNC_REPLACE);
      texture.setScale(4, 4, 0);
      texture.
          setWrapping(Texture2D.WRAP_REPEAT, Texture2D.WRAP_REPEAT);
      grass.getAppearance(0).setTexture(0, texture);
    } catch (Exception e) {
      System.out.println("Error loading texture.");
      e.printStackTrace();
    }

    return grass;
  }

  /**
   * Distributes the children of the given group randomly on the
   * x-z plane.
   *
   * @param group <code>Group</code> with children to distribute.
   * @return same object as given as parameter.
   */
  private Group distribute(Group group) {
    Random random = new Random(System.currentTimeMillis());
    for (int i=0; i<group.getChildCount(); i++) {
      float x = random.nextFloat()*3.5f - 1.75f;
      float z = random.nextFloat()*3.5f - 1.75f;
      group.getChild(i).setTranslation(x, 0.25f, z);
    }

    return group;
  }
  ...
}
```

Summary

This chapter was all about scene graphs and what you can do with the nodes inside.

World represents the root of a scene graph, which is further structured with Group nodes. If you render a scene graph in retained mode, M3G will take the camera, lighting, and background settings from the scene graph instead of `Graphics3D`. This is convenient when rendering a complex scene. The alternative is immediate mode, which lets you render individual nodes, branches of a scene graph, or submeshes. Retained and immediate modes are not exclusive, and you can switch freely back and forth between them.

After you assemble a scene graph, you can select nodes by different means: you can traverse a scene graph; tag a node with user IDs and find it with `Object3D.find()`; pick a node based on its location and shape; and use scoping to group nodes together, independent of their position in the scene graph. The final example in this chapter explored billboards with two alternative implementations for screen-aligned and axis-aligned images.

Chapter 10

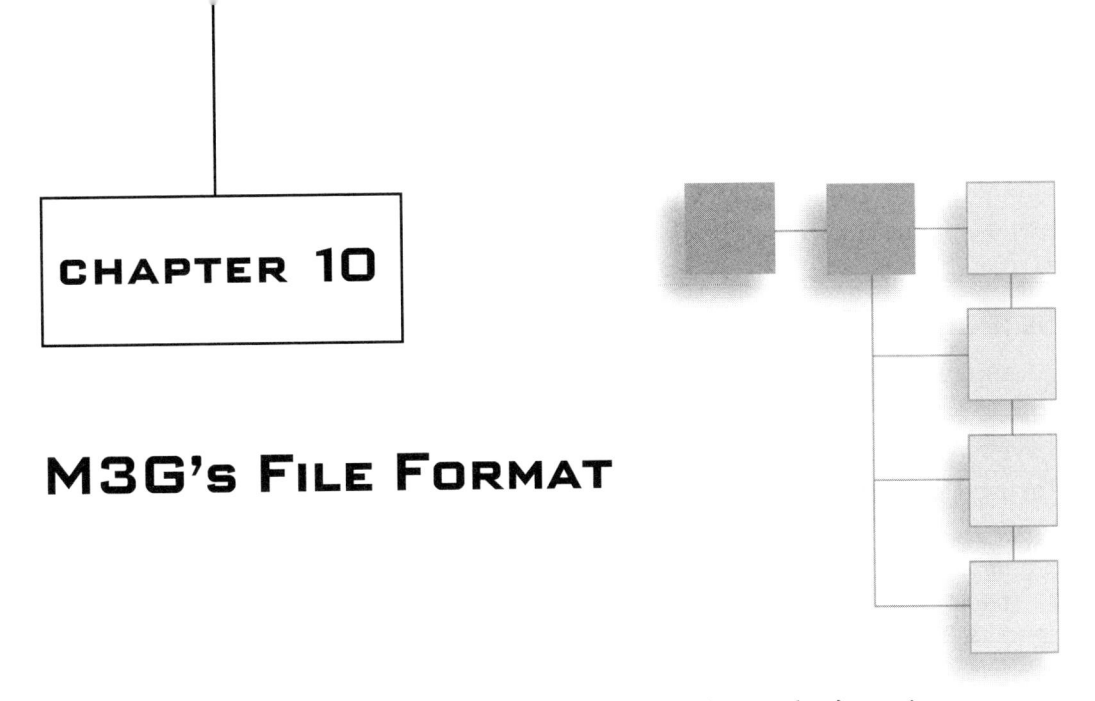

M3G's File Format

Once you get to the point where simple geometric objects don't cut it any more, digital content-creation tools come to your rescue. To help importing artwork from such tools into your application, M3G includes its own file format. M3G files can, for example, contain a scene graph in a World object that's populated with meshes, lights, and cameras.

M3G's built-in format provides a common target for tool providers. Therefore, many content-creation tools already write M3G files or you can add this functionality with a third-party plug-in. This chapter introduces you to Blender, an open source modeling package that you can extend with M3G exporting capabilities.

You learn to:

- Create a 3D scene with Blender and export the data as an M3G file.
- Load an M3G file in your application and display its contents.
- Understand M3G's binary file format.
- Add custom behavior to the M3G export.

Creating M3G Files with Blender

Blender is free of charge. Nevertheless, its features rival those of commercially available 3D content-creation tools. Most importantly for M3G, you can extend Blender with scripts written in the Python language. One such script exports Blender scenes as M3G files.

Setting Up the Environment

Although Blender comes with a Python interpreter built-in, this version doesn't include all libraries that the M3G Exporter Script requires. For this reason, you have to install a full Python environment that Blender will automatically use at the next start.

Note
Download the latest Blender version from http://www.blender.org. The release notes will tell you what Python version it works with. Python lives at http://www.python.org. The descriptions in this book refer to Blender 2.42a and Python 2.4.

To install the M3G Exporter Script, all you have to do is copy the file to the .blender\scripts directory of your Blender installation and restart the program.

Note
You can find the M3G Exporter Script at http://www.nelson-games.de/bl2m3g/. Make sure that your Blender installation has the version number that the script requires. For this book, I used version 0.6 of the script.

Getting to Know Blender

Blender helps you work with 3D artwork by providing a flexible workspace that you can configure to your needs.

Blender Short Reference

General

- Save your file with Ctrl+W.
- Undo with Ctrl+Z and redo with Ctrl+Y.
- Abort an action with Escape.
- Render your scene with F12.

Windows

- Click on the icon to the left of a window's header bar to change its type.
- Resize a window by dragging its border; right-click on this border to split or join windows.
- The current window is the one under the mouse pointer.
- Ctrl+Up arrow and Ctrl+Down arrow toggle full screen mode of the current window.

Navigating Your Scene

- Alt+left mouse button rotates your view.
- Zoom your view with Ctrl+Alt left mouse button.
- Pan with Shift+Alt+left mouse button.
- If you have a middle mouse button, you can use that instead of Alt+left mouse button.

Managing Meshes

- Select objects with right mouse button and add more with Shift+right mouse button.
- Use B (border select) to mark several objects in one go. A (all) selects/deselects all objects in a scene.
- Modify a selection with G (grab/move), R (rotate), and S (scale)
- Delete a selection with Delete or X.
- Add new meshes in the current viewport by pressing the Spacebar and selecting the Add menu.

Editing Meshes

- Switch between object and edit mode with Tab.
- Choose vertex, edge, or face selection mode with Ctrl+Tab.
- Select vertices, edges, or faces with the right mouse button and add more with the Shift+right mouse button.
- Use B (border select) to mark several items in one go. A (all) selects/deselects all items of the current object in a scene.
- Modify a selection with G (grab/move), R (rotate), and S (scale)
- Delete selection with Delete or X.

Buttons Window

- Access the Shading context with F5, the Object context with F7, the Editing context with F9, and the Scene context with F10.
- Press any context-specific hotkey several times to cycle between sub-contexts.

Blender's Workspace

Blender's user interface is divided into windows that display different information about your scene. At the top or bottom of a window, you'll find a header bar with an icon on the left that indicates the window's purpose. Clicking this icon allows you to change the window type. Context-specific menus and commands occupy the remaining space on the header line.

You can resize a window by dragging its borders. A right-click on a border opens a menu where you can split and join windows.

284 Chapter 10 ■ M3G's File Format

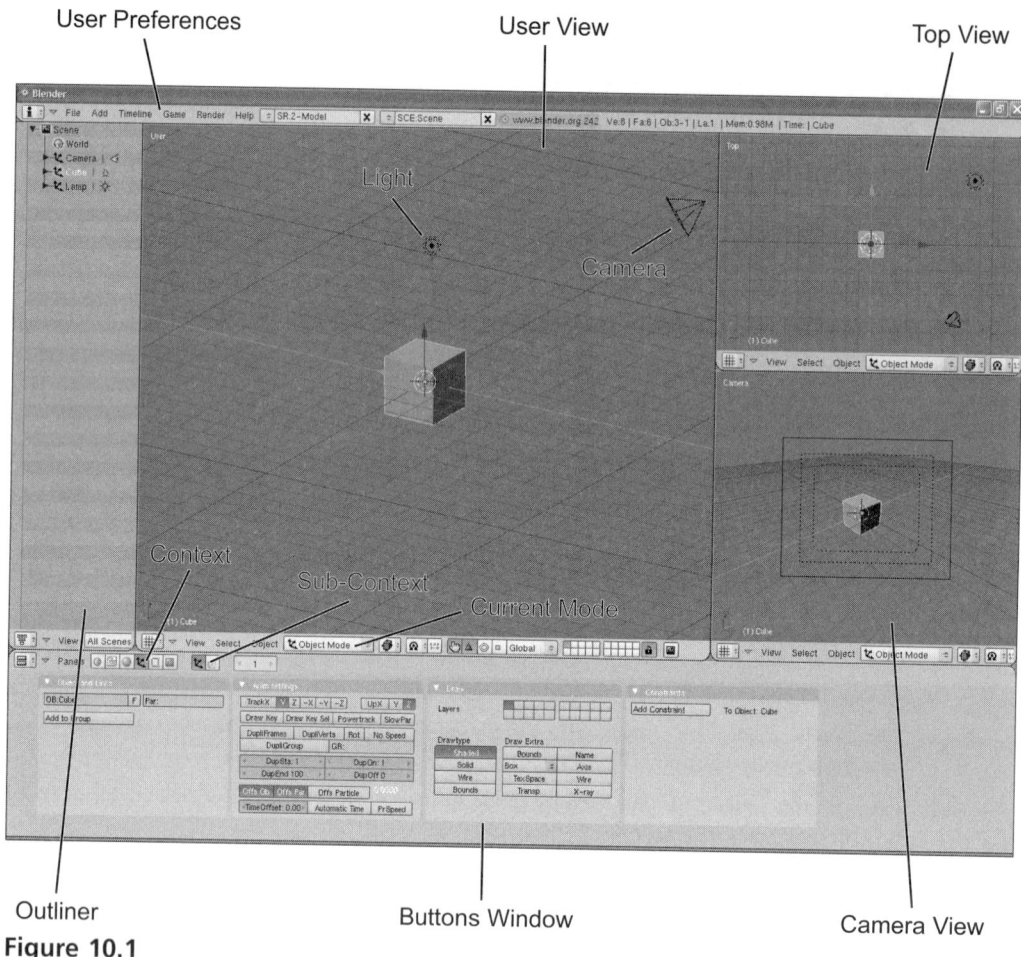

Figure 10.1
Blender's workspace.

Different layouts allow you to adapt the user interface to the current task. Figure 10.1 shows a typical setup to begin a new project.

Tip

You can start with the same configuration as in Figure 10.1 by opening the file artwork\start.blend from the CD-ROM. To set this workspace as the default one for new projects, press Ctrl+U.

This configuration has the User Preferences window at the top. Among other functions, you'll find the File menu in this window. In the middle of the workspace are three views that display your scene from different angles. A view can be perspective or orthographic, depending on whether you want foreshortening to occur. Switching between view types happens in the View menu.

Blender has pre-defined views for side, front, top, and camera view. Side, front, and top views are usually configured to be orthographic and show the scene from the respective viewing angle. The camera view, on the other hand, uses perspective and gives you a preview of the rendered scene. A soon as you make changes to a pre-defined view, it becomes a user view. This is where you can set your own options.

Because the scene is three-dimensional, it's helpful to see it from several angles. The configuration in Figure 10.1 has a top view in the upper-right corner, a camera view in the lower-right corner, and a user view to the left. It's easiest to make changes to the scene in the large user view.

To the left of the views is the Outliner, which allows you to quickly select an object from your scene. The display is similar to the hierarchy of an M3G scene graph. At the bottom of the workspace, you see the Buttons window, which has different contexts and sub-contexts with settings that change object properties. Using the buttons in this window, you manipulate most object parameters, such as when shading and texturing.

Navigating Your Scene

By default, a scene contains a cube, a light, and a camera. In the views, you'll see a light as a circle and a camera as a pyramid. To move the view to a different angle, use Alt+left mouse button. Ctrl+Alt+left mouse button zooms in and out and Shift+Alt+left mouse button pans the view. If you have a middle mouse button, you can use that instead of Alt+left mouse button.

Working with Objects

The views and the Buttons window offer different tools depending on Blender's mode. The list box in the header bar of a view next to the menus displays the mode you are currently using. If you have problems finding a specific tool, make sure you are in the right mode.

Working with meshes, lights, and cameras happens in Object mode. In this mode, the right mouse button selects an object in your scene. Holding Shift while doing this will extend the selection. When selected, Blender will highlight the object and you can press G to grab and move it. Similarly, R rotates an object and S scales it. The same hotkeys also manipulate cameras and lights.

To change vertices of a mesh, you have to select the object and switch to Edit mode with Tab. Edit mode uses the same selection and transformation hotkeys, but now you manipulate individual vertices, edges, or faces instead of entire objects.

For texturing, you will later need UV Face Select mode, which you can access by clicking the list box.

> **Tip**
>
> Sometimes, a Python script can't immediately see changes you made to your model in Edit mode. If this is the case, it helps to press Tab twice to switch to Object mode and back.

Rendering

If you press F12, Blender will open a new window and render the scene from the point of view of the camera. In the default position, the camera already points toward the cube, so you will see its shaded image in the render output.

> **Tip**
>
> For documentation and tutorials on Blender, have a look at the Blender Wiki at http://mediawiki.blender.org/. Being familiar with Blender will make it easier for you to follow the instructions in this chapter.

Monkey Business

Blender comes with a library of standard objects that you can use to assemble your scene, such as a sphere, text, or different kinds of surfaces. Included is Suzanne—a low polygon model of a monkey's head.

Creating the Mesh

To add Suzanne to your scene, you have to get rid of the cube. To do this, right-click on the cube in Object mode to select it and press X to delete. Open the context menu by pressing the Spacebar and create a new Suzanne by selecting Add>Mesh>Monkey. The 3D cursor determines where the mesh ends up. You can move the cursor by clicking anywhere in your view with the left mouse button. Press S to scale the monkey to your liking and either rotate the mesh or the camera with R so the camera faces Suzanne. You can check the result in the Camera view and render the scene with F12.

You should end up with a scene similar to the one in Figure 10.2.

User IDs

When loading the scene in your Java application later, it will be difficult to find individual objects because you don't know the order of the children in the scene graph.

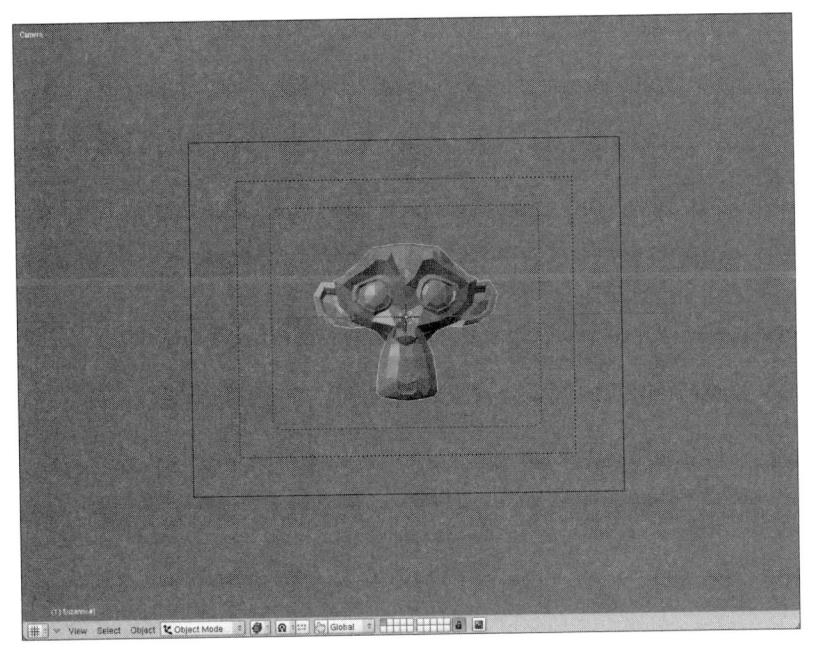

Figure 10.2
Suzanne, the monkey.

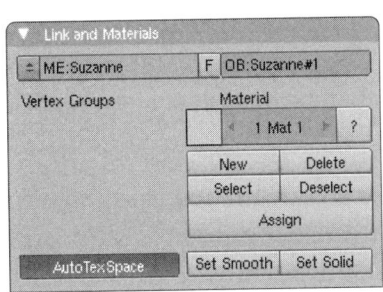

Figure 10.3
Appending an object's name with a number separated by a hash character will assign it a user ID.

Tagging an object with a user ID allows you to access it by calling `Object3D.find()`.

To give an object a user ID in Blender, you append its name with a hash character (#) and a number in the Links and Materials panel, as shown in Figure 10.3. The M3G Exporter Script will set this number as the user ID. The Links and Materials panel appears when you select the object and go to the Editing context (F9).

Light and Material

The scene already has an omnidirectional light source. Adjust the light so it produces the shading you want to achieve. To do this, select it in Object mode and use G to move it. The M3G Exporter Script can handle Blender's lamp, sun, and spot lights and will convert them into M3G's `Light.OMNI`, `DIRECTIONAL`, and `SPOT` types.

Unless you assigned a material to a mesh in Blender, the M3G Exporter Script will only write the vertex coordinates of your mesh. This means that your mesh will appear white when displayed in M3G because that's the default vertex color.

To produce normals, select Suzanne, go to the Shading context (F5), and display the Material buttons. Press the Add New button in the Links and Pipeline panel to create a new material. Once this is done, you can change the default material settings such as the diffuse color in the Material panel.

Tip
> artwork\monkey_step1.blend on the CD-ROM captures the current state of the Blender project.

Texturing

In Blender, you have two choices for adding a texture: with the Texture buttons (F6) as part of the material or by creating UV coordinates. The M3G Exporter Script requires the latter. To create new texture coordinates, switch to UV Face Select mode, which you can activate by selecting the respective entry in the list box in a view's header bar, next to the menus. Then, select all faces with A and press U. The upcoming list provides you with several ways to calculate texture coordinates.

As in Chapter 6 where you manually created texture coordinates, you have to think about how to produce coordinates that don't cause too many distortions. For irregularly shaped models such as Suzanne, the option Unwrap provides the best result. Unfortunately, Unwrap also requires the most manual work because you have to let Blender know where to cut your mesh open. Imagine cutting a milk carton so you can unfold the packaging and lay it flat on the table.

Tip
> You can find a tutorial how to unwrap Suzanne at http://mediawiki.blender.org/index.php/BlenderDev/UvUnwrapping/Suzanne. I chose to create texture coordinates so it's easy for me to color in the different face parts.

Once the texture coordinates exist, you can assign a texture. To do this, switch one of your windows to UV/Image Editor and use Image>Open to load an image.

Creating M3G Files with Blender

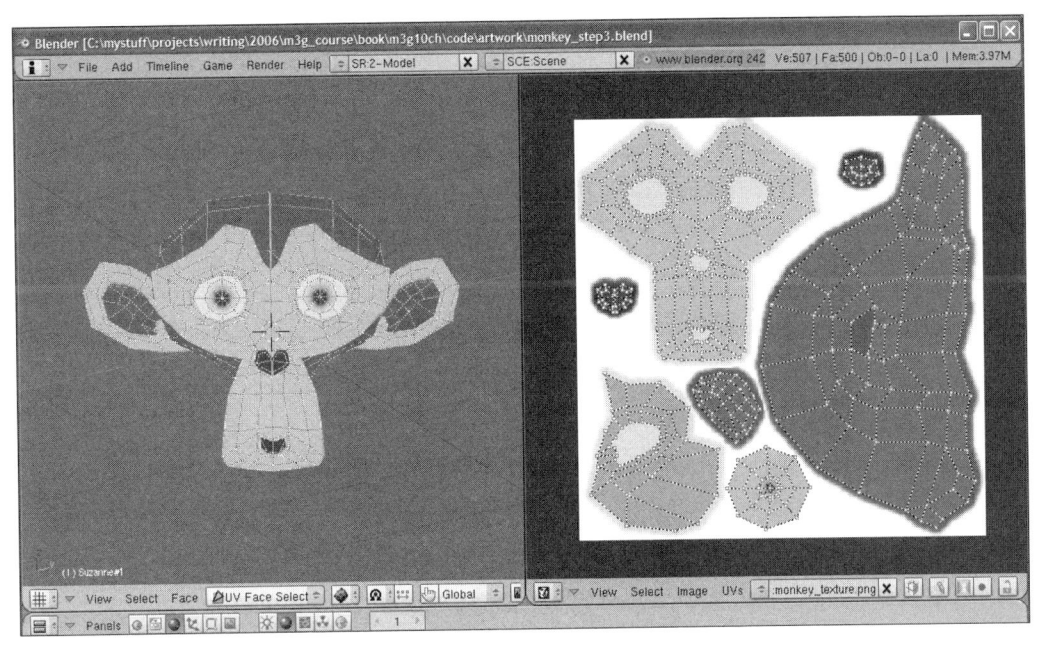

Figure 10.4
Texturing in Blender.

It's important that the image size is power-of-two as this is a requirement of M3G. The texture shouldn't be bigger than the maximum supported dimension of your handset either.

A setup similar to Figure 10.4 makes it easy to see both the model as well as the texture. To see the texture on the model, switch the draw type of the 3D View to textured (Alt+Z) and enable TexFace in the Material buttons of the Shading context (F5).

Note

You can find the textured model in artwork\monkey_step2.blend on the CD-ROM. The image file with the monkey's texture is called monkey_texture.png.

Exporting the Scene

After copying the M3G Exporter Script in the .blender\scripts directory and restarting Blender, you'll find an additional menu entry File>Export>M3G (.m3g, .java)... in the User Preferences window.

The script will present you with a dialog box that contains export options. At the moment, the default settings are fine—I'll come back to this screen later and explain what the different options mean. To accept the default settings, press OK (Return) and select a file name in the next step. Finally, press the Export M3G Binary button (Return), which will write the M3G file. You can include this file in your build and access it as a resource in your MIDlet.

Tip

> An invaluable tool at this point is HI Corporation's M3GViewer that displays M3G files and allows you to inspect the values of the exported objects. You can download the tool free of charge from http://www.mascotcapsule.com/toolkit/m3g/en/index.html.

Using M3G Files in Your Application

Creating an M3G file is the hardest part; loading and displaying it is a simple procedure. You have already seen much of the code to do this in Chapter 2 for the Hello, World! example.

Loading and Displaying the Contents

The interface to read M3G files is `Loader` and its two static methods. You can see their method signatures in Table 10.1.

When calling `load()`, you'll receive an array of deserialized objects. An M3G file can store any number of objects derived from `Object3D`. However, you'll only get unreferenced objects—objects that are part of a scene graph or otherwise referenced by an object won't be returned. For example, if you serialized an entire scene graph, you'd only receive the `World` object with the other objects as its children. That's exactly what the Blender export script does. In Figure 10.5, you can see the scene graph that results from monkey_step2.blend when it's exported with the default settings.

Apart from M3G files, images such as PNG files are also valid input to `Loader`. In this case, `load()` returns an array that contains a single `Image2D` object. As you have already seen in Chapter 6, using `Loader` to read images means you don't need an additional `Image` object that is necessary if you use `Image.createImage()` instead.

Table 10.1 Loader Class Description

Method	Description
`static Object3D[] load(byte[] data, int offset)`	Reads an M3G file from a `byte` array.
`static Object3D[] load(java.lang.String name)`	Reads an M3G file from a named resource.

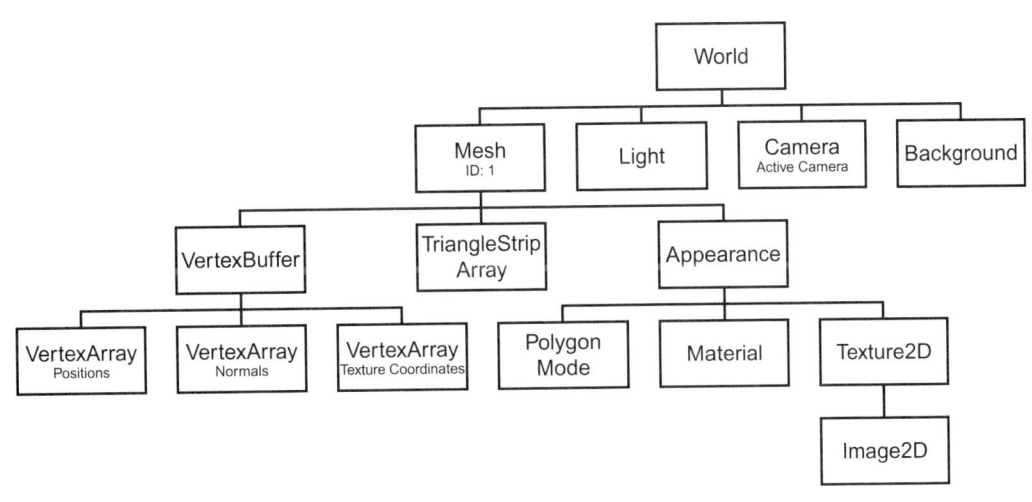

Figure 10.5
The exported M3G file from Blender includes a single scene graph with a World object as its root node.

M3G files end with .m3g, but the MIME type application/m3g is the preferred way to detect an M3G file without opening it. Also, a loader can inspect the file identifier at the start of an M3G file. Similar definitions for file ending, MIME type, and file identifier distinguish M3G files from images.

> **Note**
> You'll find this sample in M3gFileSample.java on the CD-ROM. The sample displays different versions of Suzanne—for example, before and after texturing. You can cycle through the models with the FIRE key. The M3G files are located in the res\m3g10 folder on the CD-ROM.

As input to Loader, you can use a byte array or a named resource. Most often, you'll load an M3G file from a JAR such as in the following code:

```
/**
 * Loads 3D models from M3G files that were created with Blender.
 *
 * @author Claus Hoefele
 */
public class M3gFileSample extends GameCanvas implements Sample {
    /** Object that represents the 3D world. */
    private World world;
```

```
...

/** M3G models. */
private static final String[][] MODELS = new String[][] {
   {"/m3g10/monkey_step1.m3g", "Lighting"},
   {"/m3g10/monkey_step2.m3g", "Texturing"},
   ...
};
/** Current model. */
private int currentModel;

/** 3D graphics singleton used for rendering. */
private Graphics3D graphics3d;
/** 2D graphics singleton used for rendering. */
private Graphics graphics;

/**
 * Constructor.
 */
public M3gFileSample() {
   super(false);
}

/**
 * Initializes the sample.
 */
public void init() {
   // Get the singletons for rendering.
   graphics3d = Graphics3D.getInstance();
   graphics = getGraphics();

   // Load first model.
   currentModel = 0;
   world = loadScene(MODELS[currentModel][0]);

   render(graphics);
   flushGraphics();
}

/**
 * Loads a scene graph from the given URL and adjusts the active
 * camera to match the current device. This method expects a
 * <code>World</code> object to be the first object in the M3G file.
```

```
 *
 * @param url the scene graph's URL.
 * @return scene graph.
 */
private World loadScene(String url) {
  World world = null;

  try {
    // Load scene graph.
    Object3D[] objects = Loader.load(url);
    world = (World) objects[0];

    // Change the camera's properties to match the current device.
    Camera camera = world.getActiveCamera();
    float aspect = (float) getWidth() / (float) getHeight();
    camera.setPerspective(60, aspect, 1, 1000);
    ...
  } catch (Exception e) {
    System.out.println("Error reading file " + url);
    e.printStackTrace();
  }

  return world;
}

/**
 * Renders the sample.
 *
 * @param graphics graphics context for drawing.
 */
protected void render(Graphics graphics) {
  graphics3d.bindTarget(graphics);
  graphics3d.setViewport(0, 0, getWidth(), getHeight());
  graphics3d.render(world);
  graphics3d.releaseTarget();

  drawMenu(graphics); // displays the current key assignment
}
...
}
```

`Loader` doesn't specify the order of the returned `Object3D`s. However, the M3G Exporter Script always writes a single unreferenced object into the M3G file—the

`World` object at the root of your scene graph. Therefore, the code in the previous example can directly access the first item in the array returned by `Loader.load()` and cast it into a `World` object.

> **Tip**
>
> Be careful when using the output from other exporters because M3G files can contain several unreferenced objects. If your tool supports it, the safest way to identify your object is by tagging it with a user ID. When loading, you loop through the array and check the user ID by calling `Object3D.getUserID()`. If you look for a type of object that exists only once in your file, you can also use the `instanceof` operator.

Named resources must always be absolute paths. A single forward slash (/) at the start addresses a file in the top level directory of a JAR. You can add more subdirectories in front of the file name, separated by further slashes.

The M3G specification mandates that the contents of an M3G file are valid—otherwise `Loader` will throw an `IOException`. Valid means that you can construct the same scene graph manually with M3G's API without causing an error.

The contents have to be valid, but they don't have to display correctly. You have time until rendering to modify your scene graph and bring things in order. For example, something the script can't know when it writes the M3G file is the aspect ratio of the screen on which you will display the contents. Instead, you have to set this information at runtime. For this reason, `M3gFileSample` updates the camera parameters in `loadScene()`, right after reading the scene data from file. For the same reason, the render preview in Blender might display a different detail than you'll see on the device. Rendering the contents of the M3G file in the emulator results in Figure 10.6.

Finding Nodes

Per definition, M3G ignores the transformation stored in a `World` object. This means that if you want to transform nodes inside the scene graph, you have to access them directly or via a `Group` object. If you recall, I gave Suzanne a user ID by appending the mesh's name with "#1" in Blender. This makes finding the monkey trivial:

```
/** Mesh for rotation. */
private Mesh mesh;
/** User ID to find the mesh inside the scene graph. */
private static final int USER_ID_MESH = 1;
```

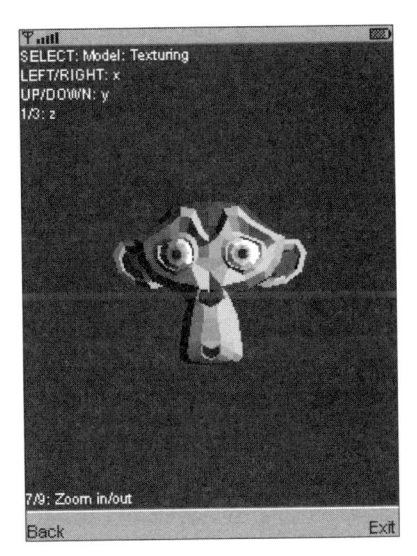

Figure 10.6
Suzanne displayed in a MIDlet.

```
private World loadScene(String url) {
   ...
   // Find mesh in scene graph.
   mesh = (Mesh) world.find(USER_ID_MESH);
   if (mesh == null) {
     System.out.println("Can't find user ID " + USER_ID_MESH);
   } ...
}
```

Coordinate Axes

Blender's coordinate system differs from M3G's. Both coordinate systems are right-handed, but the z and y axes point in different directions. Figure 10.7 shows both systems.

If you take your right hand and point the x axis (your thumb) to the right, Blender's y axis (the index finger) points away from you and the z axis (the middle finger) up. M3G's x axis is the same, but the y axis points up and the z axis toward you.

Because both the camera and Suzanne use Blender's coordinate system, the mesh displays correctly. However, your own transformations have to consider the different coordinate systems. For example, a transformation around the z axis,

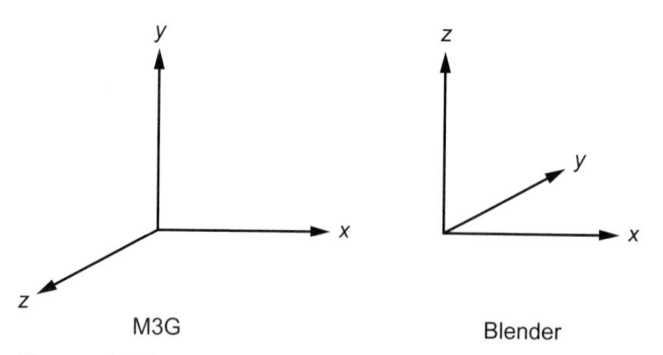

Figure 10.7
Compared to M3G, Blender's coordinate system is rotated around the x axis.

not the *y* axis, causes the monkey to rotate in an upright position. You can try this out by using the keys defined in `M3gFileSample`'s key handler:

```
/**
 * Handles key presses.
 *
 * @param keyCode key code.
 */
protected void keyPressed(int keyCode) {
  switch (getGameAction(keyCode)) {
    case FIRE:
      currentModel++;
      currentModel %= MODELS.length;
      world = loadScene(MODELS[currentModel][0]);
      break;

    case LEFT:
      mesh.postRotate(-10, 1, 0, 0);            // Model: x -> M3G: x
      break;
    case RIGHT:
      mesh.postRotate(10, 1, 0, 0);
      break;
    case DOWN:
      mesh.postRotate(-10, 0, 1, 0);            // Model: y -> M3G: -z
      break;
    case UP:
      mesh.postRotate(10, 0, 1, 0);
      break;
    case GAME_A:
```

```
      mesh.postRotate(-10, 0, 0, 1);        // Model: z -> M3G: y
      break;
    case GAME_B:
      mesh.postRotate(10, 0, 0, 1);
      break;
    case GAME_C:
      mesh.scale(1.10f, 1.10f, 1.10f);      // all axes
      break;
    case GAME_D:
      mesh.scale(0.90f, 0.90f, 0.90f);
      break;

      // no default
  }

  render(graphics);
  flushGraphics();
}
```

Improving the Result

The faceted look in Suzanne's face doesn't look too appealing. You'll also be amazed by the current file size of the exported scene. You can improve this and other features by modifying settings in Blender.

Export Options

The texture embedded inside the M3G file causes the large file size. M3G files store images as byte arrays, in the same format as required by Image2D. The M3G Exporter Script writes four bytes per pixel (RGBA), which means that Suzanne's texture with the size 256 × 256 pixels ends up as 256KB of data.

This is not as bad as it sounds, because the M3G file will shrink once you put it into the application's JAR. However, the storage techniques used for image files are superior to the more general compression algorithm a JAR uses. Thus, the better option is to store the texture as a separate image file and reference the file name from inside the M3G file. Considering the file size improvement, storing textures as external images outweighs the additional effort of keeping several files around. You are also more flexible with external files because you can modify them independently of the M3G file.

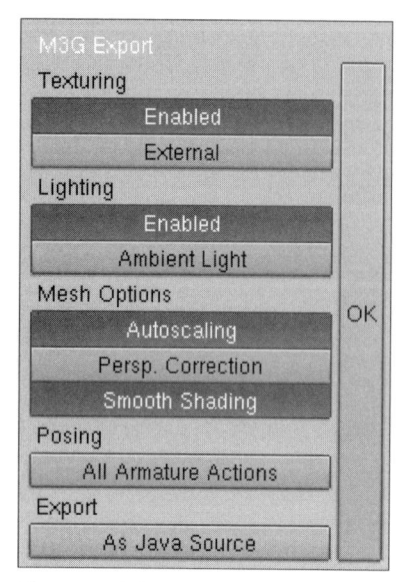

Figure 10.8
The options dialog box configures the M3G Exporter Script.

In Figure 10.8, you can see the M3G Exporter Script's default settings. Initially, the script stores images internally, but you enable textures stored as separate files with the External button. When loading the resulting M3G file, you have to put the image in the same directory, with the same name as the texture that you used in Blender. The same restrictions as for `Image2D` objects apply: you can use images such as GIF or JPEG, but only PNG support is mandated by M3G's specification.

Both texturing and lighting can be switched off with the respective Enabled button. Depending on these settings, the script will suppress texture coordinates and normals for all meshes in the entire scene. If lighting is disabled, it will also stop exporting any light sources. If lighting is switched on, an enabled Ambient Light button will create an additional light source that uses Blender's world ambient settings (World buttons in the Shading context).

In contrast to the scene-wide settings in the export options, you can also disable texturing and lighting per mesh by using the TexFace and Shadeless buttons in the Material panel, which Figure 10.9 shows. You find this panel in the Material buttons of the Shading context (F5).

Autoscaling is an option that you should always enable. Autoscaling uses the scale and bias parameters in `VertexBuffer` to maximize the precision of your mesh's vertex positions. Chapter 4 used the same technique to create shapes with fractional values.

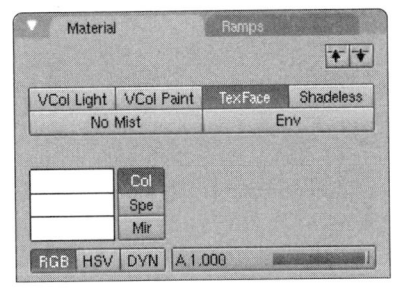

Figure 10.9
The TexFace and Shadeless buttons determine whether texture coordinates and normals are enabled for a material.

> **Tip**
> The M3G Exporter Script only exports models that are meshes. You have to convert other objects by selecting them in Object mode and pressing Alt+C repeatedly until the object ends up as a mesh. For example, I produced the text used in Chapter 2 by adding a font object and pressing Alt+C twice. The first conversion produces a curve, the second a mesh.

The two remaining options refer to features not used in this chapter. Export All Actions is useful for animated skinned meshes, which Chapter 12 will discuss. If you choose to write a Java file, the script generates the source code necessary to create your scene from M3G objects. You have to make the file part of your build and include the compiled class in your JAR file. Java source code is easier to edit than a binary M3G file. However, you'll run into problems for large meshes because the Java Virtual Machine Specification limits the code size that can be stored in a class.

Adjusting the Render Preview

Because you want to run your application on a wide range of phones, you don't know the screen size in advance. For this reason, you have to adjust the camera's aspect ratio when displaying the file contents. I showed you how to do this in the previous code example.

Blender has a much more powerful render engine than the average mobile phone. Thus the exported scene won't look exactly the same as the render output in Blender. You can, however, set the size of Blender's render output to get an idea what the scene will look like on the phone. To do this, select the Render buttons of the Scene context (F10), which Figure 10.10 displays.

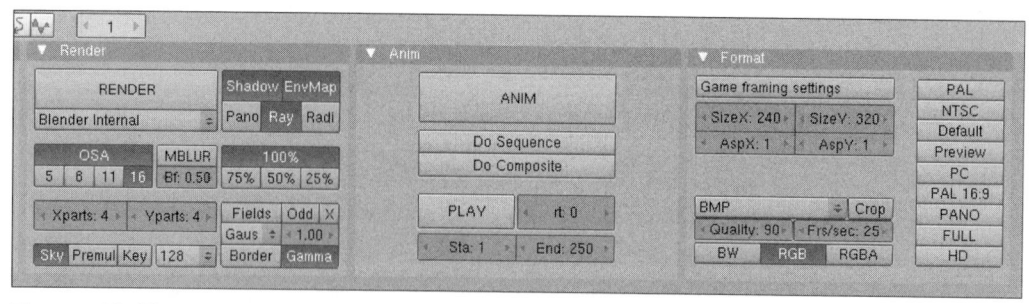

Figure 10.10
By changing the size of the render result, you can emulate a phone's screen size.

Adjust width and height in the Format box to match the screen size of your phone and set the render size in the Render box to 100%.

When rendering, Blender uses the color set for the horizon in the World panel as the background color. You reach this panel by going to the Shading context (F5) and selecting the World buttons. The M3G Exporter Script will write the same color into the M3G file. Background images, however, are not supported.

Producing the Minimum Number of Vertices

Blender's fundamental mesh-building primitive is a face, which is either a triangle or a quad. Suzanne is mostly made from quads, with a few triangles. To keep an eye on the number of polygons, Blender provides statistics of your scene in the header bar of the User Preferences window, which you can see in Figure 10.11.

In contrast to Blender, M3G only works with triangles. Therefore, if the M3G Exporter Script encounters a quad in Blender, it builds one triangle strip with two triangles made from the corners of the quad. If the face in Blender is already a triangle, the script produces one triangle strip with one triangle in it.

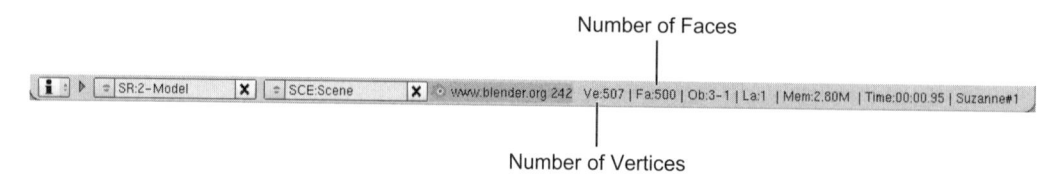

Figure 10.11
You can see the number of vertices and faces of your model in the header bar of the User Preferences window.

In other words, Blender's face count determines the number of strips you'll have in the `TriangleStripArray` of your M3G file.

Note
> The short triangle strips that the M3G Exporter Script produces are not ideal. Most devices render a small number of strips that contain many triangles quicker than many strips with few triangles. Long strips also reduce the memory that's needed for indices.

Blender's vertex count, on the other hand, relates in a more complicated way to the number of vertices stored in the `VertexBuffer`. M3G can only store mesh information per vertex; Blender on the other hand can store normals and texture coordinates per face as well. This means, although Blender can share a vertex among faces even if its normal and texture coordinates differ per face, the M3G Exporter Script has to produce separate vertices, each with its own set of information.

In the best-case scenario, vertices shared among faces have the same information. Then, the vertex count in Blender corresponds exactly to the number of vertices in the `VertexBuffer`. In the worst case, the script produces separate vertices for each face. This results in a number three to four times the face count. Most often, you have something in between, which depends on your choice of normals and texture coordinates.

A vertex's normal is the same among faces if adjacent faces use smooth shading in the Links and Materials panel of the Editing context (F9). In this case, Blender produces a normal that's the average of the normals of all faces connected to a vertex. Solid shading, on the other hand, produces hard edges because each face uses a normal orthogonal to itself. Then, a vertex can be shared only if the face normals are pointing in the same direction. In other words, it saves a lot of memory if you enable smooth shading. To do this, select your mesh in Object mode and press the Set Smooth button in the Links and Materials box of the Editing context (F9).

It's a good idea to check the normals before export. You can visualize normals by using the Mesh Tools 1 panel in the Editing context (F9). If you enable Draw Normals, Blender will display face normals used for solid shading. Checking Draw VNormals shows the vertex normals used for smooth shading. Normals pointing in the wrong direction cause unexpected shading of your model and might, in combination with backface culling, give your model holes. If you select a face in Edit Mode, Ctrl+N recalculates the face's outside normal and

W flips the direction of the normal. Backface culling of a mesh is enabled and disabled with the Double Sided button in the Mesh panel of the Editing context (F9). If the Double Sided button is pressed, the script will set the mesh's `PolygonMode` to `CULL_NONE`; otherwise, it will set to `CULL_BACK`.

> **Tip**
>
> The Double Sided button is enabled by default in Blender, so be sure to disable this option if you don't need it because it speeds up the rendering.

Figure 10.12 shows Suzanne with more natural smooth shading for the entire mesh. If you want to have hard edges, you can enable solid shading for individual faces or recreate faces with separate vertices. Note that solid shading differs from setting `PolygonMode` to `SHADE_FLAT`, which you can do in the export options. The latter is a mesh-wide setting that will simply use the information stored in the third vertex of each triangle to produce a triangle's color.

As a welcome side effect of smooth shading, you'll reduce the vertices in the M3G file drastically. With texturing enabled, the only reason left to duplicate a vertex is if the vertex has more than one set of texture coordinates. This happens at the seams where you cut the mesh open when unwrapping the mesh. All vertices on the seam will receive a second set of texture coordinates that maps to different parts of the texture.

Figure 10.12
Suzanne with smooth shading.

> **Note**
> I saved the optimized Blender settings in artwork\blender_step3.blend. When exported with external texture and smooth shading, Suzanne requires 24KB (15KB compressed, 630 vertices) compared to 291KB (22KB, 1966 vertices) with internal texture and solid shading.

Reducing the Poly Count

For Blender's standard meshes, you can adjust the number of faces at creation time. You can, for example, choose the amount of subdivisions when adding a sphere. I selected Suzanne for this chapter because she looks interesting and has a reasonable number of polygons to start with. Having an artist create a low polygon model is always the best way because he or she can take the specifics of the model into account. However, Blender also provides tools to automatically decrease the poly count.

For starters, you can remove a mesh's duplicate vertices in Edit mode by pressing W and then 6. This won't help with well constructed meshes as they shouldn't contain duplicates from the beginning.

In the Modifiers panel of the Editing context (F9), you'll find the modifier stack. With Suzanne selected, you can add a Decimate modifier by pressing the Add Modifier button. The ratio determines the amount of reduction; the face count below indicates the resulting number of faces. For example, a ratio of 0.5 will reduce the faces to about half the number that existed before.

The idea of the modifier stack is to transform objects without making permanent changes. That way, you can still work with the original mesh should you want to change settings later on. However, the M3G Exporter Script won't pick up the modifications unless you transferred them to the mesh. To do this, press the Apply button and you'll see that Blender's face count now displays the same number of faces that the Decimate tool predicted.

> **Tip**
> In addition to converting objects, pressing Alt+C on a selected mesh will also apply modifiers. (You'll have to press Alt+C several times, depending on the number of conversions your objects need.) Before you export your scene, always make sure all objects are meshes and all modifiers are applied.

With the Decimate modifier, it's important that you fix the poly count of your model before texturing because applying it will delete all UV coordinates and you'll have to start the unwrapping process anew. For this reason, I prefer a Python script that ships with Blender: the Poly Reducer.

You start the Poly Reducer by selecting the mesh in Edit mode and selecting Mesh>Script>Poly Reducer. Once executed, the script transfers the changes immediately to the mesh. It works similar to the Decimator modifier but automatically interpolates texture coordinates, and you can adjust which part of the mesh is affected the most by the reduction. For example, you can give Suzanne more detail for nose and eyes than its skull.

Both Decimate modifier and Poly Reducer work on triangles. (The Poly Reducer has an option to work with quads, but triangles produce better results.) This means that after the reduction, you'll end up with a lot of faces that increase the number of triangle strips in your M3G file. To avoid this, select the entire model with A in Edit mode and convert the triangles back to quads with Alt+J. Again, you have an alternative in the form of a script, which you'll find at Mesh>Scripts>Triangles to Quads. The script beats the built-in function because it produces fewer artifacts.

Figure 10.13 shows three examples of Suzanne after using the Poly Reducer with the default settings and converting triangles back to quads: with a reduction factor of 0.7 (457 vertices, 401 strips), a factor of 0.5 (347 vertices, 292 strips), and a factor of 0.4 (287 vertices, 247 strips). Without reduction, the model has 630 vertices and 500 strips.

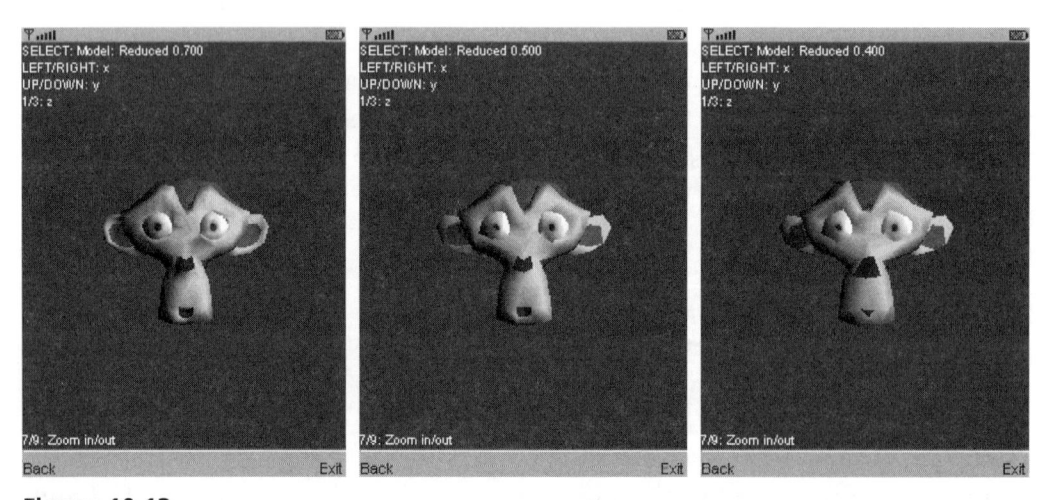

Figure 10.13
Suzanne with different levels of detail. From left to right: polygons reduced by a factor of 0.7, 0.5, and 0.4.

Analyzing M3G Files

You don't have to understand the M3G file contents to export and load M3G files—until something breaks. Knowing the innards of M3G's file format enables you to tackle problems if something goes wrong and find possibilities for optimizations.

File Structure

The first 12 bytes of the file contents constitute the file identifier. As Figure 10.14 shows, the remaining content is partitioned into sections, which are further divided into objects.

Data Types

At the basis of an M3G file are individual values encoded according to their data types. Table 10.2 lists the types you will encounter in an M3G file. They fall in two categories: fundamental and compound.

Fundamental data types exist for integer values of different sizes as well as single precision float values, text strings, and Boolean values. They correspond to Java's `byte`, `int`, `float`, `String`, and `boolean` types with the only difference that M3G's file format lets you decide whether integer values are signed or unsigned. All data types are encoded little-endian (least significant byte comes first). Combinations of fundamental data types form compound data types.

Sections

The main motivation to split data into sections is that you can choose the compression scheme independently. You can have one section that's uncompressed and can be read quickly and another that's compressed and saves storage space.

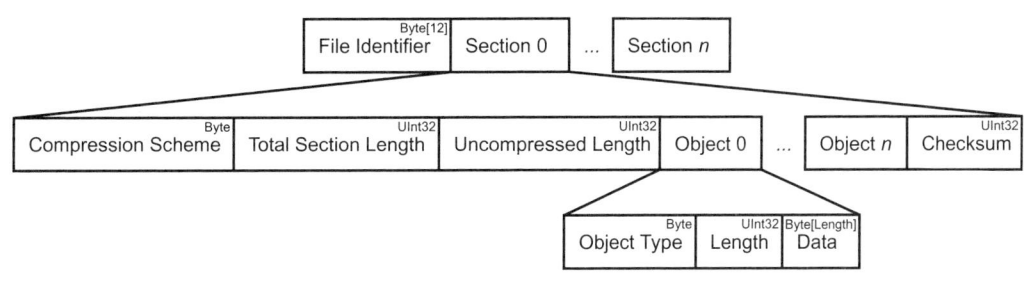

Figure 10.14
An M3G file starts with a file identifier and continues with data partitioned into sections.

Table 10.2 Data Types

Type	Description
Fundamental	
Byte	8-bit unsigned value.
Int16	16-bit signed value.
UInt16	16-bit unsigned value.
Int32	32-bit signed value.
UInt32	32-bit unsigned value.
Float32	32-bit single-precision floating point value (IEEE-754).
String	UTF-8 encoded, null terminated Unicode string.
Boolean	8-bit value (0=false, 1=true).
Compound	
Vector3D	3D vector encoded as three Float32 values (x, y, z).
Matrix	4 × 4 matrix encoded as 16 Float32 values in row-major order.
ColorRGB	Color value encoded as three Byte values (R, G, B).
ColorRGBA	Color value with transparency encoded as four Byte values (R, G, B, A).
ObjectIndex	UInt32 value indicating a reference to another object.
Type[]	Variable length array of any type encoded as one UInt32 value indicating the length, followed by the elements of the array.
Type[count]	Fixed length array of any type encoded as a list of elements of the array.

The value 0 in the compression scheme field indicates no compression. The value 1, on the other hand, specifies ZLib compression. Both schemes use an Adler32 checksum at the end of the section to validate your data.

Each section can hold one or more objects that contain serialized M3G data. Although the total section length field includes all bytes in the section, the uncompressed length relates to the number of bytes of the object fields. If this data is compressed, the uncompressed length field helps file parsers efficiently decompress the contents. Otherwise, the value is simply the number of bytes of the object fields.

Depending on the type of objects a section carries, additional requirements regarding its position and contents apply.

Objects

The actual payload of an M3G file is contained in the object fields. Each consists of the object type that describes the contents, the length of the data field, and the data itself.

M3G's file format assigns each class that it can serialize an object type value between 1 and 22. Valid input includes all classes derived from `Object3D`, except for abstract classes. Because you can't instantiate abstract classes such as `Transformable`, they are serialized as part of superclass data but don't have an object type value. For example, the value 14 (0x0E) signifies a `Mesh` object. The data field would then contain the serialized object properties of `Mesh` and those of its superclasses `Node`, `Transformable`, and `Object3D`.

Note

For each class that M3G's file format can serialize, the javadoc documentation has a link to further information that specifies its binary structure.

If the object type doesn't indicate an M3G object, it must correspond to one of two special cases: the type value 0 is reserved for the header object and the value 255 (0xFF) for external references.

The header object contains information about the M3G file such as the format's version number and the total file size. Its contents must be the only object in the first, uncompressed section of the file. A valid M3G file comprises at least two sections: one with the header object and another non-empty section.

An external reference, on the other hand, is a unified resource identifier (URI) that points to another M3G compatible file. "http://www.example.com/example.m3g" is a valid absolute URI for example. When reading a named resource with `Loader.load(String)`, external references may also use path names relative to the referrer. When reading an M3G file from a `byte` array, on the other hand, all external references must be absolute paths. When exporting Suzanne with external textures, you have already seen external references in action. However, external references are not restricted to images—you can also store any other part of your scene graph in a separate file.

If a file has external references, they must appear in section 1, right after the section with the header object. This ensures that a parser can check and load all external references before continuing with the rest for the file. The contents of the references are then merged with the referrer.

Object Relationships

Starting from index 1, each object in a file is implicitly assigned a number based on the position in the file. The numbering starts with the header object because it's always the first object in the first section. Next are the reference objects if the file has any and afterward all objects in all further sections. The index 0 is reserved for `null` references. These indices are used in an M3G file as the data type `ObjectIndex`.

If an object such as `World` references another object such as the active camera, the camera's index substitutes the object. To simplify file parsing, an object must only reference indices that preceded it. Hence the root of a tree is written last, after all its leaves. You can have any number of roots in one section. It is these non-referenced objects that you'll receive when calling `Loader.load()`.

To be able to write referenced objects first, the serialized data mustn't contain cycles. This is the case for an M3G scene graph with the exception of node alignment. A cycle exists if a child node uses a parent in the scene graph as an alignment target. A file writer must erase this problem by inserting a dummy node and redirecting the alignment target to it.

Contents of the Blender Generated File

The file written by the Blender exporter contains the scene graph for the monkey, but also M3G specific data such as section headers and file information. Figure 10.15 shows the contents of the M3G file generated by the M3G Exporter Script with external textures enabled.

Note
You'll find this file with the name monkey_step3.m3g on the CD-ROM in the folder res\m3g10.

File Identifier

The first 12 bytes comprise the file identifier; it's identical for every M3G file. It contains a human readable text, but also non-ASCII characters to distinguish the file as binary. (If you have a look in Chapter 6, you'll find that PNG files have a similar signature.)

Section 0: Header Object

The first section after the file identifier contains the header object. The information from the section data (compression scheme, total section length, uncompressed length, and checksum) indicates no compression, as is required for the first section with the header object.

Analyzing M3G Files 309

File Identifier

```
0:   AB 4A 53 52 31 38 34 BB  0D 0A 1A 0A          «JSR184»....
```

Section 0: File Header

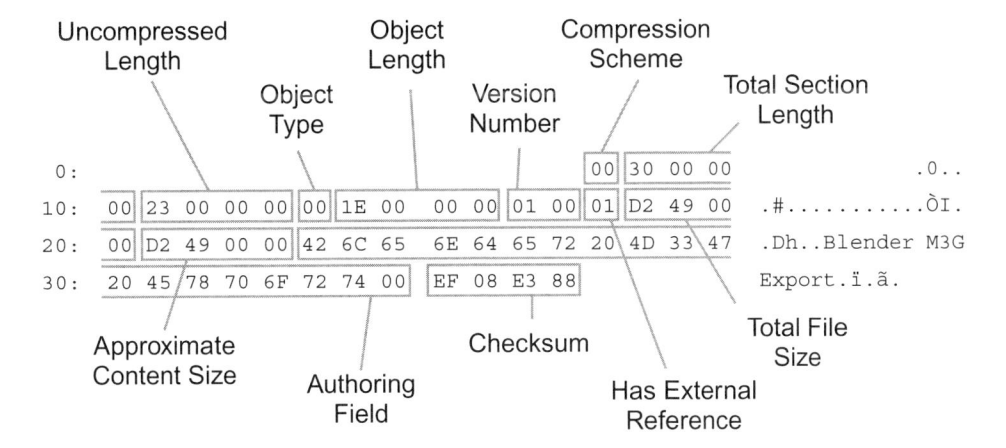

```
 0:                                        00 30 00 00        .0..
10:  00 23 00 00 00 00 1E 00  00 00 01 00 01 D2 49 00  .#...........ÒI.
20:  00 D2 49 00 00 42 6C 65  6E 64 65 72 20 4D 33 47  .ÒI..Blender M3G
30:  20 45 78 70 6F 72 74 00  EF 08 E3 88              Export.ï.ã.
```

- Uncompressed Length
- Object Type
- Object Length
- Version Number
- Compression Scheme
- Total Section Length
- Approximate Content Size
- Authoring Field
- Checksum
- Has External Reference
- Total File Size

Section 1: External References

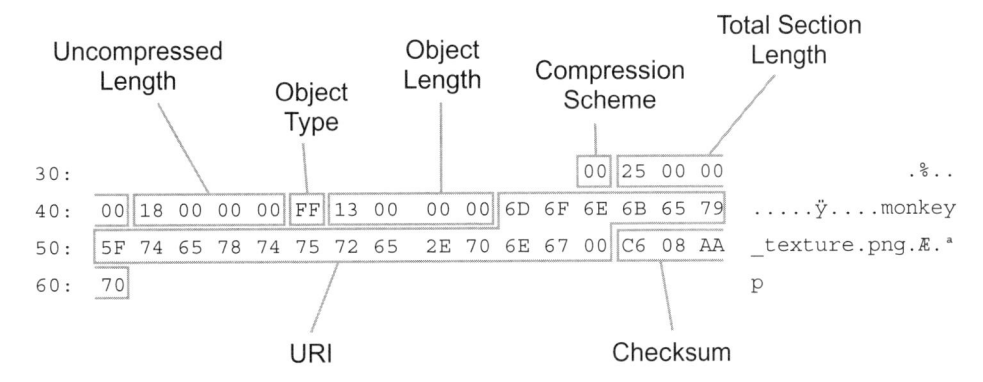

```
30:                                        00 25 00 00        .%..
40:  00 18 00 00 00 FF 13 00  00 00 6D 6F 6E 6B 65 79  .....ÿ....monkey
50:  5F 74 65 78 74 75 72 65  2E 70 6E 67 00 C6 08 AA  _texture.png.Æ.ª
60:  70                                                p
```

- Uncompressed Length
- Object Type
- Object Length
- Compression Scheme
- Total Section Length
- URI
- Checksum

Section 2: Scene Objects

```
60:          00 71 49 00 00 64 49 00 00                       .qI..dI...
                <2546 bytes of scene data>
49C0:                                      93 EA                .ê
49D0:  FD 58                                                    ýX
```

- Compression Scheme
- Total Section Length
- Uncompressed Length
- Checksum

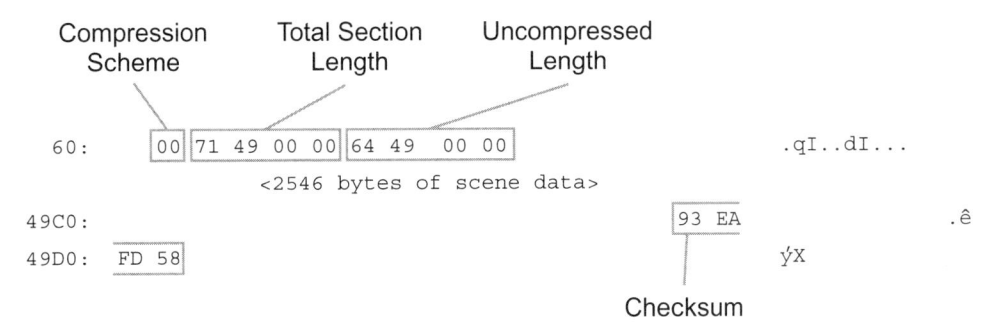

Figure 10.15
Contents of the M3G file monkey_step3.m3g; generated with Blender and the M3G Exporter Script.

The section is 48 bytes long; the uncompressed length is 13 bytes smaller because this field doesn't include the section header. The object data (object type and length) indicate that the section contains the object header because of the value 0 written in the type field.

The header object's payload starts with the version number. Both M3G 1.0 and 1.1 use the same version number because the file format didn't change. The first byte indicates the major version number, the next byte the minor version number. The next field is of Boolean type. The value 1 indicates that the file uses external references. These references will follow in section 1.

Total file size and approximate content size specify the file length. Whereas the total file size relates to the current file, the content size includes external references. It's only a hint because external files might change without update to the referrer. Because the field is optional, the M3G Exporter Script never includes external files in this value. The field is, however, useful to suggest the overall download size of a scene. The total file size, on the other hand, must be correct as the file parser needs to know the file length.

Finally, the authoring field contains a null-terminated UTF-8 string. As in this example, the text usually indicates the software that wrote the file, but can also contain a copyright notice of the author.

Section 1: External References

The file has external references, so these references must appear in this section. From the compression scheme field, you can see that this section is uncompressed as well.

Tip

M3G's file format supports compression, but you are better off without it, because the M3G file will be compressed anyway when it's added to the application's JAR file.

You can recognize the external reference by its object type 0xFF. The object data itself comprises the null-terminated URI of the file the reference points to. In this case, this is the file name of the texture without any path identifier. Hence, you must place the texture and the M3G file in the same directory.

Section 2: Scene Objects

The file continues with the scene objects. According to M3G's file format rules, the M3G Exporter Script writes referenced objects first, before the referring objects.

The script uses a depth-first algorithm, which recursively descends down each branch of the scene graph and writes the objects from bottom to top. The following table lists the objects in the order they appear in the M3G file.

Object	Type	File Position	Object Length (Bytes)	Comment
Camera	0x05	0x006A	103	
Background	0x04	0x00D6	40	
VertexArray	0x14	0x0103	3797	Positions (3*2 bytes per vertex)
VertexArray	0x14	0x0FDD	1907	Normals (3*1 byte per vertex)
VertexArray	0x14	0x1755	2537	UV coordinates (2*2 bytes per vertex)
VertexBuffer	0x15	0x2143	68	630 vertices
TriangleStripArray	0x0B	0x218C	9893	968 triangles in 500 strips
PolygonMode	0x08	0x4836	18	
Material	0x0D	0x484D	30	
Texture2D	0x11	0x4871	26	Uses external reference in section 1 for Image2D
Appearance	0x03	0x488F	37	
Mesh	0x0E	0x48B9	102	
Light	0x0C	0x4924	114	
World	0x16	0x499B	46	

A large chunk of data stems from the TriangleStripArray and the three VertexArrays. For this reason, you should strive for a minimum of vertices and faces in your model. Another possibility is to reduce the data per vertex. By using light maps instead of dynamic lighting as described in Chapter 8, you can get rid of the normals, for example.

Extending the M3G Exporter Script

What if you had an idea for a great new feature, you want to optimize the existing script, or you want to adapt it to your specific needs? All this is possible because you can modify the script's source code under the GNU Public License.

Writing Blender Scripts

Before this section goes into the details of the existing M3G Exporter Script, let's review how you can extend Blender with Python code. Blender makes executing

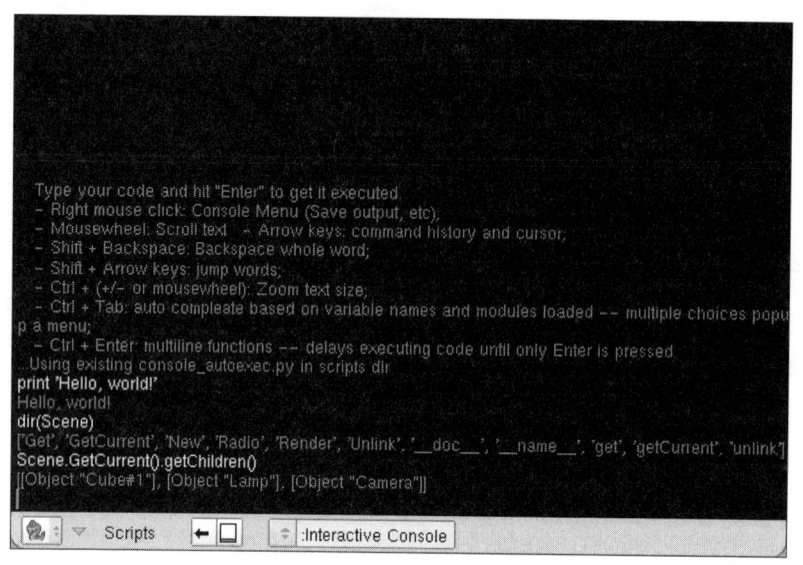

Figure 10.16
You can explore Blender's Python API by typing commands into the Interactive Console.

scripts easy by shipping with a Python interpreter and providing an extensive API to access Blender's state. A text editor is enough to write a script and Blender will pick up changes immediately—no additional compilation step needed. Scripts will run on all operating systems that both Blender and Python support.

Using the Interactive Console

The easiest way to have a go at Blender's Python API is by using the Interactive Console shown in Figure 10.16. You open one by switching a window's type to a Scripts window and selecting Scripts>System>Interactive Console.

You can directly enter code to see what it does. `Scene.GetCurrent().getChildren()`, for example, returns a list of all objects in the current scene. If you activate the Outliner (Alt+Shift+F9), you'll see that Blender provides the same hierarchy of objects to your Python application as the Outliner displays. Two Python functions might help you in the beginning: `dir()`, which prints an object's attributes, and `help()`, which prints an object's documentation.

Tip

You can find Blender's Python API reference at http://mediawiki.blender.org/. To learn Python, have a look at http://docs.python.org/tut/tut.html.

Executing Scripts

You can turn a Blender window into a simple script editor by selecting Text editor from a window's type icon. After typing in Python code or loading it from a file, you can execute a script with Alt+P. Here's a simple example:

```
import Blender

print 'Objects in the current scene:'
for object in Blender.Scene.GetCurrent().getChildren():
    print object.getName() + ':', object.getType()
```

That's similar to the code that I used before in the Interactive Console. In a script, however, you have to declare the `Blender` module before use with an `import` statement. The rest of the script loops through Blender's scene objects and prints each object's name and type. The output ends up in Blender's console window. (The console window is the one that opens when Blender starts, not the Interactive Console.)

Writing Exporter Scripts

The only missing piece of information to get a working exporter script is how to get a Python script in to Blender's menu. The answer is in the following lines:

```
#!BPY

"""
Name: 'Simple Exporter'
Blender: 242
Group: 'Export'
Tooltip: 'M3G Chapter 10'
"""

import Blender

def write(filename):
    out = file(filename, 'w')
    for object in Blender.Scene.GetCurrent().getChildren():
        out.write(object.getName() + ': ' + object.getType() + '\n')

Blender.Window.FileSelector(write, 'Export')
```

To qualify for inclusion in the menu, you have to save the file in the .blender\ scripts directory of your Blender installation. This is the same place where you installed the M3G Exporter Script. You can either restart Blender or click Scripts>Update Menus in the Scripts window (the one with the Interactive Console) to let the new menu entry File>Exporter>Simple Exporter appear in Blender's menu.

Blender recognizes Python scripts by scanning for the #!BPY identifier at the beginning of the file. The rest of the preamble tells Blender more details about the script. It includes the name of the script that's used in the menu, the Blender version it's written for, the group it belongs to, and a tooltip. The group determines in which menu the script will show. Different types of scripts such as importers or mesh editing tools each have their unique location in Blender's menu.

Upon invocation, Python executes the parts of your script that are not embedded in a function or class. Most exporter scripts start with a call to Blender.Window.FileSelector() to open a window where the user can select a file name that will contain the exported contents. In the callback to this function, Blender notifies you of the file's name, and you can write your output.

The remaining task for an exporter is to read Blender's object hierarchy and export it into the format that your application requires. That's where the M3G Exporter Script gives you a jump start because it already contains a lot of functionality. In the next section, I show you how to extend this functionality with a new feature.

Data-Driven Applications

Data-driven applications let data control functionality. For example, if you keep the level information of a game separate from your code, a game designer can modify the game without rebuilding it and add more levels even after development is completed. Although the scene in an M3G file can hold the look of the level, what about data that controls the game's logic? For example, whether a scene object is a door that the player can open or just a picture on the wall. This information should also end up in the M3G file, together with the scene data.

Tip

Remember that you need a full Python installation to execute the M3G Exporter Script because Blender doesn't ship with all of the standard Python libraries.

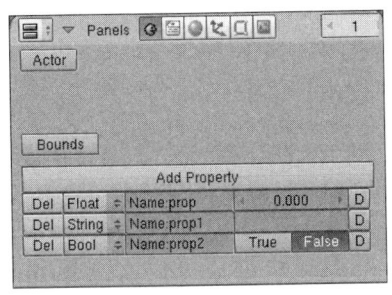

Figure 10.17
You can assign properties to Blender objects in the Logic panel.

Annotating Scene Objects

In Blender, you have a built-in mechanism to annotate scene objects. If you select an object in Blender and display the Logic context (F4), you'll find an interface that is part of Blender's physics simulation. For example, you can simulate how two meshes collide. Of interest in this panel is the Add Property button where you can associate named properties with an object.

Figure 10.17 shows the Logic context with three properties added. The idea is to take these properties and provide them to your Java application. This way, you can communicate additional metadata about your scene objects from Blender to M3G.

On the M3G side, user data provides a convenient mechanism for metadata. By calling getUserObject(), you can retrieve application specific data from your Object3D. When stored in a file, M3G restricts a user object to a Hashtable. If M3G supported arbitrary objects, the scope of its file format would extend considerably because CLDC doesn't support Java's standard object serialization mechanism. The Hashtable is further restricted to Integers as keys and byte arrays as values; each key/value pair is called a user parameter.

In order to transform Blender properties into user data, you need to do three things: read the properties from Blender, translate them into a format understood by M3G, and write this data into the M3G file. First, you have to extend the data structures the M3G Exporter Script uses.

Serializing User Data

All serializable M3G classes have corresponding types in the M3G Exporter Script. For the class Object3D, for example, you'll find M3GObject3D in Python. M3G associates user data with Object3D, so this is the right place to put it in Python as well.

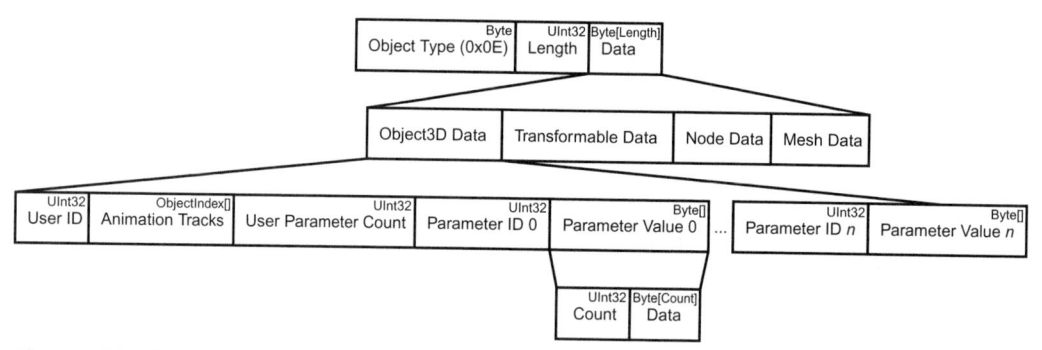

Figure 10.18
Serializing Object3D as part of a Mesh object.

An `Object3D`, however, is never serialized by itself, but always as part of another object because it's an abstract class. Say you want to serialize a `Mesh` object (object type 0x0E). You'll need to write the mesh's properties including those that it inherits from superclasses such as `Object3D`. Thus, if you look up the file format for a `Mesh` in M3G's javadoc, you'll find the structure that is displayed in Figure 10.18.

Because the Python script has a similar class structure, all you really need to care about is the user data related fields in `M3GObject3D`—the script will take care of the rest. These fields comprise the user parameter count that indicates the number of parameters and a parameter ID/parameter value for each property. As the parameter value is a `byte` array, this field is further split into the count of the array length and the data itself.

Note
You'll find the Python script in src\m3g_export_06_userdata.py on the CD-ROM. It's based on version 0.6 of the M3G Exporter Script.

This is what `M3GObject3D` looks like after adding a new field `userData`:

```
class M3GObject3D(M3GProxy):
  def __init__(self):
    M3GProxy.__init__(self)
    self.userID=0                    # UInt32
    self.animationTracks=[]          # ObjectIndex[]
    self.userParameterCount=0        # UInt32
    self.userData={}                 # User data

  ...

  def getData(self):
```

```python
        data = struct.pack('<I',self.userID)
        data += struct.pack('<I',len(self.animationTracks))
        for element in self.animationTracks:
            data += struct.pack('<I',getId(element))

        data += \
            struct.pack('<I', len(self.userData))      # userParameterCount
        for key in self.userData.keys():
            data += struct.pack('<I', int(key))        # parameterID
            value = self.userData[key]
            data += struct.pack('<I', len(value))      # parameterValue count
            data += str(value)                         # parameterValue
        return data

    def getDataLength(self):
        value = struct.calcsize('<2I')
        if len(self.animationTracks) > 0:
            value += struct.calcsize('<'+str(len(self.animationTracks))+'I')

        value += struct.calcsize('<I')                 # userParameterCount
        for key in self.userData:
            value += struct.calcsize('<I')             # parameterID
            value += struct.calcsize('<I')             # parameterValue count
            value += len(str(self.userData[key]))      # parameterValue
        return value
```

In Python, the brackets indicate that userData is a dictionary with key/value pairs, similar to a Hashtable in Java—ideal for this purpose. When the serialization process starts, the script calls getData() and getDataLength() for all M3G objects. The former returns an object's data as a byte array and the latter the length of this array. For M3GObject3D, these two methods are responsible to turn the userData's key/value pairs into binary data. To help you with this task, Python offers the struct module.

struct.pack() takes a format string that determines the conversion of Python types. struct.pack('<I', i), for example, takes an unsigned int (four bytes) and encodes it in little-endian format indicated by the "less than" sign. struct.calcsize() works similar except that it returns the length of the resulting binary data rather than the data itself.

In a next step, you need to fill the userData field with data from Blender's properties.

Translating Blender Properties

The M3G Exporter Script splits its functionality into three main classes: `M3GExporter`, `M3GWriter`, and `M3GTranslator`.

Each time you start the script, it creates a new `M3GExporter` object and passes its constructor a new `M3GWriter` as an argument. Afterward, the script calls `M3GExporter.start()`, which creates a new `M3GTranslator`. To write an M3G file, `M3GExporter` asks `M3GTranslator` to transform Blender's scene into an M3G scene graph. It then creates a list of M3G objects out of this scene graph in the order they will appear in the file. In the final step, `M3GWriter` calls `getData()` and `getDataLength()` for each object in the list and serializes the data.

> **Tip**
>
> Winpdb can debug Python scripts running inside Blender, which might help you understand the control flow of the script. Read more about this tool at http://www.digitalpeers.com/pythondebugger/blender.htm.

`M3GTranslator` splits its work into methods that start with `translate`. In essence, `M3GTranslator` loops through the scene objects it retrieves from `Blender.Scene.GetCurrent().getChildren()` and calls a different method depending on the object's type. For example, it calls `translateMesh()` when the script encounters a mesh object. `translateMesh()` in turn calls further methods to translate specific parts of a mesh.

However, Blender properties not only exist for meshes, but also for all scene objects such as cameras and lights. Thus, the best place to translate user data is a method that's called for all those objects. As it turns out, this method is `translateToNode()`.

```
def translateToNode(self,obj,node):
    self.translateUserData(obj, node)

    # more node translation
    ...

def translateUserData(self, object, node):
    """Translates Blender object properties into user data."""

    # Mark all numbers that are used by property names as used.
    usedInts = [int(p.getName()) for p in \
```

```
      object.getAllProperties() if p.getName().isdigit()]

# Loop through properties.
for index, property in enumerate(object.getAllProperties()):
  if property.getName().isdigit():
    # If a property uses an integer as its name, this
    # is used as the key.
    key = int(property.getName())
    constant = str(index)
  else:
    # Otherwise, assign an automatic number.
    key = 0
    while key in usedInts:
      key += 1
    usedInts.append(key)
    constant = property.getName()
  node.userData[key] = str(property.getData())

# Print a Java constant based on the property name.
# Underscores replace symbols illegal in Java.
print 'private static final int USER_PARAM_' \
    + re.sub('[^\w]', '_', object.name.upper()) \
    + '_' \
    + re.sub('[^\w]', '_', constant.upper()) \
    + ' = ' + str(key) + ';'
```

translateUserData() is a new method that takes care of the Blender properties. Apart from a pointer to self, its parameters are object, the Blender scene object, and node, the M3G object that resulted from the translation process so far. object.getAllProperties() retrieves a list of Blender properties that translateUserData() stores in the right format in node.userData. Here you will encounter a problem because Blender allows properties to have arbitrary names while M3G only allows Integers as keys to parameters.

To solve the problem, translateUserData() either uses the property name as the key if the name is a number or automatically assigns a number if the name is not. You now have a choice in Blender's user interface: if you add a property with the name "100," for example, this is exactly the key that the script will use. If you use a property name such as "myName," on the other hand, the script will automatically determine a number. Its value is predictable as it's based on the order the properties appear in the Logic context. Thus, if you don't change this order, you'll always get the same key. To help you figure out what key the script used in the end, it prints out a Java constant with the key value. You can copy and paste this information into your Java application and refer to this constant when retrieving the values stored in the Hashtable.

Deserializing User Data

What's left is to retrieve the user data stored in the M3G file in your Java application. You'll get access to the user parameters by calling Object3D .getUserObject() on the scene node that owns the user data and casting the result into a Hashtable.

Blender properties can be of type String, Float, Timer (a kind of Float), Int, and Bool. You can set the type in the first drop-down list of every property in the Logic context. translateUserData() converts all of these types as strings; for example, a float value of 1.0 becomes "1.0". Java provides convenient methods for the reverse process. Float.parseFloat(), for example, turns the string back into a float. Slightly special are Boolean values because there's no parseBoolean() in CLDC. Thus when reading such a user parameter, the value is true if the string contains "1" and false if it contains "0". These are the strings Python writes when converting a Boolean value.

The following class implements methods to retrieve the user parameters for you:

```
/**
 * Utility methods that deserialize user parameters stored in a
 * user object.
 *
 * @author Claus Hoefele
 */
public class UserData {
  /**
   * Constructor has private access because class contains static
   * methods exclusively.
   */
  private UserData() {}

  /**
   * Deserializes a user parameter as String from user data.
   *
   * @param userObject hashtable with user data.
```

```java
 * @param keyValue key to get the user parameter.
 * @param defaultValue value if parameter doesn't exist.
 * @return deserialized data or default value.
 */
public static String getString(Hashtable userObject,
    int keyValue, String defaultValue) {
  Integer key = new Integer(keyValue);
  if (userObject != null && userObject.containsKey(key)) {
    byte[] data = (byte[]) userObject.get(key);
    defaultValue = new String(data);
  }

  return defaultValue;
}

/**
 * Deserializes a user parameter as int from user data.
 *
 * @param userObject hashtable with user data.
 * @param keyValue key to get the user parameter.
 * @param defaultValue value if parameter doesn't exist.
 * @return deserialized data or default value.
 */
public static int getInt(Hashtable userObject,
    int keyValue, int defaultValue) {
  Integer key = new Integer(keyValue);
  if (userObject != null && userObject.containsKey(key)) {
    byte[] data = (byte[]) userObject.get(key);
    defaultValue = Integer.parseInt(new String(data));
  }

  return defaultValue;
}

/**
 * Deserializes a user parameter as boolean from user data.
 *
 * @param userObject hashtable with user data.
 * @param keyValue key to get the user parameter.
 * @param defaultValue value if parameter doesn't exist.
 * @return deserialized data or default value.
 */
public static boolean getBoolean(Hashtable userObject,
```

```
      int keyValue, boolean defaultValue) {
    Integer key = new Integer(keyValue);
    if (userObject != null && userObject.containsKey(key)) {
      byte[] data = (byte[]) userObject.get(key);
      defaultValue = (new String(data)).equals("1");
    }

    return defaultValue;
  }

  /**
   * Deserializes a user parameter as float from user data.
   *
   * @param userObject hashtable with user data.
   * @param keyValue key to get the user parameter.
   * @param defaultValue value if parameter doesn't exist.
   * @return deserialized data or default value.
   */
  public static float getFloat(Hashtable userObject,
      int keyValue, float defaultValue) {
    Integer key = new Integer(keyValue);
    if (userObject != null && userObject.containsKey(key)) {
      byte[] data = (byte[]) userObject.get(key);
      defaultValue = Float.parseFloat(new String(data));
    }

    return defaultValue;
  }
}
```

Playing Memory

To end with a nice example that demonstrates user data, I implemented a memory game. The rules are simple: Initially, all cards are covered. In each turn, users can uncover two cards. If the images on the front sides of the cards match, the cards stay uncovered. Otherwise, they return to their initial state. Users win the game by finding all pairs. Users should avoid the action card hidden in the deck: If they uncover this card, they lose all their pairs and have to start anew.

The application reads in the game data from an M3G file. Instead of hard coding which cards match, each mesh object contains that information in a description parameter. Each time users uncover a card, the game displays this description at the bottom. Two cards match if their description is the same. In addition, the key code that uncovers a card is also stored in the M3G file. The game tells the action card apart from the others with a third parameter.

Note
> The memory game is implemented in UserData.java, UserDataSample.java, CardDeck.java, and Card.java, which you'll find on the CD-ROM. Have a look in `UserDataSample.init()` and `Card`'s constructor to see how the application reads the user data from memory.m3g.

I provided a sample level that lays out nine cards in a grid and assigns each card a key code that corresponds to its position on the keyboard. For example, the number 1 key activates the upper-left card. Figure 10.19 displays this layout.

I created the scene in Blender and textured the cards with images. Each card is a mesh and contains the user data as the named properties `keyCode`, `description`, and `trigger`. I prefer to use names instead of numbers because it's easier to tell the properties apart. For each mesh, I ordered the properties the same way so they end up with identical key values.

Because no information is hard coded, you can change the layout of the cards and the card images without touching the code. The simple rules can be extended with additional action cards that have negative or positive effects.

Figure 10.19
The memory game uses information stored in the user objects of the meshes in the scene.

You could then provide game levels of different difficulty by varying the number of action cards. Another idea is to provide additional game levels with another set of images for download.

Summary

The big advantage of M3G files exported from 3D tools is that you can split the work between developers and artists. When you create more complex models in Blender, you'll soon realize that this needs a complementary skill set to software development.

When creating M3G files with Blender, it's important that the resulting file is as small as possible—I showed you several options in Blender to achieve this goal. You should closely watch the number of faces and vertices of your model as this will not only increase the file size, but will also slow down the rendering of the model. If the model is too complex, you can reduce the polygons with one of Blender's tools such as the Poly Reducer. I also showed you the contents of an M3G file created by Blender. Analyzing M3G files can help you find problems and give you clues to optimizations.

The M3G Exporter Script is available in source code, which makes it possible to adapt it to your needs. In the last section of this chapter, I showed you how you can extend the script to support a data-driven tool chain. Ideally, by controlling functionality in a game with metadata stored in M3G files, a level designer can make changes to a game without any developer intervention.

CHAPTER 11

Keyframe Animations

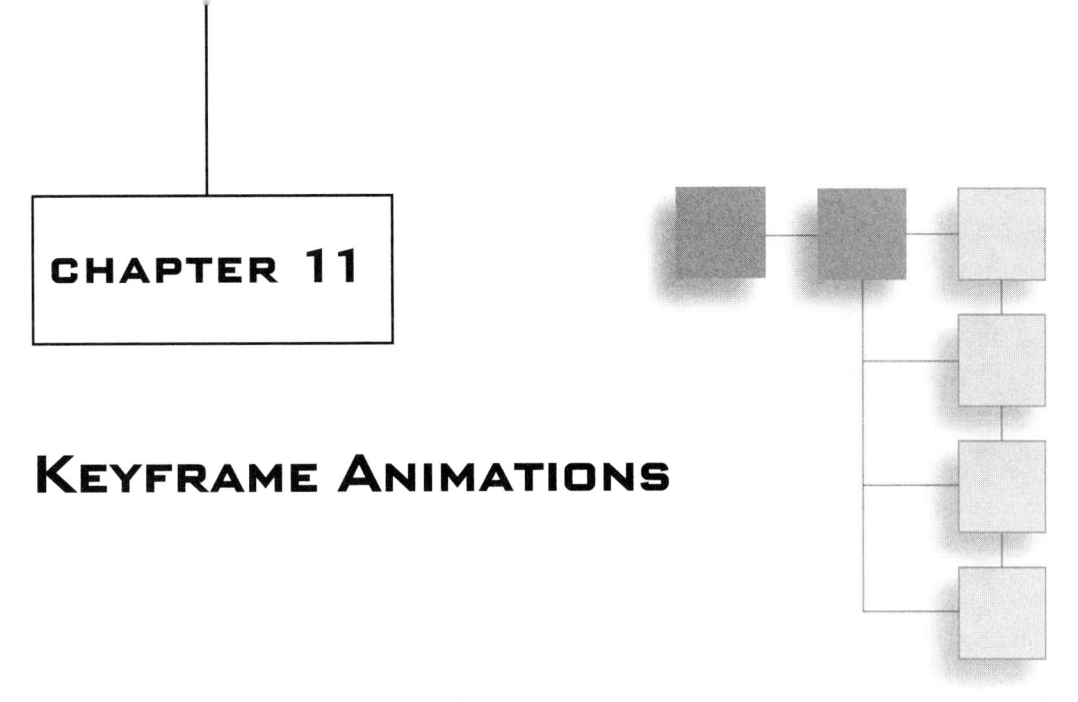

Keyframing is a concept taken from cartoon animations. At a time when all images for a film had to be drawn by hand, it was very costly and time consuming to let the most experienced artists draw all the frames that comprise a movie. Instead, a senior artist would draw only the keyframes that were most important. Other artists would add the in-between frames to complete the animation. In computer animation, the same concept is employed, except that the intermediate frames are automatically generated.

In this chapter, you learn:

- The concepts of keyframes and interpolation.
- How to create animations with M3G.
- What properties you can animate.
- How you can use textures to create animated images.

Keyframes

A keyframe consists of a time stamp and one or more values. For example, a position comprises three values: one each for x, y, and z axis. If you wanted to move a mesh around, you'd use one position with three values for each keyframe and associate it with the time you want the values to change.

Creating Keyframe Sequences

Keyframe values are usually plotted as functions over time such as in Figure 11.1.

A succession of keyframes is stored in KeyframeSequence, whose interface you can see in Table 11.1. You add keyframes like this:

```
KeyframeSequence sequence
    = new KeyframeSequence(2, 3, KeyframeSequence.STEP);
sequence.setRepeatMode(KeyframeSequence.LOOP);
sequence.setDuration(1000);
sequence.setKeyframe(0,   0, new float[] {-1, 0, 0});
sequence.setKeyframe(1, 500, new float[] { 1, 0, 0});
```

The code defines two keyframes: one for $t=0$, and one for $t=500$. It's up to you what units the time stamps represent, but it's easiest to think of them as milliseconds. The data associated with a time stamp always represent absolute values.

You can include a subset of your keyframes in the animation with setValidRange(). This method takes indices to the first and last valid keyframe number. Figure 11.1 shows these values as t_{first} and t_{last}. By default, the valid range spans all existing keyframes.

The duration passed to setDuration() specifies the length of the animation. By definition, the duration is always counted starting from $t=0$. To be valid, it must be greater than t_{last}. The previous code example sets the duration to 1000, which results in both keyframes being played for 500 ms.

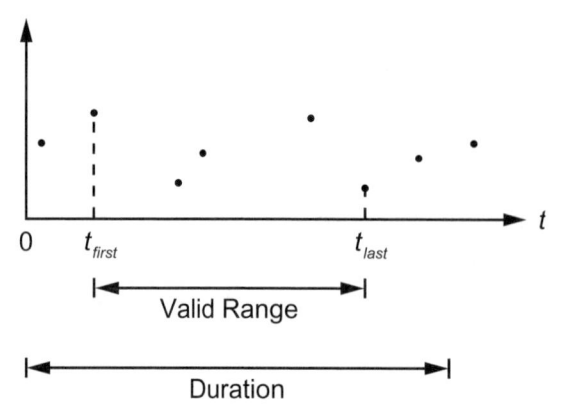

Figure 11.1
Keyframe sequence.

Table 11.1 KeyframeSequence Class Description

Method	Since	Description
Repeat Modes		
static int LOOP		Repeats an animation endlessly.
static int CONSTANT		Plays an animation once.
Interpolation Modes		
static int STEP		Steps from one keyframe to the next; no interpolation for values in-between.
static int LINEAR		Interpolates linearly between keyframes.
static int SPLINE		Uses spline interpolation.
static int SLERP		Spherical linear interpolation for quaternions.
static int SQUAD		Spline interpolation for quaternions.
Construction		
KeyframeSequence(int numKeyframes, int numComponents, int interpolation)		Defaults: CONSTANT repeat mode; valid range spans all frames.
int getKeyframeCount()	1.1	Getter for number of keyframes.
int getComponentCount()	1.1	Getter for component count.
int getInterpolationType()	1.1	Getter for interpolation mode.
Animation Properties		
void setDuration(int duration)		Sets the duration of the animation.
int getDuration()		Getter for duration.
void setRepeatMode(int mode)		Sets the repeat mode (CONSTANT or LOOP).
int getRepeatMode()		Getter for repeat mode.
Keyframe Data		
void setKeyframe(int index, int time, float[] value)		Sets the keyframe values.
int getKeyframe(int index, float[] value)	1.1	Getter for keyframe values.
void setValidRange(int first, int last)		Sets the range of valid keyframe indices.
int getValidRangeFirst()	1.1	Getter for first valid index.
int getValidRangeLast()	1.1	Getter for last valid index.

You can play an animation once by calling setRepeatMode() with KeyframeSequence.CONSTANT or repeatedly by using KeyframeSequence.LOOP.

When constructing a new KeyframeSequence, you have to specify the number of keyframes, the number of values for each keyframe, and the interpolation mode. In the previous code example, there were two keyframes with three values each.

The `KeyFrameSequence` doesn't know what the values represent. You will assign this meaning in a separate step. However, the class receives the interpolation mode in its constructor, which determines how to calculate values in-between keyframes.

Interpolation Modes

Once you have defined the keyframe values, M3G gives you three choices of how to progress from one frame to the next. Figure 11.2 contains a graphical representation of these options.

- **Step:** Each keyframe value is valid until it's overridden by the value for the next frame.

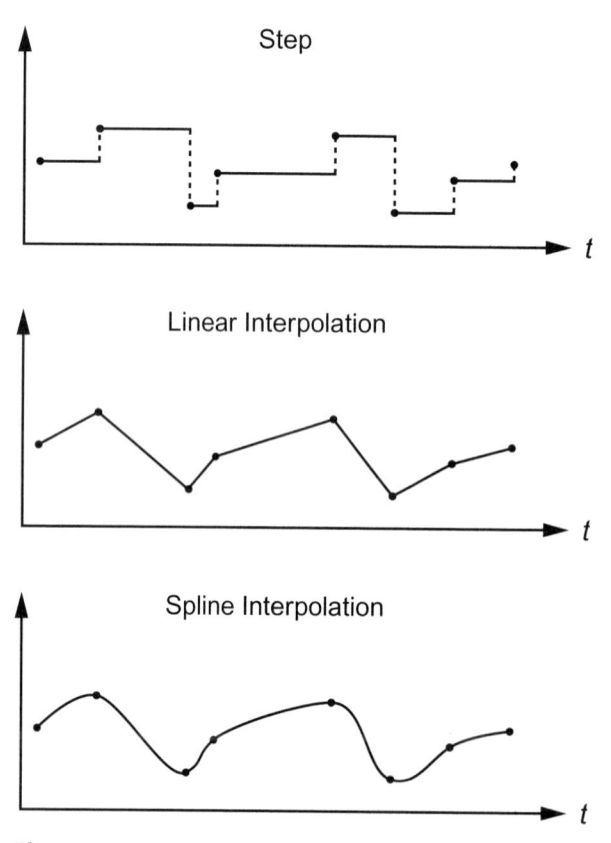

Figure 11.2
Interpolation modes.

- **Linear:** Calculates in-between values as linear interpolation between the current keyframe and the next. This connects each value with the next by a line.

- **Spline:** Interpolates values with a spline function, which generates a smooth curve out of the keyframe values. This avoids sudden changes that occur with linear interpolation when the keyframe values change.

For spline interpolation, M3G uses *Catmull-Rom splines*. The idea is the same as for the Bézier curves introduced in Chapter 4: You define control points, and the intermediate points are generated by a curve algorithm. However, the curve formula differs and M3G generates tangents for each control point automatically. This leaves you less flexibility in shaping the curve segments, but guarantees that the curve will go through all keyframe values and the curve segments are connected continuously.

You set the interpolation mode when creating a new KeyframeSequence, for example KeyframeSequence.STEP steps between keyframe values. LINEAR and SPLINE are the respective interpolation modes as described previously. You can use these modes to interpolate any values.

For values in quaternion format, KeyframeSequence knows two additional interpolation modes. Because a unit quaternion represents a rotation, you can use these modes in case of animating orientations (AnimationTrack.ORIENTATION). SLERP stands for *spherical linear interpolation*, which results in a constant rate of rotation. This is preferable to LINEAR because you want your rotation to change at a constant speed. SQUAD is the analogous spline interpolation for quaternions. When interpolating quaternions, M3G automatically takes care of normalization.

Note

Have a look at the section in Chapter 5 called "Orientation Representations" to find out more about quaternions.

Each time stamp in a KeyframeSequence must be greater than or equal to the preceding time stamp, otherwise the interpolation is undefined. However, several keyframes with the same time stamp are explicitly allowed. The keyframe with the lowest index is used for the animation leading to this time stamp. The highest index is then used to continue. With this feature, you can, for example, achieve a cut between two camera positions.

Table 11.2 AnimationTrack Class Description

Method	Description
Construction	
AnimationTrack(KeyframeSequence sequence, int property)	Constructs a new AnimationTrack. The values in the sequence for each keyframe must match the number of components required for the animation property.
KeyframeSequence getKeyframeSequence()	Getter for sequence.
int getTargetProperty()	Getter for animation property.
Animation Controller	
void setController(AnimationController controller)	Associates an animation controller with a track.
AnimationController getController()	Getter for animation controller.

Animation Targets

Each keyframe contains the values of an animation sequence for a specific point in time. The number of values per frame and how to interpret them are dependent on the property you want to animate. Translating a mesh, for example, will need three values—one for each coordinate axis. Transparency, on the other hand, needs a single value that represents the alpha component of a color. Binding a KeyFrameSequence to an animation property is the task of AnimationTrack. Its interface is listed in Table 11.2.

When creating a new KeyframeSequence, you have to pass the number of values that each frame requires. This number depends on the animation target and is checked when calling AnimationTrack's constructor. Table 11.3 lists the targets defined in AnimationTrack together with the necessary number of components and the classes you can use as the receiver of the animation.

Because keyframe values are floats, so are the results from the animation interpolation. Hence, the result needs a conversion if the animation property uses a different type. A boolean property, such as the rendering enable flag animated by AnimationTrack.VISIBILITY, is set to true if the interpolation result is greater than or equal to 0.5 and false otherwise. int properties, such as the cropping parameters animated by CROP, are rounded to the closest integer. In general, M3G takes care that an animation always results in valid data. Color data is restricted to the interval [0, 1] for example.

Table 11.3 Animation Targets

Method	Components	Applicable Classes
static int ALPHA	1	Node (alpha factor), Background, VertexBuffer, or Material (diffuse color)
static int AMBIENT_COLOR	3 (RGB)	Material
static int COLOR	3 (RGB)	Light, Background, Fog, VertexBuffer, or Texture2D (texture blend color)
static int CROP	2 (x, y) or 4 (x, y, width, height)	Sprite3D or Background
static int DENSITY	1	Fog
static int DIFFUSE_COLOR	3 (RGB)	Material
static int EMISSIVE_COLOR	3 (RGB)	Material
static int FAR_DISTANCE	1	Camera or Fog
static int FIELD_OF_VIEW	1	Camera
static int INTENSITY	1	Light
static int MORPH_WEIGHTS	Number of morph targets	MorphingMesh
static int NEAR_DISTANCE	1	Camera or Fog
static int ORIENTATION	4 (quaternion)	Transformable
static int PICKABILITY	1	Node
static int SCALE	1 or 3 (x, y, z)	Transformable
static int SHININESS	1	Material
static int SPECULAR_COLOR	3 (RGB)	Material
static int SPOT_ANGLE	1	Light
static int SPOT_EXPONENT	1	Light
static int TRANSLATION	3 (x, y, z)	Transformable
static int VISIBILITY	1	Node

Note

AnimationSample.java contains the complete source code, which you can find on the accompanying CD-ROM together with a working MIDlet. In this section, I explain how to set up `KeyframeSequence` and `AnimationTrack`. The next section, "Controlling Animations," shows how to add the code to perform the actual animation.

The following sample code picks `AnimationTrack.TRANSLATION` to animate the position of a mesh:

```
/**
 * Simple animation with different interpolation modes.
 *
 * @author Claus Hoefele
 */
```

Chapter 11 ■ Keyframe Animations

```java
public class AnimationSample extends GameCanvas
    implements Sample, Runnable {
  ...

  /** Steps through keyframe values. */
  private static final int INTERPOLATION_STEP        = 0;
  /** Linear interpolation of keyframe values. */
  private static final int INTERPOLATION_LINEAR      = 1;
  /** Spline interpolation of keyframe values. */
  private static final int INTERPOLATION_SPLINE      = 2;
  /** Number of interpolation modes. */
  private static final int NUMBER_OF_INTERPOLATIONS  = 3;
  /** Current interpolation mode. */
  private int currentMode;

  /** Controls animation speed. */
  private AnimationController animationController;

  /** 3D graphics singleton used for rendering. */
  private Graphics3D graphics3d;
  /** 2D graphics singleton used for rendering. */
  private Graphics graphics;

  /**
   * Constructor.
   */
  public AnimationSample() {
    super(false);
  }

  /**
   * Initializes the sample.
   */
  private void reset() {
    graphics3d = Graphics3D.getInstance();
    graphics = getGraphics();

    // Set up animation.
    currentMode = INTERPOLATION_STEP;
    animationController = new AnimationController();
    createAnimation(mesh, currentMode, animationController);

    // Create a camera with perspective projection.
    Camera camera = new Camera();
```

```
      float aspect = (float) getWidth() / (float) getHeight();
      camera.setPerspective(60, aspect, 1, 1000);
      Transform cameraTransform = new Transform();
      cameraTransform.postTranslate(0, 0, 4.5f);
      graphics3d.setCamera(camera, cameraTransform);
  }

  /**
   * Animates the translation component of the given mesh.
   *
   * @param mesh mesh for animation.
   * @param interpolationMode interpolation mode.
   * @param controller animation controller.
   */
  private void createAnimation(Mesh mesh,
        int interpolationMode, AnimationController controller) {
      // Keyframe data for translation.
      float[][] positions = new float[][] {
          { 1,  0, 0},    // east
          { 0, -1, 0},    // south
          {-1,  0, 0},    // west
          { 0,  1, 0}     // north
      };

      // Create the keyframe sequence.
      KeyframeSequence sequence = null;

      switch (interpolationMode) {
        case INTERPOLATION_STEP:
          sequence = new KeyframeSequence(positions.length, 3,
              KeyframeSequence.STEP);
          break;

        case INTERPOLATION_LINEAR:
          sequence = new KeyframeSequence(positions.length, 3,
              KeyframeSequence.LINEAR);
          break;

        case INTERPOLATION_SPLINE:
          sequence = new KeyframeSequence(positions.length, 3,
              KeyframeSequence.SPLINE);
          break;

          // no default
      }
```

```
      sequence.setRepeatMode(KeyframeSequence.LOOP);
      sequence.setDuration(positions.length * 500);
      for (int i=0; i<positions.length; i++) {
        sequence.setKeyframe(i, i*500, positions[i]);
      }

      // Remove all previous animation tracks.
      while (mesh.getAnimationTrackCount() > 0) {
        mesh.removeAnimationTrack(mesh.getAnimationTrack(0));
      }

      // Attach new animation track.
      AnimationTrack track
          = new AnimationTrack(sequence, AnimationTrack.TRANSLATION);
      mesh.addAnimationTrack(track);
      track.setController(controller);
    }
    ...
  }
```

First of all, you have to define the keyframe values. In `createAnimation()`, each frame has three values representing the absolute *x*, *y*, and *z* values of a translation. The animation property TRANSLATION indicates that the animation result is set with `Transformable.setTranslation()`.

You specify the interpolation mode when creating the KeyframeSequence and afterward set the data with `setKeyframe()`. Each of the frames must have an associated time stamp; `setAnimation()` sets each frame at 500 ms intervals. As with the keyframe data, the time must be set in absolute values. It's also important to set the duration, otherwise the animation won't play.

The sequence is bound to the TRANSLATION target in the constructor of AnimationTrack. To tell which object to use as the target of the animation, `addAnimationTrack()` adds this track to mesh. The last lines of the code add a new animation controller, which is used to manage the animation playback. You will see how to do this in the following section. Associating a controller with a track ensures that the target is updated by the animation.

Controlling Animations

If KeyframeSequence is the celluloid and AnimationTrack the film roll of a movie, AnimationController is the projector, and the animation target is the screen. But the actual animation won't play until you advance the frames in regular intervals.

The Animation Loop

To drive the animation, `AnimationSample` implements the `Runnable` interface.

Note

> Alternatively to implementing `Runnable` and starting your own thread, you can also use `Timer` and `TimerTask` in the `java.util` package to drive your animation. I prefer to implement my own thread because it allows me to have better control of what happens. At the same time, you avoid creating an additional class (the one derived from `TimerTask`), which makes your application smaller.

```java
public class AnimationSample extends GameCanvas
    implements Sample, Runnable {
  /** Flag whether thread is running. */
  private boolean isRunning;
  ...

  /**
   * Initializes the sample.
   */
  public void init() {
    reset();

    Thread thread = new Thread(this);
    isRunning = true;
    thread.start();
  }

  /**
   * Destroys the sample.
   */
  public void destroy() {
    isRunning = false;
  }

  /**
   * Animation loop.
   */
  public void run() {
    while(isRunning) {
      int worldTime = (int) System.currentTimeMillis();
      checkKeys(worldTime);
      mesh.animate(worldTime);
```

```
      render(graphics);
      flushGraphics();

      try {
        Thread.sleep(20);
      } catch (Exception e) {}
    }
  }
  ...
}
```

`AnimationSample` ties starting the thread to the `init()` method, which is called before the sample is displayed on the screen. The method creates a new `Thread` and sets `isRunning` to `true`. This `boolean` value serves as a flag to stop the thread and is used by `destroy()` to end the animation.

The actual animation loop is implemented in `run()`, which periodically updates the *world time*. This is the time `AnimationSample` passes to the `animate()` method of the mesh object. Each time you call this method, M3G evaluates the animation tracks associated with the object and calculates a new interpolation value from the keyframe sequence. The result is then used to update the animation target. In case of `AnimationSample`, this will change the position of the mesh. A call to `animate()` also animates children of the object if it has any. A call to `World.animate()`, for example, updates all meshes in the world that have animation tracks.

`run()` derives the world time from the system time, which is the reason it's convenient to use milliseconds for the time stamps of the keyframe sequence. Using the system time also decouples the world time from the frame rate. No matter how fast your device's processor is, the system time will tick along in regular intervals.

The return value of `animate()` indicates when the animation will make the next change to the animated object or any of its children. You can use this information to advance the animation depending on the characteristic of the keyframe sequence. Instead, the sample code simply sleeps for a specific amount of time. This gives the Java system time to process other events such as key input.

Tip

You should always set an upper limit to the frame rate. Increasing the frame rate to a higher value than what's needed for a smooth animation will drain the device's battery unnecessarily.

Before advancing the animation with `animate()`, `checkKeys()` allows you to change parameters with key presses. Afterward, the result of the animation is rendered to the screen with `render()`.

```java
/**
 * Receives key presses.
 *
 * @param keyCode key code.
 */
protected void keyPressed(int keyCode) {
  lastKey = getGameAction(keyCode);
}

/**
 * Processes key presses.
 *
 * @param worldTime current world time.
 */
private void checkKeys(int worldTime) {
  if (lastKey == FIRE) {
    reset();
  } else if (lastKey == GAME_A) {
    currentMode++;
    currentMode %= NUMBER_OF_INTERPOLATIONS;
    createAnimation(mesh, currentMode, animationController);
  } else if (lastKey == GAME_B) {
    toggleSpeed(animationController, worldTime);
  }
  lastKey = 0;
}

/**
 * Renders the sample.
 *
 * @param graphics graphics context for drawing.
 */
private void render(Graphics graphics) {
  graphics3d.bindTarget(graphics);
  graphics3d.setViewport(0, 0, getWidth(), getHeight());
  graphics3d.clear(null);

  // When animating a mesh's transformation and rendering the mesh
  // in immediate mode, you have to copy the animation result from
  // the Transformable into a Transform object.
```

```
    mesh.getCompositeTransform(meshTransform);
    graphics3d.render(mesh, meshTransform);
    graphics3d.releaseTarget();

    drawMenu(graphics); // displays the current key assignment
}
```

`AnimationSample` implements its own thread and therefore needs to protect its state from accesses form another thread, such as the key handler. Although `GameCanvas` offers `getKeyStates()`, which you can call from within your animation loop, `AnimationSample` uses a different strategy to receive key presses. If you called `getKeyStates()` every frame, it would trigger changes too often. Instead, `AnimationSample` receives a key event in `keyPressed()` and stores the current event in the member variable `lastKey`. Because `int` read and write operations are atomic, the animation loop implemented in `run()` can access `lastKey` with the `checkKeys()` method and update the animation.

In `AnimationSample`, the `GAME_A` key switches among the interpolation modes. When running the sample, you can see a disc that changes positions. With `KeyframeSequence.STEP`, the circle jumps between positions; with `LINEAR`, the circle moves in a straight line; and with `SPLINE`, the circle moves in a curve between positions. You can see a screenshot in Figure 11.3.

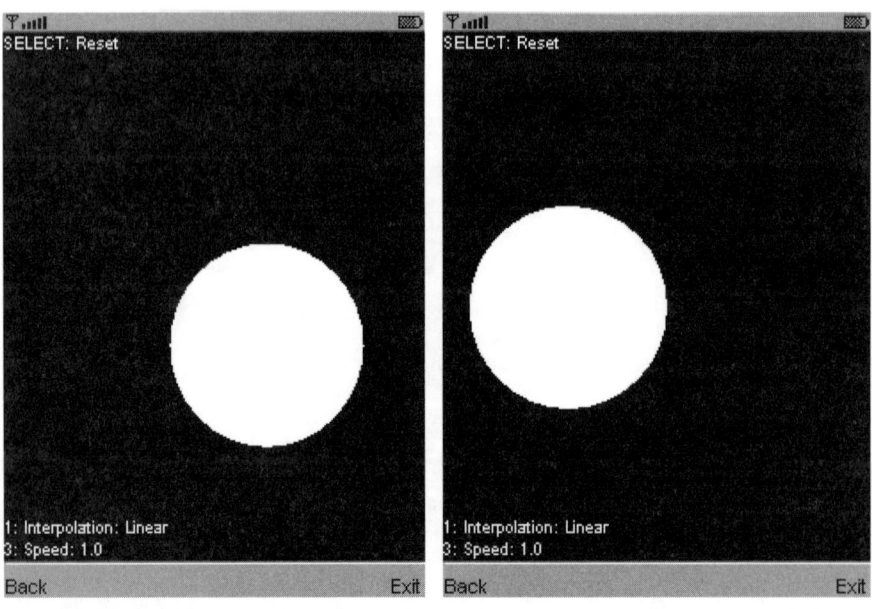

Figure 11.3
The animation of the disc's translation property causes it to change position.

In `run()`, the translation component of the mesh's `Transformable` property is updated by calling `animate()`. If you render your mesh as a part of `Group` or `World`, this is all you have to do. To draw the mesh in immediate mode, you have to copy the information in `Transformable` with `getCompositeTransform()` to a `Transform` object. You can then use this object in `render()`.

This demonstrates how you can read back interpolation values, which is a useful feature independent of doing animations. The spline interpolation essentially provides you with a smoothing filter. This could be used to beautify the slopes of hills by smoothing height values representing a terrain, for example.

By choosing the right values for `animate()`, you can jump to any position of the animation or vary the playback speed. `AnimationController`, which you adjust with the `GAME_B` key, provides an easier interface to do this.

World versus Sequence Time

Figure 11.4 shows the relationships between the objects involved in an animation.

`KeyframeSequence` contains the animation data. `AnimationTrack` knows the animation target and is owned by the target `Object3D`. An `Object3D` can have any number of animation tracks, but one track is associated with at most one `KeyframeSequence`.

Each animation track also has one `AnimationController`. If an `Object3D` has several tracks, you can assign the same controller to each track or use separate ones. In the latter case, if two or more tracks animate the same property, the contribution of each track is weighted by the value you set in `AnimationController.setWeight()`. Most important, `AnimationController` allows you to control animation playback. You can see its methods in Table 11.4.

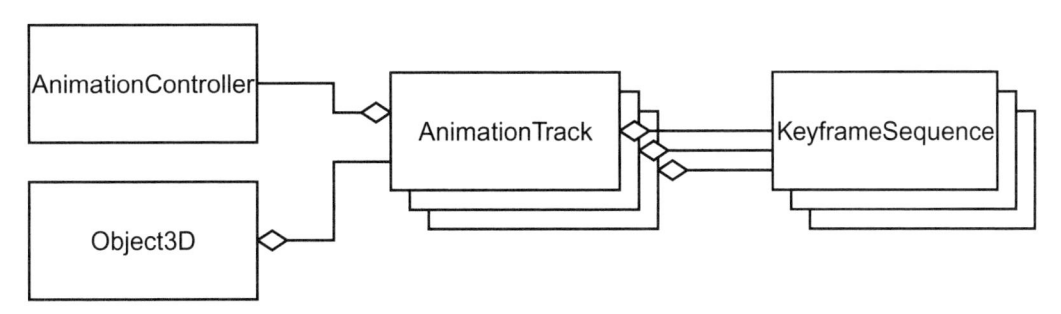

Figure 11.4
Associations for an animation.

Table 11.4 AnimationController Class Description

Method	Description
Construction	
`AnimationController()`	Default values: (0, 0) for active interval and reference point; 1.0 for blending weight and speed.
Active Interval	
`void setActiveInterval(int start, int end)`	Sets the active interval in world time. If both parameters are the same value, controller is always active.
`int getActiveIntervalStart()`	Getter for start of active interval.
`int getActiveIntervalEnd()`	Getter for end of active interval.
Animation Properties	
`void setPosition(float sequenceTime, int worldTime)`	Sets the current reference position for world and sequence time.
`int getRefWorldTime()`	Getter for reference world time. (Since 1.1.)
`float getPosition(int worldTime)`	Converts world time to sequence time.
`void setSpeed(float speed, int worldTime)`	Sets the execution speed of the animation. If the current world time is passed to this method, the sequence time is automatically adjusted to avoid jumps in the animation.
`float getSpeed()`	Getter for animation speed.
`void setWeight(float weight)`	Sets the blending weight for this controller.
`float getWeight()`	Getter for blending weight.

World time is what you pass to `Object3D.animate()`. When defining the keyframe values, you already provided time stamps when values are to be changed. M3G calls this the *sequence time*. `AnimationController` allows you to change how world time maps to sequence time.

When looking up the current value of an animation, M3G uses two reference points: t_{wref} for world time and t_{sref} for sequence time. With these two values, you can define when to start the animation as well as adjust the current playback position of the sequence. The formula to compute the sequence time t_s from a given world time t_w is given by

$$t_s = t_{sref} + s(t_w - t_{wref})$$

where s is the scaling factor that determines the speed of your animation.

For example, if you set the reference times to $t_{wref} = 1000$ and $t_{sref} = 0$, the animation would start to play from the beginning as soon as the world time reaches 1000 time units.

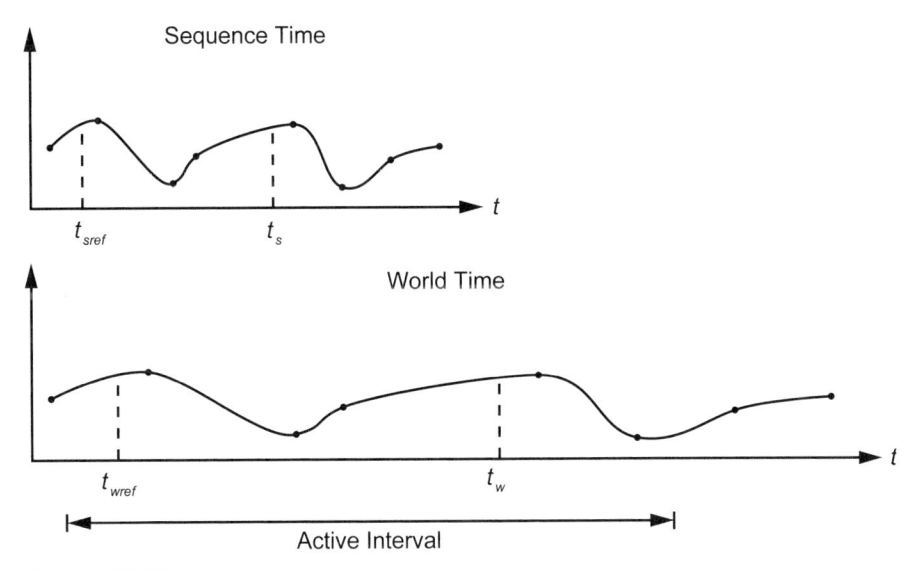

Figure 11.5
Relation between world and sequence time.

Setting the scaling factor to the value 2 would double the playback speed; setting it to 0.5, on the other hand, would decrease the speed by half.

Figure 11.5 compares sequence time with world time. It also shows the active interval, a parameter that you can set with `setActiveInterval()`, which determines the interval in world time units for which the animation is played back.

In the case of Figure 11.5, the choice of reference values causes the animation to start at a position between the first two keyframes. You can set the reference values with `setPosition()`.

Because of the chosen scaling factor, which you can change with `setSpeed()`, the animation will play at half the speed. Hence the world time t_w would map to a sequence time t_s at the indicated positions.

Here is sample code to change the playback speed:

```
/**
 * Toggles animation between slow, fast, and reverse speed.
 *
 * @param animationController controller for animation.
 * @param worldTime current world time.
 */
private void toggleSpeed(AnimationController animationController,
```

```
      int worldTime) {
  float speed = animationController.getSpeed();

  if (speed == 1) {
    animationController.setSpeed(2, worldTime);
  } else if (speed == 2) {
    animationController.setSpeed(-1, worldTime);
  } else {
    animationController.setSpeed(1, worldTime);
  }
}
```

`toggleSpeed()` circles among double, single, and reverse speed. You achieve reverse speed by setting the speed to a negative value. When calling `setSpeed()`, you also pass the current world time. This automatically updates the reference values to avoid sudden jumps in the animation.

Moving Images

In a game, you often see an animated sky or tree leaves moving in the wind. It would be very resource consuming to model all of this with geometry. Instead, you can use a mesh with an animated texture. This makes the mesh look as if a movie was projected on it.

Drawing into Textures

One approach to create an animated texture is to update its contents in regular intervals.

M3G allows you to render directly into an `Image2D`. However, because textures are two-dimensional, you'll most likely want a MIDP graphics context with 2D functionality. To get such a context, you create and draw into a MIDP `Image` object and update the texture by using one of `Image2D`'s constructors.

The problem here is that when constructing a new `Image2D` object from a MIDP image, you copy the `Image` contents. Each frame of your animation allocates a new object the size of the image and makes the old one available to garbage collection. Allocating many objects not only takes time, but can also lead to fragmented memory and little pauses in the animation when the garbage collector frees unused memory.

> **Tip**
>
> Pre-allocate all memory for your animation outside the animation loop to speed up your animation.

To avoid this problem, the following code constructs an empty mutable `Image2D` object and updates its contents with `set()`:

```
// Image dimension: 128x128 pixels.
private Image midpImage = Image.createImage(128, 128);
private Image2D m3gImage = new Image2D(Image2D.RGB, 128, 128);
private Texture2D texture = new Texture2D(m3gImage);
private byte[] byteImage = new byte[128*128*3];
private int[] pixels = new int[128];          // one row of data

private void render(Graphics graphics) {
  int width = midpImage.getWidth();
  int height = midpImage.getHeight();

  // Draw into image.
  Graphics imgGraphics = midpImage.getGraphics();
  imgGraphics.setColor(0x0000FF);          // black
  imgGraphics.fillRect(0, 0, width, height);
  imgGraphics.setColor(0xFFFFFF);          // white
  imgGraphics.drawString("" + System.currentTimeMillis(), 0, 0, 0);

  // Copy image from MIDP to M3G format.
  for (int i=0; i<height; i++) {
    midpImage.getRGB(pixels, 0, width, 0, i, width, 1);
    for (int j=0; j<width; j++) {
      int position = 3*(i*width + j);
      byteImage[position + 0] = (byte) (pixels[j]>>16 & 0xFF); // R
      byteImage[position + 1] = (byte) (pixels[j]>> 8 & 0xFF); // G
      byteImage[position + 2] = (byte) (pixels[j]>> 0 & 0xFF); // B
    }
  }

  // By modifying the Image2D object, the associated Texture2D is
  // automatically updated.
  m3gImage.set(0, 0, width, height, byteImage);

  // Render mesh with texture.
  ...
}
```

All memory is now allocated only once, which comes at the cost of an additional image copy. The same image exists three times: as `Image` object, as `Image2D` object, and as `byte` array. In addition, you need a buffer to convert the image format because you receive the `Image` contents as `int`s, but `Image2D` requires `byte`s.

You can imagine that you'll run out of memory sooner rather than later with this approach. Depending on your contents, you might be able to save some memory by updating only parts of the texture or storing pre-rendered images in `byte` arrays. But even if the memory usage is acceptable to you, rebinding a texture might trigger costly operations in the M3G implementation. A hardware accelerated system has to transfer the new texture to the GPU for example.

If you know the contents of the animation beforehand, you can avoid all these issues by using UV animations.

UV Animations

In a UV animation, one static texture stores the entire animation. Instead of updating the image contents, you modify the texture coordinates so that a changing detail of the image is visible. If you do this quickly enough, you'll create a movie that uses a mesh as the screen.

UV animations come in two flavors: One possibility is to select a visible detail and scroll the image underneath. The image wraps around at the border and moves as if attached to a conveyor belt. The other possibility is a flip-book animation, where you split an image into several frames that you show in quick succession.

> **Note**
>
> You'll find the UV animation example in TextureAnimationSample.java and UvAnimation.java on the CD-ROM.

Conveyor Belt Animations

Conveyor belt animations work great if all animated objects move at the same speed and in the same direction, such as clouds or tumble weeds. Figure 11.6 shows how the image revolves around imaginary rolls to display a different part of the image in the viewport.

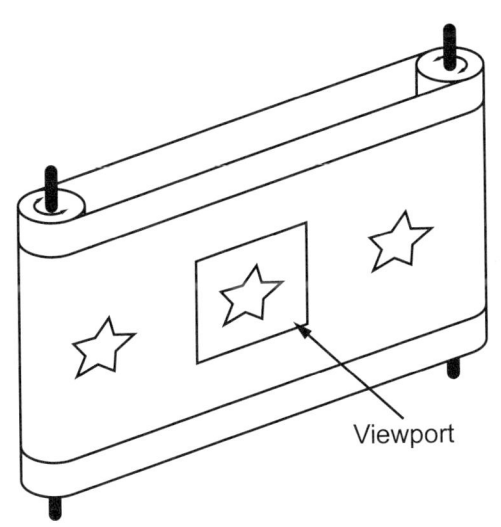

Figure 11.6
In a conveyor belt animation, the viewport shows a changing detail of the revolving source image.

`UvAnimation` implements the setup of the animation:

```java
/**
 * Encapsulates a UV animation. UV animations display sequences of
 * images by modifying texture coordinates.
 *
 * @author Claus Hoefele
 */
public class UvAnimation {
  /** Controller for animation. */
  private AnimationController controller;
  /** Duration of animation. */
  private int duration;

  /**
   * Protected because a new <code>UvAnimation</code> object must be
   * created with one of the static <code>create</code> methods.
   *
   * @param controller animation controller.
   * @param duration duration of animation.
   * @see #createConveyorBeltAnimation
   * @see #createFlipBookAnimation
   */
  protected UvAnimation(AnimationController controller, int duration){
    this.controller = controller;
    this.duration = duration;
  }
```

```java
/**
 * Creates a UV animation based on the given parameters.
 *
 * @param mesh mesh to use for UV animation.
 * @param image image to use for UV animation.
 * @param sequence animation sequence.
 * @param scaleX scaling factor of texture in x direction.
 * @param scaleY scaling factor of texture in y direction.
 * @return new UvAnimation object.
 */
private static UvAnimation createAnimation(
    Mesh mesh, Image2D image, KeyframeSequence sequence,
    float scaleX, float scaleY) {
  // Set texture with high quality settings.
  Texture2D texture = new Texture2D(image);
  texture.scale(scaleX, scaleY, 0);
  texture.setFiltering(
      Texture2D.FILTER_LINEAR, Texture2D.FILTER_LINEAR);
  mesh.getAppearance(0).setTexture(0, texture);
  PolygonMode polygonMode = new PolygonMode();
  polygonMode.setPerspectiveCorrectionEnable(true);
  mesh.getAppearance(0).setPolygonMode(polygonMode);

  // Automatically enable blending if image contains alpha channel.
  int format = image.getFormat();
  if (format == Image2D.ALPHA ||
      format == Image2D.LUMINANCE_ALPHA ||
      format == Image2D.RGBA) {
    CompositingMode compositingMode = new CompositingMode();
    compositingMode.setBlending(CompositingMode.ALPHA);
    mesh.getAppearance(0).setCompositingMode(compositingMode);
  }

  // Attach new animation track.
  AnimationTrack track
      = new AnimationTrack(sequence, AnimationTrack.TRANSLATION);
  AnimationController controller = new AnimationController();
  track.setController(controller);
  texture.addAnimationTrack(track);

  return new UvAnimation(controller, sequence.getDuration());
}
```

```
/**
 * Creates an animation where an image is scrolled horizontally
 * as if it were attached to a conveyor belt.
 *
 * @param mesh mesh to use for UV animation.
 * @param image image to use for UV animation.
 * @param duration duration of one entire rotation.
 * @param scaleX scaling factor of texture in x direction.
 * @return new UvAnimation object.
 */
public static UvAnimation createConveyorBeltAnimation(Mesh mesh,
    Image2D image, int duration, float scaleX) {
  KeyframeSequence sequence
      = new KeyframeSequence(3, 3, KeyframeSequence.LINEAR);
  sequence.setRepeatMode(KeyframeSequence.LOOP);
  sequence.setDuration(duration);
  sequence.setKeyframe(0,        0, new float[] {0, 0, 0});
  sequence.setKeyframe(1, duration, new float[] {1, 0, 0});
  sequence.setKeyframe(2, duration, new float[] {0, 0, 0});

  return createAnimation(mesh, image, sequence, scaleX, 1);
}
...
}
```

`createAnimation()` prepares the texture and creates the animation track. The flip-book animation will later reuse this method.

`createConveyorBeltAnimation()` implements the actual animation sequence. Two keyframes with a linear interpolation suffice to scroll the image once. This implementation modifies only the *x* coordinate of the translation component of a texture, which causes the image to move horizontally. The third frame is necessary to repeat the sequence. It has the same time stamp as the second frame, but the value of the first. Hence, the sequence restarts anew.

The texture wraps around because a new instance of `Texture2D` automatically has `WRAP_REPEAT` set. To avoid visible lines where the image starts and ends, you have to use a texture that's seamless in the animation direction.

The parameters that you pass in `createConveyorBeltAnimation()` determine speed and what is displayed in the viewport. With `duration`, you can adjust the time it takes for one loop to complete. `scale` stretches the texture in the *x* direction.

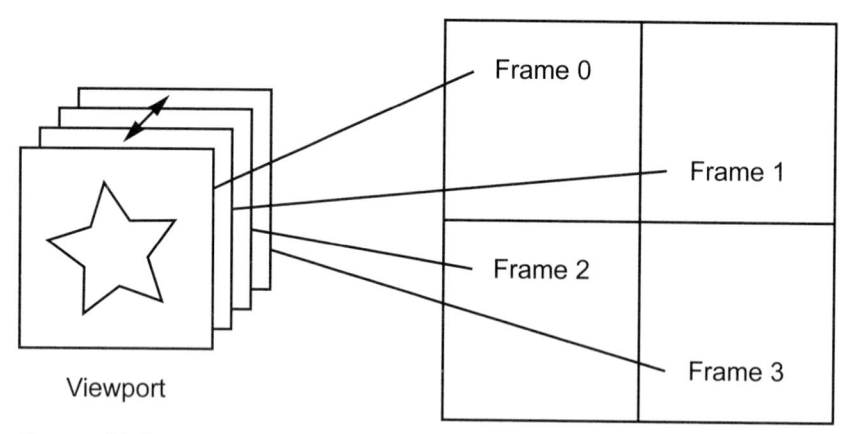

Figure 11.7
Flip-book animations show individual frames in quick succession.

For example, if the texture animation is assigned to a square quad and the texture is double the width, the scale must be 0.5. This means the texture will take twice the time to repeat itself.

Flip-Book Animations

Flip-book animations are more versatile than those using a conveyor belt system because one frame updates the complete viewport. On the other hand, the amount of memory needed for the image grows with each frame. Figure 11.7 shows an animation where the content of an image is split into four frames.

The following code demonstrates how to use texture coordinates to split an image into frames and create an animation. `createFlipBookAnimation()` is implemented in `UvAnimation` and reuses its `createAnimation()` method listed in the previous conveyor belt animation example.

```
/**
 * Creates an animation where frames inside an image are displayed
 * successively like in a flip-book animation.
 *
 * @param mesh mesh to use for UV animation.
 * @param image image to use for UV animation.
 * @param delay delay between successive frames.
 * @param framesX number of frames inside the image in x direction.
 * @param framesY number of frames inside the image in y direction.
 * @return new UvAnimation object.
 */
```

```java
public static UvAnimation createFlipBookAnimation(
    Mesh mesh, Image2D image, int delay,
    int framesX, int framesY) {
  // Set up detail of one frame based on the number of frames.
  float scaleX = 1.0f/framesX;
  float scaleY = 1.0f/framesY;

  // Create flip-book sequence. Frames are read left to right,
  // top to bottom. It is assumed that the image contains the
  // maximum possible number of frames that fit in it. Repeat mode
  // is set to CONSTANT by default.
  int numberOfFrames = framesX*framesY;
  KeyframeSequence sequence
      = new KeyframeSequence(numberOfFrames, 3, KeyframeSequence.STEP);
  sequence.setDuration(delay*numberOfFrames);

  for (int i=0; i<framesX; i++) {
    for (int j=0; j<framesY; j++) {
      int frame = i*framesX + j;
      sequence.setKeyframe(frame, delay*frame,
          new float[] {j*scaleX, i*scaleY, 0});
    }
  }

  return createAnimation(mesh, image, sequence, scaleX, scaleY);
}
```

`createFlipBookAnimation()` assumes that image frames are distributed left to right, top to bottom, and creates a new keyframe for each of them. To determine the speed of the animation, you can set the delay between successive frames.

Controlling the Animation

`UvAnimation` simplifies the process of controlling the animation by offering three methods:

```java
public class UvAnimation {
  /** Controller for animation. */
  private AnimationController controller;
  /** Duration of animation. */
  private int duration;

  ...
```

```java
/**
 * Stops the animation.
 */
public void stop() {
  controller.setSpeed(0, 0);
}

/**
 * Plays the animation in forward direction.
 *
 * @param worldTime current world time.
 */
public void playForward(int worldTime) {
  controller.setPosition(0, worldTime);
  controller.setSpeed(1, worldTime);
}

/**
 * Plays the animation in backward direction.
 *
 * @param worldTime current world time.
 */
public void playBackward(int worldTime) {
  controller.setPosition(duration, worldTime);
  controller.setSpeed(-1, worldTime);
  }
}
```

stop() halts the animation by setting the speed to zero; playForward() and playBackward(), on the other hand, restart the playback. Whereas playForward() rewinds the animation and plays it in normal direction, playBackward() does the opposite: it fast forwards the animation to the end and reverses the playback. Both play methods need the current world time to avoid sudden jumps in the animation.

UV Animations in Action

TextureAnimationSample uses both types of UV animations: the scene depicted in Figure 11.8 contains a conveyor belt animation that scrolls the clouds in the background and a flip-book animation to open and close the lower window sash. Although it's possible to use multitexturing, the implementation uses two layers of textured planes for the different animations. This makes TextureAnimationSample compatible with devices that do not support this feature.

Figure 11.8
A flip-book animation opens and closes the window, whereas a conveyor belt animation moves the clouds.

```java
/**
 *  Displays a scene with UV animations.
 *
 *  @author Claus Hoefele
 *  @see UvAnimation
 */
public class TextureAnimationSample extends GameCanvas
        implements Sample, Runnable {
    /** Window animation controller. */
    private UvAnimation windowAnimation;
    /** State of window. */
    private boolean isWindowOpen;

    /** Object that represents the scene graph. */
    private World world;

    /** Flag whether thread is running. */
    private boolean isRunning;
    /** Stores the last game action key. */
    private int lastKey = 0;

    /** 3D graphics singleton used for rendering. */
    private Graphics3D graphics3d;
    /** 2D graphics singleton used for rendering. */
    private Graphics graphics;
```

Chapter 11 ■ Keyframe Animations

```java
/**
 * Constructor.
 */
public TextureAnimationSample() {
  super(false);
}

/**
 * Initializes the sample.
 */
public void init() {
  reset();

  Thread thread = new Thread(this);
  isRunning = true;
  thread.start();
}

/**
 * Initializes the sample.
 */
private void reset() {
  // Get the singletons for rendering.
  graphics3d = Graphics3D.getInstance();
  graphics = getGraphics();

  // Set up scene with one group node.
  world = new World();
  Group group = new Group();
  group.postRotate(25, 0, 1, 0);
  world.addChild(group);

  try {
    // Window animation. Picture is loaded with Image class to
    // force RGBA format.
    Image image = Image.createImage("/m3g11/window.png");
    Image2D windowImage = new Image2D(Image2D.RGBA, image);
    Mesh window = MeshFactory2D.createQuad(true);
    windowAnimation = UvAnimation.createFlipBookAnimation(
        window, windowImage, 100, 2, 2);
    windowAnimation.stop();
    isWindowOpen = false;
    window.scale(8, 8, 0);
    group.addChild(window);
```

```java
      // Clouds animation. Handle for clouds animation isn't needed as
      // the animation will go on forever.
      Image2D cloudsImage
          = (Image2D) Loader.load("/m3g11/clouds.png")[0];
      Mesh clouds = MeshFactory2D.createQuad(true);
      UvAnimation.createConveyorBeltAnimation(clouds, cloudsImage,
          128000, 0.5f);
      clouds.translate(0, 1, -1);
      clouds.scale(3, 3, 0);
      group.addChild(clouds);
    } catch (Exception e) {
      e.printStackTrace();
    }

    // Create a camera with perspective projection.
    Camera camera = new Camera();
    float aspect = (float) getWidth() / (float) getHeight();
    camera.setPerspective(60, aspect, 1, 1000);
    camera.setTranslation(0, 0, 10);
    world.addChild(camera);
    world.setActiveCamera(camera);
  }

  /**
   * Destroys the sample.
   */
  public void destroy() {
    isRunning = false;
  }

  /**
   * Animation loop.
   */
  public void run() {
    while(isRunning) {
      int worldTime = (int) System.currentTimeMillis();
      checkKeys(worldTime);
      world.animate(worldTime);
      render(graphics);
      flushGraphics();

      try {
        Thread.sleep(20);
      } catch (Exception e) {}
```

        }
    }

    /**
     * Renders the sample on the screen.
     */
    private void render(Graphics graphics) {
        graphics3d.bindTarget(graphics);
        graphics3d.setViewport(0, 0, getWidth(), getHeight());
        graphics3d.render(world);
        graphics3d.releaseTarget();

        drawMenu(graphics); // displays the current key assignment
    }

    /**
     * Receives key presses.
     *
     * @param keyCode key code.
     */
    protected void keyPressed(int keyCode) {
        lastKey = getGameAction(keyCode);
    }

    /**
     * Processes key presses.
     *
     * @param worldTime current world time.
     */
    private void checkKeys(int worldTime) {
        if (lastKey == FIRE) {
            if (isWindowOpen) {
                windowAnimation.playBackward(worldTime);
            } else {
                windowAnimation.playForward(worldTime);
            }

            isWindowOpen = !isWindowOpen;
            lastKey = 0;
        }
    }
    ...
}
```
```

Alternatives

You can embed UV animated meshes easily into your scene, at any position and in any orientation you like. However, textures also have their limitations. M3G restricts textures to a power-of-two dimension, and, furthermore, the quality of the texture filters and the maximum texture size depend on the implementation. M3G only mandates point sampling and a minimum texture dimension of 256×256 pixels.

If you can live with the restriction of screen-aligned images, Sprite3D and Background are alternatives. Both classes allow you to change the cropping rectangle, which achieves the same effect as scaling and translating texture coordinates. When using Sprite3D in unscaled mode or Background, the display quality is the same as the original image. There's also no restriction on the dimension of the source images.

Background works great for sky animations. However, you can't have several layers with independent animations as in the case of textures.

In combination with the billboards technique from Chapter 9, Sprite3Ds can be effective impostors such as animated enemies attacking you. You are restricted to flip-book animations because Sprite3D doesn't support a repeat mode.

Summary

Keyframes define time-stamped, absolute values of an animatable property. Stored in a KeyframeSequence, a collection of keyframes defines how this property changes over time. M3G then steps from keyframe to keyframe or interpolates in-between frames with linear or spline functions.

To associate an animation with an object, you have to create an AnimationTrack. AnimationTrack remembers which property you want to animate and ties it together with one KeyframeSequence and one AnimationController. The latter manages the execution of the animation such as playback direction and speed.

Calling the object's animate() method in regular intervals drives the animation. By using the system time to advance the animation, you can control playback speed and frame rate independently. Hence your animation runs at the same speed no matter what processor your device employs.

The end of the chapter showed you how you can put animations to good use: UV animated textures are an effective tool for creating movie-like shows.

CHAPTER 12

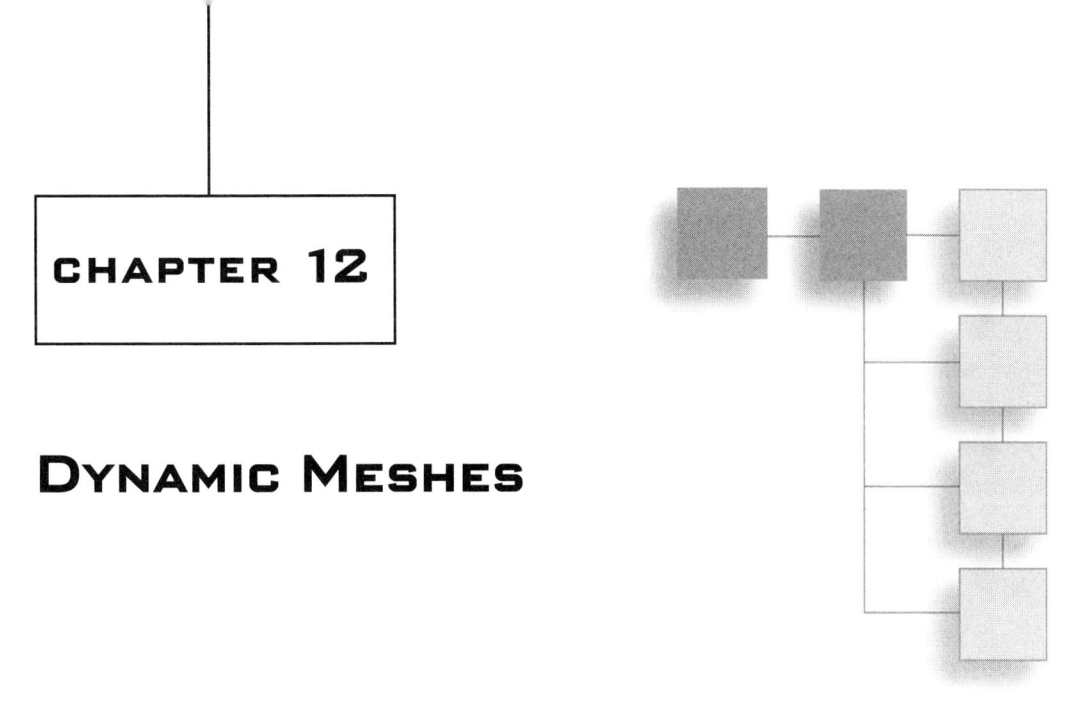

Dynamic Meshes

M3G provides two subclasses of Mesh that contain extra features useful for animations: MorphingMesh and SkinnedMesh. A MorphingMesh blends one mesh into another. For example, you can morph the model of a person with a neutral face expression into a model with a smile. A SkinnedMesh, on the other hand, emulates the anatomy of humans and animals by letting you define a mesh as the skin and a hierarchy of scene graph nodes as the skeleton. When connected, the skeleton deforms the skin according to the bone movements. Two bones can flex an arm at the elbow for example.

This chapter shows you how to:

- Define a base mesh and the targets for a MorphingMesh.
- Combine the animation of several morph targets.
- Produce skin and skeleton to create a SkinnedMesh.
- Pose a SkinnedMesh.
- Build an animated robot in Blender and articulate the figure.

Morphing

Like the metamorphosis of a caterpillar into a butterfly, morphing turns one mesh property into another.

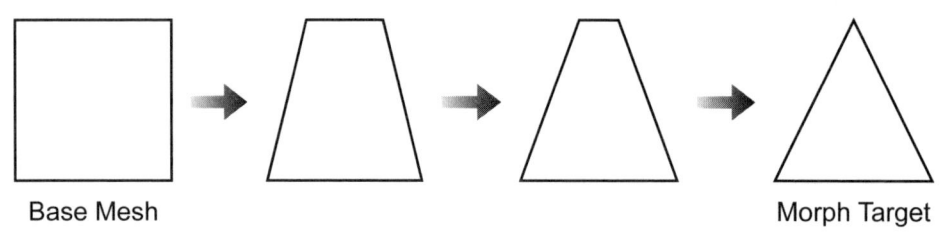

Figure 12.1
Morphing blends one mesh into another.

Basic Morphing

All vertex attributes (positions, colors, normals, and texture coordinates) as well as the default color of a mesh can be the target of morphing. Figure 12.1 shows an example whereby a quad's vertex positions are morphed into a triangle.

You start by defining a base mesh with the initial mesh properties and a morph target that contains the vertex attributes of the end result. You adjust the progress by setting a blending weight. You can also provide several targets, in which case M3G allows you to adjust how much each target affects the result. More formally, the morphing result **R** is defined as

$$\mathbf{R} = \mathbf{B} + \sum_{i=0}^{n-1} w_i (\mathbf{T}_i - \mathbf{B})$$

In other words, the result is a linear interpolation of the base mesh **B** and the sum of n morph targets denoted by $\mathbf{T}_i$, where the influence of each target on the result is weighted with w_i.

The weight serves two purposes: For one, it adjusts the progression of the morph process. Say you have a base mesh that models a face with a neutral face expression. In addition, you design the same face with a smile as a morph target. Initially, the weight is set to zero, which means the base mesh is visible. Increasing the weight would blend the mesh into the target until the smile is fully visible when the value reaches one. Weights outside the range [0, 1] are allowed, however. A negative value, for example, gives the face a sad expression.

The second purpose of the weight is to vary the influence of targets relative to each other. This enables you to create complex morphing results by combining separate morph targets. Consider the example of the smiling face again. If you added another version of the face with closed eyes, you could create a face that smiles, blinks, or does both at the same time.

Because the morph result is computed per vertex and the weight can take on any value, the result might overflow the 8-bit or 16-bit range of your vertex attributes. To avoid this, you would usually select weights so that individual values as well as the sum of all weights stay within the range [0, 1]. This ensures that the morph result doesn't grow bigger than the initial values.

Creating a MorphingMesh

A `MorphingMesh` is a `Mesh` with the addition of `VertexBuffers` that define the morph targets. You start by defining the base mesh with all the attributes that a regular `Mesh` object would also require. Then, you add targets that contain a subset of the base mesh's `VertexBuffer` with the attributes you want to morph. Figure 12.2 shows `MorphingMesh`'s structure; Table 12.1 lists its interface.

All `VertexBuffers` of the targets must have the exact same kind of properties—the number and type of vertex arrays, the number of vertices, as well as a vertex

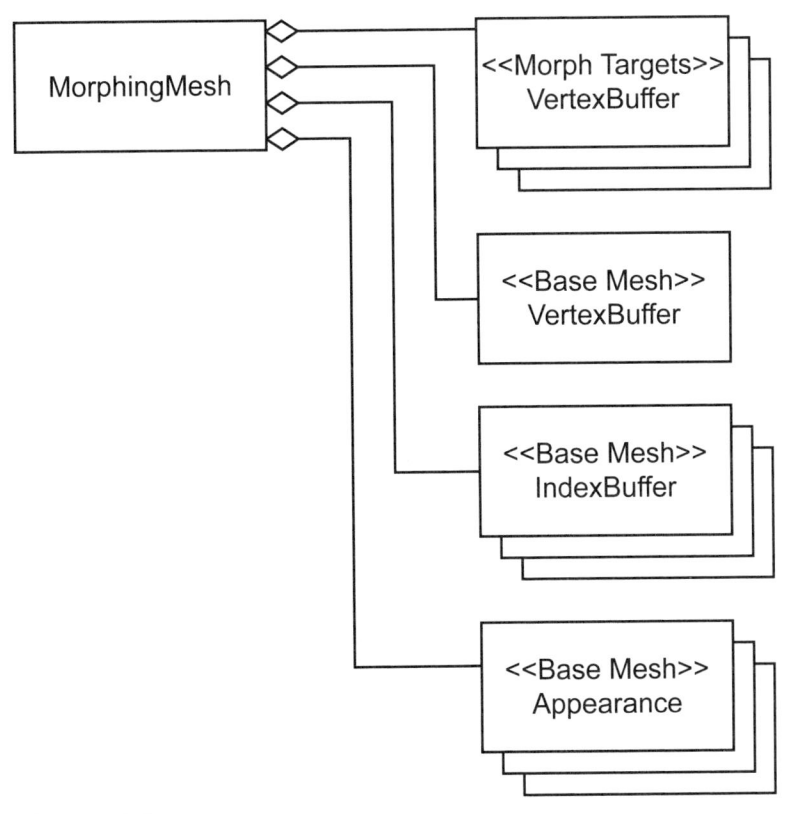

Figure 12.2
`MorphingMesh` associations.

Table 12.1 MorphingMesh Class Description

Method	Description
MorphingMesh(VertexBuffer base, VertexBuffer[] targets, IndexBuffer[] submeshes, Appearance[] appearances)	Initializes the class with a base mesh, morph targets, and submeshes.
MorphingMesh(VertexBuffer base, VertexBuffer[] targets, IndexBuffer submesh, Appearance appearance)	Initializes the class with a base mesh, morph targets, and one submesh.
VertexBuffer getMorphTarget(int index)	Returns the morph target at the given index.
int getMorphTargetCount()	Returns the number of morph targets.
void setWeights(float[] weights)	Sets the weights that determine how much a morph target contributes to the resulting mesh.
void getWeights(float[] weights)	Getter for morph target weights.

Figure 12.3
For the morph targets, the two vertices at one side of the quad are moved to the same position.

array's component number and size must all be the same. The properties of VertexArrays that exist in base mesh and targets must also match, but the targets only have to contain the vertex attributes that you want to morph. The example depicted by Figure 12.3 illustrates these requirements.

In this example, a quad is the base mesh and two triangles pointing at opposite sides are the targets. Even though the triangle needs only three vertices, you'll have to model it with four—otherwise, the vertex count of base and target meshes wouldn't be the same. For this reason, the two outer vertices are co-located at the tip of each triangle to turn the quad into the new shape. The following code achieves this constellation:

```
/**
 * Creates a new MorphingMesh that has a quad as the base mesh and
 * two triangles as morph targets.
 *
```

```java
 * @return new MorphingMesh.
 */
private MorphingMesh createMorphingMesh() {
  // Create a quad as base mesh. Its scale and bias arguments are
  // automatically used for the morph targets as well.
  byte h = Byte.MAX_VALUE;
  byte l = -Byte.MAX_VALUE;
  byte[] base = {1, 1, 0, h, 1, 0, 1, h, 0, h, h, 0};
  VertexArray vertexBase = new VertexArray(base.length/3, 3, 1);
  vertexBase.set(0, base.length/3, base);
  VertexBuffer vertexBufferBase = new VertexBuffer();
  vertexBufferBase.setPositions(vertexBase, 1.0f/h, null);
  TriangleStripArray triangles
      = new TriangleStripArray(0, new int[] {4});

  byte c = (byte) 255;
  byte[] colors = {0, 0, 0,  0, 0, 0, c, 0, 0,  0, 0, c};
  VertexArray vertexColors = new VertexArray(colors.length/3, 3, 1);
  vertexColors.set(0, colors.length/3, colors);
  vertexBufferBase.setColors(vertexColors);

  Appearance appearance = new Appearance();
  PolygonMode polygonMode = new PolygonMode();
  polygonMode.setShading(PolygonMode.SHADE_FLAT);
  appearance.setPolygonMode(polygonMode);

  // Create first morph target (triangle with tip at the top).
  byte[] target1 = {1, 1, 0, h, 1, 0, 0, h, 0, 0, h, 0};
  VertexArray vertexTarget1=new VertexArray(target1.length/3, 3, 1);
  vertexTarget1.set(0, target1.length/3, target1);
  VertexBuffer vertexBufferTarget1 = new VertexBuffer();
  vertexBufferTarget1.setPositions(vertexTarget1, 1, null);

  // Create second morph target (triangle with tip at the bottom).
  byte[] target2 = {0, 1, 0, 0, 1, 0, 1, h, 0, h, h, 0};
  VertexArray vertexTarget2=new VertexArray(target2.length/3, 3, 1);
  vertexTarget2.set(0, target2.length/3, target2);
  VertexBuffer vertexBufferTarget2 = new VertexBuffer();
  vertexBufferTarget2.setPositions(vertexTarget2, 1, null);

  return new MorphingMesh(vertexBufferBase,
      new VertexBuffer[] {vertexBufferTarget1, vertexBufferTarget2},
      triangles, appearance);
}
```

Because this example only wants to change the mesh geometry, the morph targets defined in `createMorphingMesh()` require vertex positions but need not repeat the vertex colors from the base mesh. Note also that the scale and bias arguments you pass to the `VertexBuffer` are ignored for the morph targets because they are taken from the base mesh. It's important to set scale and bias to values that let the outcome of the morphing calculations (most likely fractional numbers) have enough precision to produce the intended result. That's why `createMorphingMesh()` scales the quad to the maximum values allowed by the 8-bit range of the vertex positions.

Animating Morph Targets

To animate the morph process, you can create an `AnimationTrack` that uses the `MORPH_WEIGHTS` target property, such as in the following code:

```
/**
 * Creates a new animation that morphs the MorphingMesh's base and
 * target meshes.
 *
 * @param mesh mesh for animation.
 */
private void createAnimation(MorphingMesh mesh) {
  // Keyframe data for the two morph targets.
  float[][] weights = new float[][] {
    {0, 0},                    // quad
    {1, 0},                    // triangle with tip at the top
    {0, 1},                    // triangle with tip at the bottom
    {0, 0}                     // quad
  };

  // Create the keyframe sequence.
  KeyframeSequence sequence = new KeyframeSequence(
      weights.length, 2, KeyframeSequence.LINEAR);
  sequence.setRepeatMode(KeyframeSequence.LOOP);
  sequence.setDuration((weights.length - 1) * 2000);
  for (int i=0; i<weights.length; i++) {
    sequence.setKeyframe(i, i*2000, weights[i]);
  }

  // Attach new animation track.
  AnimationTrack track
```

```
      = new AnimationTrack(sequence, AnimationTrack.MORPH_WEIGHTS);
   mesh.addAnimationTrack(track);
   track.setController(new AnimationController());
}
```

The `KeyframeSequence` for the animation comprises as many values per frame as morph targets exist. The reason I chose two morph targets is to demonstrate that a `MorphingMesh` can blend together independent targets. In each keyframe, the first value specified for `weights` is for morph target 1, the second value for morph target 2.

The animation defined by `createAnimation()` morphs the quad to a triangle with the tip pointing up (morph target 1), and then to a triangle with the tip pointing down (morph target 2), and finally back to the quad again. In the middle of the animation—when blending from one triangle to the other—both morph targets are active. During the animation, you can retrieve the current weights with `MorphingMesh.getWeights()`. The screenshots of the morph animation in Figure 12.4 display these weights at the bottom of the screen.

Note

The CD-ROM contains the entire MorphingSample.java together with a MIDlet, ready for execution.

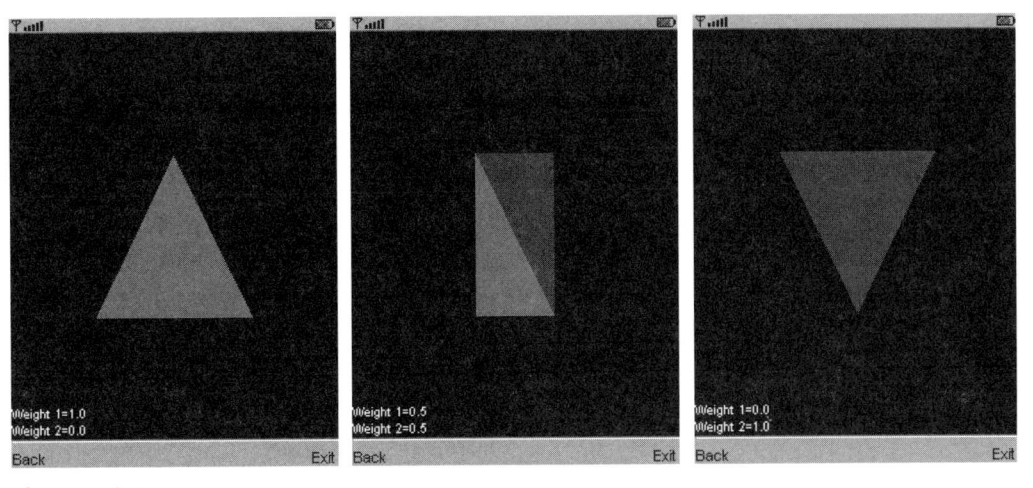

Figure 12.4
Selected states of the morph animation. From left to right: morph target 1 visible (weights: 1.0, 0.0), halfway between morph target 1 and 2 (0.5, 0.5), and morph target 2 (0.0, 1.0).

Chapter 12 ■ Dynamic Meshes

The previously explained code is tied together by `MorphingSample`, as follows:

```java
/**
 * Defines an animation that blends mesh shapes into each other by
 * using morphing.
 *
 * @author Claus Hoefele
 */
public class MorphingSample extends GameCanvas
        implements Sample, Runnable {
  /** Mesh for display. */
  private MorphingMesh morphingMesh;

  /** Flag whether thread is running. */
  private boolean isRunning;

  /** 3D graphics singleton used for rendering. */
  private Graphics3D graphics3d;
  /** 2D graphics singleton used for rendering. */
  private Graphics graphics;

  /**
   * Constructor.
   */
  public MorphingSample() {
    super(false);
  }

  /**
   * Initializes the sample.
   */
  public void init() {
    reset();

    Thread thread = new Thread(this);
    isRunning = true;
    thread.start();
  }

  /**
   * Initializes the sample.
   */
  private void reset() {
    graphics3d = Graphics3D.getInstance();
```

```
    graphics = getGraphics();

    // Set up morphing mesh and its animation.
    morphingMesh = createMorphingMesh();
    createAnimation(morphingMesh);

    // Create a camera with parallel projection.
    Camera camera = new Camera();
    float aspect = (float) getWidth() / (float) getHeight();
    camera.setParallel(5, aspect, 1, 1000);
    Transform cameraTransform = new Transform();
    cameraTransform.postTranslate(0, 0, 4);
    graphics3d.setCamera(camera, cameraTransform);
}

...

/**
 * Destroys the sample.
 */
public void destroy() {
    isRunning = false;
}

/**
 * Animation loop.
 */
public void run() {
    while(isRunning) {
        morphingMesh.animate((int) System.currentTimeMillis());
        render(graphics);
        flushGraphics();

        try {
            Thread.sleep(20);
        } catch (Exception e) {}
    }
}

/**
 * Renders the sample.
 *
 * @param graphics graphics context for drawing.
 */
```

```
  private void render(Graphics graphics) {
    graphics3d.bindTarget(graphics);
    graphics3d.setViewport(0, 0, getWidth(), getHeight());
    graphics3d.clear(null);
    graphics3d.render(morphingMesh, null);
    graphics3d.releaseTarget();
  }
}
```

Skinned Meshes

A `MorphingMesh` gives you fine-grained control over individual vertices. This flexibility isn't always required. For example, the entire skin on your forearm will follow the forearm's bone. Following this analogy, a `SkinnedMesh` allows you to define a mesh as the skin and a hierarchy of nodes as the skeleton. When a bone moves, it will move all parts of the skin attached to it. Because one bone can transform many vertices, it efficiently encodes the transformations required to animate vertebrates.

Creating Skin and Skeleton

The following code serves as an example of how to create a skin and a skeleton, which Figure 12.5 represents.

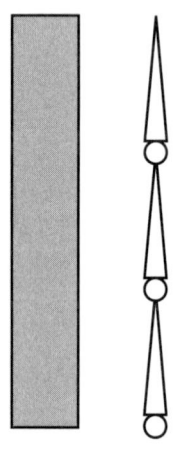

Figure 12.5
Skin and skeleton.

```java
/**
 * Creates a new rectangular mesh that serves as skin.
 *
 * @param subdivisions number of vertical subdivisions.
 * @return mesh.
 */
private Mesh createSkin(int subdivisions) {
  final short length = Short.MAX_VALUE;
  final short halfWidth = Short.MAX_VALUE/16;
  final double diff = length/(subdivisions-1.0);
  short[] positions = new short[subdivisions*2*3];

  for (int i=0; i<subdivisions; i++) {
    short currentDiff = (short) (i*diff);
    positions[i*2*3 + 0] = (short) (-halfWidth);
    positions[i*2*3 + 1] = currentDiff;
    positions[i*2*3 + 3] = halfWidth;
    positions[i*2*3 + 4] = currentDiff;
  }

  VertexArray vertexPositions
      = new VertexArray(positions.length/3, 3, 2);
  vertexPositions.set(0, positions.length/3, positions);
  VertexBuffer vertexBuffer = new VertexBuffer();
  vertexBuffer.setPositions(vertexPositions, 1.0f/length, null);

  TriangleStripArray triangles
      = new TriangleStripArray(0, new int[] {2*(subdivisions-1)});

  byte[] colors = new byte[positions.length];
  VertexArray vertexColors = new VertexArray(colors.length/3, 3, 1);
  vertexColors.set(0, colors.length/3, colors);
  vertexBuffer.setColors(vertexColors);

  Appearance appearance = new Appearance();
  PolygonMode polygonMode = new PolygonMode();
  polygonMode.setShading(PolygonMode.SHADE_FLAT);
  appearance.setPolygonMode(polygonMode);

  return new Mesh(vertexBuffer, triangles, appearance);
}

/**
 * Creates a hierarchy of Groups that serves as skeleton.
 *
```

```
 * @param numBones number of bones.
 * @return skeleton.
 */
private Group createSkeleton(int numBones) {
  Group rootBone = new Group();
  Group parent = rootBone;

  for (int i=0; i<(numBones-1); i++) {
    Group bone = new Group();
    bone.translate(0, 1.0f/numBones, 0);
    parent.addChild(bone);
    parent = bone;
  }

  return rootBone;
}
```

createSkin() constructs a rectangular mesh with subdivisions that allow the skin to stretch. In addition, createSkeleton() creates Group nodes that build the skeleton. Any Node can serve as a bone, but as in this chapter's example you will most often use Group objects because they can model chains of bones such as a human arm where the upper arm is connected to the forearm at the elbow.

So far, skin and skeleton are independent structures. Hence, transformations done to the bones will not yet affect the skin. Instead, the transformations in createSkeleton() form the initial pose of the skeleton. This example distributes the bones in equal distances over the same length as the skin mesh.

Attaching the Skin to the Skeleton

A Node doesn't have a length, but rather describes a position. Thus, initially it might be easier to think of skeleton nodes as joints rather than bones. In the next step, however, you'll form a unit between skin and skeleton by attaching a bone with a number of the skin's vertices. In Figure 12.6, you can see what this looks like if you attach all vertices between two joints to the same bone. When you rotate the bone, the associated vertices will also rotate around the joint and the bone works as if it had a length.

Similar to a MorphingMesh, a SkinnedMesh is a Mesh with additional attributes. In this case, the standard Mesh properties build the skin and the skeleton exists as a hierarchy of Node objects with a Group as the root bone. Figure 12.7 shows this structure.

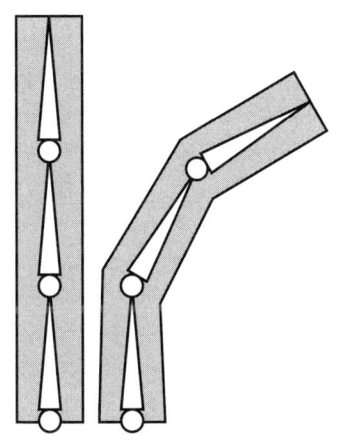

Figure 12.6
A transformation of the bones will result in a deformation of the attached skin.

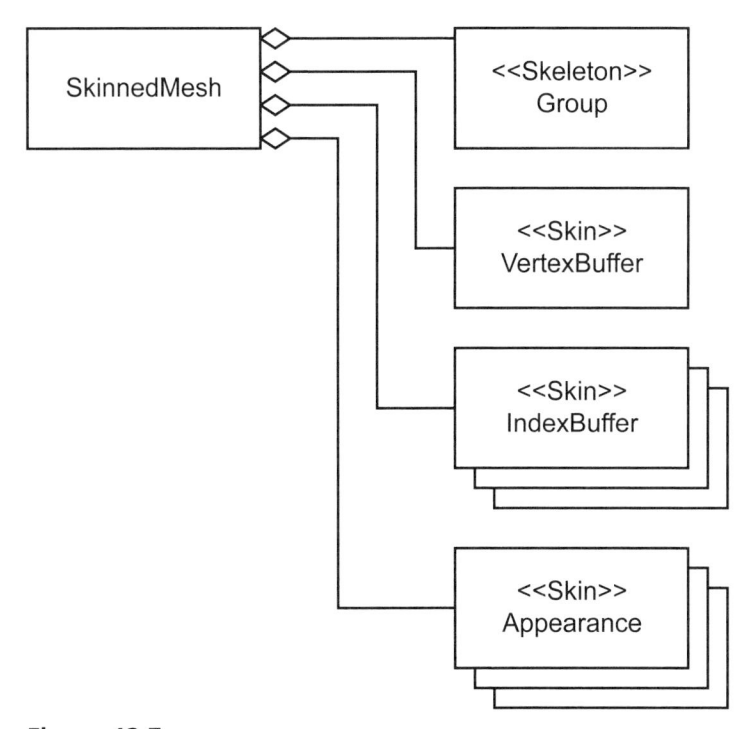

Figure 12.7
`SkinnedMesh` associations.

Because the skeleton is an arbitrary scene graph structure, you can also combine bone and non-bone objects. You could, for example, model a knight with the armor as the skin and a skeleton that allows the knight to move. The sword could be modeled as a separate mesh and made part of the skeleton as the child of the hand. Now, if the knight moves the arm, the sword will follow.

Table 12.2 SkinnedMesh Class Description

Method	Description
`SkinnedMesh(VertexBuffer vertices, IndexBuffer[] submeshes, Appearance[] appearances, Group skeleton)`	Initializes the class with a skin mesh, submeshes, and a skeleton.
`SkinnedMesh(VertexBuffer vertices, IndexBuffer submesh, Appearance appearance, Group skeleton)`	Initializes the class with a skin mesh, one submesh, and a skeleton.
`void addTransform(Node bone, int weight, int firstVertex, int numVertices)`	Attaches the given bone to a number of vertices.
`void getBoneTransform(Node bone, Transform transform)`	Returns the transformation for a bone in its initial pose. (Since 1.1.)
`int getBoneVertices(Node bone, int[] indices, float[] weights)`	Returns the vertices that are attached to a bone. (Since 1.1.)
`Group getSkeleton()`	Returns the skeleton.

To attach skin and skeleton, you'll need to create a `SkinnedMesh` out of the two data structures that you created in `createSkin()` and `createSkeleton()`. In addition, you'll have to bind bones to vertices. Table 12.2 displays `SkinnedMesh`'s methods to achieve these tasks.

```
/**
 * Attaches skin to skeleton to create a SkinnedMesh.
 *
 * @param skin mesh used as skin.
 * @param skeleton hierarchy used as skeleton.
 * @param numBones number of bones.
 * @param twoBonesPerVertex enables vertices to share bones.
 * @return SkinnedMesh.
 */
private SkinnedMesh attachSkin(Mesh skin, Group skeleton,
    int numBones, boolean twoBonesPerVertex) {
  SkinnedMesh skinnedMesh = new SkinnedMesh(skin.getVertexBuffer(),
      skin.getIndexBuffer(0), skin.getAppearance(0), skeleton);
  Group bone = skeleton;
  final int vertexCount = skin.getVertexBuffer().getVertexCount();
  final int numVerts = vertexCount / numBones;
  final int rest = vertexCount % numBones;

  // Adjusts the number of vertices that a bone influences. Minimum
  // is 1 or addTransform() will throw an exception.
  final int overlap = Math.max(numVerts/2, 1);
```

```
// Changes the influence of the inner bone on a vertex compared
// to the outer bones.
final int weight = 3;

// Vertex sharing only works with at least three bones.
if (numBones < 3) {
  twoBonesPerVertex = false;
}

// Colors for bones.
VertexArray colors = skin.getVertexBuffer().getColors();
byte[] red  = new byte[(numVerts+rest)*3];
byte[] blue = new byte[(numVerts+rest)*3];
for (int i=0; i<(numVerts+rest); i++) {
  red [i*3 + 0] = (byte) 255;
  blue[i*3 + 2] = (byte) 255;
}

// Attach bones to skin.
for (int i=0; i<(numBones-1); i++) {
  // Attach inner bone vertices.
  int first = i*numVerts;
  skinnedMesh.addTransform(bone, weight, first, numVerts);
  // Color each bone's skin in an alternating color.
  colors.set(first, numVerts, i%2 == 0 ? red : blue);

  // Attach outer bone vertices.
  if (twoBonesPerVertex) {
    if (i > 1) {                          // overlap to previous bone
      skinnedMesh.addTransform(bone, 1, first-overlap, overlap);
    }
    if (i<(numBones-2)) {                 // overlap to next bone
      skinnedMesh.addTransform(bone, 1, first+numVerts, overlap);
    }
  }

  bone = (Group) bone.getChild(0);        // next bone in hierarchy
}

// Add remaining vertices to the last bone.
int last = (numBones-1);
int first = last*numVerts;
skinnedMesh.addTransform(bone, weight, first, numVerts + rest);
colors.set(first, numVerts + rest, last%2 == 0 ? red : blue);
```

```
    if (twoBonesPerVertex) {                  // overlap to previous bone
      skinnedMesh.addTransform(bone, 1, first-overlap, overlap);
    }

    return skinnedMesh;
  }
```

A straightforward approach to attaching vertices comprises dividing the skin into segments of the same length. Then, you attach each segment to a bone that's positioned at the start of the segment. In `attachSkin()`, the skin's vertex colors serve to identify where the bones are attached to the skin in a color that alternates between red and blue. The number of bones in the skeleton is up to you; as is the number of vertices of the skin. The more bones you add, the more bendy the skeleton. The more vertices you define, the smoother the skin can deform.

After attaching the skin to the skeleton, moving a bone will always move the associated vertices with it. That's why it's important to distinguish between transforming bones before and after calling `SkinnedMesh.addTransform()`. In the former case, you define the pose where the bones are at rest. In the latter, you bend the skeleton to achieve the target pose.

The formula to transform a vertex **v** is

$$\mathbf{v}' = \sum_{i=0}^{n-1} w_i \mathbf{M}_i \mathbf{B}_i \mathbf{v}$$

where n is the number of bones that influence a vertex. For each bone, the vertex is multiplied with the at-rest transformation **B**, the transformation of the bone to world coordinates **M**, and the normalized weight w.

Having one bone per vertex creates edges at the joints because the vertices change abruptly from one bone to the next. Alternatively, you can attach a vertex to more than one bone. If you call `attachSkin()` with the method's parameter `twoBonesPerVertex` set to `true`, the example code extends the reach of a bone to include more vertices at the top and the bottom—this smooths the skin deformation where the influence areas of adjacent bones overlap. Figure 12.8 shows three bones where the middle part of the mesh is attached to the outer bones in addition to the inner bone.

You can fine-tune the process by adjusting bone weights. You'll get a really smooth result when two bones share vertices at their joints at even weights and a

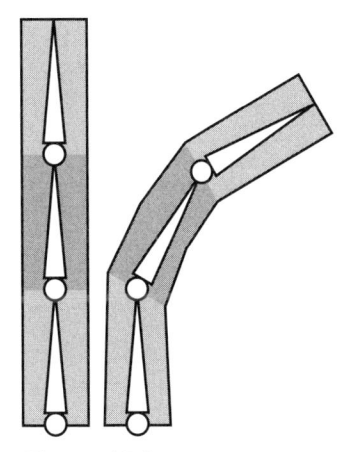

Figure 12.8
Using two bones per vertex smooths out the transition between bones.

bone's influence vanishes with the distance from the bone. In the example, however, you can only set a fixed blending ratio: The influence of the inner bone is increased by setting its weight to three and that of the outer bones decreased by setting their weights to one. M3G automatically normalizes a vertex's bone weights by dividing each weight by the sum of all weights attached to it. In the example, the inner bone influence would be 0.75 and that of the outer bones 0.25.

> **Tip**
>
> You can use automatic normalization of weights to reduce the number of addTransform( ) calls. If you want vertices to shares bones with the same weight, just call addTransform( ) once for each bone with all the vertices. In my example, however, a ratio of 3:1 results in a smoother deformation.

You can also use even more bones per vertex. An implementation is, however, allowed to restrict the number of bones that have an effect on a vertex to the value in the property maxTransformsPerVertex. If you add more bones, it chooses those with the highest weights. If several bones use the same weights, the selection process is undefined, but must be deterministic. Every implementation must at least support two bones per vertex.

Rotating Bones with Quaternions

As most bones connect via joints to the next bone, you'll often pose the skeleton with rotations. If you remember, you can rotate an object using axis-angle format, Euler angles, or quaternions. When rotating an object directly, you can choose how to rotate it; when doing animations, M3G requires quaternions.

Because it's more intuitive, I want to specify the bone rotations in the axis-angle format. You therefore need a helper class that converts this format to a quaternion.

Note

> You'll find this class implemented in Quaternion.java on the CD-ROM. The section in Chapter 5 called "Orientation Representations" introduced the equations used in this implementation.

```java
/**
 * Quaternion implementation.
 *
 * @author Claus Hoefele
 */
public class Quaternion {
  /** Quaternion element. */
  private float x, y, z, w;

  /**
   * Creates a new quaternion and initializes it to the identity.
   */
  public Quaternion() {
    setIdentity();
  }

  /**
   * Resets this quaternion to the identity.
   */
  public void setIdentity() {
    set(0, 0, 0, 1);
  }

  /**
   * Sets this quaternion to the given values.
   *
   * @param x x value.
   * @param y y value.
   * @param z z value.
   * @param w w value.
   */
  public void set(float x, float y, float z, float w) {
    this.x = x;
    this.y = y;
    this.z = z;
```

```
    this.w = w;
}

/**
 * Getter for x value.
 *
 * @return x value.
 */
public float getX() { return x; }

/**
 * Getter for y value.
 *
 * @return y value.
 */
public float getY() { return y; }

/**
 * Getter for z value.
 *
 * @return z value.
 */
public float getZ() { return z; }

/**
 * Getter for w value.
 *
 * @return w value.
 */
public float getW() { return w; }
}
```

First of all, the quaternion class needs the four elements x, y, z, and w and setters and getters for these values. The constructor sets these values to the identity quaternion. The only operation you need is a conversion from axis-angle to quaternion format:

```
/**
 * Sets the values of this quaternion by converting the given
 * axis-angle values.
 *
 * @param angle angle of rotation around the axis, in degrees.
 * @param ax x component of the rotation axis.
```

```
 * @param ay y component of the rotation axis.
 * @param az z component of the rotation axis.
 * @return reference to this quaternion.
 */
public Quaternion setAxisAngle(float angle,
    float ax, float ay, float az) {
  double length = Math.sqrt(ax*ax + ay*ay + az*az);

  if (length == 0) {
    // If axis of rotation is zero vector, set to identity.
    setIdentity();
  } else {
    // Convert from deg to rad and divide by 2.
    angle *= Math.PI / 360;

    double cangle = Math.cos(angle);
    double sangle = Math.sin(angle);
    double scale = sangle / length;        // axis must be unit length

    set((float) (scale * ax),              // x
        (float) (scale * ay),              // y
        (float) (scale * az),              // z
        (float) cangle);                   // w
  }

  return this;
}
```

Animating the Skeleton

You can still transform the entire mesh by calling `SkinnedMesh`'s transformation methods. Because this chapter's example places the root bone at the same origin as the skin and attaches all vertices, transforming the mesh is equivalent to transforming the root bone of the skeleton. However, depending on the way you attached the vertices, this distinction can make a difference.

This example leaves the position of the mesh unchanged, but instead rotates the bones to achieve an animation. With the quaternion class from the previous section, you can use `AnimationTrack.ORIENTATION` for this purpose.

```
/**
 * Creates a new animation that interpolates between two
 * orientations.
 *
```

```java
 * @return animation track.
 */
private AnimationTrack createAnimation() {
  Quaternion q = new Quaternion();
  q.setAxisAngle(30, 0, 0, 1);

  float[][] orientations = new float[][] {
    { q.getX(),  q.getY(),  q.getZ(), q.getW()},    //  30 degrees
    {-q.getX(), -q.getY(), -q.getZ(), q.getW()}     // -30 degrees
  };

  // Create the keyframe sequence.
  KeyframeSequence sequence = new KeyframeSequence(
      orientations.length, 4, KeyframeSequence.SQUAD);
  sequence.setRepeatMode(KeyframeSequence.LOOP);
  sequence.setDuration((orientations.length) * 2000);
  for (int i=0; i<orientations.length; i++) {
    sequence.setKeyframe(i, i*2000, orientations[i]);
  }

  track
      = new AnimationTrack(sequence, AnimationTrack.ORIENTATION);
  track.setController(new AnimationController());

  return track;
}

/**
 * Attaches the animation to the bones of the SkinnedMesh's
 * skeleton.
 *
 * @param skinnedMesh mesh with skeleton.
 * @param track animation track.
 */
private void attachAnimation(SkinnedMesh skinnedMesh,
    AnimationTrack track) {
  Group parent = skinnedMesh.getSkeleton();
  while (parent.getChildCount() != 0) {
    Group bone = (Group) parent.getChild(0);
    bone.addAnimationTrack(track);
    parent = bone;
  }
}
```

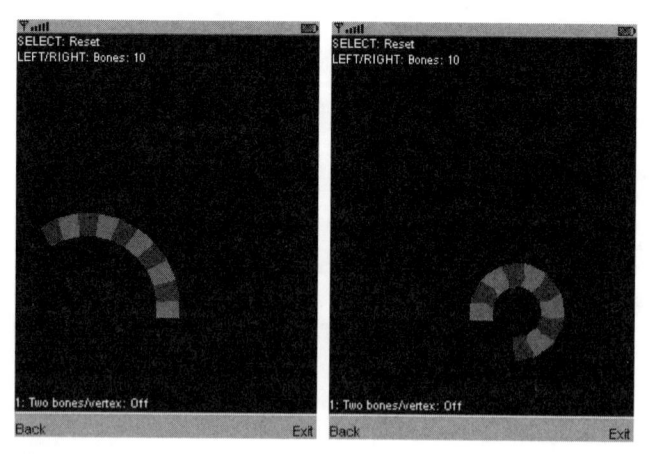

Figure 12.9
The bending shape in action.

`createAnimation()` creates an `AnimationTrack` that rotates a bone 30 degrees back and forth around the *z* axis. The `Quaternion` class converts this angle into the proper format and the result ends up as keyframe values.

Tip

You get the inverse rotation of a normalized quaternion by negating its vector part.

`attachAnimation()` then makes the animation part of each bone. By increasing the number of bones, you'll get a more flexible version of the shape, as displayed in Figure 12.9 with 10 bones.

Note

You'll find SkinnedMeshSample.java and Quaternion.java on the CD-ROM.

Here is the remaining code of `SkinnedMeshSample` that pulls together the methods explained so far:

```
/**
 * <code>SkinnedMesh</code> animation that bends a skeleton with an
 * adjustable number of bones.
 *
 * @author Claus Hoefele
 */
public class SkinnedMeshSample extends GameCanvas
    implements Sample, Runnable {
  /** Representation of the skin. */
  private Mesh skin;
```

```java
/** Mesh with skin and skeleton. */
private SkinnedMesh skinnedMesh;
/** Bone animation. */
private AnimationTrack track;
/** Number of bones for skeleton. */
private int numBones;
/** Enables vertices to share two bones. */
private boolean twoBonesPerVertex;

/** Flag whether thread is running. */
private boolean isRunning;
/** Stores the last game action key. */
private int lastKey = 0;

/** 3D graphics singleton used for rendering. */
private Graphics3D graphics3d;
/** 2D graphics singleton used for rendering. */
private Graphics graphics;

/**
 * Constructor.
 */
public SkinnedMeshSample() {
  super(false);
}

/**
 * Initializes the sample.
 */
public void init() {
  reset();

  Thread thread = new Thread(this);
  isRunning = true;
  thread.start();
}

/**
 * Destroys the sample.
 */
public void destroy() {
  isRunning = false;
}
```

```java
/**
 * Animation loop.
 */
public void run() {
  while(isRunning) {
    int worldTime = (int) System.currentTimeMillis();
    checkKeys(worldTime);
    skinnedMesh.animate(worldTime);
    render(graphics);
    flushGraphics();

    try {
      Thread.sleep(20);
    } catch (Exception e) {}
  }
}

/**
 * Initializes the sample.
 */
private void reset() {
  graphics3d = Graphics3D.getInstance();
  graphics = getGraphics();

  // Set up skinned mesh and its animation.
  numBones = 4;
  twoBonesPerVertex = false;
  skin = createSkin(100);
  Group skeleton = createSkeleton(numBones);
  skinnedMesh
      = attachSkin(skin, skeleton, numBones, twoBonesPerVertex);
  track = createAnimation();
  attachAnimation(skinnedMesh, track);

  // Create a camera with parallel projection.
  Camera camera = new Camera();
  float aspect = (float) getWidth() / (float) getHeight();
  camera.setParallel(2, aspect, 0.5f, 1000);
  Transform cameraTransform = new Transform();
  cameraTransform.postTranslate(0, 0.5f, 2);
  graphics3d.setCamera(camera, cameraTransform);
}

...
```

```
/**
 * Receives key presses.
 *
 * @param keyCode key code.
 */
protected void keyPressed(int keyCode) {
  lastKey = getGameAction(keyCode);
}

/**
 * Processes key presses.
 *
 * @param worldTime current world time.
 */
private void checkKeys(int worldTime) {
  boolean updateSkeleton = false;

  if (lastKey == FIRE) {
    reset();
  } else if (lastKey == RIGHT) {
    numBones++;
    updateSkeleton = true;
  } else if (lastKey == LEFT) {
    if (numBones > 1) numBones-;
    updateSkeleton = true;
  } else if (lastKey == GAME_A) {
    twoBonesPerVertex = !twoBonesPerVertex;
    updateSkeleton = true;
  }

  if (updateSkeleton) {
    Group skeleton = createSkeleton(numBones);
    skinnedMesh
        = attachSkin(skin, skeleton, numBones, twoBonesPerVertex);
    attachAnimation(skinnedMesh, track);
  }

  lastKey = 0;
}

/**
 * Renders the sample.
 *
```

```
 * @param graphics graphics context for drawing.
 */
private void render(Graphics graphics) {
  graphics3d.bindTarget(graphics);
  graphics3d.setViewport(0, 0, getWidth(), getHeight());
  graphics3d.clear(null);
  graphics3d.render(skinnedMesh, null);
  graphics3d.releaseTarget();

  drawMenu(graphics);    // displays the current key assignment
  }
}
```

An Articulated Robot

`MorphingMeshes` are often used for face expressions because you can model fine details into the meshes of the morph targets. Given the fact that most mobile phone screens are too small to fully appreciate delicate animations, games usually spend their computing resources on other effects. A `SkinnedMesh`, on the other hand, suits a number of tasks such as animating a human in a third-person shooter or monsters that attack the player.

The following example guides you through the process of creating a `SkinnedMesh` animation with Blender. You'll create a walking robot that you can control interactively.

Rigging the Robot Model

You can see the textured model of the robot in Figure 12.10. The first step when preparing a 3D model for animation is the setup of the skeleton. This process is referred to as *rigging*.

Note

artwork\robot.blend on the CD-ROM contains the completed robot project and artwork\robot_texture.png contains the robot's texture.

When rigging, you have to think about how much control you want to have over the model. For this example, I decided to use seven bones in total: two bones for each leg, one bone for each arm, and one bone for the back. This allows the robot to bend its knees when walking and to swing its arms back and forth.

Figure 12.10
The robot model.

In Blender, a skeleton is called an *armature*. To create a new armature, follow these steps:

1. Before you start, make sure to apply scale and rotation to the mesh by using Ctrl+A. This will simplify transforming the mesh when you import it into your application.

2. Left-click in a 3D View window to move the cursor to the position where you want to place the root of the first bone. It doesn't matter which bone you start with; for example, you can position the cursor at the hip to start with the back bone.

3. With the cursor positioned, press Spacebar and select Add>Armature. This will create the first bone and automatically put you in Edit mode. By default, a bone is displayed as an octahedron. You can move the ends of the bone by selecting either side's tip and pressing G. Selecting the middle of the bone and pressing G will move the entire bone.

4. In Edit mode, you have two choices to add more bones to an armature: One possibility is to right-click the sphere at the tip of a bone and extrude it with E. This will connect the beginning of the new bone to the end of the existing one. Extruding creates a hierarchy, which you'll need for the second bone of each leg. Another possibility is to position the cursor, press Spacebar, and select Add>Bone. This will add a new bone to the armature with no connections to any other bone. You'll need this to start a new chain of bones.

5. Position the bone in the desired location.

6. Repeat steps 4 and 5 until you have created all bones. The end result should look similar to Figure 12.11.

7. At the end, select the armature in Object mode and press Ctrl+A to apply scale and rotation to the skeleton.

To avoid confusion, I named all bones according to their position. You can do that by selecting a bone in Edit mode and going to the Armature Bones panel of the Editing context (F9). For example, the upper-left leg bone is called "UpLeg.L".

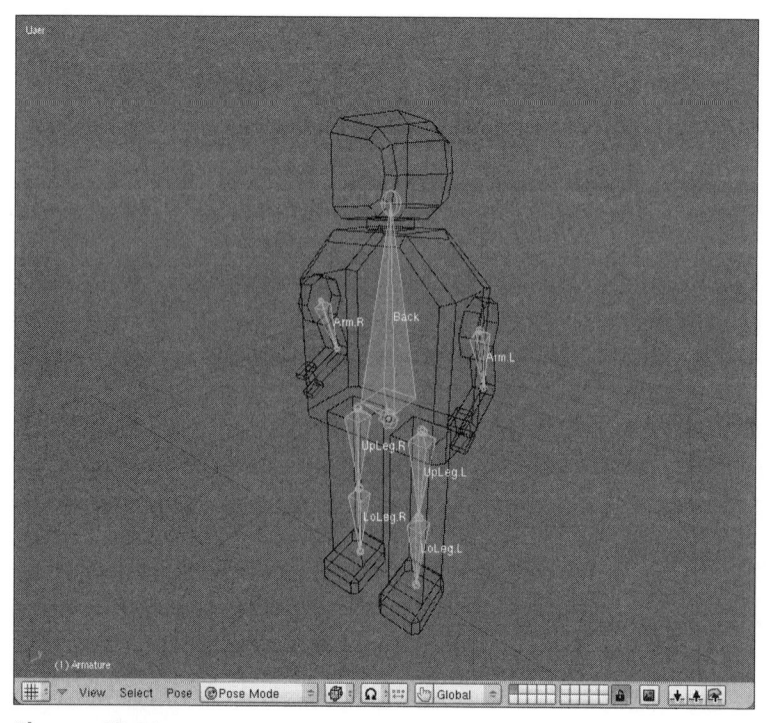

Figure 12.11
Seven bones form the robot's skeleton.

The suffixes .L and .R are a Blender naming convention to indicate the side of the skeleton where a bone is located (from the robot's point of view). This will help you later when animating the skeleton.

Skinning the Mesh

When connecting the armature to the mesh, you'll have to decide which bone affects what vertices. You can achieve this by gathering vertices in a *vertex group*. A bone deforms a vertex group with the same name. For example, the bone named Back deforms all vertices that are contained in the group Back. Because there are seven bones, you'll have to create seven groups.

Here are the next steps in more detail:

1. Start by parenting the mesh to the armature: right-click the mesh in Object mode, right-click the armature, and press Ctrl+P. In the first upcoming dialog box, select Armature as the parent. In the second dialog box, choose Name Groups when asked whether to create vertex groups. The parent-child relationship is indicated by a dashed line between mesh and armature.

2. In the previous step, the option Name Groups created an empty vertex group with the correct name for each bone. To add vertices to a group, select the robot and switch to Edit mode. Hold down Shift and select all vertices that you want to assign to a group with the right mouse button. Then, go to the Link and Materials panel of the Editing Context (F9). From the list in this panel, choose the name of the vertex group you want to add them to and press Assign. You can see this panel in Figure 12.12.

3. Repeat step 2 for all bones.

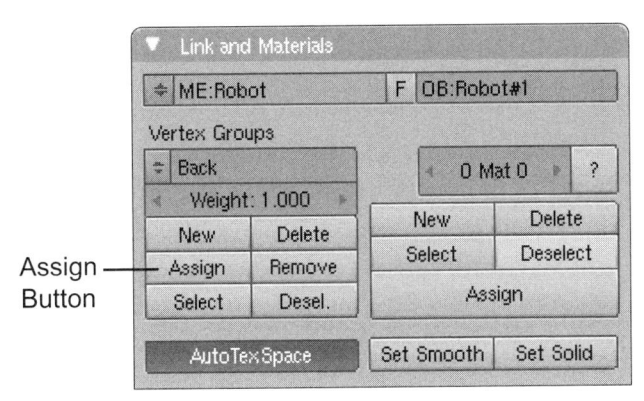

Figure 12.12
Vertices in a vertex group are attached to the bone with the same name.

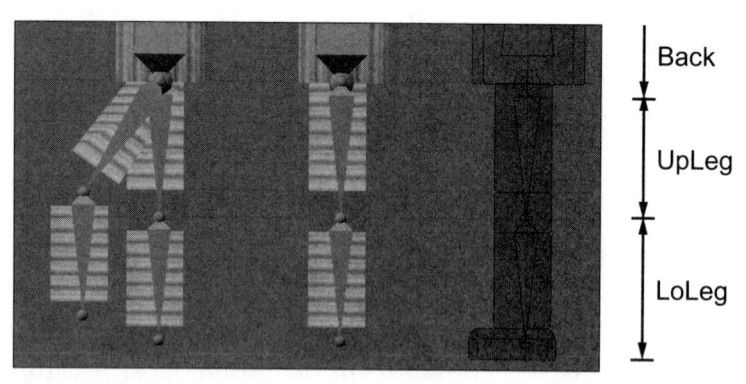

Figure 12.13
The vertices at the robot's legs are attached to three bones so the mesh bends at the knee.

When assigning vertices, you connect those closest to the bone. As an example, you can see how I skinned the robot's legs in Figure 12.13: the foot, calf, and the bottom part of the knee are attached to the lower leg bone; the top part of the knee and thigh to the upper leg bone; and the root of the leg to the backbone. In a similar way, you go through the remaining bones: because the robot has only one arm bone, you attach the entire arm to it; the remaining vertices such as body and head belong to the backbone.

You have to pay special attention to the transitions from one bone to the next where the mesh will deform. Flexing the leg bones, for example, will bend the mesh at the knees. For this reason, I gave the area around the knee a single color. If I had assigned a patterned texture, it would stretch together with the movement of the bones and start looking weird. There's some distortion happening at the thigh because its upper vertices are assigned to the back bone and don't join the movement of the leg bones. On the other hand, this gives the viewer the impression that the robot's legs are firmly connected to the body. I found the distortion acceptable because it's at the side of the legs.

At the end, all vertices should be connected to at least one bone. If you correctly attached the mesh to the bones, moving the armature will take the entire mesh with it. To check, right-click on the armature and select Pose mode. Relocating the bones when pressing G shouldn't leave any vertices behind. You activate Pose mode by selecting the respective entry in the list box in a view's header bar, next to the menus.

Posing the Walk Animation

Blender's Pose mode is where you move bones in a specific position—you create poses at different points in time to build an animation. Because you skinned the robot's mesh in the previous step, the animated skeleton will also deform the attached vertices and thus produce the walking robot.

Individual bones are transformed with a combination of rotations and translations. The skeleton itself is posed with rotations because the intention is to make it look as if the robot's legs and arms were attached to the body at joints. However, the translations are necessary to move the robot forward and correct its position.

From Chapter 11, you'll remember that it's not necessary to create each frame of an animation. Instead, you create keyframes and let the interpolation calculate the in-between values. You can see some of the robot's poses overlaid on top of each other in Figure 12.14.

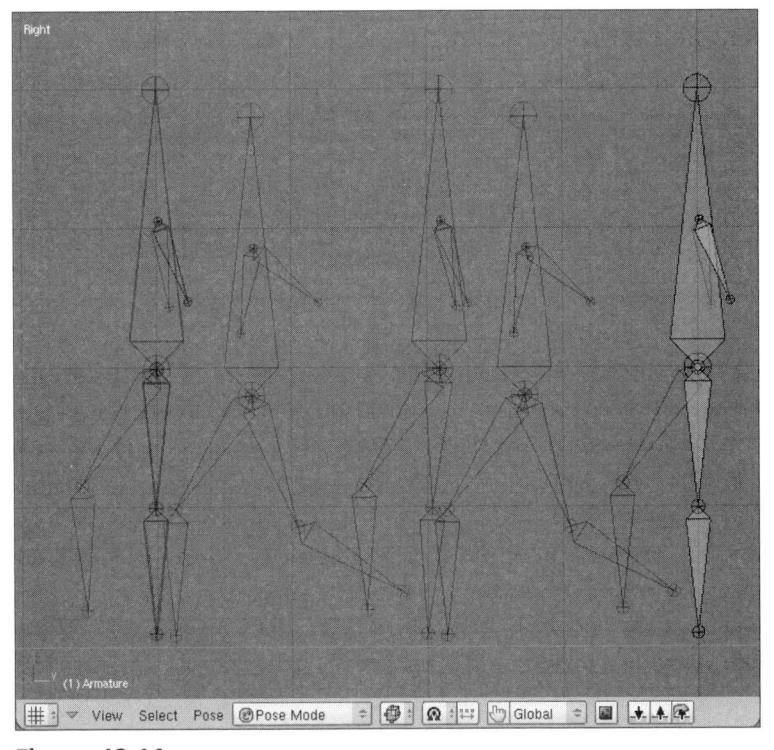

Figure 12.14
The robot's walking animation at different points in time.

Figure 12.15
The frame counter indicates the current position of the animation.

I created seven poses that represent the keyframes of the animation: the robot standing, its left leg lifted, walking one step with each foot (three poses), left leg lifted, and finally the stand again. The animation includes a full walking sequence from start to stop positions, but is also designed to allow the middle part to cycle seamlessly. For this reason, the second and sixth pose is the same, which lets you walk several steps in a row by repeating the middle frames. I'll come back to this point when playing back the animation inside the Java application.

To let you know your current position in the animation, Blender displays the frame counter next to the header line of the Buttons window. In Figure 12.15, you can see the frame counter at position one, which is the start of the animation. You can change the counter either by clicking on the button or using the cursor keys: Left and Right keys move the counter by one frame, Up and Down keys move it by 10 frames.

Because it's easy to navigate with Up and Down keys, I created each pose of the animation 10 frames apart. By using narrower or wider gaps, you can increase or decrease the speed of the animation. You can still configure the overall walking speed later when playing back the animation in your application. However, I recommend that you make sure the animation speed is consistent across all poses of your animation in Blender, because changing the speed within the animation is difficult to control. For example, if you want the robot to pick up speed while doing its first step, build this into the animation right now.

To create one frame of your animation, you position the frame counter at the intended position, pose the skeleton to your liking, and create a new keyframe. This process repeats until you create all keyframes. Here are the details:

1. Select the armature and go into Pose mode. Because all bones are at rest, you don't need to move anything for the first pose.

2. Press A to select all bones. Afterward, press I to insert a new keyframe and select LocRot in the upcoming dialog box. This creates a new keyframe with location (translation) and rotation information.

3. Advance the frame counter by 10 (Up key).

4. Move the bones into the next position by selecting each of them individually and use G to translate or R to rotate.

5. Press A to select all the bones and create a new keyframe with I. Select LocRot.

6. Repeat steps 3 to 5 for each pose.

You can save yourself time by copying poses between frames; you'll find the Copy Current Pose command in the Pose menu. Don't forget to set the frame counter to the intended position before using Paste Pose or Paste Flipped Pose in the same menu. Paste Pose copies the pose unchanged, which you can use for frames one and seven and two and six. Paste Flipped Pose mirrors the pose—if you used the .L and .R suffixes when naming the bones. Blender will exchange transformations between bones that have the same name but differ in their suffixes. With this mechanism, you can create pose five based on pose three and pose four based on pose two.

Tip
> In a chain of bones, such as the robot's legs, the transformation of the upper bone influences the end position of the lower one. One way to get to the end pose is to fix the start of the chain first and work down toward the end. This process is called *forward kinematics*. Blender also offers support for *inverse kinematics*, where you position the end of the chain and the connected bones are automatically positioned to fulfill the desired configuration. If you want to pose more sophisticated models than the robot, you might want to read about Blender's support for inverse kinematics at http://mediawiki.blender.org/index.php/Manual/Inverse_Kinematics.

Once you created all the poses, moving the frame counter back and forth should animate the robot. To play the entire animation, rewind the frame counter to one and press Alt+A with the mouse pointer in a 3D View window.

Tip
> You can find more detailed instructions for how to rig and animate a model in the second part of the two-part tutorial at http://mediawiki.blender.org/index.php/Manual/Your_First_Animation_in_30_plus_30_Minutes_Part_II.

Importing the Robot Model

Importing the robot's scene graph into your Java application is the same as reading any other M3G file. Before exporting the scene in Blender, I tagged the robot with the user ID 1 to make it accessible to `world.find()`.

Note

The exported M3G file is stored in res\m3g12\robot.m3g on the CD-ROM.

In contrast to the example in Chapter 10, however, the returned object is a `SkinnedMesh` instance and you have to deal with the animation as well. Here's the code:

```
/**
 * Displays a walking robot that can be controlled with the game keys.
 *
 * @author Claus Hoefele
 */
public class RobotSample extends GameCanvas
    implements Sample, Runnable {

  /** File that stores the scene graph. */
  private static final String M3G_FILE = "/m3g12/robot.m3g";
  /** User ID to find the mesh inside the scene graph. */
  private static final int USER_ID_MESH = 1;

  ...

  /** Object that represents the 3D world. */
  private World world;
  /** Robot. */
  private SkinnedMesh mesh;
  /** The robot's animation controller. */
  private AnimationController controller;
  /** The robot's position. */
  private Group position;
  /** Current walking direction. */
  private float direction;
  /** Helper object for transformation. */
  private Transform transform = new Transform();

  /** Flag for stopping the animation thread.*/
  private boolean isRunning;

  /** 3D graphics singleton used for rendering. */
  private Graphics3D graphics3d;
  /** 2D graphics singleton used for rendering. */
  private Graphics graphics;
```

```java
/**
 * Constructor.
 */
public RobotSample() {
  super(true);
}

/**
 * Initializes the sample.
 */
public void init() {
  reset();

  Thread thread = new Thread(this);
  isRunning = true;
  thread.start();
}

/**
 * Initializes the sample.
 */
public void reset() {
  // Get the singletons for rendering.
  graphics3d = Graphics3D.getInstance();
  graphics = getGraphics();

  try {
    // Load scene graph from M3G binary file.
    Object3D[] objects = Loader.load(M3G_FILE);
    world = (World) objects[0];

    // Change the camera's properties to match the current device.
    Camera camera = world.getActiveCamera();
    float aspect = (float) getWidth() / (float) getHeight();
    camera.setPerspective(60, aspect, 1, 1000);

    // Find mesh in scene graph.
    mesh = (SkinnedMesh) world.find(USER_ID_MESH);
    world.removeChild(mesh);
    position = new Group();
    position.addChild(mesh);
    world.addChild(position);
  } catch (Exception e) {
```

```
      System.out.println("Error loading " + M3G_FILE + ".");
      e.printStackTrace();
    }

    // All tracks have the same animation controller. This code finds
    // the first one, which is used to manage the animation.
    Group parent = mesh.getSkeleton();
    while (parent.getChildCount() != 0) {
      Group bone = (Group) parent.getChild(0);
      if (bone.getAnimationTrackCount() != 0) {
        controller = bone.getAnimationTrack(0).getController();
        break;
      }
      parent = bone;
    }
  }

  /**
   * Destroys the sample.
   */
  public void destroy() {
    isRunning = false;
  }

  ...

  /**
   * Renders the sample.
   *
   * @param graphics graphics context for drawing.
   */
  protected void render(Graphics graphics) {
    graphics3d.bindTarget(graphics);
    graphics3d.setViewport(0, 0, getWidth(), getHeight());
    graphics3d.render(world);
    graphics3d.releaseTarget();

    drawMenu(graphics);
  }
}
```

Because of the animation, `RobotSample` implements `Runnable` and contains a render loop to advance the frames. You'll see the `run()` method and how to cope with the walk cycle in the next section.

The skeleton transformations are stored in `AnimationTracks` attached to the robot's bones. The M3G Exporter Script creates two tracks per bone: one for the translations and one for the rotations. All of them reference a single instance of `AnimationController`. You can play this pre-recorded scene graph animation by simply calling `world.animate()`. For a game, however, you'll need to interactively control what's happening. That's why `reset()` obtains the `AnimationController` and stores it for future use. `RobotSample` will need this controller to manage the walking cycle.

Switching Between Animation Sequences

The animation created in Blender contains a full walking cycle—including start and stop sequences. In order to walk several steps in a row, you'll have to repeat the middle part before coming to the stop sequence. `RobotSample` achieves this by changing the playback position in the `AnimationController` obtained in `reset()`. Figure 12.16 shows where the different sequences start and end.

As mentioned previously, I set the keyframes in Blender 10 frames apart. However, M3G requires time stamps for each keyframe. The M3G Exporter Script thus divides the frame value with the number of frames per second that Blender uses to render the animation. You'll find this value in the Format panel of the Scene context (F10). Adjusting this number changes the overall speed of the animation, which by default is 25 fps (40 ms per frame).

The first frame in Blender starts with index 1. The M3G Exporter Script counts this frame, so the animation begins at 40 ms.

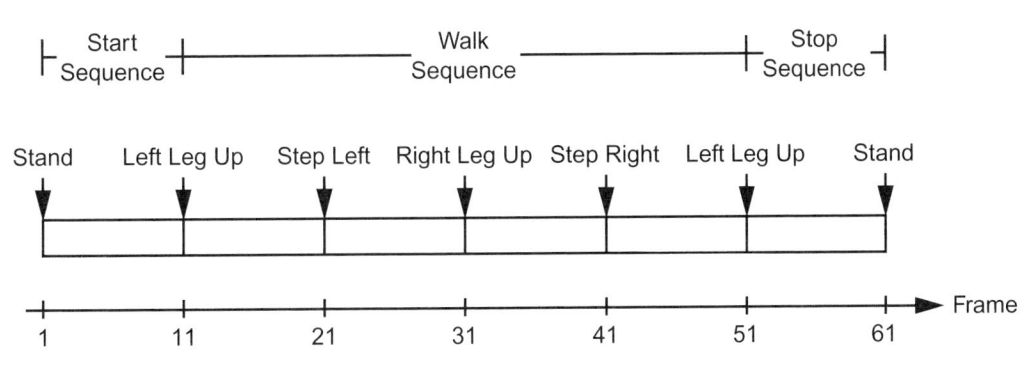

Figure 12.16
The animation comprises three sequences.

Chapter 12 ■ Dynamic Meshes

If you derive the start and duration times for all sequences, you'll come to the following result:

Sequence	Start	Duration
Start	40 ms	400 ms
Walk	440 ms	1600 ms
Stop	2040 ms	400 ms

To change to a new sequence, you can set the start value in `Animation Controller.setPosition()` and let the animation play for the specified duration. Either automatically or based on key input, you then switch to the next sequence. In `RobotSample`, pressing the UP key will trigger the start sequence and automatically switch to the walk sequence. As long as you press the UP key, the walking sequence repeats. Without input, the animation will finish the current walk sequence and switch to the stop sequence.

> **Tip**
>
> Alternatively to creating one animation with all the frames in it, Blender also lets you divide animation sequences into *actions* such as walking, jumping, or shooting. This is more flexible because you can combine actions to walk and shoot at the same time or blend actions to transition smoothly from walking to running. However, exporting several actions is not fully supported by the M3G Exporter Script v0.6.

```
/** State index for invalid state. */
private static final int STATE_INVALID   = -1;
/** State index for idle state. */
private static final int STATE_IDLE = 0;
/** State index for starting state. */
private static final int STATE_STARTING  = 1;
/** State index for walking state. */
private static final int STATE_WALKING   = 2;
/** State index for stopping state. */
private static final int STATE_STOPPING  = 3;

/** State data. Contains start time of animation, duration, speed,
 * key assignment, true state, false state, and walking distance. */
private static final int[][] STATE_DATA = {
   {    0,    0, 0, UP_PRESSED, STATE_STARTING, STATE_INVALID,  0},
   {   40,  400, 1,       0xFF, STATE_WALKING,  STATE_INVALID,  0},
   {  440, 1600, 1, UP_PRESSED, STATE_WALKING,  STATE_STOPPING, -4},
   { 2040,  400, 1,       0xFF, STATE_IDLE,     STATE_INVALID, -4},
};
```

```java
/** State data index for animation start time. */
private static final int DATA_START       = 0;
/** State data index for animation duration. */
private static final int DATA_DURATION    = 1;
/** State data index for animation speed. */
private static final int DATA_SPEED       = 2;
/** State data index for key to move to the next state. */
private static final int DATA_KEY         = 3;
/** State data index for next state if key was pressed. */
private static final int DATA_TRUE_STATE  = 4;
/** State data index for next state if key was not pressed. */
private static final int DATA_FALSE_STATE = 5;
/** State data index for walking distance. */
private static final int DATA_DISTANCE    = 6;

/** Time since last state update. */
private int stateTime;
/** Current state. */
private int state;

/**
 * Returns data for the current state.
 *
 * @param index type of state data.
 * @return data.
 */
private int getData(int index) {
  return STATE_DATA[state][index];
}

/**
 * Changes state and updates the animation position.
 *
 * @param state new state.
 * @param worldTime current world time.
 * @param error delta between the animation start and current
 *              world time.
 */
private void changeState(int state, int worldTime, int error) {
  this.stateTime = worldTime - error;
  this.state = state;
  controller.setPosition(getData(DATA_START) + error, worldTime);
  controller.setSpeed(getData(DATA_SPEED), worldTime);
}
```

`RobotSample` uses a state machine with a state for every part of the animation. Each state has an entry in the `STATE_DATA` array, which holds information such as the start and duration values of its animation sequence. The state data also comprises more information that I'll explain in a minute.

You can switch to a new state by calling `changeState()`, which positions the animation and sets the playback speed. The latter is a means to freeze the animation when the robot is idle. This method also stores the time when the new state began because you'll need to know when you can switch to the next sequence.

That's where a small error can happen if you catch the transition too late. Say the render loop draws a frame every 20 ms. If the last frame was 2 ms before a transition, the next frame will exceed the duration by 18 ms. `changeState()` adjusts for that with the `error` parameter and correcting the animation state. You have to make sure then to call `changeState()` before `world.animate()` to render the correct frame.

This is implemented in the `run()` method, which drives the animation, and `process()`, which advances the state machine:

```
/** The robot's position. */
private Group position;
/** Current walking direction. */
private float direction;
/** Helper object for transformation. */
private Transform transform = new Transform();

/**
 * Animation loop.
 */
public void run() {
  int worldTime = (int) System.currentTimeMillis();
  changeState(STATE_IDLE, worldTime, 0);

  while(isRunning) {
    process(worldTime, worldTime - stateTime);
    world.animate(worldTime);
    render(graphics);
    flushGraphics();

    try {
      Thread.sleep(20);
    } catch (Exception e) {}
```

```
      worldTime = (int) System.currentTimeMillis();
  }
}

/**
 * Checks for key presses and advances the state machine.
 *
 * @param worldTime current world time.
 * @param stateDelta time since last state change.
 */
private void process(int worldTime, int stateDelta){
  int keyStates = getKeyStates();

  // Update walking direction.
  int deltaDirection = 0;
  if ((keyStates & LEFT_PRESSED) != 0) {
    direction += 10;
    deltaDirection = 10;
  } else if ((keyStates & RIGHT_PRESSED) != 0) {
    direction -= 10;
    deltaDirection = -10;
  }

  // The rotation pivot takes the animation progress into account.
  float factor = 0;
  if (state == STATE_WALKING) {
    factor = stateDelta/(float) getData(DATA_DURATION);
  } else if (state == STATE_STOPPING) {
    factor = 1;
  }

  mesh.getTransform(transform);
  transform.postTranslate(0, getData(DATA_DISTANCE) * factor, 0);
  transform.postRotate(deltaDirection, 0, 0, 1);
  transform.postTranslate(0, -getData(DATA_DISTANCE) * factor, 0);
  mesh.setTransform(transform);

  // Check for state changes.
  if (stateDelta > getData(DATA_DURATION)) {
    int newState;

    if ((getData(DATA_KEY) == 0xFF)
    || (keyStates & getData(DATA_KEY)) != 0) {
      newState = getData(DATA_TRUE_STATE);
```

```
      // Update walking position.
      if (getData(DATA_DISTANCE) != 0) {
        position.getTransform(transform);
        transform.postRotate(direction, 0, 0, 1);
        transform.postTranslate(0, getData(DATA_DISTANCE), 0);
        transform.postRotate(-direction, 0, 0, 1);
        position.setTransform(transform);
      }
    } else {
      newState = getData(DATA_FALSE_STATE);
    }

    // Update state.
    if (newState != STATE_INVALID) {
      int error = 0;
      if (state != STATE_IDLE) {
        error = stateDelta - getData(DATA_DURATION);
      }
      changeState(newState, worldTime, error);
    }
  }
}
```

The `process()` method monitors the time that passed in the current state. If that time exceeds the current state's animation duration, it either checks the currently pressed key or advances automatically to the next sequence if that is required. The values to do this are stored in the `STATE_DATA` array. When walking, for example (`STATE_WALKING`), the `UP_PRESSED` event will trigger another walking sequence. If no key is pressed, on the other hand, `process()` will activate `STATE_STOPPING` and switch to this part of the walk animation.

Because the translation is built into the animation, the robot will move forward during the walk animation. It will, however, jump back to the start when a new cycle begins. Before that happens, you'll have to move the robot forward by the distance covered in the animation. The easiest way to do this is to measure that distance in Blender. As it turns out, this value is exactly four units and is stored in `STATE_DATA`. The distance is negated because of the differences in coordinate systems between M3G and Blender.

Independent of the forward movement, you'll also want to change the walking direction. This is the second task of the `process()` method and is controlled by `LEFT` and `RIGHT` keys. A complicating factor here is that you want the robot to

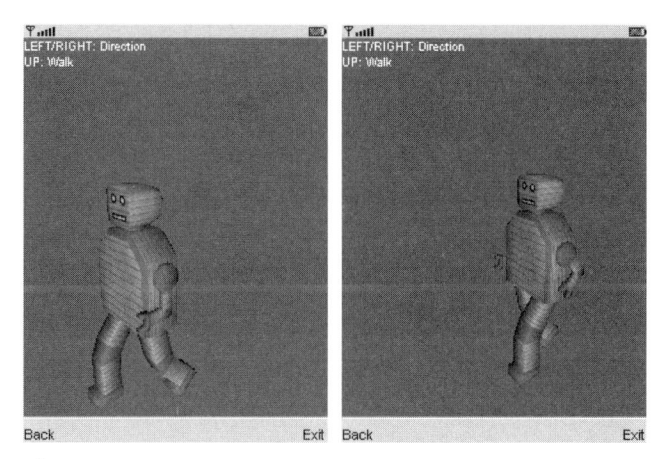

Figure 12.17
The walking robot inside the Java application.

rotate around itself, but the robot's center moves forward, together with the animation. If you don't take this into account, the robot will rotate around the start position, which looks more awkward the farther the animation advances. The cure is to divide the overall distance by the time spent in the current state to calculate the current walking distance and use this as the pivot point. Figure 12.17 shows two screenshots of the animated robot.

Summary

This chapter explained two subclasses of `Mesh` that come in handy for animations.

A `MorphingMesh` allows you to blend among vertex attributes of a base mesh and its morph targets, which is often used to animate face expressions. This flexibility comes at the price of high memory consumption because each morph target must duplicate the base mesh's vertex data that is used for morphing.

A `SkinnedMesh`, on the other hand, uses an approach based on the anatomy of humans and animals. A hierarchy of scene graph nodes provides the skeleton. When connected to a mesh that serves as the skin, the animated skeleton will deform the mesh to create realistic looking vertebrates. The animation data for this technique grows per keyframe but only requires information per bone rather than per vertex.

With Blender and the M3G Exporter Script, you can create your own `SkinnedMesh` animations and import them into your applications. This feature built the foundation for the example at the end of this chapter, where you saw how to create a walking robot that you can control interactively.

APPENDIX A

REFERENCE GEOMETRY AND FRAGMENT PIPELINES

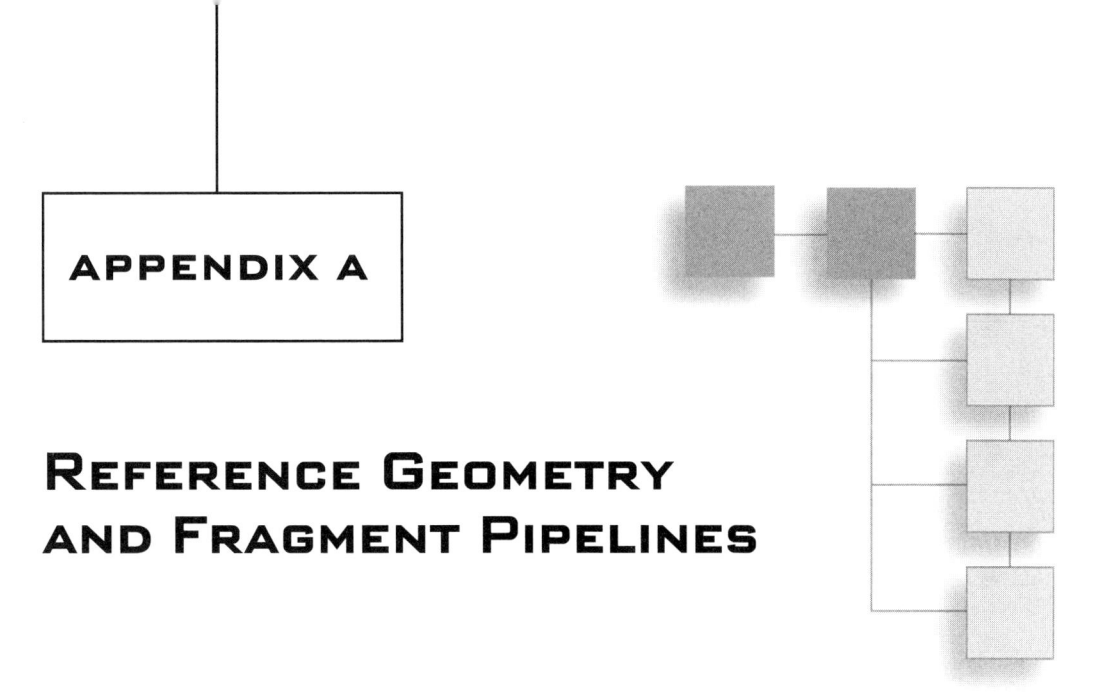

The reference geometry pipeline in Figure A.1 and the fragment pipeline in Figure A.2 show M3G's order of operation. The illustrations are part of M3G's specification and are also included in its javadoc documentation. M3G's specification allows implementations to vary this order but requires them to produce the same result as the reference pipelines would.

In the pipeline model, you enter 3D data at one end in the form of vertex and pixel data and receive the result at the other end in the frame buffer. At different stages of the process, M3G's API allows you to influence the outcome. At these points, the illustrations contain references to M3G's classes and functionality, which you can use to find more detailed explanations in this book.

The process starts with the transformation of vertex positions, texture coordinates, and normals. The vertices are then assembled into triangles, and the colors and normals are used to produce the triangles' color. After further processing that transforms the geometric primitives and prepares them to be displayed on the screen, the final step in the geometry pipeline rasterizes triangles into fragments. Fragments have an associated screen coordinate and are destined to become pixels in the frame buffer.

At this point, the geometry pipeline leads into the fragment pipeline, where textures and fog are applied. Before it is written into the color buffer, a fragment must pass the alpha and the depth test. If it passes, it's blended together with the existing value in the color buffer. The render result can then be displayed on the screen.

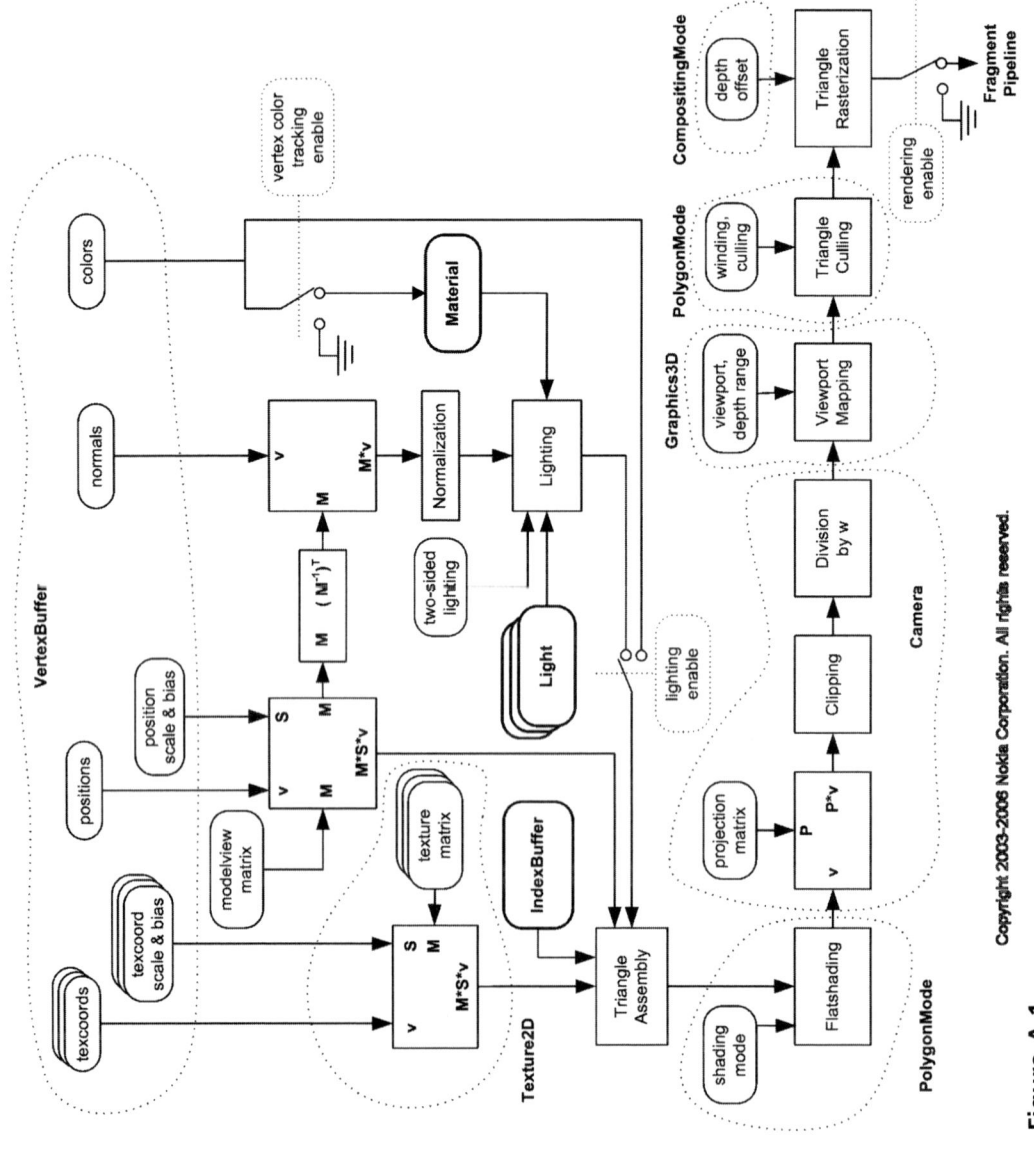

Figure A.1
M3G's geometry pipeline.

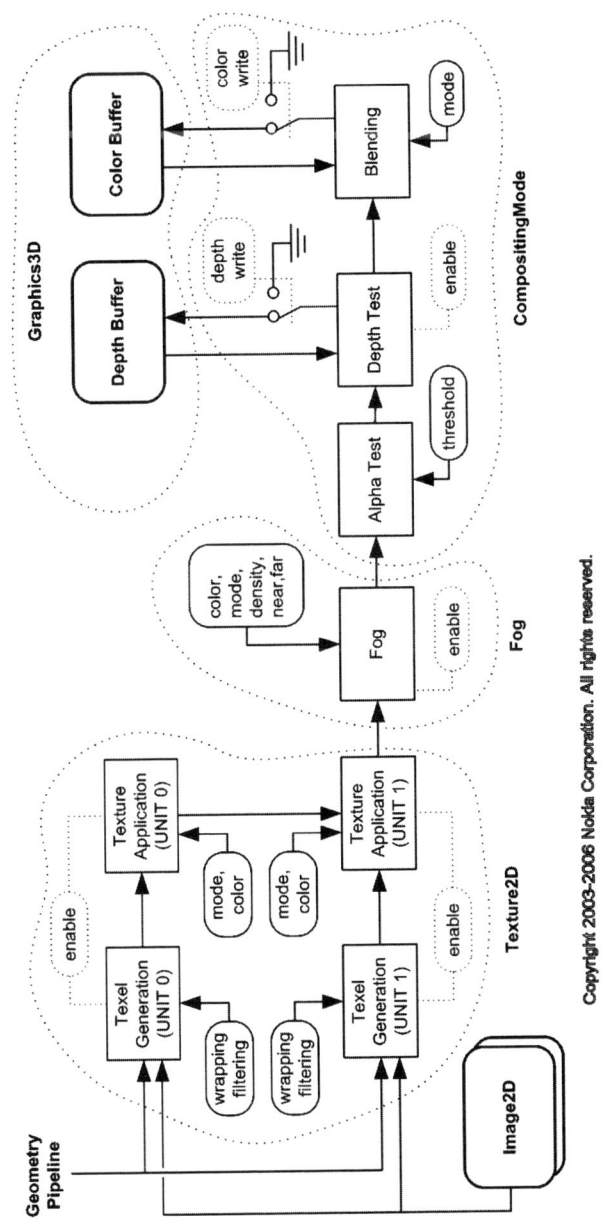

Figure A.2
M3G's fragment pipeline.

APPENDIX B

MascotCapsule V3 API

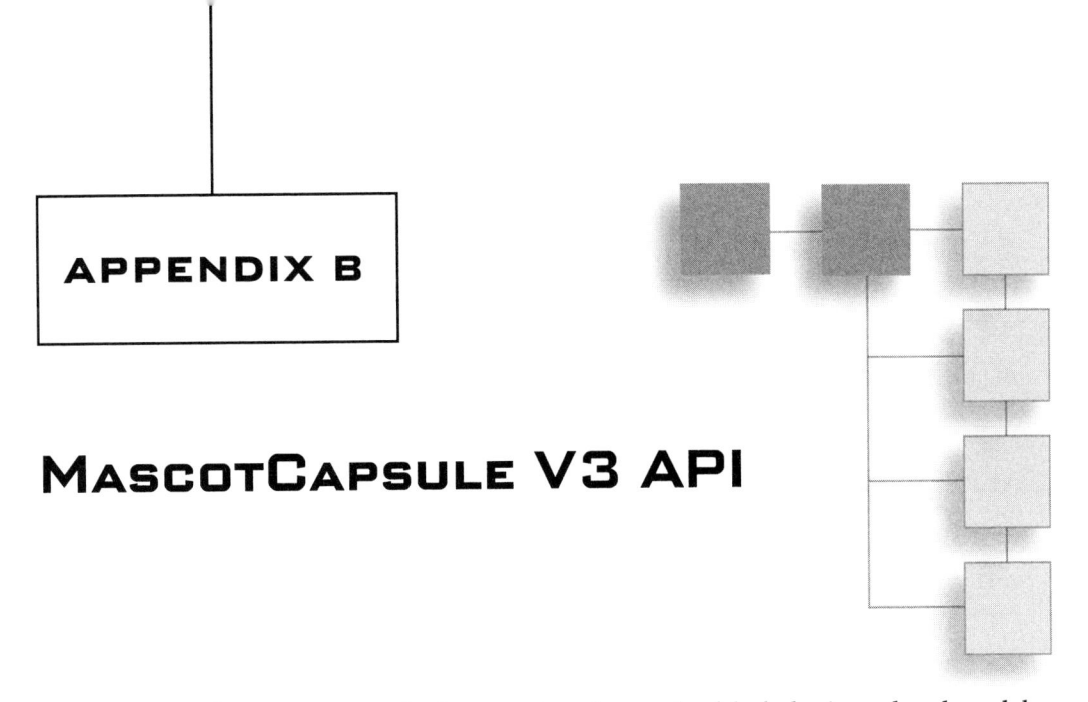

MascotCapsule is a 3D rendering engine for embedded devices developed by Japan-based HI Corporation. It first shipped commercially in 2001.

Among other interfaces, version V4 offers M3G API support and is also backward compatible to HI's own Java interface from V3 of the engine. Compared to M3G 1.1, the MascotCapsule V3 API has fewer features. However, this simplicity is its greatest strength as it leads to improved performance. V3 bridges the gap between low-end and more capable devices.

MascotCapsule V3 Features

MascotCapsule V3 exclusively uses fixed-point numbers in its interface, represented by an `int` value. Rotations, for example, use 12 bits for fractional values; a value of 1.0 corresponds to 4096. The use of fixed-point arithmetic improves performance on devices that don't support floating-point operations in hardware. These devices currently represent the majority of mobile phones.

Another item that sets MascotCapsule apart is the use of a polygon-sorting algorithm to hide obscured objects. Instead of using a depth buffer, MascotCapsule sorts polygons by their z value and draws them back to front. This decreases memory accesses and thus speeds up rendering, but can lead to artifacts where polygons overlap.

Other features of MascotCapsule V3 include:

- Support for point, line, triangle, and quad render primitives.
- Point sprites.
- One light supported with directional and ambient attributes.
- Flat, Gouraud, and toon shading.
- Texture sizes don't have to be power of two (maximum 256 × 256 pixels; 8 bits per pixel).
- Texture animation.
- Sphere mapping.
- Limited support for transparency and blending.

Class Library Overview

The same MascotCapsule version offers different programming interfaces depending on the phone manufacturer and the operator that deploys the engine. You should consult the operator or manufacturer documentation to find out which particular API your phone offers.

This appendix refers to the interface found in `com.mascotcapsule.micro3d.v3`. This API consists of 10 classes, which you can see in Table B.1.

Table B.1 MascotCapsule V3 API

Class	Description
ActionTable	Represents animation data loaded from MTRA files.
AffineTrans	Matrix math operations.
Effect3D	Appearance-related properties such as transparency and shading parameters.
Figure	Encapsulates 3D model data loaded from MBAC files.
FigureLayout	Defines the model/view and projection transformation of 3D models.
Graphics3D	Graphics context for rendering 3D objects.
Light	Encapsulates light properties.
Texture	Encapsulates a texture loaded from a BMP file.
Util3D	Utility class for fixed-point math operations.
Vector3D	Vector math operations.

`AffineTrans`, `Vector3D`, and `Util3D` offer various math routines for matrix, vector, and fixed-point operations.

Appearance properties are stored in `Effect3D`—for example, transparency settings and shading options. Lighting itself is represented by `Light`. You can store geometry transformations in `FigureLayout`, which also stores the projection transformation.

`ActionTable`, `Figure`, and `Texture` read in binary files for animation, model, and texture data, respectively. Rendering occurs on a graphics context represented by `Graphics3D`.

Rendering with MascotCapsule V3

Although MascotCapsule V3 doesn't offer a retained mode, it is very flexible in the way you can render data. Conveniently, MascotCapsule uses the same coordinate systems for rendering as M3G.

Rendering Primitives

The simplest way of rendering uses 3D model data stored in individual arrays for vertex coordinates, normals, texture coordinates, and colors. This works similar to immediate mode rendering in M3G.

You can render up to 255 primitives, such as triangles, in a batch. In addition to the vertex data, you pass appearance and transformation attributes that change the look and position of your 3D objects. The source code at the end of this appendix provides an example of how to render primitives with the `Graphics3D.renderPrimitives()` method.

Command Lists

The drawback of immediate mode rendering is that a method call has to be done for each state change. When using command lists, you pack all data into one array and pass it all together to `Graphics3D.drawCommandList()`. A list can consist of vertex data, but also of appearance and transformation parameters. One batch of render primitives still contains a maximum of 255 elements. However, you can concatenate several batches in one command list.

With the combination of separate command lists, you can mimic a retained mode. Used in this way, command lists work similarly to OpenGL's display lists.

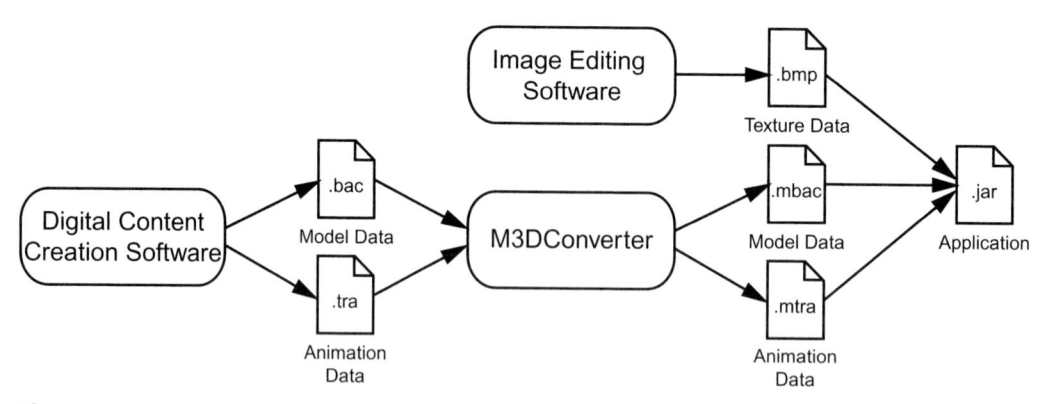

Figure B.1
Tool chain for using 3D models in MascotCapsule's binary data format.

You can, for example, store the data for a cube in a command list and render the cube at different positions in your scene.

Binary Files

MascotCapsule can import model, animation, and texture data from binary files. This works similar to M3G's binary file support and simplifies importing 3D models created by artists. Figure B.1 depicts the tool chain used for this process.

Textures can be authored with any image-editing software that can save 8-bit BMP files. These textures also work in combination with rendering primitives and command lists.

The 3D data is split into model (files ending with .bac) and animation files (files ending with .tra). HI offers exporter plug-ins that can write files in this format for many popular content-creation tools. The files are then converted into MBAC and MTRA files by a tool called M3DConverter. It is these files that you can import into your application and render with the `Graphics3D.renderFigure()` and `drawFigure()` methods. In addition to exporters, HI also provides tools to display and edit 3D data in MascotCapsule's format.

Example Using MascotCapsule V3 API

The following example uses `Graphics3D.renderPrimitives()` to render a rotating, textured cube in combination with lighting. Figure B.2 shows the output.

Figure B.2
Sample demonstrating the usage of MascotCapsule V3 API.

Note

> You can build and test applications for MascotCapsule V3 API with Sony Ericsson's Java emulator, which you can download from http://developer.sonyericsson.com. The installation package also contains the javadoc for the API. The tools provided by HI are located at http://www.mascotcapsule.com.
>
> The build steps are the same as for M3G applications. You can find MascotSample.java together with a working MIDlet on the accompanying CD-ROM.

```
/*
 * Mobile 3D Graphics
 * Learning 3D Graphics with the Java Micro Edition
 */

package m3gab;

import javax.microedition.lcdui.*;
import javax.microedition.lcdui.game.*;
import com.mascotcapsule.micro3d.v3.*;

/**
 * Demonstrates 3D rendering using the MascotCapsule V3 API
 * (com.mascotcapsule.micro3d.v3).
 *
```

```
 * @author Claus Hoefele
 */
public class MascotSample extends GameCanvas implements Runnable {
  /** Flag whether thread is running. */
  private boolean isRunning;

  /** 3D graphics singleton used for rendering. */
  private Graphics3D graphics3d;
  /** 2D graphics singleton used for rendering. */
  private Graphics graphics;

  /** Texture. */
  private Texture texture;
  /** Transformation. */
  private FigureLayout figureLayout;
  /** Appearance settings. */
  private Effect3D effect;

  /** Matrix used for rotation. */
  private AffineTrans rotation;

  /** Vertex positions. */
  private static final int[] VERTEX_POSITIONS = new int[] {
    -128, -128,  128,  128, -128,  128,            // front
     128,  128,  128, -128,  128,  128,
     128, -128, -128, -128, -128, -128,            // back
    -128,  128, -128,  128,  128, -128,
     128, -128,  128,  128, -128, -128,            // right
     128,  128, -128,  128,  128,  128,
    -128, -128, -128, -128, -128,  128,            // left
    -128,  128,  128, -128,  128, -128,
    -128,  128,  128,  128,  128,  128,            // top
     128,  128, -128, -128,  128, -128,
    -128, -128, -128,  128, -128, -128,            // bottom
     128, -128,  128, -128, -128,  128
  };

  /** Normals (unit length 4096). */
  private static final int[] FACE_NORMALS = new int[] {
       0,    0, 4096,                              // front
       0,    0,-4096,                              // back
    4096,    0,    0,                              // right
   -4096,    0,    0,                              // left
```

```
       0,  4096,     0,                      // top
       0, -4096,     0                       // bottom
};

/** Texture coordinates (in pixels). */
private static final int[] VERTEX_TEX_COORDS = new int[] {
  0, 255,  255, 255,  255, 0,  0, 0,    // front
  0, 255,  255, 255,  255, 0,  0, 0,    // back
  0, 255,  255, 255,  255, 0,  0, 0,    // right
  0, 255,  255, 255,  255, 0,  0, 0,    // left
  0, 255,  255, 255,  255, 0,  0, 0,    // top
  0, 255,  255, 255,  255, 0,  0, 0     // bottom
};

/** Colors are not used in this example. However, MascotCapsule
 * still requires a non-null argument when calling
 * renderPrimitives(). */
private static final int[] COLORS = new int[] {};

/**
 * Constructor.
 */
public MascotSample() {
  super(true);
}

/**
 * Initializes the sample.
 */
public void init() {
  // Get the singletons for rendering.
  graphics3d = new Graphics3D();
  graphics = getGraphics();

  try {
    // The texture is an 8-bit BMP image; max 256x256 pixels.
    texture = new Texture("/m3gab/texture.bmp", true);
  } catch (Exception e) {
    e.printStackTrace();
  }

  // Effect3D contains appearance settings such as lighting.
  effect = new Effect3D();
```

```java
        Light light = new Light(
            new Vector3D(0, 0, 4096),       // directional light vector
            4096,                            // directional light intensity
            0);                              // ambient intensity
        effect.setLight(light);

        // FigureLayout is the model/view and projection transformation.
        figureLayout = new FigureLayout();
        figureLayout.setPerspective(
            1,                               // near plane
            32767,                           // far plane
            60*4096/360);                    // field of view
        figureLayout.setCenter(getWidth()/2, getHeight()/2);

        AffineTrans viewTransformation = new AffineTrans();
        viewTransformation.setIdentity();
        viewTransformation.lookAt(
            new Vector3D(0, 256, 512),       // position
            new Vector3D(0, -2048, -4096),   // view direction
            new Vector3D(0, 4096, 0));       // up vector
        figureLayout.setAffineTrans(viewTransformation);

        // Matrix used to rotate the cube.
        rotation = new AffineTrans();
        rotation.setIdentity();
        rotation.rotationY(1*4096/360);

        // Start animation.
        Thread thread = new Thread(this);
        isRunning = true;
        thread.start();
    }

    /**
     * Stops the animation thread.
     */
    public void destroy() {
        isRunning = false;
    }

    /**
     * Animation loop.
     */
```

```
public void run() {
  while(isRunning) {
    figureLayout.getAffineTrans().mul(rotation);
    render(graphics);
    flushGraphics();

    try {
      Thread.sleep(20);              // max 50 fps
    } catch(InterruptedException e) {}
  }
}

/**
 * Renders the sample.
 *
 * @param graphics graphics context for rendering.
 */
private void render(Graphics graphics) {
  // Clear background with 2D commands.
  graphics.setColor(0x000000);       // black
  graphics.fillRect(0, 0, getWidth(), getHeight());

  // Render 3D data.
  graphics3d.bind(graphics);
  graphics3d.renderPrimitives(
      texture,                              // texture
      0, 0,                                 // offset in x/y direction
      figureLayout,                         // transformation
      effect,                               // appearance
      Graphics3D.PRIMITVE_QUADS |           // quad list
      Graphics3D.PDATA_NORMAL_PER_FACE |    // one normal per face
      Graphics3D.PDATA_TEXURE_COORD |       // texture coordinates
      Graphics3D.PATTR_LIGHTING,            // enable lighting
      6,                                    // number of primitives
      VERTEX_POSITIONS,                     // vertex positions
      FACE_NORMALS,                         // face normals
      VERTEX_TEX_COORDS,                    // texture coordinates
      COLORS);                              // colors
  graphics3d.flush();
  graphics3d.release(graphics);
 }
}
```

APPENDIX C

JAVA BINDING FOR THE OPENGL ES API

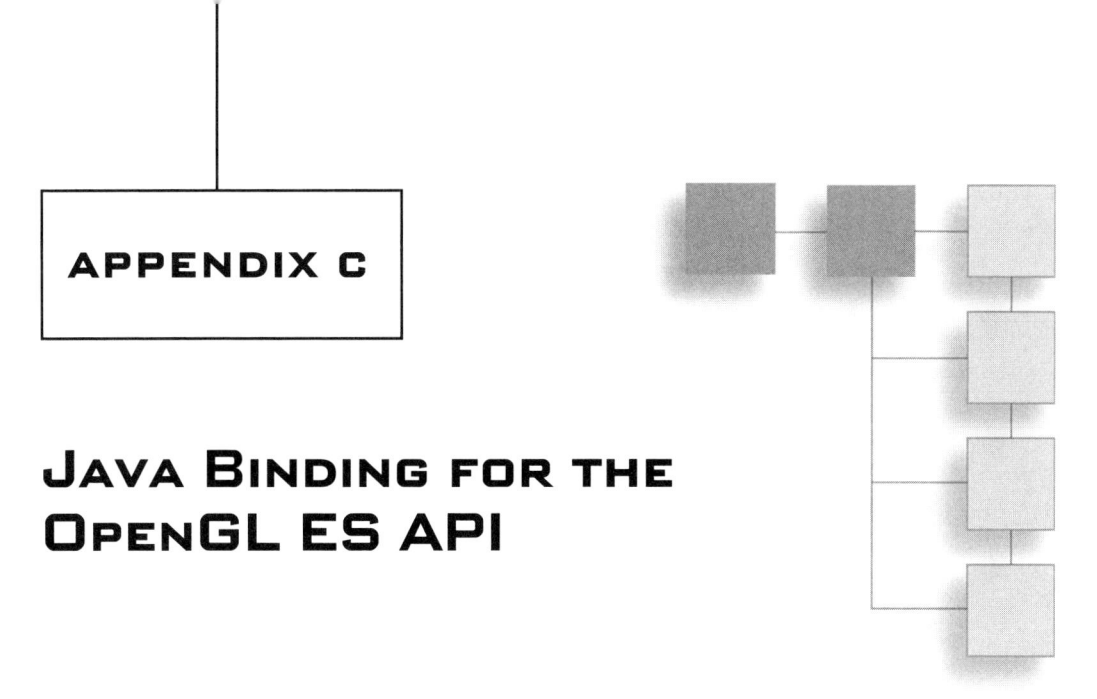

OpenGL ES is a subset of the widely known OpenGL 3D graphics API for embedded systems, such as video game consoles and mobile phones. It's defined as a royalty-free and cross-platform API by the industry consortium Khronos, which comprises most major hardware and software vendors in the 3D graphics area. The Java Binding for the OpenGL ES API in JSR 239 defines a Java API that resembles OpenGL ES's C interface, making it easy to port existing OpenGL content.

Compared to M3G, OpenGL ES lacks high-level features such as a scene graph API, but on the other hand includes more low-level features such as compressed textures or anti-aliasing. Although the particular version supported by an implementation depends on the device, JSR 239 provides bindings for OpenGL ES 1.0, 1.1, and 1.1 Extension Pack, including all additions and extensions. It also specifies access to the OpenGL ES Native Platform Graphics Interface, so-called EGL, in version 1.0 and 1.1.

The OpenGL ES Native Platform Graphics Interface (EGL)

The OpenGL ES API provides graphics operations exclusively. Applications, however, also need platform-specific functionality—to define the target of the render output or synchronize OpenGL ES with native drawing operations, for example. EGL complements OpenGL ES by providing a standard way to access the underlying native window system.

Note

You can download the EGL specifications from http://www.khronos.org/egl/.

Most important, EGL provides you with a drawing surface that you can use for rendering. EGL defines three types of surfaces: *windows* for onscreen rendering, *pbuffers* for off-screen rendering, and *pixmaps* for off-screen rendering, where the result is accessible to the native platform.

When writing an application for MIDP, window surfaces map to `javax.microedition.lcdui.Canvas` or `javax.microedition.lcdui.game.GameCanvas` instances, and pixmap surfaces map to mutable `javax.microedition.lcdui.Image`s. To synchronize access to these surfaces, you must enclose OpenGL ES operations in between calls to `eglWaitNative()` and `eglWaitGL()`. The former completes MIDP drawing commands, whereas the latter finishes OpenGL ES rendering. In contrast to window and pixmap surfaces, pbuffer surfaces are not accessible by MIDP. Only EGL-based APIs can access pbuffers, which might be faster for this reason.

EGL operations exist in interfaces defined in the `javax.microedition.khronos.egl` package, which Table C.1. shows. The package also defines additional classes that encapsulate EGL data and functionality. `EGLContext.getGL()`, for example, returns an object to access OpenGL ES operations.

Table C.1 javax.microedition.khronos.egl

Class/Interface	Description
EGL	Parent interface for EGL bindings.
EGL10	Bindings for EGL 1.0.
EGL11	Bindings for EGL 1.1.
EGLConfig	Encapsulates a frame buffer configuration.
EGLContext	Context that provides access to EGL and GL interfaces.
EGLDisplay	Encapsulates a display.
EGLSurface	Encapsulates a rendering surface.

Using OpenGL ES in Java

As a result of the EGL operations, you have a window surface for rendering and an object that implements an interface derived from `javax.microedition.khronos.opengles.GL` for OpenGL ES functionality. JSR 239 requires you to use this object only from within the thread that also bound the EGL context to a render surface. Depending on the OpenGL ES version your device supports, you can cast this object into an interface that's listed in Table C.2.

Note

You can access the OpenGL ES specifications from http://www.khronos.org/opengles/.

Naming Conventions

To ease the transition, JSR 239 preserves the exact naming of the OpenGL functions. This includes the OpenGL convention to indicate the type of function parameters with a suffix. For example, you'll find `glRotatex()` in `GL10`. The x at the end of the function indicates a fixed-point parameter; `glRotatef()` is the respective floating point version.

The distinction between fixed-point and floating-point functionality is important for devices that lack hardware floating-point support. On these devices, using fixed-point functionality will improve performance. To support a variety of devices, OpenGL ES 1.x defines two profiles: the Common-Lite profile, which supports 32-bit fixed-point numbers with 16 bits for fractional values, and the Common profile, which includes the Common-Lite profile with the addition of single precision floating-point support. JSR 239 provides one common binding for both profiles.

Table C.2 javax.microedition.khronos.opengles

Interface	Description
GL	Parent interface for OpenGL ES bindings.
GL10	Bindings for OpenGL 1.0, including core additions and required profile extensions.
GL10Ext	Bindings for OpenGL ES 1.0's optional profile extensions.
GL11	Bindings for OpenGL 1.1, including core additions and required profile extensions.
GL11Ext	Bindings for OpenGL ES 1.1's optional profile extensions.
GL11ExtensionPack	Bindings for OpenGL ES 1.1 Extension Pack.

Passing Data

As function parameters, JSR 239 uses Java's native types where appropriate. For example, Java's int replaces OpenGL's fixed-point type GLfixed and float replaces GLfloat. Pointer arguments in OpenGL require a more sophisticated mapping. JSR 239 substitutes pointer arguments with arrays of the respective native type and Buffer objects.

A Buffer wraps a sequence of primitive types and contains additional information about the contents such as the current position that will be used for the next read or write operation. Buffers were introduced in Java 1.4 as part of the New I/O (NIO) APIs to speed up input/output operations. JSR 239 includes a subset of this API that you can see in Table C.3. As a side effect, these classes also need Comparable from the java.lang package that's shown in Table C.4. This package includes UnsupportedOperationException, which is thrown if you call the method of an unsupported OpenGL ES extension.

Buffers exist for byte, float, int, and short types; an IntBuffer, for example, holds int values. A ByteBuffer distinguishes itself from the others in being able

Table C.3 java.nio

Class	Description
Buffer	Parent interface for buffers.
ByteBuffer	Buffer backed up by a byte array. Contains additional features to allocate the Buffer as a direct buffer and read/write any type of primitive data.
FloatBuffer	Buffer backed up by a float array.
IntBuffer	Buffer backed up by an int array.
ShortBuffer	Buffer backed up by a short array.
BufferOverflowException	Thrown if a put operation fails to write more data.
BufferUnderflowException	Thrown if a get operation fails to read more data.

Table C.4 java.lang

Class/Interface	Description
Comparable	Implemented by the Buffer derived classes to compare a buffer to another.
UnsupportedOperationException	Thrown by methods of an OpenGL ES optional profile extension that's not supported by the device.

to read and write any of the supported primitive types along with `byte` values. In addition, you can allocate a `ByteBuffer` as a *direct* buffer. The Java virtual machine will make a best effort to accelerate direct buffer operations by allocating its memory on the native heap and executing I/O operations directly on it. You can convert a `ByteBuffer` into another type such as an `IntBuffer`, which allows these buffers to be direct as well.

The API specification will guide you whether a method takes an array of a native type, a direct `Buffer`, or a non-direct `Buffer`. `glVertexPointer()` is an example of a method that requires a direct buffer. You'll need to use this function to render primitives.

Rendering

OpenGL ES did away with the begin/end paradigm and display lists that you might know from OpenGL. Instead, you have to use `glVertexPointer()` to define a vertex array with vertex coordinates—similar to what you do in M3G with a `VertexArray`. For normals, texture coordinates, and colors, you can choose between using vertex arrays and setting individual current values.

Rendering occurs with `glDrawArrays()` and `glDrawElements()` that produce different kinds of point, line, and triangle primitives. The former function uses vertices in the same order as they were specified in the vertex array. The latter allows you to define a list of indices to construct a sequence in any order. (These two functions correspond to implicit and explicit indices in M3G's `TriangleStripArray`.)

OpenGL ES 1.0 Example

The example in this appendix uses OpenGL ES 1.0 features to render a rotating, textured cube in combination with lighting. The code uses fixed-point operations and renders the output to a window surface that's bound to the graphics context of a `GameCanvas`. Figure C.1 shows a screenshot of the result.

Note that OpenGL ES defines the origin of the texture coordinate system at the lower-left corner and the *y* axis extends up, whereas MIDP images use the upper-left corner and the *y* axis extends down. The example compensates for this difference by adjusting the *y* axis when it loads the texture image.

Figure C.1
Sample demonstrating the use of JSR 239.

Note

> The CD-ROM contains OpenGLSample.java together with a working MIDlet. To build and run the sample, you can use Sun's Java Wireless Toolkit 2.5 Beta 2 or later, which includes support for JSR 239. The build steps are the same as for M3G applications. You can download the API specification from http://jcp.org/en/jsr/detail?id=239.

```
/*
 * Mobile 3D Graphics
 * Learning 3D Graphics with the Java Micro Edition
 */

package m3gac;

import java.nio.*;
import javax.microedition.khronos.egl.*;
import javax.microedition.khronos.opengles.*;
import javax.microedition.lcdui.*;
import javax.microedition.lcdui.game.*;

/**
 * Demonstrates 3D rendering using the Java Binding for the OpenGL ES
 * API (JSR 239). This sample uses OpenGL ES 1.0 features with fixed-
 * point variants of functions. To run this sample, the device must
```

```
 * support a texture size of 256x256 pixels.
 *
 * @author Claus Hoefele
 */
public class OpenGLSample extends GameCanvas implements Runnable {
  /** Vertex positions. */
  private static final byte[] VERTEX_POSITIONS = {
    -1, -1,  1,  1, -1,  1, -1,  1,  1,  1,  1,  1,   // front
     1, -1, -1, -1, -1, -1,  1,  1, -1, -1,  1, -1,   // back
     1, -1,  1,  1, -1, -1,  1,  1,  1,  1,  1, -1,   // right
    -1, -1, -1, -1, -1,  1, -1,  1, -1, -1,  1,  1,   // left
    -1,  1,  1,  1,  1,  1, -1,  1, -1,  1,  1, -1,   // top
    -1, -1, -1,  1, -1, -1, -1, -1,  1,  1, -1,  1    // bottom
  };

  /** Vertex texture coordinates (origin at the lower left corner). */
  private static final byte[] VERTEX_TEX_COORDS = {
    0, 0, 1, 0, 0, 1, 1, 1,                           // front
    0, 0, 1, 0, 0, 1, 1, 1,                           // back
    0, 0, 1, 0, 0, 1, 1, 1,                           // right
    0, 0, 1, 0, 0, 1, 1, 1,                           // left
    0, 0, 1, 0, 0, 1, 1, 1,                           // top
    0, 0, 1, 0, 0, 1, 1, 1,                           // bottom
  };

  /** Face normals. */
  private static final byte[] FACE_NORMALS = {
     0,  0,  1,                                       // front
     0,  0, -1,                                       // back
     1,  0,  0,                                       // right
    -1,  0,  0,                                       // left
     0,  1,  0,                                       // top
     0, -1,  0                                        // bottom
  };

  /** Triangle strip information.*/
  private static final byte[] STRIPS = {4, 4, 4, 4, 4, 4};

  /** The cube's current rotation angle. */
  private int angle;

  /** Flag whether thread is running. */
  private boolean isRunning;
```

```java
/** 2D graphics context for rendering. */
private Graphics graphics;
/** Object for executing EGL operations. */
private EGL10 egl;
/** Object for executing OpenGL operations. */
private GL10 gl;
/** EGL Display used for rendering. */
private EGLDisplay eglDisplay;
/** EGL context used for rendering. */
private EGLContext eglContext;
/** EGL surface used for rendering. */
private EGLSurface eglWindowSurface;

/**
 * Constructor.
 */
public OpenGLSample() {
  super(true);
}

/**
 * Starts the animation.
 */
public void init() {
  Thread thread = new Thread(this);
  isRunning = true;
  thread.start();
}

/**
 * Stops the animation.
 */
public void destroy() {
  isRunning = false;
}

/**
 * Animation loop.
 */
public void run() {
  // Initialize context data. All calls to the GL context must
  // execute in the thread that bound the EGL context.
  initGL();
```

```
    initCube();
    initLight();
    initTexture("/m3gac/texture.png");
    initCamera(60, (float) getWidth() / (float) getHeight(), 1, 100);

    // Animation loop.
    while(isRunning) {
      angle += toX(1);
      render(graphics);
      flushGraphics();

      try {
        Thread.sleep(20);                    // max 50 fps
      } catch(InterruptedException e) {}
    }

    // Destroy context data.
    if (egl != null && eglDisplay != null) {
      egl.eglMakeCurrent(eglDisplay, EGL10.EGL_NO_SURFACE,
          EGL10.EGL_NO_SURFACE, EGL10.EGL_NO_CONTEXT);
      if (eglContext != null) {
        egl.eglDestroyContext(eglDisplay, eglContext);
      }
      if (eglWindowSurface != null) {
        egl.eglDestroySurface(eglDisplay, eglWindowSurface);
      }
      egl.eglTerminate(eglDisplay);
    }
  }

  /**
   * Initializes the EGL, GL, and Graphics contexts.
   */
  private void initGL() {
    // Initialize EGL.
    egl = (EGL10) EGLContext.getEGL();
    eglDisplay = egl.eglGetDisplay(EGL10.EGL_DEFAULT_DISPLAY);
    egl.eglInitialize(eglDisplay, null);

    // Locate a configuration with eight bits per color channel. The
    // default value for EGL_SURFACE_TYPE is EGL_WINDOW_BIT.
    int[] configAttributes = {
      EGL10.EGL_RED_SIZE, 8,
```

```
            EGL10.EGL_GREEN_SIZE, 8,
            EGL10.EGL_BLUE_SIZE, 8,
            EGL10.EGL_DEPTH_SIZE, EGL10.EGL_DONT_CARE,
            EGL10.EGL_NONE
        };
        int[] numConfigs = new int[1];
        egl.eglGetConfigs(eglDisplay, null, 0, numConfigs);
        EGLConfig[] eglConfigs = new EGLConfig[numConfigs[0]];
        egl.eglChooseConfig(eglDisplay, configAttributes, eglConfigs,
            eglConfigs.length, numConfigs);
        eglContext = egl.eglCreateContext(eglDisplay, eglConfigs[0],
            EGL10.EGL_NO_CONTEXT, null);

        // Create a window surface that's bound to the graphics context of
        // this GameCanvas.
        graphics = getGraphics();
        eglWindowSurface = egl.eglCreateWindowSurface(eglDisplay,
            eglConfigs[0], graphics, null);
        egl.eglMakeCurrent(eglDisplay, eglWindowSurface,
            eglWindowSurface, eglContext);
        gl = (GL10) eglContext.getGL();
    }

    /**
     * Initializes the cube's vertex data. The vertex arrays created in
     * this method are later used for rendering.
     */
    private void initCube() {
        gl.glEnableClientState(GL10.GL_VERTEX_ARRAY);
        ByteBuffer vertexPositions
            = ByteBuffer.allocateDirect(VERTEX_POSITIONS.length);
        vertexPositions.put(VERTEX_POSITIONS).rewind();
        gl.glVertexPointer(3, GL10.GL_BYTE, 0, vertexPositions);

        gl.glEnableClientState(GL10.GL_TEXTURE_COORD_ARRAY);
        ByteBuffer vertexTexCoords
            = ByteBuffer.allocateDirect(VERTEX_TEX_COORDS.length);
        vertexTexCoords.put(VERTEX_TEX_COORDS).rewind();
        gl.glTexCoordPointer(2, GL10.GL_BYTE, 0, vertexTexCoords);

        gl.glEnable(GL10.GL_CULL_FACE);
        gl.glCullFace(GL10.GL_BACK);
    }
```

```java
/**
 * Creates a directional light.
 */
private void initLight() {
  // By default, LIGHT0 is initialized as a directional light
  // and points toward the negative z axis.
  gl.glMatrixMode(GL10.GL_MODELVIEW);
  gl.glLoadIdentity();
  int[] diffuse =new int[]{toX(0.9f), toX(0.9f), toX(0.9f), toX(1)};
  gl.glLightxv(GL10.GL_LIGHT0, GL10.GL_DIFFUSE, diffuse, 0);

  gl.glEnable(GL10.GL_LIGHTING);
  gl.glEnable(GL10.GL_LIGHT0);
  gl.glEnable(GL10.GL_COLOR_MATERIAL);
}

/**
 * Loads an image from the given resource and uses it as texture.
 * This method automatically adjusts the y axis so that the image's
 * coordinate system has its origin at the lower left corner. The
 * image's transparency channel is ignored.
 *
 * @param resource named resource.
 */
private void initTexture(String resource) {
  try {
    // Load the image and convert it into Buffer object.
    Image image = Image.createImage(resource);
    int width = image.getWidth();
    int height = image.getHeight();
    int[] pixels = new int[width];         // one row of data
    ByteBuffer buffer = ByteBuffer.allocateDirect(width*height*3);
    for (int i=(height-1); i>=0; i-) {    // change y coordinate
      image.getRGB(pixels, 0, width, 0, i, width, 1);
      for (int j=0; j<width; j++) {
        buffer.put((byte) ((pixels[j]>>16) & 0xFF));
        buffer.put((byte) ((pixels[j]>> 8) & 0xFF));
        buffer.put((byte) ((pixels[j]>> 0) & 0xFF));
      }
    }
    buffer.rewind();
```

```java
        // Use the image as texture.
        gl.glEnable(GL10.GL_TEXTURE_2D);
        gl.glDisable(GL10.GL_DITHER);
        gl.glHint(GL10.GL_PERSPECTIVE_CORRECTION_HINT, GL10.GL_NICEST);
        int[] textures = new int[1];
        gl.glGenTextures(1, textures, 0);
        gl.glBindTexture(GL10.GL_TEXTURE_2D, textures[0]);
        gl.glTexImage2D(GL10.GL_TEXTURE_2D, 0, GL10.GL_RGB,
            width, height, 0, GL10.GL_RGB, GL10.GL_UNSIGNED_BYTE, buffer);
        gl.glTexParameterx(GL10.GL_TEXTURE_2D,
            GL10.GL_TEXTURE_MIN_FILTER, GL10.GL_LINEAR);
        gl.glTexParameterx(GL10.GL_TEXTURE_2D,
            GL10.GL_TEXTURE_MAG_FILTER, GL10.GL_LINEAR);
      } catch (Exception e) {
        System.out.println("Error creating texture.");
        e.printStackTrace();
      }
    }

    /**
     * Initializes the camera with a perspective projection matrix.
     *
     * @param fovy field of view in the vertical direction, in degrees.
     * @param aspectRatio the viewport's width divided by its height.
     * @param near distance to the front clipping plane.
     * @param far distance to the back clipping plane.
     */
    private void initCamera(float fovy, float aspectRatio,
        float near, float far) {
      gl.glViewport(0, 0, getWidth(), getHeight());
      gl.glMatrixMode(GL10.GL_MODELVIEW);
      gl.glLoadIdentity();
      gl.glRotatex(toX(25), toX(1), 0, 0);
      gl.glTranslatex(0, toX(-2), toX(-4));

      float top = near * (float) Math.tan(fovy*Math.PI/360.0);
      float bottom = -top;
      float left = bottom * aspectRatio;
      float right = top * aspectRatio;
      gl.glMatrixMode(GL10.GL_PROJECTION);
      gl.glLoadIdentity();
      gl.glFrustumx(toX(left), toX(right), toX(bottom), toX(top),
          toX(near), toX(far));
```

}

/**
 * Renders the sample.
 *
 * @param graphics graphics context for drawing.
 */
private void render(Graphics graphics) {
  // Wait until MIDP graphics commands are dispatched and start
  // OpenGL ES drawing.
  egl.eglWaitNative(EGL10.EGL_CORE_NATIVE_ENGINE, graphics);

  // Clear with default background color (black).
  gl.glClear(GL10.GL_COLOR_BUFFER_BIT | GL10.GL_DEPTH_BUFFER_BIT);

  // Transform cube.
  gl.glMatrixMode(GL10.GL_MODELVIEW);
  gl.glPushMatrix();
  gl.glRotatex(angle, 0, toX(1), 0);

  // The cube consists of six triangle strips—one for each face.
  // Normals exist per face while positions and texture coordinates
  // use vertex arrays and exist per vertex.
  int position = 0;
  for (int i=0; i<STRIPS.length; i++) {
    gl.glNormal3x(toX(FACE_NORMALS[i*3+0]),
        toX(FACE_NORMALS[i*3+1]), toX(FACE_NORMALS[i*3+2]));
    gl.glDrawArrays(GL10.GL_TRIANGLE_STRIP, position, STRIPS[i]);
    position += STRIPS[i];
  }
  gl.glPopMatrix();

  // Flush OpenGL ES commands and return to MIDP drawing.
  egl.eglWaitGL();
}

/**
 * Converts an int to a fixed-point value (GLfixed).
 *
 * @param value conversion value.
 * @return result.
 */
private static int toX(int value) {
```
```

```java
      return value<<16;
   }

   /**
    * Converts a float to a fixed-point value (GLfixed).
    *
    * @param value conversion value.
    * @return result.
    */
   private static int toX(float value) {
      return (int) (value*(1<<16));
   }
}
```

APPENDIX D

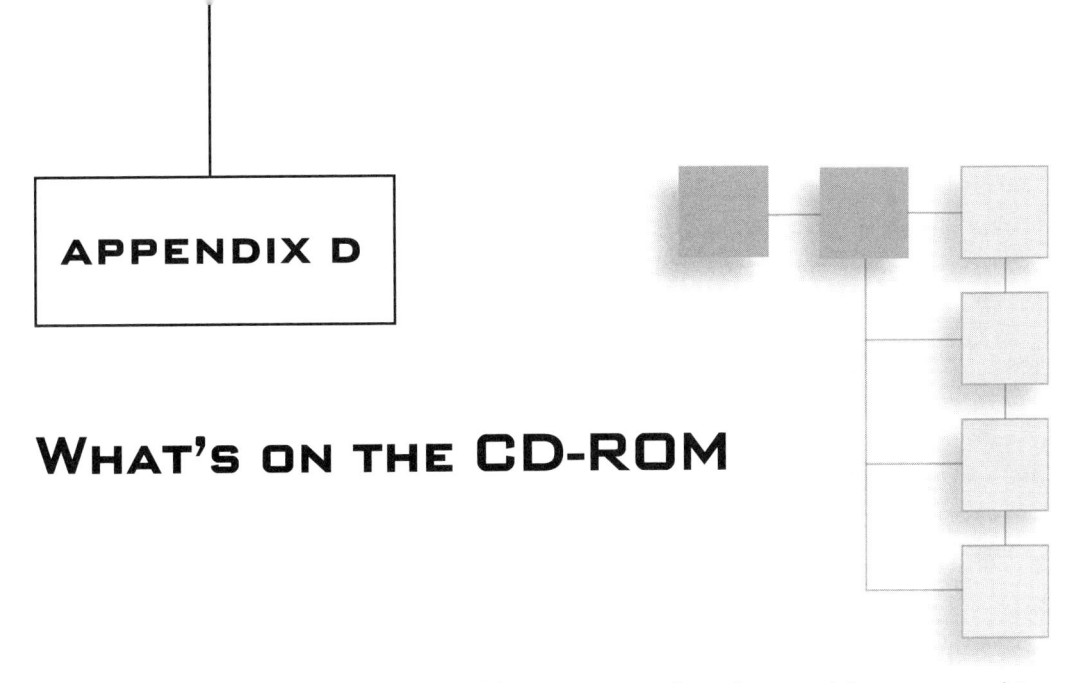

WHAT'S ON THE CD-ROM

The CD-ROM contains the book's source code, along with any graphics resources and data files you need to build and run the examples in this book. You'll also find software and links to Web sites that I find useful when developing my own 3D graphics applications.

Note

For up-to-date information regarding this book, please visit the publisher's Web site (http://www.course.com) and the author's homepage (http://www.claushoefele.com).

Examples

The source code and other data files used in the book are located in the examples folder on the CD-ROM.

Directory Layout

Each chapter and appendix in the book with source code has its own directory named chapter<number> or appendix<letter>. In each folder, you'll find the following directories:

- **src:** Java source files. All Java classes use a chapter-specific package.
- **res:** If an example uses resource files such as images, they are located here.
- **artwork**: If applicable, the original artwork to create the resources.
- **dist:** Prebuilt binary of the application (JAD/JAR file).
- **javadoc:** The Javadoc formatted documentation.

The chapters come with a MIDlet, implemented in a class called `Main`, which provides an application to execute the examples. If the chapter has several examples, this MIDlet will present you with a list from which you can choose which sample to run.

Each example is implemented in a separate class whose name ends with "Sample" and demonstrates a specific feature of the M3G API. The MIDlet requires each sample to implement the interface `Sample`, which defines the methods `init()` and `destroy()`. The MIDlet calls the former method before the class is displayed and the latter before it's destroyed.

You'll find pre-compiled binaries of the applications (JAD/JAR files) in the dist folder. The folder examples\all\dist contains a binary that includes all the examples from the book in one application. As a minimum environment, the M3G examples require CLDC 1.1, MIDP 2.0, and M3G 1.0. The examples are also compatible with M3G 1.1.

For further information on how to build and run CLDC/MIDP applications, see Chapter 2 and the readme.txt file in the examples folder on the CD-ROM.

List of Examples

The following table lists the examples by chapter:

Chapter 2: Hello, World!	
m3g02.HelloWorldSample	Animates a three-dimensional Hello, World! text that's stored in a binary file.
Chapter 3: Before You Start	
m3g03.midp1.Main	Test application to find out whether a phone supports M3G.
m3g03.midp2.CanvasKeyEvents	Displays key events received from `Canvas.keyPressed()`.
m3g03.midp2.GameCanvasKeyStates	Displays key states read from `GameCanvas.getKeyStates()`.
m3g03.midp2.M3gProperties	Displays M3G properties obtained from `Graphics3D.getProperties()`.
m3g03.midp2.MidpProperties	Displays MIDP properties.
Chapter 4: Rendering Geometric Objects	
m3g04.ColoredGeometrySample	Sample displaying a cube with per-vertex colors.
m3g04.GeometricShapesSample	Sample displaying different meshes. Also see mesh classes in the m3g04.mesh package.
Chapter 5: Transformations	
m3g05.DepthBufferSample	Sample demonstrating depth buffer and projection.

`m3g05.ModelTransformationsSample`	Sample displaying a cube that can be transformed interactively.
`m3g05.ProjectionSample`	Sample demonstrating parallel and perspective projection.
`m3g05.ViewTransformationsSample`	Demonstrates switching between portrait and landscape rendering by changing the camera transformation.
`m3g05.WireframeSample`	Demonstrates manual transformation of vertices by displaying wireframe objects. Also see `m3g05.WireframeEngine`.

Chapter 6: Textures

`m3g06.EnvironmentMappingSample`	Demonstrates environment mapping. Also see `m3g06.EnvironmentMap`.
`m3g06.Image2DTypesSample`	Loads PNG images with different color types and transparency combinations by using `Loader.load()` and displays the resulting `Image2D` pixel format.
`m3g06.TexturingSample`	Displays different shapes with textures and allows changing texture parameters interactively.

Chapter 7: Blending and Transparency

`m3g07.CompositingSample`	Demonstrates compositing with different blending modes.
`m3g07.EmbossingSample`	Demonstrates embossing. See also `m3g07.EmbossEffect`.
`m3g07.FogSample`	Sample demonstrating fog.

Chapter 8: Lighting

`m3g08.EmulatingLightSample`	Shows alternatives to real lighting.
`m3g08.LightingSample`	A sphere lit with different light sources.
`m3g08.MaterialsSample`	Demonstrates how different materials change the look of a mesh.

Chapter 9: Scene Graphs

`m3g09.BillboardSample`	This sample displays a field of flowers to demonstrate two alternative billboard techniques.
`m3g09.PickingSample`	Picks meshes in viewport coordinates.
`m3g09.SceneGraphSample`	Uses a scene graph tree to structure a hierarchy of 3D objects.

Chapter 10: M3G's File Format

`m3g10.M3gFileSample`	Loads 3D models from M3G files that were created with Blender.
`m3g10.UserDataSample`	Memory game that uses information serialized in a model's user data. Also see `UserData`, `Card`, and `CardDeck` in the `m3g10` package as well as `m3g_export_06_userdata.py`.

Chapter 11: Keyframe Animations

`m3g11.AnimationSample`	Simple animation with different interpolation modes.
`m3g11.TextureAnimationSample`	Displays a scene with UV animations. See also `m3g11.UvAnimation`.

Chapter 12: Dynamic Meshes

m3g12.MorphingSample	Defines an animation that blends mesh shapes into each other by using morphing.
m3g12.RobotSample	Displays a walking robot that can be controlled with the game keys.
m3g12.SkinnedMeshSample	SkinnedMesh animation that bends a skeleton with an adjustable number of bones. See also m3g12.Quaternion.

Appendix B: MascotCapsule V3 API

m3gab.MascotSample	Demonstrates 3D rendering using the MascotCapsule V3 API.

Appendix C: Java Binding for the OpenGL ES API

m3gac.OpenGLSample	Demonstrates 3D rendering using the Java Binding for the OpenGL ES API (JSR 239).

Tools

On the CD-ROM, you'll find software to help you with application development in the tools folder. Please review relevant licensing information for each application by their respective creators.

Links

The CD-ROM also contains links to additional resources that might help you in developing mobile 3D applications. Please have a look at the provided application that runs automatically when you insert the CD (Windows) as well as the readme.txt file in the top-level folder of the CD-ROM.

INDEX

2D coordinate systems, 48–49
3D coordinate systems
    manual transformation, 141
    overview, 48

ActionTable class, 406–407
active interval methods, AnimationController class, 340
active state, MIDlets, 14
addAnimationTrack() method, 334
addCommand() method, 21
addLight() method, 226, 252
addTransform() method, 373
affine transformation, 98
AffineTrans class, 406–407
align() method, 271, 277
alignment
    Node class methods, 260
    node (scene graphs), 270–271
alpha texture format, blending modes, 197
ambient light, 227
ambient reflection, 238
animate() method, 336–337
animation methods, Object3D class, 262
animation targets, keyframe animations, 330–334
AnimationController class, 340
animations. *See also* keyframe animations
    frame rate, 23
    Hello, World! example, 22–23
    morphing, 362–366
    skeleton, skinned meshes, 376–382
    UV
        conveyor belt animations, 344–348
        flip-book animations, 348–350
        TextureAnimationSample, 350–354
AnimationTrack class, 330
API Selection dialog box, 28
appearance attributes, Appearance class, 60

Appearance class, 60
application development tools, CD-ROM contents, 432
application management software, 7
architecture, M3G, 7
art asset compression, M3G future features, 11
attachAnimation() method, 378
attachSkin() method, 372
attenuation methods, Light class, 222
axis-aligned billboards, 273–279
axis-angle format, transformations, 102–104

Background class, 69
background objects
    color, 68
    geometric objects, rendering, 68–71
Bézier surfaces
    Bézier curves, 81–82
    forward differencing, 82–85
    rendering, 85–88
    Utah Teapot example, 88–93
billboards
    axis-aligned, 273–279
    screen-aligned, 271–272
binary files, 408
bindTarget() method, 72, 74, 134, 137, 139
Blender tool
    coordinate system, 295–297
    discussed, 281
    export options, 297–299
    file contents
        external references, 310
        file identifier, 308
        header object, 308, 310
        scene objects, 310–311
    general options, 282
    header bar, 283
    light and material sources, 288
    mesh creation, 286–287

433

434   Index

Blender tool (*continued*)
  mesh editing options, 283
  mesh management options, 283
  nodes, finding, 294
  Poly Reducer feature, 303–304
  render preview, adjusting, 299–300
  scene export options, 289–290
  scene navigation options, 283, 285–286
  scripts, 311–314
  texturing in, 288–289
  user IDs, 286–287
  user interface, 283–285
  User Preferences window, 284
  vertices, producing minimum
    number of, 300–302
  views, 285
  windows options, 282
  workspace, 283–285
blending
  blending functions, Texture2D class, 165
  blending modes, 190–195
  compositing, 187
  CompositingMode class
    blending modes, 189
  embossing
    image creation, 206–207
    textures, 207–211
  fog
    blending modes, 202–205
    creation, 198–202
    density, 202
    exponential, 201
    linear, 201
    parameters, 200–201
  fragment tests and, 188, 190
  multi-texturing, 195–196
  texture, 196–198
  transparency values, 191
Bluetooth support (JSR 82), 7
bone-joint connections, skinned meshes, 373–376
Boolean data type, 306
**Boolean type, implementation-specific
  properties, 38**
build process
  CLDC tool chain, 24
  MIDlet suite creation, 25–26
Byte data type, 306

Camera class
  geometry pipeline, 402
  methods associated with, 129
**camera coordinates, view transformations,
  122–123**
camera methods, Graphics3D class, 64
Canvas class, 17, 19
canvas properties, 40

CDC (Connected Device Configuration), 5
CD-ROM contents
  application development tools, 432
  chapter examples, 430–432
  directory layout, 429–430
  links and resources, 432
  source code example, 429
changeState() method, 396
chapter examples, CD-ROM contents, 430–432
checkHit() method, 268
checkKeys() method, 337–338
chunks, 155
circles, parametric equation, 78
class file verification, 24
classes
  ActionTable, 406–407
  AffineTrans, 406–407
  AnimationController, 340
  AnimationTrack, 330
  Appearance, 60
  Background, 69
  Camera
    geometry pipeline, 402
    methods associated with, 129
  Canvas, 17, 19
  CompositingMode
    fragment pipeline, 403
    geometry pipeline, 402
    methods associated with, 189
  Effect3D, 406–407
  Figure, 406–407
  FigureLayout, 406–407
  Fog
    fragment pipeline, 403
    methods associated with, 201
  GameCanvas, 17
  Graphics3D
    discussed, 63
    fragment pipeline, 403
    geometry pipeline, 402
    MascotCapsule V3 API, 406–407
    methods associated with, 64–65
    rendering hints, 73
  Group, 253
  Image2D
    discussed, 151
    fragment pipeline, 403
    methods associated with, 152
  IndexBuffer, 55–56
  KeyframeSequence, 327
  Light
    MascotCapsule V3 API, 406–407
    methods associated with, 222
  Loader, 290
  Material, 232
  Mesh, 51

Index

MorphingMesh
  associations, 359
  methods associated with, 360
Node, 260
Object3D, 262
PolygonMode
  geometry pipeline, 402
  methods associated with, 58–59
RayIntersection, 263
Screen, 17
SkinnedMesh, 370
Sprite3D
  methods associated with, 175
  scaled images, 174
Texture, 406–407
Texture2D
  fragment pipeline, 403
  geometry pipeline, 402
  methods associated with, 165
Transform, 99
Transformable, 254
Util3D, 406–407
Vector3D, 406–407
VertexArray, 53
VertexBuffer
  geometry pipeline, 402
  methods associated with, 54
World, 253
CLDC (Connected, Limited Device Configuration), 5, 7, 24
clear() method, 73, 255
code
  Bézier surfaces
    forward differencing, 83–85
    rendering, 86–88
    Utah Teapot example, 89–92
  billboards
    axis-aligned, 273–279
    screen-aligned, 271–272
  blending
    blending modes, 191–195
    texture blending, 196–197
  embossing, 208–214
  environment mapping
    applying to meshes, 182–185
    normals, transforming into texture coordinates, 176–179
  fog
    modes, switching between, 203–205
    properties of, 199–200
  geometric objects
    color, 62
    Graphics3D class, 66
  Hello, World! example
    animation, 22–23
    commands, user input, 20–21

GameCanvas class, 17–19
JAD file example, 25
screens, displaying, 15–16
keyframe animations
  animation loop, 335–338
  animation targets, 332–334
  UV animations, 345–354
lighting
  creation, 223–224, 226
  emulating with vertex colors, 242
  light maps, 244–245
  material types, 232–237
  normals, finding, 217–218
  texture baking, 240–241
M3G properties, retrieving, 37
MascotCapsule V3 API, 408–413
morphing, 362, 364–366
OpenGL ES, 420–428
polygon-level attributes, 59–60
projection transformations, 132–134
rectangles, drawing, 145–148
render targets, 71–72
scene graphs
  creation, 250–252
  picking, 265–268
  rendered scene graph example, 256–258
shapes, fractional positions, 79–80
skinned meshes
  bone-joint connections, 374–376
  skeleton animation, 376–382
  skin and skeleton creation, 366–368
  skin, attaching to skeleton, 370–372
textures
  creation, 162–164
  filters, 173–174
  perspective correction, 172
  wrapping modes, 169–170
transformations
  axis-angle format, 102–103
  depth buffer, 138
  Euler angles, 104–105
  model, 110–112
  rotation, 117–119
  scaling, 116–117
  view, 124–129
wireframe meshes, 142–145
collection standards, 6–7
color buffer methods, CompositingMode class, 189
color methods, Background class, 69
ColorRGB data type, 306
ColorRGBA data type, 306
colors
  background objects, 68
  emulating light with, 241–243
  geometric objects, 61–63
combining transformations, 119–120

Index

command lists, MascotCapsule 3D rendering engine, 407–408
commandAction() method, 21
CommandListener interface, 20–21
commands, user input, 20–21
components, vertex data, 52
compositing, 187
CompositingMode class
    fragment pipeline, 403
    geometry pipeline, 402
    methods associated with, 189
Connected Device Configuration (CDC), 5
Connected, Limited Device Configuration (CLDC), 5, 7, 24
construction methods
    AnimationController class, 340
    AnimationTrack class, 330
    Appearance class, 60
    Background class, 69
    CompositingMode class, 189
    Fog class, 201
    Group class, 253
    Image2D class, 152
    KeyframeSequence class, 327
    Light class, 222
    Material class, 232
    Polygon class, 58
    RayIntersection class, 263
    Sprite3D class, 175
control points, Bézier curves, 81–82
convex hull, Bézier curves, 81–82
conveyor belt animations, 344–348
coordinate systems
    2D/3D, 47–49
    Blender tool, 295–297
coordinates, texture, 167–168
create() method, 92
Create Package command, 31
createAnimation() method, 334, 347, 363, 378
createBackground() method, 68
createCube() method, 53, 80
createCylinder() method, 80
createDisc() method, 79
createMesh() method, 166–167, 185
createMorphingMesh() method, 362
createQuad() method, 79
createSkeleton() method, 368
createSkin() method, 368
createSphere() method, 80
createSprite3D() method, 273
createTextureQuad() method, 273, 275
createTriangle() method, 79
createTriStrips() method, 92
cropping methods
    Background class, 69
    Sprite3D class, 175

cube example
    triangle strip, 55–58
    vertex positions, 53–54
cube mapping, 176–177
culling methods, Polygon class, 58
curves, Bézier, 81–82
cylinders, 80

data setting methods, Image2D class, 152
data types, 305–306
data-driven applications
    discussed, 314
    scene objects, annotating, 315
    user data, deserializing, 320–321
    user data, serializing, 315–317
density, fog, 202
depth buffer
    CompositingMode class, 189
    discussed, 136
    enabling/disabling, 137–138
    resolution, 139–140
depth range methods, Graphics3D class, 65
destroy() method, 19, 66
destroyApp() method, 15–16, 19
destroyed state, MIDlets, 15
development, MIDlets, 13
device compatibility, JSR 248, 11
diffuse reflection, 238
dir() method, 312
directional light, 227–228
directory layout, CD-ROM contents, 429–430
disc creation, 78–79
display properties, 40
double-buffering, 17
draw() method, 145
drawing graphics, 17–19
drawLine() method, 19
drawMenu() method, 75
drifting, transformations, 103

Eclipse, 32
Effect3D class, 406–407
EGL. *See* OpenGL ES
embossing
    EmbossingSample, 211–214
    image creation, 206–207
    textures, 207–211
emission reflection, lighting, 237
Enterprise edition, Java, 4
environment mapping
    applying to meshes, 182–186
    cube mapping, 176–177
    normals, transforming, 177–181
    sphere mapping, 176–177

Euler angles, 104–105
evaluateCubicCurve() method, 85
example code. *See* code
explicit indices, 57
exponential fog, 201
export options, Blender tool, 289–290, 297–299
external references, Blender generated file, 310

face-specific attributes, Polygon class, 58–59
fields methods, Camera class, 129
Figure class, 406–407
FigureLayout class, 406–407
file structure
    Blender generated file contents
        external references, 310
        file identifier, 308
        header object, 308, 310
        scene objects, 310–311
    data types, 305
    data-driven applications
        discussed, 314
        scene objects, annotating, 315
        user data, deserializing, 320–321
        user data, serializing, 315–317
    object fields, 306–307
    object relationships, 307–308
    sections, 305–306
files, class file verification, 24
filters
    filter modes, Texture2D class, 165
    texture, 172–174
find() method, 262
fixed point numbers, 8
flicker, 17
flip-book animations, 348–350
float type, 8
Float32 data type, 306
floating point numbers, 8
fog
    blending modes, 202–205
    creation, 198–202
    density, 202
    parameters, 200–201
Fog class
    fragment pipeline, 403
    methods associated with, 201
forward differencing, 82–85
forward kinematics, 389
fractional positions, shapes, 78–80
fragment pipeline, 402
fragment tests, blending and, 188, 190
frame rate, animation, 23
framebuffer test methods, Background class, 69

game actions
    discussed, 21–22
    mappings, 39–41

GameCanvas class, 17
general functionality methods
    Fog class, 201
    Graphics3D class, 64
    Light class, 222
    Object3D class, 262
    Sprite3D class, 175
    Transform class, 99
generic matrix methods, Transformable class, 254
generic transformations, 120–122
geometric objects, rendering
    2D coordinate systems, 48–49
    3D coordinate systems, 48
    background objects, 68–71
    colors, 61–63
    coordinate systems, 47–48
    immediate mode rendering, 63, 65–67
    mesh creation, 49–50
    polygon-level attributes, 58–61
    render targets, 71–77
    shapes
        Bézier surfaces, 81–93
        cylinders, 80
        discussed, 77
        fractional positions, 78–80
        sphere, 80–81
    vertex arrays, 51–53
    vertex buffers, 51–53
geometry pipeline, 402
getChild() method, 261
getChildCount() method, 261
getChildren() method, 312
getCompositeTransform() method, 339
GetCurrent() method, 312
getGraphics() method, 19
getHeight() method, 135
getKeyName() method, 22
getKeyStates() method, 23–24, 338
getProperties() method, 72, 175, 252
getReferences() method, 261
getWeights() method, 363
getWidth() method, 135
gimbal lock problem, transformations, 105
Gourand shading, 220
GPUs (graphics processing units), 8
graphics, drawing, 17–19
Graphics3D class
    discussed, 63
    fragment pipeline, 403
    geometry pipeline, 402
    MascotCapsule V3 API, 406–407
    methods associated with, 64–65
    rendering hints, 73
Group class, 253

Index

hardware considerations, phone, 41–42
header bar, Blender tool, 283
header object, Blender generated file, 308, 310
Hello, World! example
    animation, 22–23
    graphics, drawing, 17–19
    JAR file example, 25
    screens, displaying, 15–17
    user input, receiving, 20–22
help() method, 312
high-level user interfaces, 17
homogeneous coordinates, transformations, 97–98

image methods
    Background class, 69
    Image2D class, 152
image mode methods, Background class, 69
Image2D class
    discussed, 151
    fragment pipeline, 403
    methods associated with, 152
images. *See also* textures
    creation, 153–155
    immutable, 153
    JPEG, 158
    loading, 154
    mutable, 153
    pixel formats, 151–153
    PNG files, 155–158
immediate mode rendering, 63, 65
immediate mode, scene graphs, 258–259
immutable images, 153
implementation-specific properties, 36–37
implicit indices, 57
IndexBuffer class, 55–56
inherited property methods, Node class, 260
init() method, 19, 23, 66–68, 111, 114, 116
installation
    Java Wireless Toolkit, 26–27
    M3G Exporter Script, 282
    Over the Air User, 32–33
Int16 data type, 306
Int32 data type, 306
Integer type, implementation-specific properties, 38–39
interoperability issues, new features, 11
interpolation modes
    keyframe animations, 328–329
    KeyframeSequence class, 327
intersection result methods, RayIntersection class, 263
inverse kinematics, 389
invert() method, 101

JAR (Java Archive File), 25
Java
    Enterprise Edition, 4
    Java Community Process, 4
    JSR (Java Specification Request), 4
    Micro Edition
        configurations, 5
        optional packages, 6
        overview, 4
        profiles, 5–6
    mobile support and, 3–4
    Standard Edition, 4
Java Archive File (JAR), 25
Java Bindings for OpenGL ES (JSR 239), 12
Java Technology for the Wireless Industry (JTWI), 6–7
Java Wireless Toolkit
    game action mappings, 39–41
    KToolbar
        new project creation, 27–28
    KToolbar, new project creation, 27–28
    software installation, 26–27
javax.microedition.khronos.egl, 416
JPEG images, 11, 158
JRS 135 (Mobile Media API), 6
JSR 82 (Bluetooth support), 7
JSR 239 (Java Bindings for OpenGL ES), 12
JSR 248 (Mobile Service Architecture), 6, 11
JSR (Java Specification Request), 4
JTWI (Java Technology for the Wireless Industry), 6–7

key events, 21–22
keyframe animations
    animation loop, 335–338
    animation targets, 330–334
    associations, 339–342
    control, 334
    discussed, 325
    interpolation modes, 328–329
    moving images, 342–344
    sequences, 326–328
    world versus sequence time, 339–342
KeyframeSequence class, 327
keyPressed() method, 21–23, 75, 113–114, 128, 338
keyReleased() method, 21–22
KToolbar
    API Selection dialog box, 28
    building and running application, 30–31
    Create Package command, 31
    new project creation, 27–28
    source code and resources, 29

landscape and portrait mode, view transformations, 123–129

layer methods, Appearance class, 60
LCDUI interface API, 5
light and material sources, Blender tool, 288
Light class
    MascotCapsule V3 API, 406–407
    methods associated with, 222
light methods, Graphics3D class, 64–65
lighting
    ambient, 227
    ambient reflection, 238
    creation, 221, 223–227
    diffuse reflection, 238
    directional, 227–228
    discussed, 215
    emission reflection, 237
    emulating
        texture baking, 239–241
        with vertex colors, 241–243
    light maps, 243–245
    lighting model, 216
    material types, 231–237
    normals, computing, 219–220
    normals, finding, 216–219
    omnidirectional, 228–229
    quality, 220
    scoping and, 269
    sources, 221
    specular reflection, 238–239
    spot light, 230
linear fog, 201
linear interpolation, 329
linear transformations, 97
links and resources, CD-ROM contents, 432
load() method, 154, 290, 294
Loader attribute, 70
Loader class, 290
loading images, 154
loadScene() method, 294
luminance texture format, blending modes, 197
luminance_alpha texture format, blending modes, 197

M3G Exporter Script
    default settings, 298
    installation, 282
M3G (Mobile 3D Graphics API)
    alternatives to, 12
    architecture, 7
    features in, 9
    future of, 11–12
    new features, 10–11
MascotCapsule 3D rendering engine
    binary files, 408
    classes, 406–407
    code, 408–413
    command lists, 407–408
    discussed, 12
    features, 405–406
    rendering primitives, 407
Material class, 232
material types, lighting, 231–237
matrices, transformation, 96–97
matrix calculations, transformations, 98–101
Matrix data type, 306
maxLights key, 38
maxSpriteCropDimension key, 39
maxTextureDimension key, 39
maxTransformsPerVertex key, 39
maxViewportDimension key, 38
maxViewportHeight key, 38
maxViewportWidth key, 38
memory game, 322–323
Mesh class, 51
mesh creation, Blender tool, 286–287
meshes
    appearance of, 51
    applying environment mapping to, 182–186
    associations with, 50
    overview, 49–50
    skinned
        bone-joint connections, 373–376
        robot model, 382–388, 390–392
        skeleton animation, 376–382
        skin and skeleton creation, 366–368
        skin, attaching to skeleton, 368–373
    wireframe, 141–145
methods
    addAnimationTrack(), 334
    addCommand(), 21
    addLight(), 226, 252
    addTransform(), 373
    align(), 271, 277
    animate(), 336–337
    animation target, 331
    AnimationTrack class associated, 330
    Appearance class associated, 60
    attachAnimation(), 378
    attachSkin(), 372
    Background class associated, 69
    bindTarget(), 72, 74, 134, 137, 139
    Camera class associated, 129
    changeState(), 396
    checkHit(), 268
    checkKeys(), 337–338
    clear(), 73, 255
    commandAction(), 21
    CompositingMode class associated, 189
    create(), 92
    createAnimation(), 334, 347, 363, 378
    createBackground(), 68

methods (*continued*)
    createCube() method, 53, 80
    createCylinder(), 80
    createDisc(), 79
    createMesh(), 166–167, 185
    createMorphingMesh(), 362
    createQuad(), 79
    createSkeleton(), 368
    createSkin(), 368
    createSphere(), 80
    createSprite3D(), 273
    createTextureQuad(), 273, 275
    createTriangle(), 79
    createTriStrips(), 92
    destroy(), 19, 66
    destroyApp(), 15–16, 19
    dir(), 312
    draw(), 145
    drawLine(), 19
    drawMenu(), 75
    evaluateCubicCurve(), 85
    find(), 262
    Fog class associated, 201
    getChild(), 261
    getChildCount(), 261
    getChildren(), 312
    getCompositTransform(), 339
    GetCurrent(), 312
    getGraphics(), 19
    getHeight(), 135
    getKeyName(), 22
    getKeyStates(), 23–24, 338
    getProperties(), 72, 175, 252
    getReferences(), 261
    getWeights(), 363
    getWidth(), 135
    Graphics3D class associated, 64–65
    Group class associated, 253
    help(), 312
    Image2D class associated, 152
    IndexBuffer class associated, 55–56
    init(), 19, 23, 66–68, 111, 114, 116
    invert(), 101
    KeyframeSequence class associated, 327
    keyPressed(), 21–23, 75, 113–114, 128, 338
    keyReleased(), 21–22
    Light class associated, 222
    load(), 154, 290, 294
    Loader class associated, 290
    loadScene(), 294
    Material class associated, 232
    Mesh class associated, 51
    MorphingMesh class associated, 360
    Node class associated, 260
    notifyDestroyed(), 15
    notifyPaused(), 15
    Object3D class associated, 262
    pauseApp(), 14–16
    playBackward(), 350
    playForward(), 350
    PolygonMode class associated, 58–59
    postRotate(), 101–102, 118, 120, 123, 168
    postRotateQuat(), 101–102, 120, 123
    postScale(), 101–102, 120
    postTranslate(), 101–102, 115, 120, 123
    preRotate(), 168
    RayIntersection class associated, 263
    releaseTarget(), 74, 139
    render(), 19, 68, 73–74, 112, 114, 126, 138
    reset(), 255, 393
    resumeRequest(), 15
    run(), 23–24, 336
    scale(), 168
    setActiveCamera(), 253
    setActiveInterval(), 341
    setAlignment(), 271, 275
    setAlphaThreshold(), 190
    setAnimation(), 334
    setAttenuation(), 228
    setBackground(), 254
    setBlending(), 193
    setCamera(), 126, 252
    setColor(), 234, 236
    setColorClear(), 71
    setCrop(), 70, 175
    setCulling(), 61
    setDensity(), 202
    setDepthClearEnable(), 71, 139
    setDuration(), 326
    setFogMode(), 200
    setGap(), 210–211
    setGeneric(), 129–130
    setIdentity(), 100–101
    setImage(), 70
    setImageMode(), 71
    setLayer(), 60
    setLightMode(), 224
    setLinear(), 202
    setMaterial(), 234
    setParallel(), 129–130
    setPerspective(), 67, 130
    setPolygonMode(), 60–61
    setPosition(), 341
    setRepeatMode(), 327
    setScope(), 74
    setSpeed(), 341
    setSpotExponent(), 230
    setTexCoords(), 52
    setTransformationValues(), 114, 116, 118, 121
    setTwoSidedLightingEnabled(), 61
    setUserID(), 262

Index   441

setUserObject(), 262
setValidRange(), 326
setViewport(), 73, 134–135
setWinding, 61
SkinnedMesh class associated, 370
sleep(), 23
startApp(), 14–16
TestEnabled(), 139
Texture2D class associated, 165
transform(), 100, 112, 114, 117–118
Transform class associated, 99
Transformable class associated, 254
translate(), 168
translateMesh(), 318
transpose(), 101
VertexArray class associated, 53
VertexBuffer class associated, 54
World class associated, 253

Micro Edition, Java
configurations, 5
optional packages, 6
overview, 4
profiles, 5–6

MIDlets
active state, 14
destroyed state, 15
development, 13
MIDlet suites, 25–26
MIDP and, 5
paused state, 14
state transitions, 14–15

MIDP (Mobile Information Device Profile)
overview, 5–7
properties, 39–40
security checks mandated by, 11

mipmaps, 165, 173
Mobile Media API (JSR 135), 6
Mobile Service Architecture (JSR 248), 6, 11
mobile support, Java and, 3–4
model transformations, 109–114
morphing
basic functionality, 358–359
discussed, 357
morph targets, animating, 362–366
MorphingMesh associations, 359–361

MorphingMesh class
associations, 359
methods associated with, 360

moving images, keyframe animations, 342–344
multiplication methods, Transform class, 99
multi-texturing, 193, 195
mutable images, 153

naming conventions, OpenGL ES, 417
NetBeans Mobility Pack, 32

new features, M3G, 10–11
New Project dialog box, 27
new state, 14
node alignment, scene graphs, 270–271
Node class, 260
node properties, scene graphs, 260–261
node selection, scene graphs, 261
node transformations, scene graphs, 254–255
normals, lighting fundamentals
computing, 219–220
finding, 216–219
notifyDestroyed() method, 15
notifyPauses() method, 15
numTextureUnits key, 39

object fields, 306–307
object relationships, 307–308
Object3D class, 262
ObjectIndex data type, 306
omnidirectional light, 228–229
OpenGL, 9
OpenGL ES, 8
example code, 420–428
javax.microedition.khronos.egl, 416
JSR 239 (Java Bindings for OpenGl ES), 12
naming conventions, 417
operations, 415–416
passing data, 418–419
rendering, 419
optional packages, Java Micro Edition, 6
orientation representations, transformations
axis-angle format, 102–104
Euler angles, 104–105
gimbal lock problem, 105
quaternions, 105–107
Over the Air User Initiated Provisioning Specification, 32–33
OVERWRITE hint flag, new features, 10

packages, Create Package command, 31
parallel projection, projection transformation, 131–134
parametric equation, circles, 78
pauseApp() method, 14–16
paused state, MIDlets, 14
perspective corrections, textures, 171–172
perspective projection, projection transformation, 131–134
phone
hardware considerations, 41–42
M3G support, 35–36
system software, M3G architecture, 7
Phong shading, 220
picking
general method of, 263–264
scoping and, 269
in viewport coordinates, 264–268

Index

pixel format methods, Image2D class, 152
pixel formats, 151–153
playBackward() method, 350
playForward() method, 350
PNG files, 155–158
PNGGauntlet tool, 157
Poly Reducer feature, 303–304
polygon-level attributes, 58–61
PolygonMode class
    geometry pipeline, 402
    methods associated with, 58–59
portrait and landscape mode, view transformations, 123–129
postRotate() method, 101–102, 118, 120, 123, 168
postRotateQuat() method, 101–102, 120, 123
postScale() method, 101–102, 120
postTranslate() method, 101–102, 115, 120, 123
preRotate() method, 168
preverification, CLDC tool chain, 5
primitives, rendering, 407
profiles
    Java Micro Edition, 5–6
    MIDP, 5–6
projection matrix methods, Camera class, 129
projection transformations
    parallel projection, 131–134
    perspective projection, 131–134
    viewing volume, setting, 129–131
properties
    canvas, 40
    display, 40
    MIDP, 39–40
    system, 40

quaternions, 105–107

RayIntersection class, 263
Record Management System, 6
reference fragment pipeline, 402
reference geometry pipeline, 402
releaseTarget() method, 74, 139
render() method, 19, 68, 73–74, 112, 114, 126, 138
render targets
    geometric objects, 71–77
    Graphics3D class, 64
rendering
    geometric objects
        2D coordinate systems, 48–49
        3D coordinate systems, 48
        background objects, 68–71
        Bézier surfaces, 81–93
        colors, 61–63
        coordinate systems, 47–48
        cylinders, 80
        immediate mode rendering, 63, 65–67
        mesh creation, 49–50
        polygon-level attributes, 58–61
        render targets, 71–77
        shapes, discussed, 77
        shapes, fractional positions, 78–80
        sphere shapes, 80–81
        vertex arrays, 51–53
        vertex buffers, 51–53
    Graphics3D class rendering methods, 64
    MascotCapsule 3D rendering engine
        binary files, 408
        classes, 406–407
        code, 408–413
        command lists, 407–408
        discussed, 12
        features, 405–406
        rendering primitives, 407
    OpenGL ES, 419
    primitives, 407
    scoping and, 269
repeat modes, KeyframeSequence class, 327
reset() method, 255, 393
resolution, depth buffer, 139–140
resources and links, CD-ROM contents, 432
resumeRequest() method, 15
retained mode, scene graphs, 249, 258–259
RGB texture format, blending modes, 197
RGBA texture format, blending modes, 197
rigging, 382–384
robot model
    importing, 389–393
    rigging, 382–384
    vertex group, 385–386
    walking animation, 387–389
rotation, 117–119
rotation methods, Transformable class, 254
run() method, 23–24, 336
Runnable interface, 22–23, 335
runtime exceptions, new features, 10

scale() method, 168
scale methods, Transformable class, 254
scaled images, Sprite3D class, 174
scaling, 116–117
scene export options, Blender tool, 289–290
scene graphs
    billboards
        axis-aligned, 273–279
        screen-aligned, 271–272
    creation, 250–254
    immediate mode, 258–259
    node alignment, 270–271

Index

node properties, 260–261
node selection, 261
node transformations, 254–255
picking
    general method of, 263–264
    in viewport coordinates, 264–268
retained mode, 249, 258–259
scoping, 269
traversing, 261
user IDs, 262
World objects, 255–258
scene navigation options, Blender tool, 285–286
scene objects, Blender generated file, 310–311
Screen class, 17
screen-aligned billboards, 271–272
screens, displaying, 15–17
scripts, writing, 311–314
sections, file structure, 305–306
security checks, MIDP mandated, 11
sequences, keyframe animations, 326–328
setActiveCamera() method, 253
setActiveInterval() method, 341
setAlignment() method, 271, 275
setAlphaThreshold() method, 190
setAnimation() method, 334
setAttenuation() method, 228
setBackground() method, 254
setBlending() method, 193
setCamera() method, 126, 252
setColor() method, 234, 236
setColorClear() method, 71
setCrop() method, 70, 175
setCulling() method, 61
setDensity() method, 202
setDepthClearEnable() method, 71, 139
setDuration() method, 326
setFogMode() method, 200
setGap() method, 210–211
setGeneric() method, 129–130
setIdentity() method, 100–101
setImage() method, 70
setImageMode() method, 71
setLayer() method, 60
setLightMode() method, 224
setLinear() method, 202
setMaterial() method, 234
setParallel() method, 129–130
setPerspective() method, 67, 130
setPolygonMode() method, 60–61
setPosition() method, 341
setRepeatMode() method, 327
setScope() method, 74
setSpeed() method, 341
setSpotExponent() method, 230
setTexCoords() method, 52
setTransformationValues() method, 114, 116, 118, 121
setTwoSidedLightingEnable() method, 61
setUserID() method, 262
setUserObject() method, 262
setValidRange() method, 326
setViewport() method, 73, 134–135
setWinding() method, 61
shading
    Gourand, 220
    Phong, 220
    Polygon class methods, 58
shapes
    Bézier surfaces
        Bézier curves, 81–82
        forward differencing, 82–85
        rendering, 85–88
        Utah Teapot example, 88–93
    cylinders, 80
    disc example, 78–79
    discussed, 77
    fractional positions, 78–80
    sphere, 80–81
skeleton, skinned meshes
    animation, 376–382
    creation, 366–368
skinned meshes
    bone-joint connections, 373–376
    robot model
        animation sequences, switching between, 393–398
        importing, 389–393
        rigging, 382–384
        vertex group, 385–386
        walking animation, 387–389
    skeleton animation, 376–382
    skin and skeleton creation, 366–368
    skin, attaching to skeleton, 368–373
SkinnedMesh class, 370
sleep() method, 23
software installation, Wireless Toolkit, 26–27
source code example, CD-ROM contents, 429
specular reflection, 238–239
sphere, 80–81
sphere mapping, 176–177
spherical linear interpolation, 329
spline function, 329
spot light, 230
spot light methods, Light class, 222
Sprite3D class
    methods associated with, 175
    scaled images, 174
Standard Edition, Java, 4
startApp() method, 14–16
state transitions, MIDlet, 14–15
String data type, 306

444 Index

supportAntialiasing key, 38
supportDithering key, 38
supportLocalCameraLighting key, 38
supportMipMapping key, 38
supportPerspectiveCorrection key, 38
supportTrueColor key, 38
system properties, 40

Technology Compatibility Kit, 43
TestEnabled() method, 139
texels, 158
texture baking, light emulation, 239–241
texture blending, 196–198
Texture class, 406–407
texture image methods, Texture2D class, 165
Texture2D class
    fragment pipeline, 403
    geometry pipeline, 402
    methods associated with, 165
textures
    coordinates, 167–168
    creation, 161–164, 167
    embossing, 207–211
    environment mapping
        applying to meshes, 182–186
        cube mapping, 176–177
        normals, transforming, 177–181
        sphere mapping, 176–177
    filtering, 172–174
    multi-texturing, 195–196
    perspective correction, 171–172
    texture mapping, 158–161
    wrapping modes, 169–170
texturing, in Blender tool, 288–289
tiling, 169
Timer, 335
TimerTask, 335
Transform class, 99
transform() method, 100, 112, 114, 117–118
Transformable class, 254
transformations
    3D coordinates, manual transformation, 141
    affine, 98
    combining, 119–120
    depth buffer
        discussed, 136
        enabling/disabling, 137–138
        resolution, 139–140
    drifting, 103
    generic, 120–122
    homogeneous coordinates, 97–98
    linear, 97
    matrices, 96–97
    matrix calculations, 98–101
    model, 109–114

    orientation representations
        axis-angle format, 102–104
        Euler angles, 104–105
        gimbal lock problem, 105
        quaternions, 105–107
    projection, viewing volume, 129–131
    rotation, 117–119
    scaling, 116–117
    stages of, 107–109
    texture coordinates, 168
    translation, 114–115
    transparent objects, 140
    vectors, 95–96
    view
        camera coordinates, 122–123
        portrait and landscape mode, switching between, 123–129
    viewport, 134–136
translate() method, 168
translateMesh() method, 318
translation, 114–115
translation methods, Transformable class, 254
transparency values, blending modes, 191
transparent objects, transformations, 140
transpose() method, 101
traversing scene graphs, 261
triangle strip, cube example, 55–58
triangles, drawing, 145–148
TweakPNG tool, 157
Type data type, 306

UInt16 data type, 306
UInt32 data type, 306
user data methods, Object3D class, 262
user IDs, Blender tool, 286–287
user IDs, scene graphs, 262
user input, receiving
    commands, 20–21
    discussed, 19
    game actions, 21–22
    key events, 21–22
user interface, Blender tool, 283–285
User Preferences window, Blender tool, 284
Utah Teapot, as Bézier surface example, 88–93
Util3D class, 406–407
UV animations
    conveyor belt animations, 344–348
    flip-book animations, 348–350
    TextureAnimationSample, 350–354

vector transformation, 95–96
Vector3D class, 406–407
Vector3D data type, 306
vertex arrays, 51–53

vertex buffers, 51–53
vertex colors, emulating light with, 241–243
vertex defined, 50
vertex group, 385–386
VertexArray class, 53
VertexBuffer class
    geometry pipeline, 402
    methods associated with, 54
view transformations
    camera coordinates, 122–123
    portrait and landscape mode, switching between, 123–129
viewing volume, projection transformations, 129–131
viewport coordinates, picking in, 264–268

viewport methods, Graphics3D class, 65
viewport transformations, 134–136
views, Blender tool, 285

walking animation, robot model, 387–389
winding methods, Polygon class, 58
wireframe meshes, 141–145
Wireless Toolkit
    game action mappings, 39–41
    software installation, 26–27
workspace, Blender tool, 283–285
World class, 253
World objects, scene graphs, 255–258
wrapping modes
    texture, 169–170
    Texture2D class, 165

License Agreement/Notice of Limited Warranty

By opening the sealed disc container in this book, you agree to the following terms and conditions. If, upon reading the following license agreement and notice of limited warranty, you cannot agree to the terms and conditions set forth, return the unused book with unopened disc to the place where you purchased it for a refund.

License

The enclosed software is copyrighted by the copyright holder(s) indicated on the software disc. You are licensed to copy the software onto a single computer for use by a single user and to a backup disc. You may not reproduce, make copies, or distribute copies or rent or lease the software in whole or in part, except with written permission of the copyright holder(s). You may transfer the enclosed disc only together with this license, and only if you destroy all other copies of the software and the transferee agrees to the terms of the license. You may not decompile, reverse assemble, or reverse engineer the software.

Notice of Limited Warranty

The enclosed disc is warranted by Thomson Course Technology PTR to be free of physical defects in materials and workmanship for a period of sixty (60) days from end user's purchase of the book/disc combination. During the sixty-day term of the limited warranty, Thomson Course Technology PTR will provide a replacement disc upon the return of a defective disc.

Limited Liability

THE SOLE REMEDY FOR BREACH OF THIS LIMITED WARRANTY SHALL CONSIST ENTIRELY OF REPLACEMENT OF THE DEFECTIVE DISC. IN NO EVENT SHALL THOMSON COURSE TECHNOLOGY PTR OR THE AUTHOR BE LIABLE FOR ANY OTHER DAMAGES, INCLUDING LOSS OR CORRUPTION OF DATA, CHANGES IN THE FUNCTIONAL CHARACTERISTICS OF THE HARDWARE OR OPERATING SYSTEM, DELETERIOUS INTERACTION WITH OTHER SOFTWARE, OR ANY OTHER SPECIAL, INCIDENTAL, OR CONSEQUENTIAL DAMAGES THAT MAY ARISE, EVEN IF THOMSON COURSE TECHNOLOGY PTR AND/OR THE AUTHOR HAS PREVIOUSLY BEEN NOTIFIED THAT THE POSSIBILITY OF SUCH DAMAGES EXISTS.

Disclaimer of Warranties

THOMSON COURSE TECHNOLOGY PTR AND THE AUTHOR SPECIFICALLY DISCLAIM ANY AND ALL OTHER WARRANTIES, EITHER EXPRESS OR IMPLIED, INCLUDING WARRANTIES OF MERCHANTABILITY, SUITABILITY TO A PARTICULAR TASK OR PURPOSE, OR FREEDOM FROM ERRORS. SOME STATES DO NOT ALLOW FOR EXCLUSION OF IMPLIED WARRANTIES OR LIMITATION OF INCIDENTAL OR CONSEQUENTIAL DAMAGES, SO THESE LIMITATIONS MIGHT NOT APPLY TO YOU.

Other

This Agreement is governed by the laws of the State of Massachusetts without regard to choice of law principles. The United Convention of Contracts for the International Sale of Goods is specifically disclaimed. This Agreement constitutes the entire agreement between you and Thomson Course Technology PTR regarding use of the software.